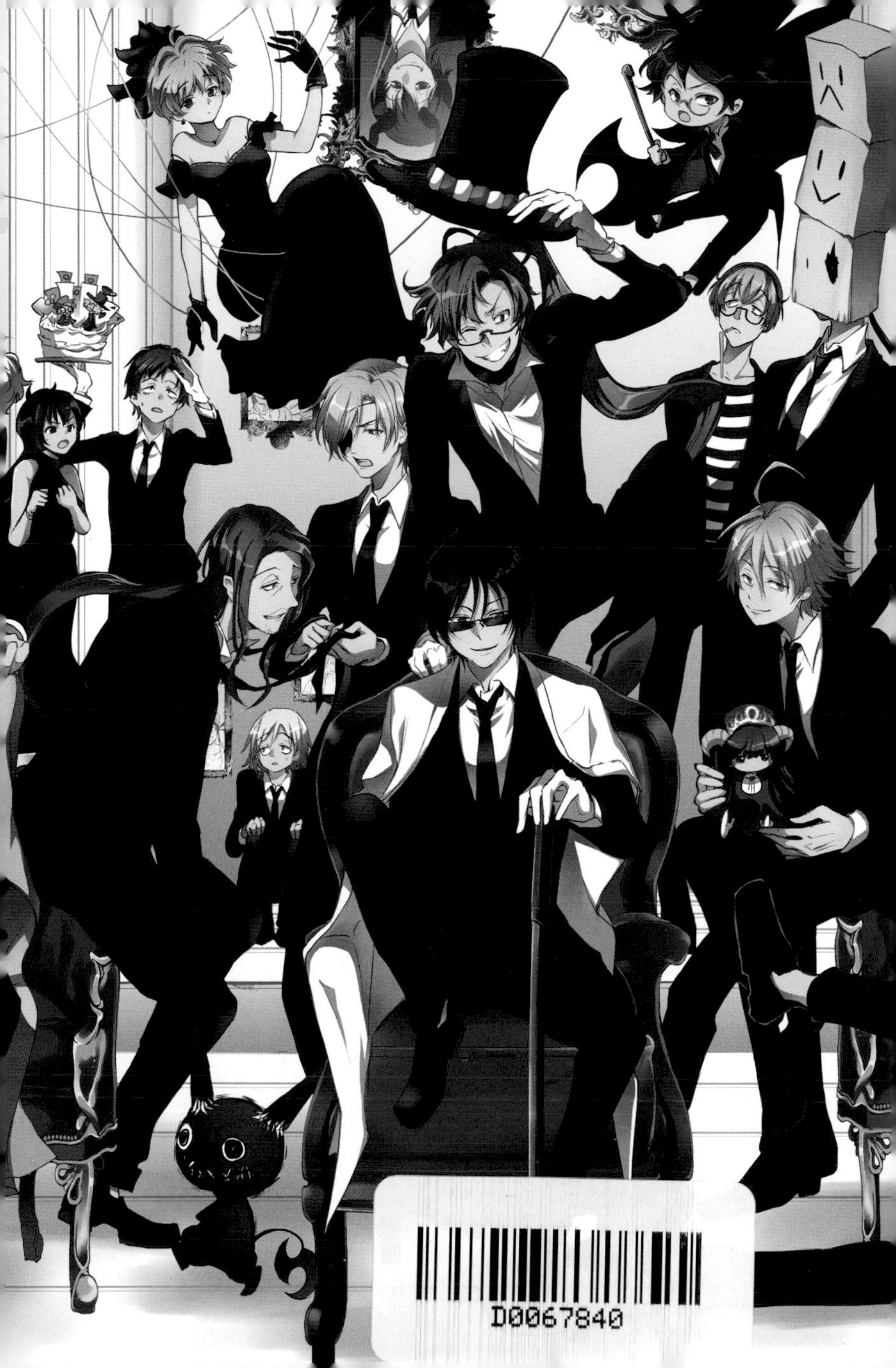

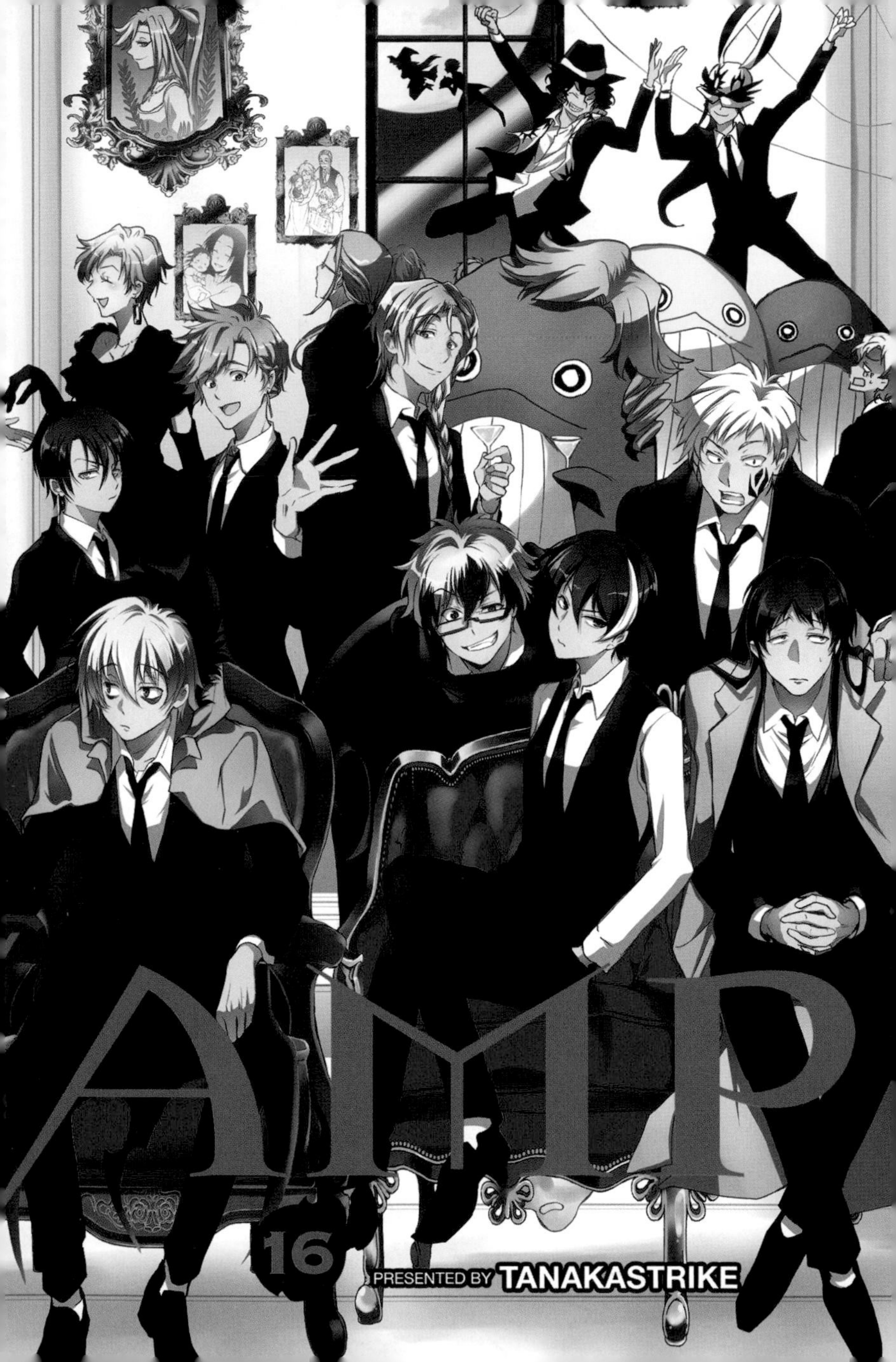
AMP
16
PRESENTED BY TANAKASTRIKE

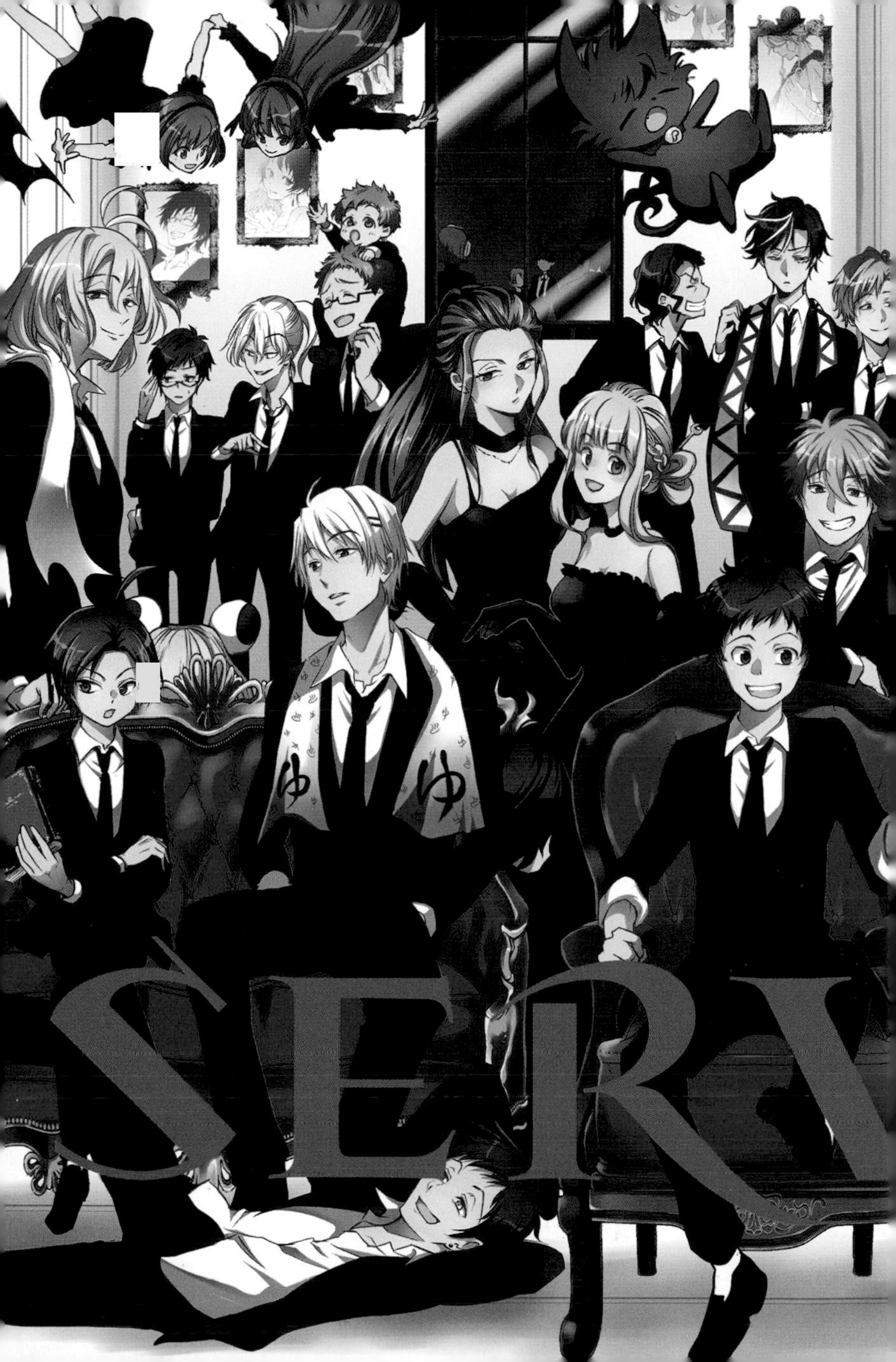
SERV

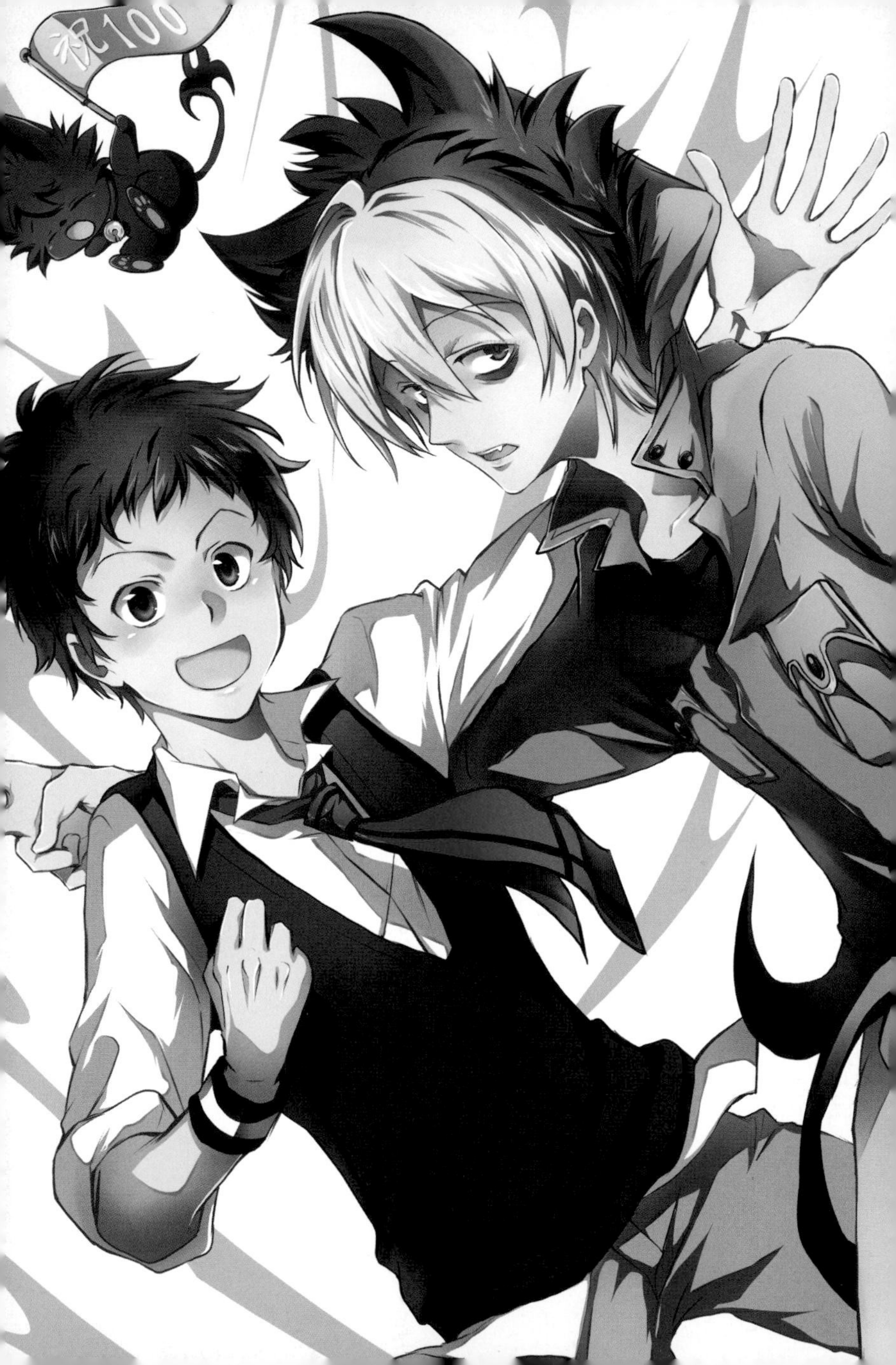
祝100

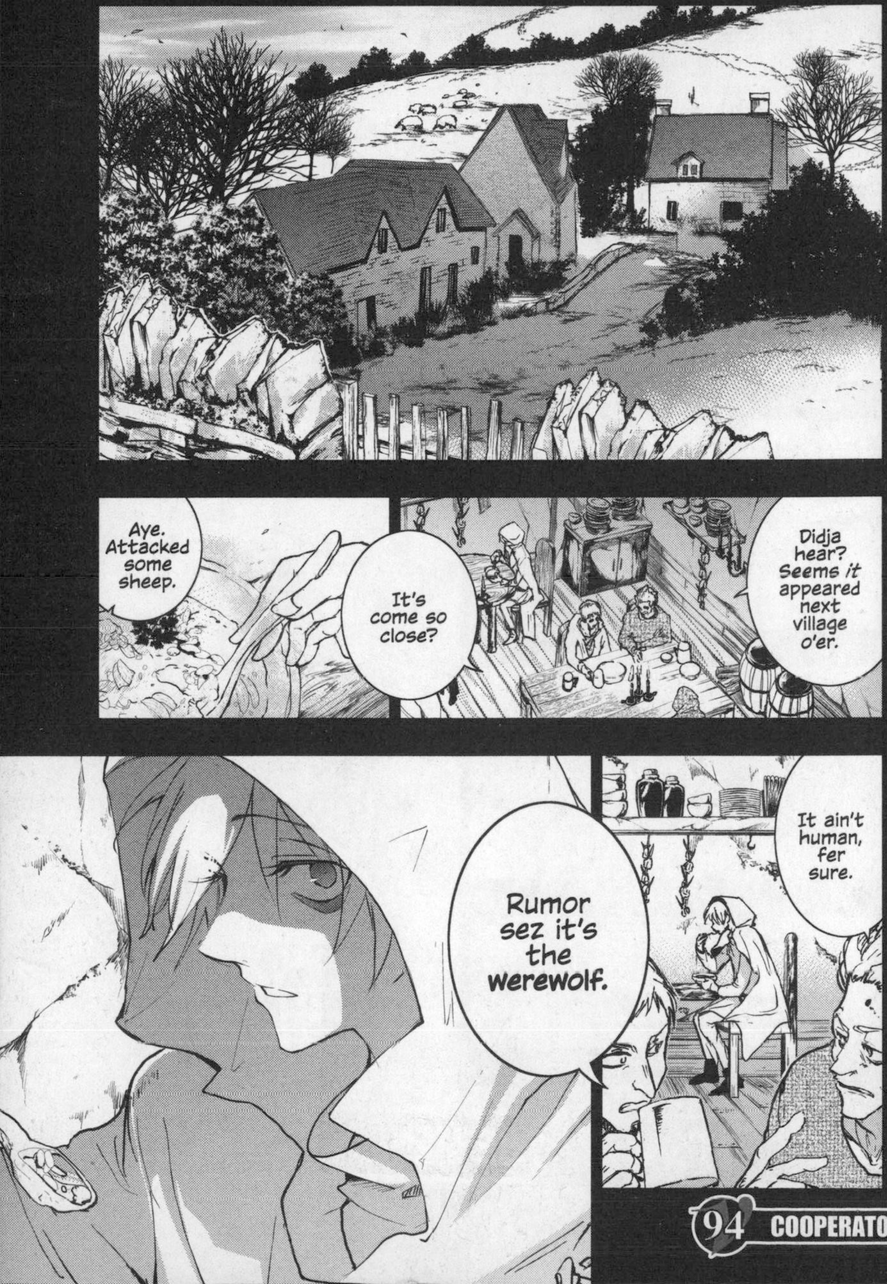
Didja hear? Seems *it* appeared next village o'er.
It's come so close?
Aye. Attacked some sheep.
It ain't human, fer sure.
Rumor sez it's the werewolf.

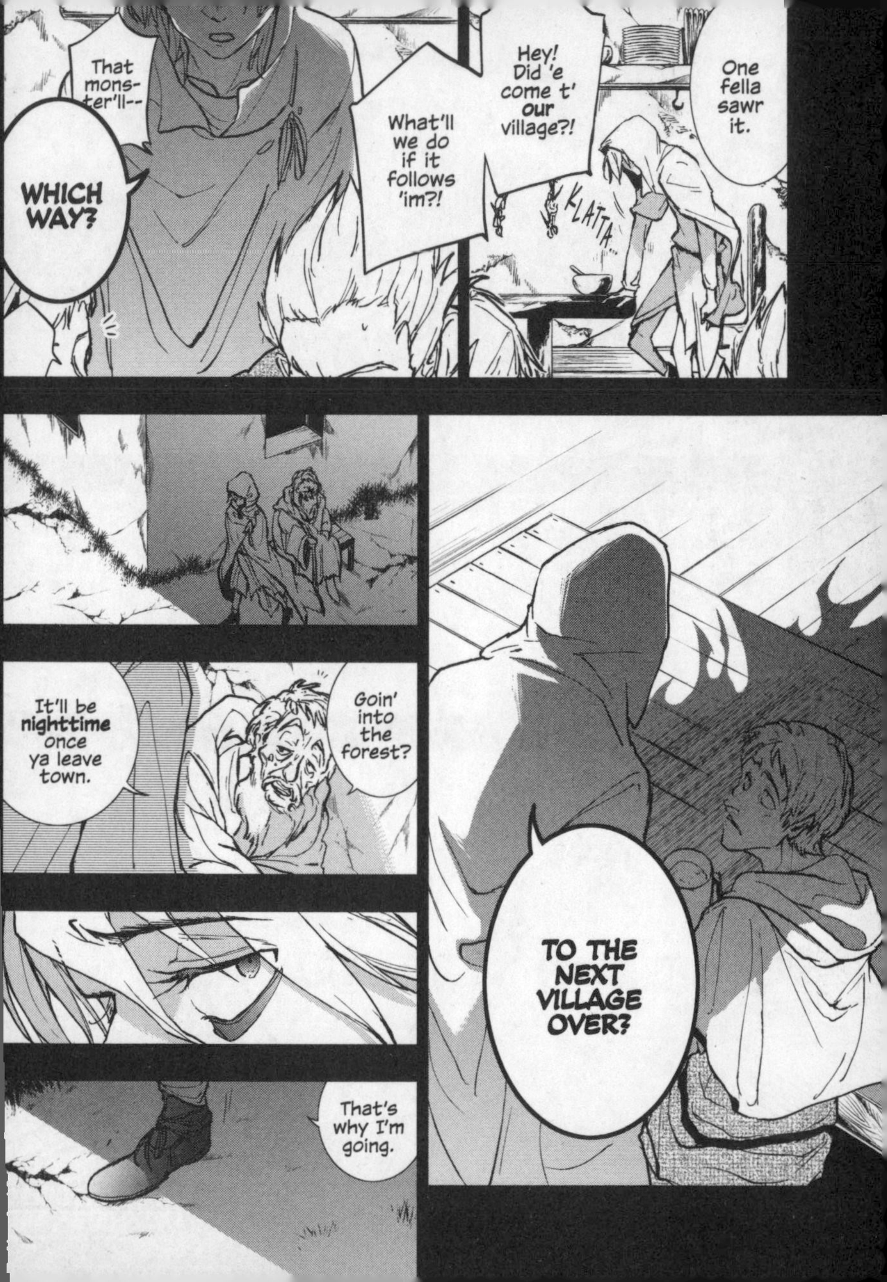
One fella sawr it.
KLATTA...
Hey! Did 'e come t' our village?!
What'll we do if it follows 'im?!
That monster'll--
WHICH WAY?
TO THE NEXT VILLAGE OVER?
Goin' into the forest?
It'll be nighttime once ya leave town.
That's why I'm going.

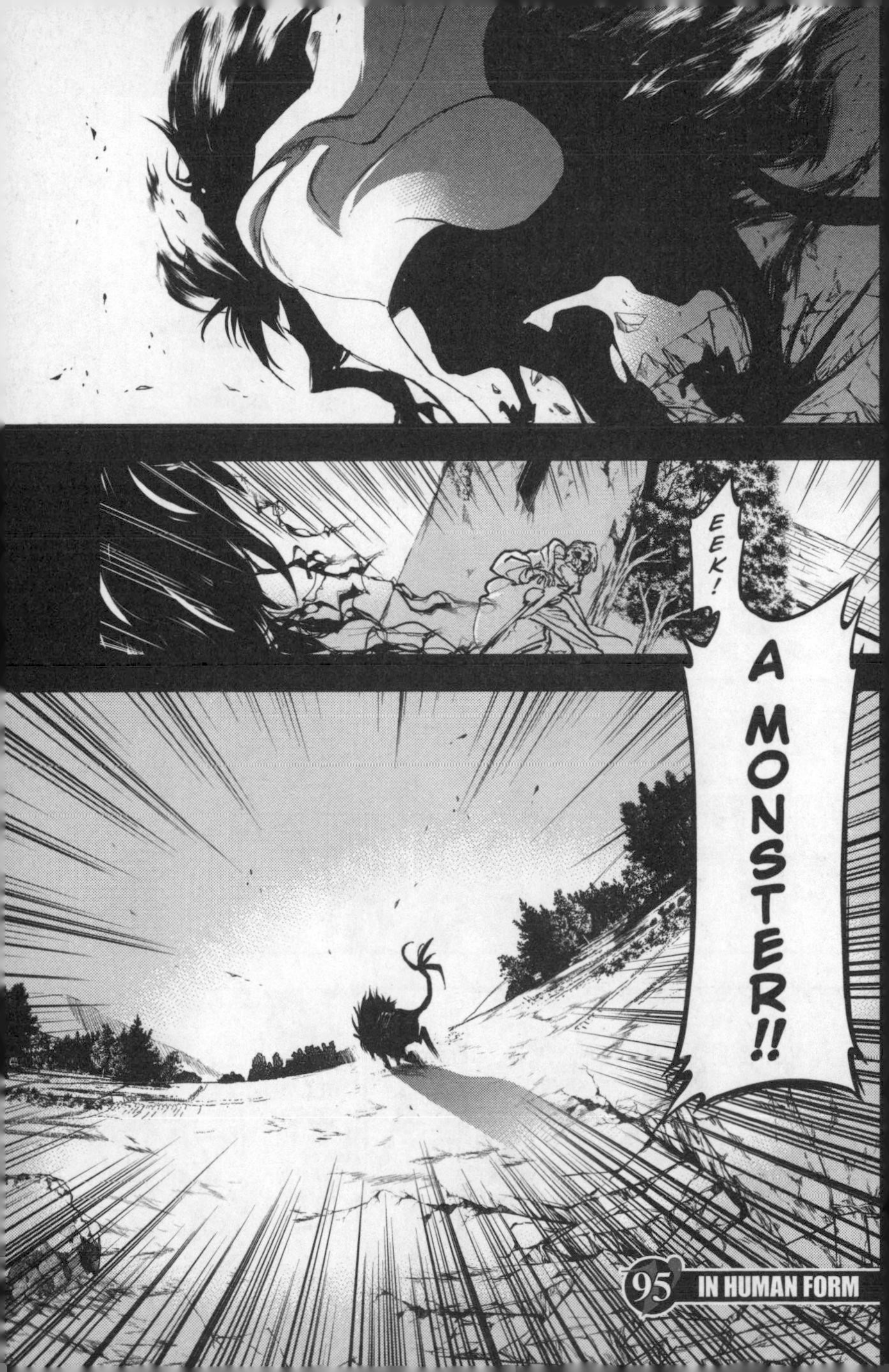
EEK!
A MONSTER!!
95 IN HUMAN FORM

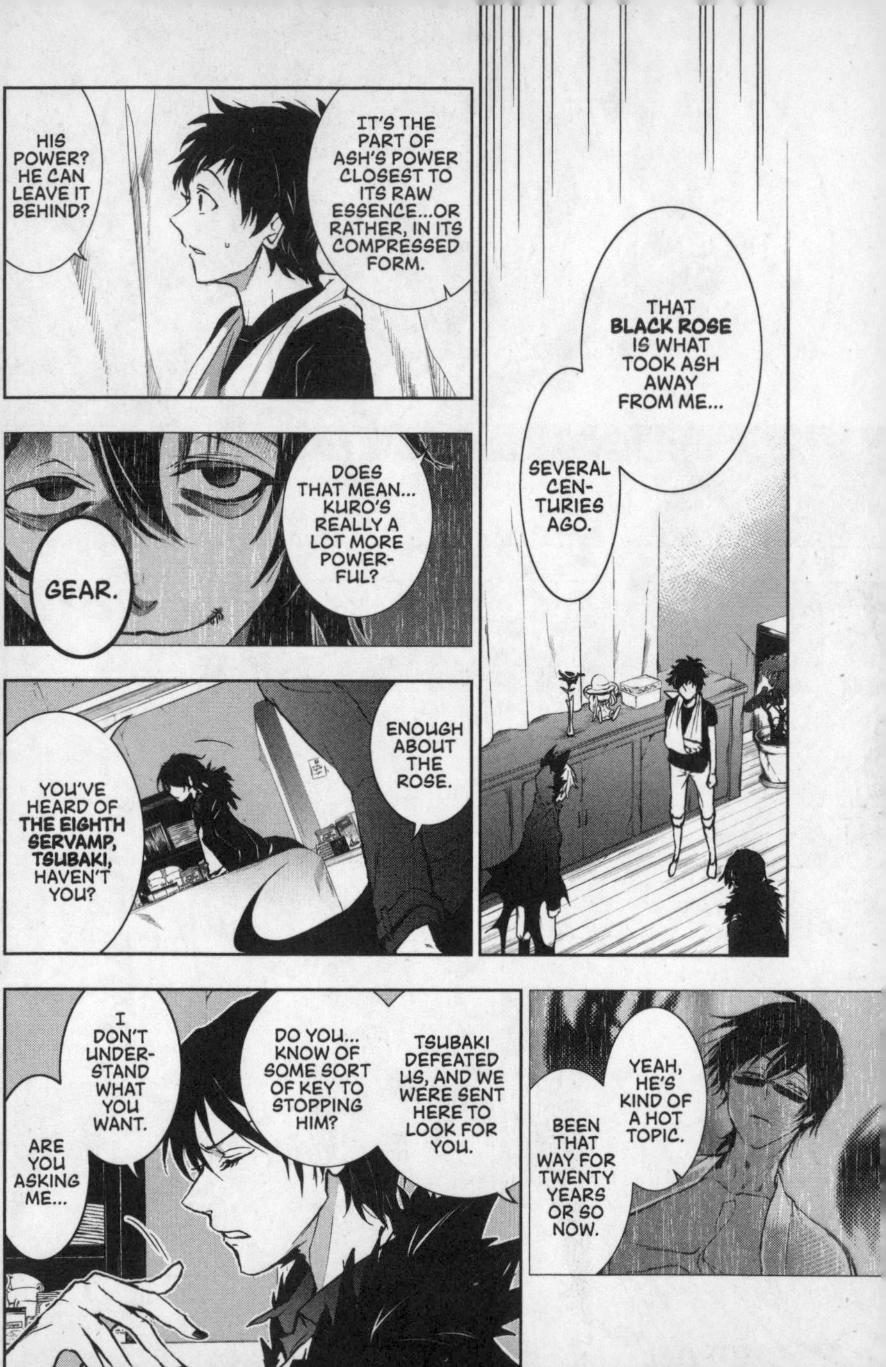

THAT **BLACK ROSE** IS WHAT TOOK ASH AWAY FROM ME...
SEVERAL CEN-TURIES AGO.
IT'S THE PART OF ASH'S POWER CLOSEST TO ITS RAW ESSENCE...OR RATHER, IN ITS COMPRESSED FORM.
HIS POWER? HE CAN LEAVE IT BEHIND?
DOES THAT MEAN... KURO'S REALLY A LOT MORE POWER-FUL?
GEAR.
ENOUGH ABOUT THE ROSE.
YOU'VE HEARD OF **THE EIGHTH SERVAMP, TSUBAKI,** HAVEN'T YOU?
YEAH, HE'S KIND OF A HOT TOPIC.
BEEN THAT WAY FOR TWENTY YEARS OR SO NOW.
TSUBAKI DEFEATED US, AND WE WERE SENT HERE TO LOOK FOR YOU.
DO YOU... KNOW OF SOME SORT OF KEY TO STOPPING HIM?
I DON'T UNDER-STAND WHAT YOU WANT.
ARE YOU ASKING ME...

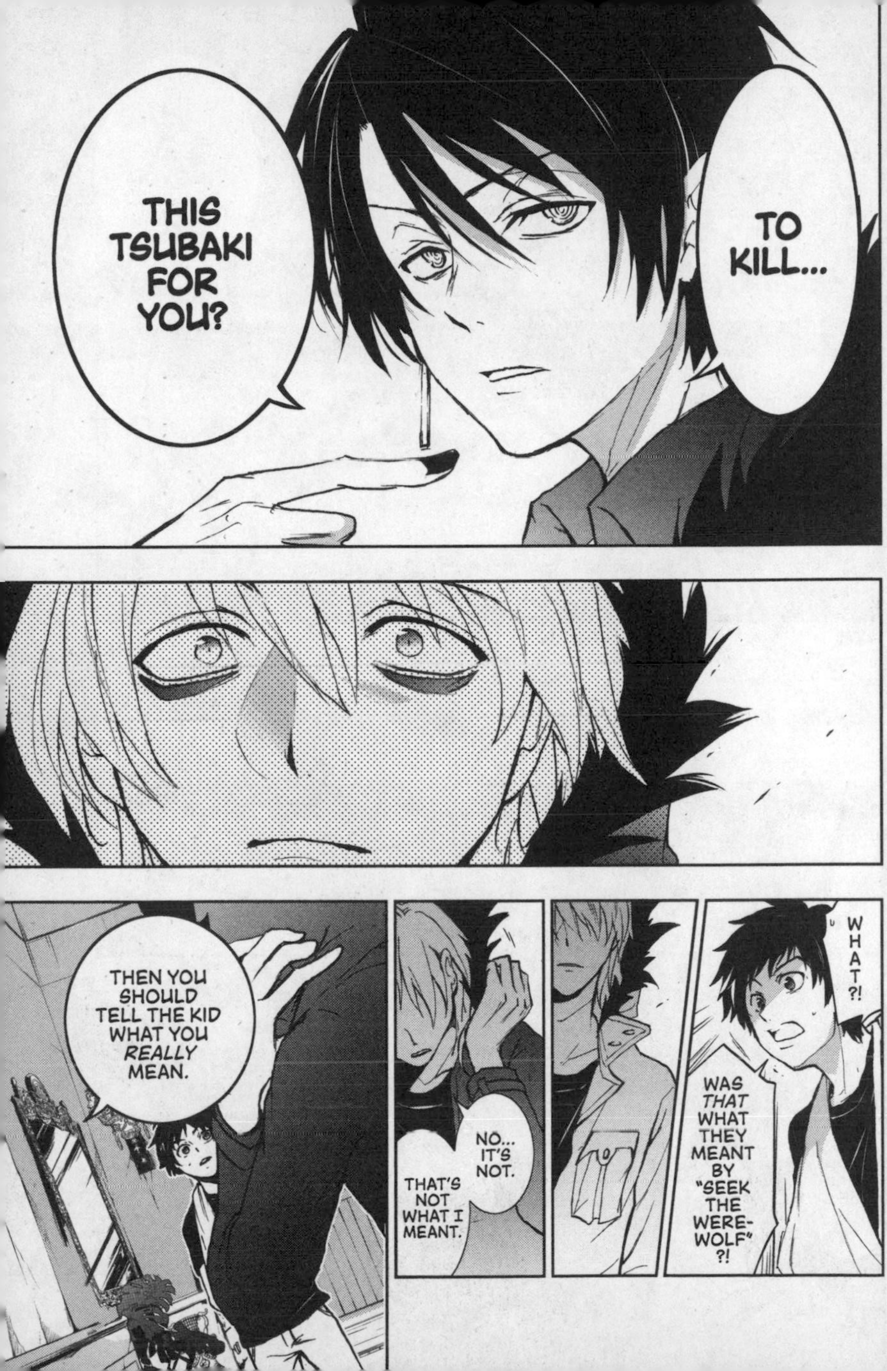
TO KILL...
THIS TSUBAKI FOR YOU?
WHAT?!
WAS *THAT* WHAT THEY MEANT BY "SEEK THE WERE-WOLF"?!
NO... IT'S NOT.
THAT'S NOT WHAT I MEANT.
THEN YOU SHOULD TELL THE KID WHAT YOU *REALLY* MEAN.

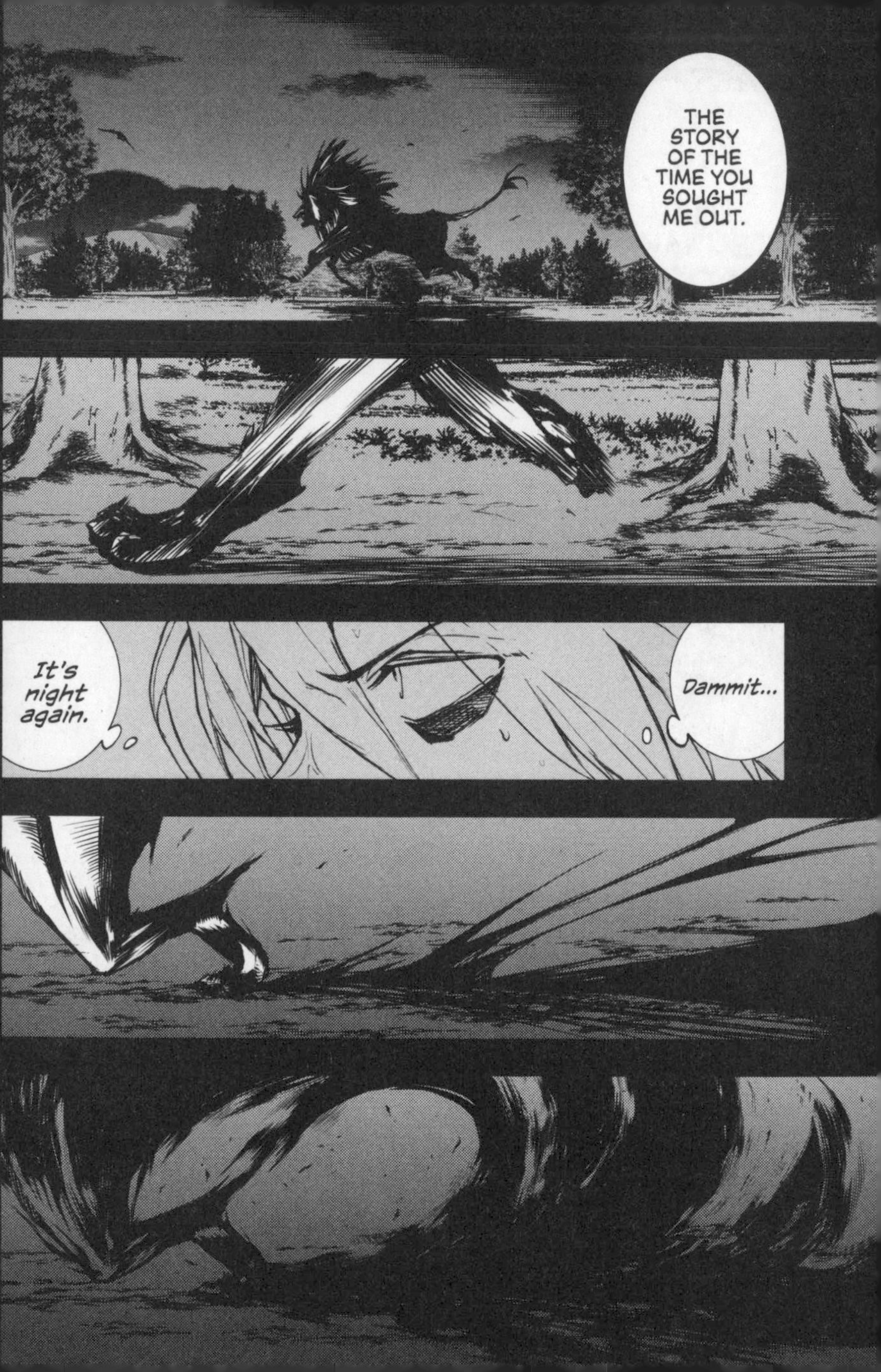
THE STORY OF THE TIME YOU SOUGHT ME OUT.
Dammit...
It's night again.

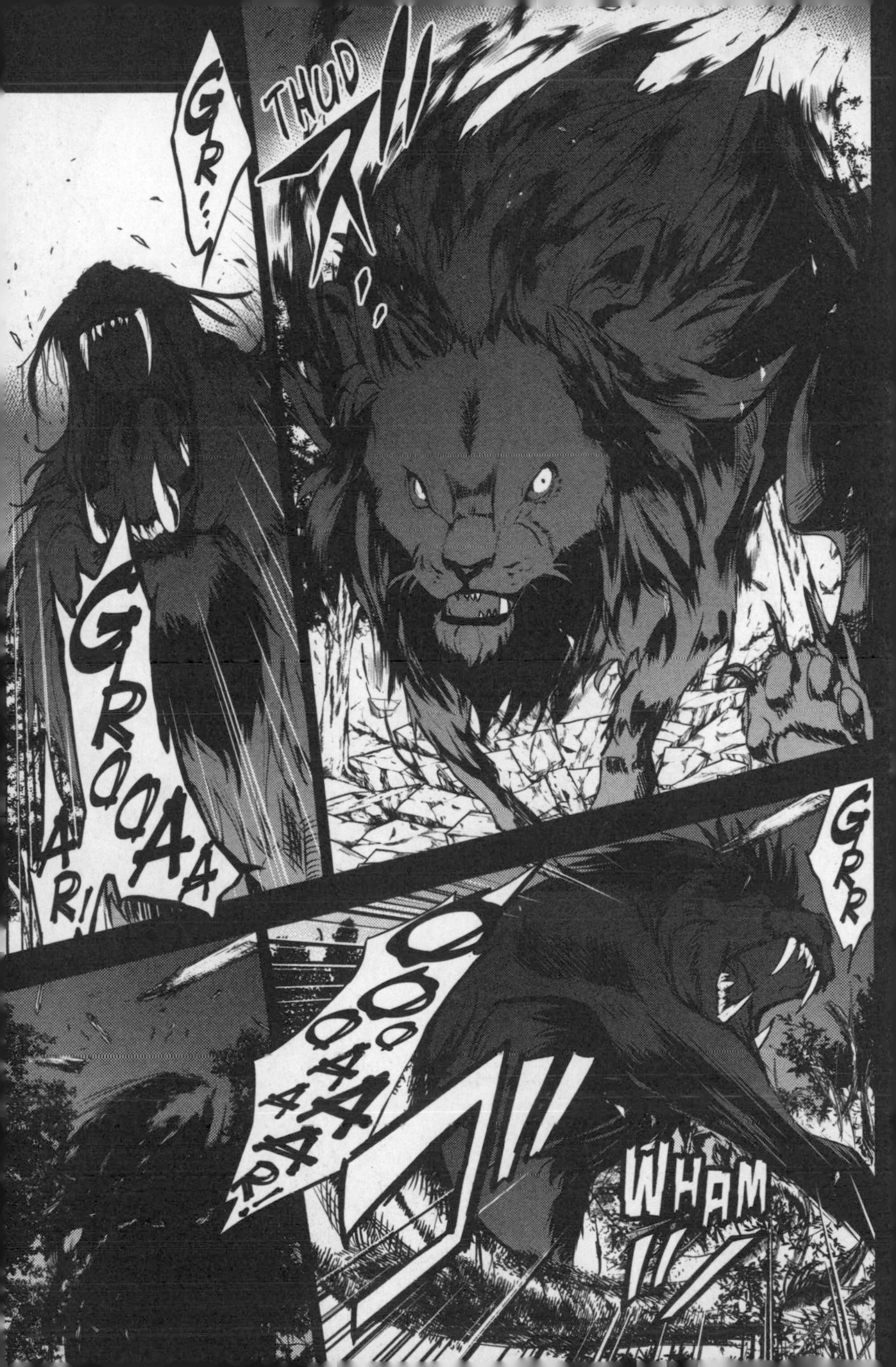
THUD
GR...
GROOAAAR!
GRR
OOOAAAAR!
WHAM

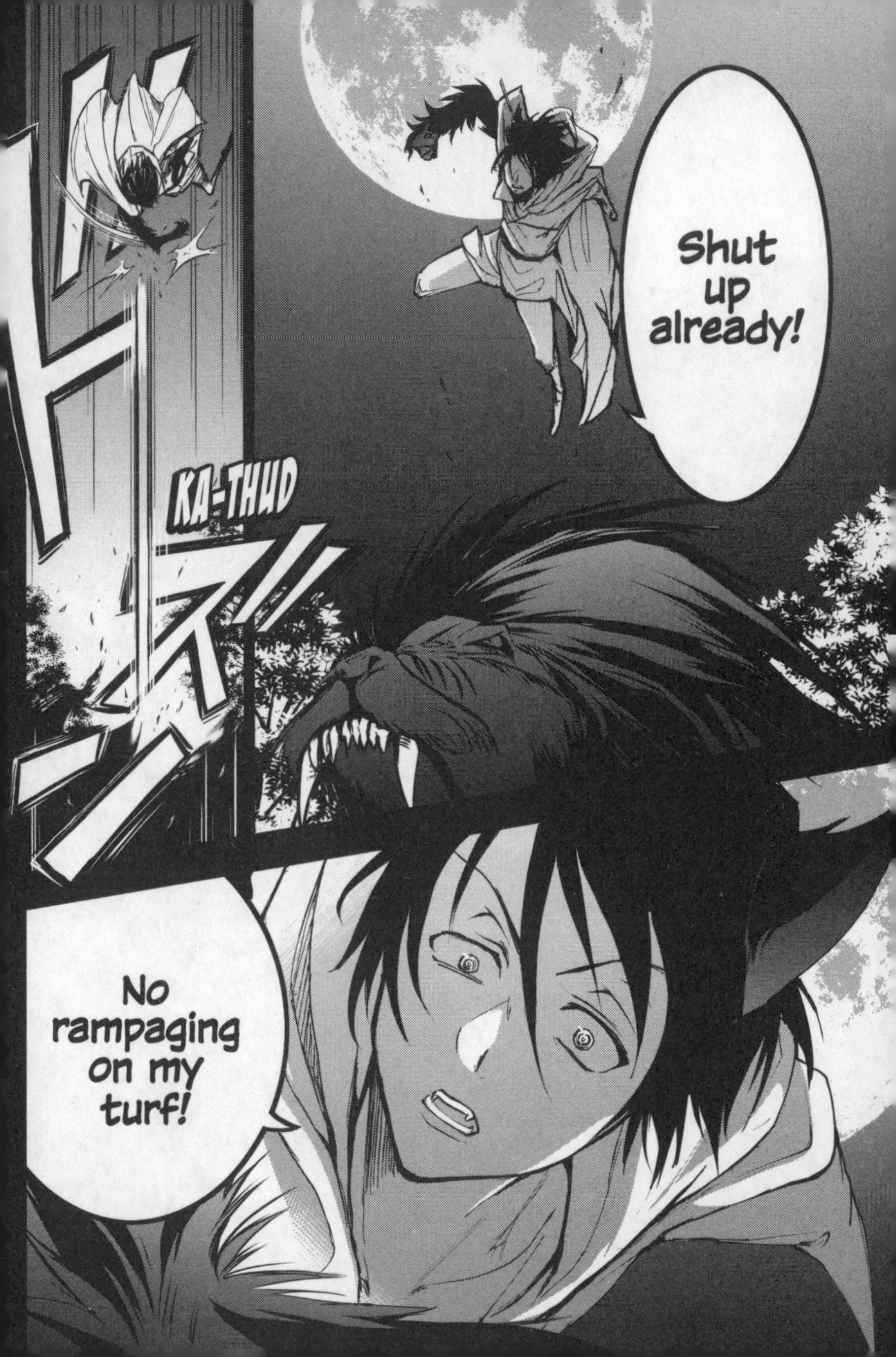
Shut up already!
KA-THUD
No rampaging on my turf!

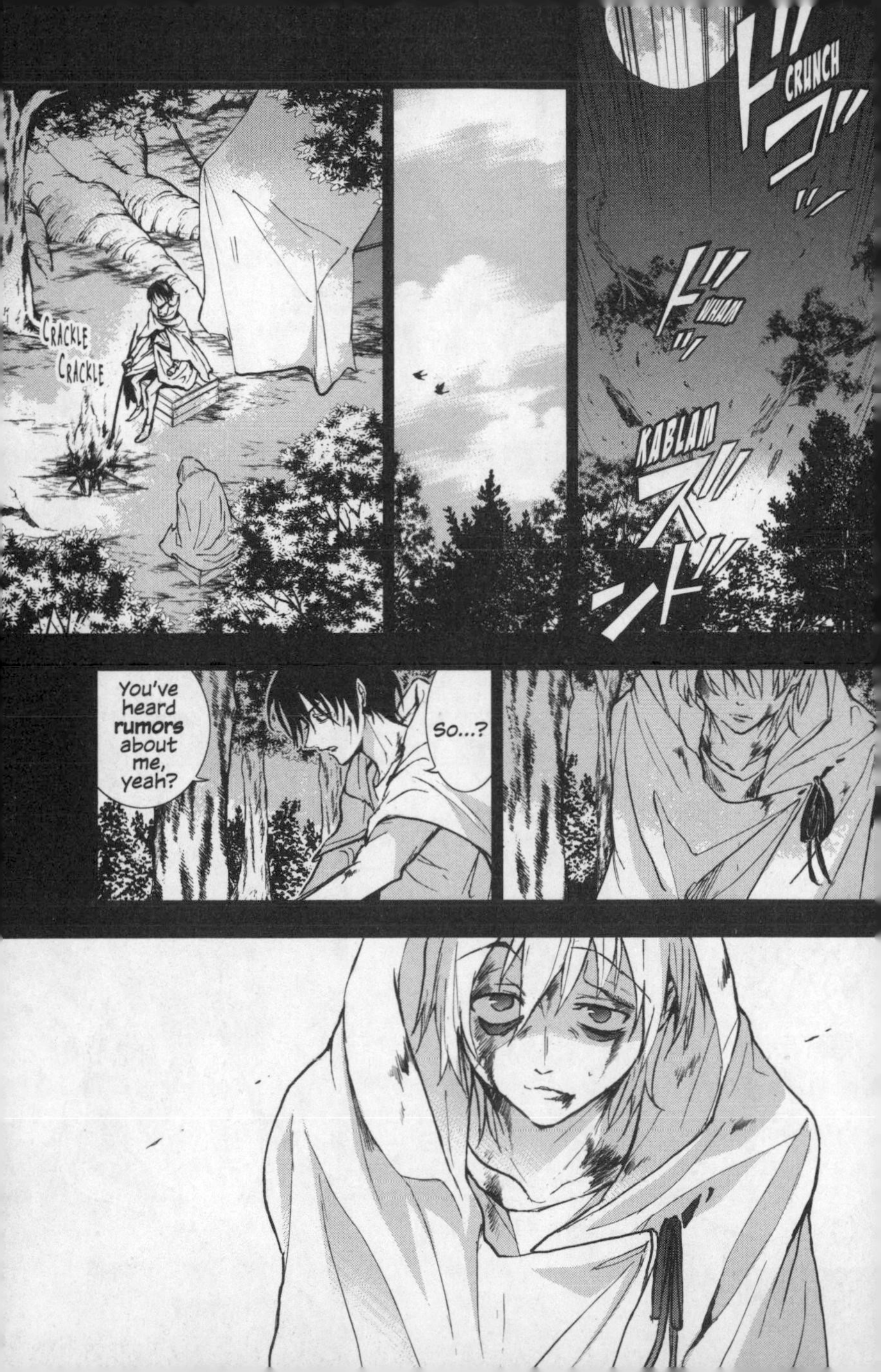

CRUNCH
WHAM
KABLAM
CRACKLE
CRACKLE
You've heard rumors about me, yeah?
So...?

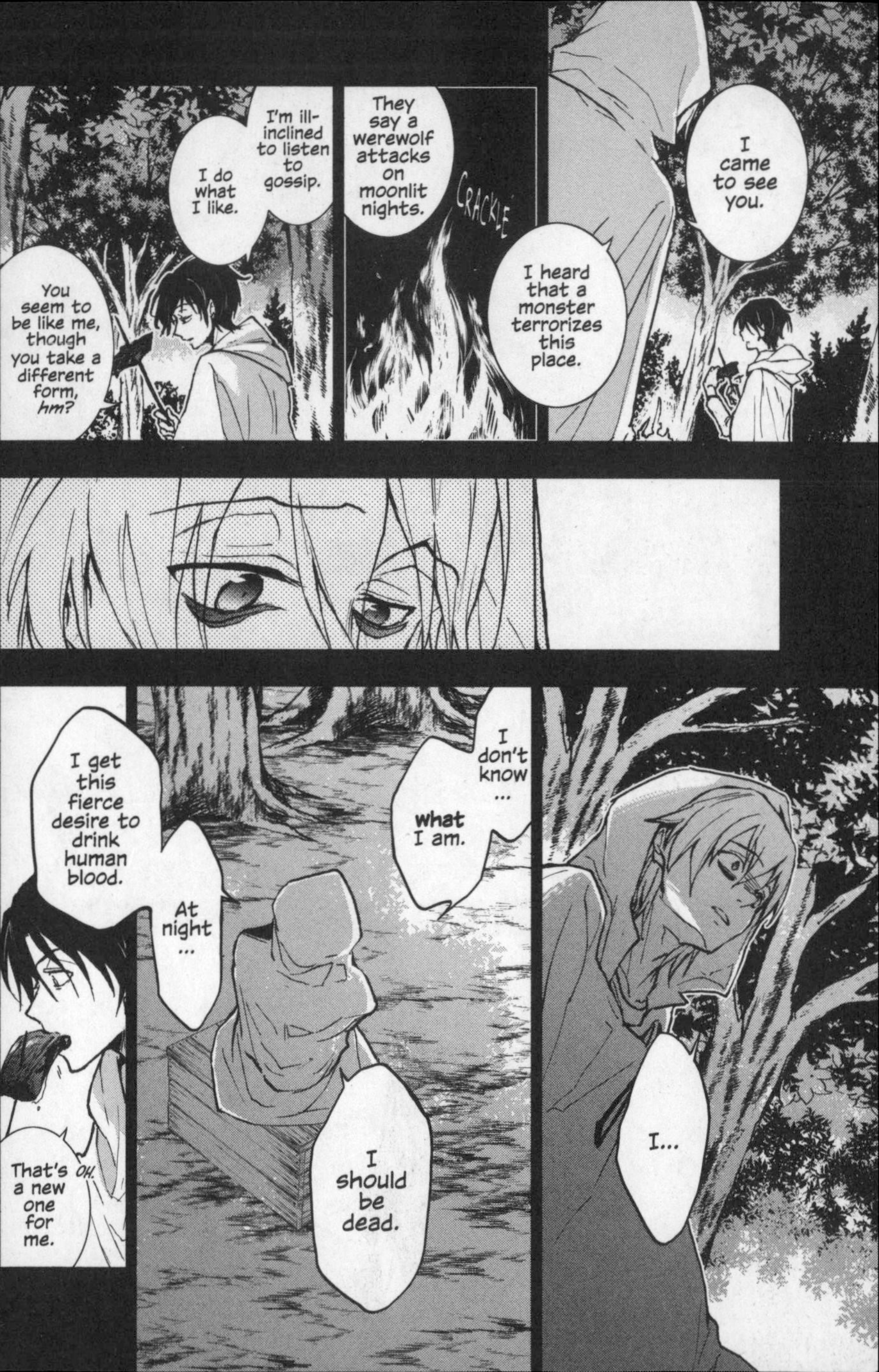
I came to see you.
I heard that a monster terrorizes this place.
They say a werewolf attacks on moonlit nights.
CRACKLE
I'm ill-inclined to listen to gossip.
I do what I like.
You seem to be like me, though you take a different form, *hm?*
I...
I don't know... **what** I am.
I should be dead.
At night...
I get this fierce desire to drink human blood.
OH.
That's a new one for me.

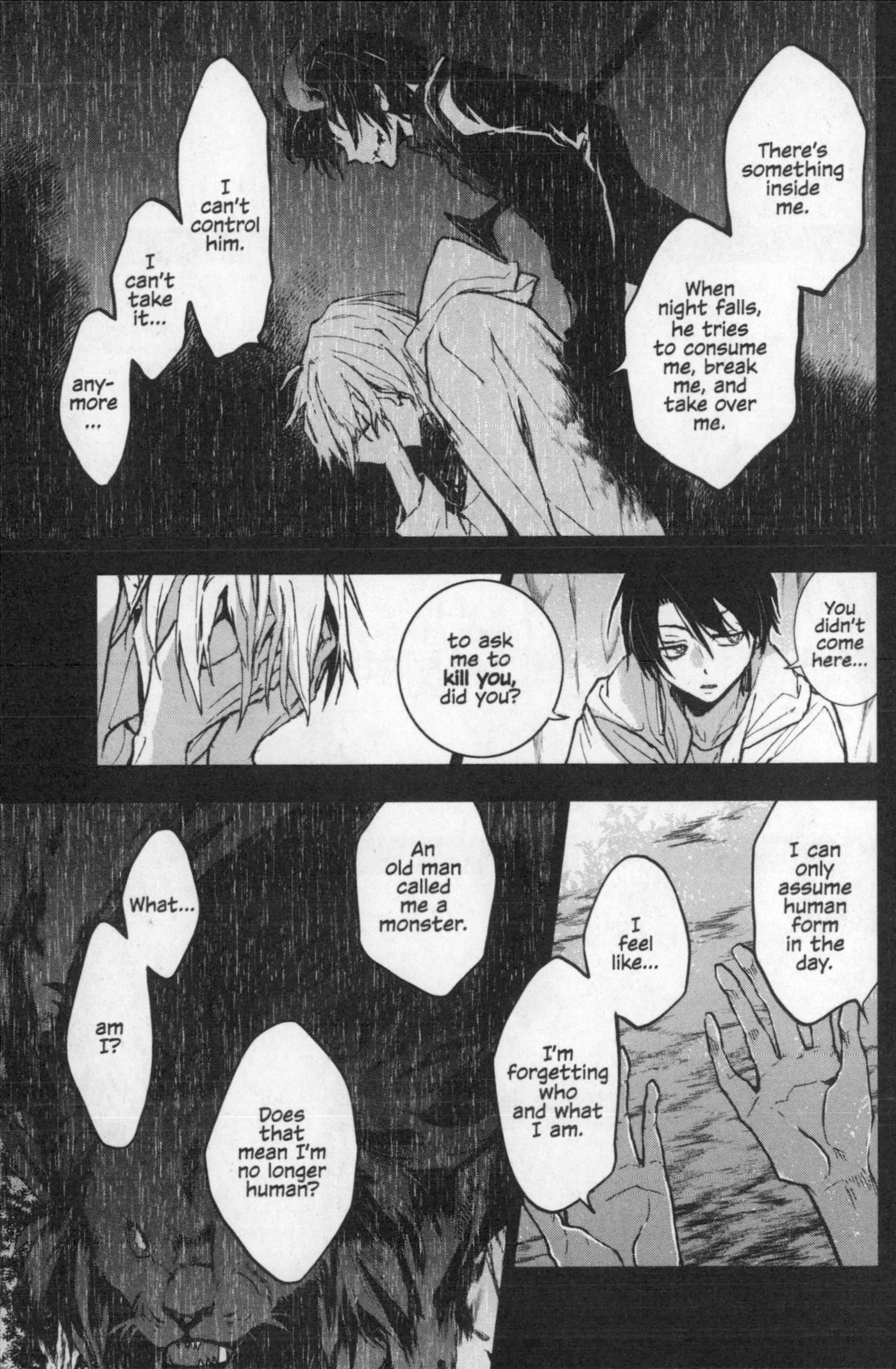
There's something inside me.
When night falls, he tries to consume me, break me, and take over me.
I can't control him.
I can't take it...
anymore...
You didn't come here...
to ask me to **kill you,** did you?
I can only assume human form in the day.
I feel like...
I'm forgetting who and what I am.
An old man called me a monster.
What...
am I?
Does that mean I'm no longer human?

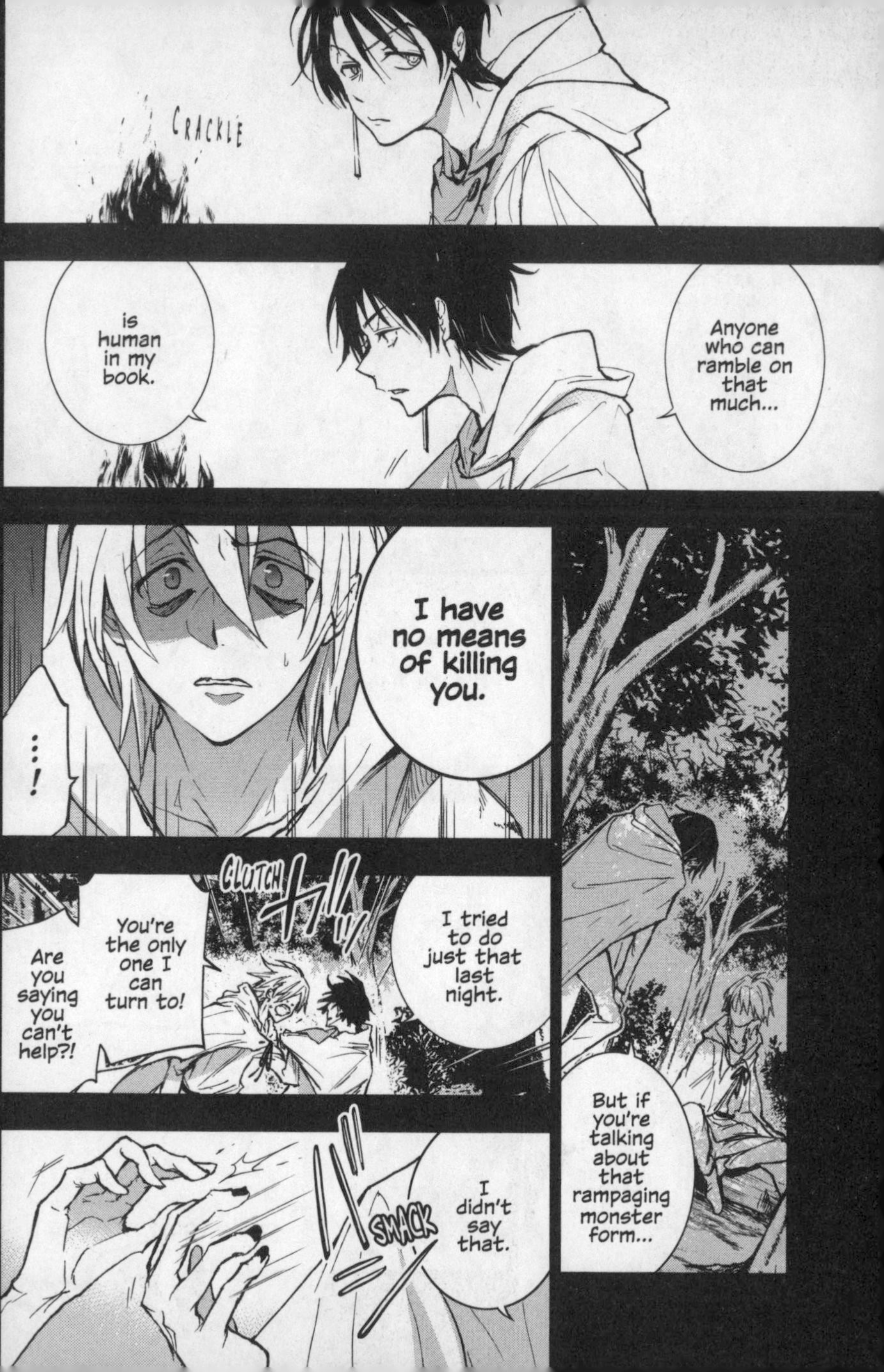
CRACKLE
Anyone who can ramble on that much...
is human in my book.
I have no means of killing you.
...!
CLUTCH
I tried to do just that last night.
You're the only one I can turn to!
Are you saying you can't help?!
SMACK
I didn't say that.
But if you're talking about that rampaging monster form...

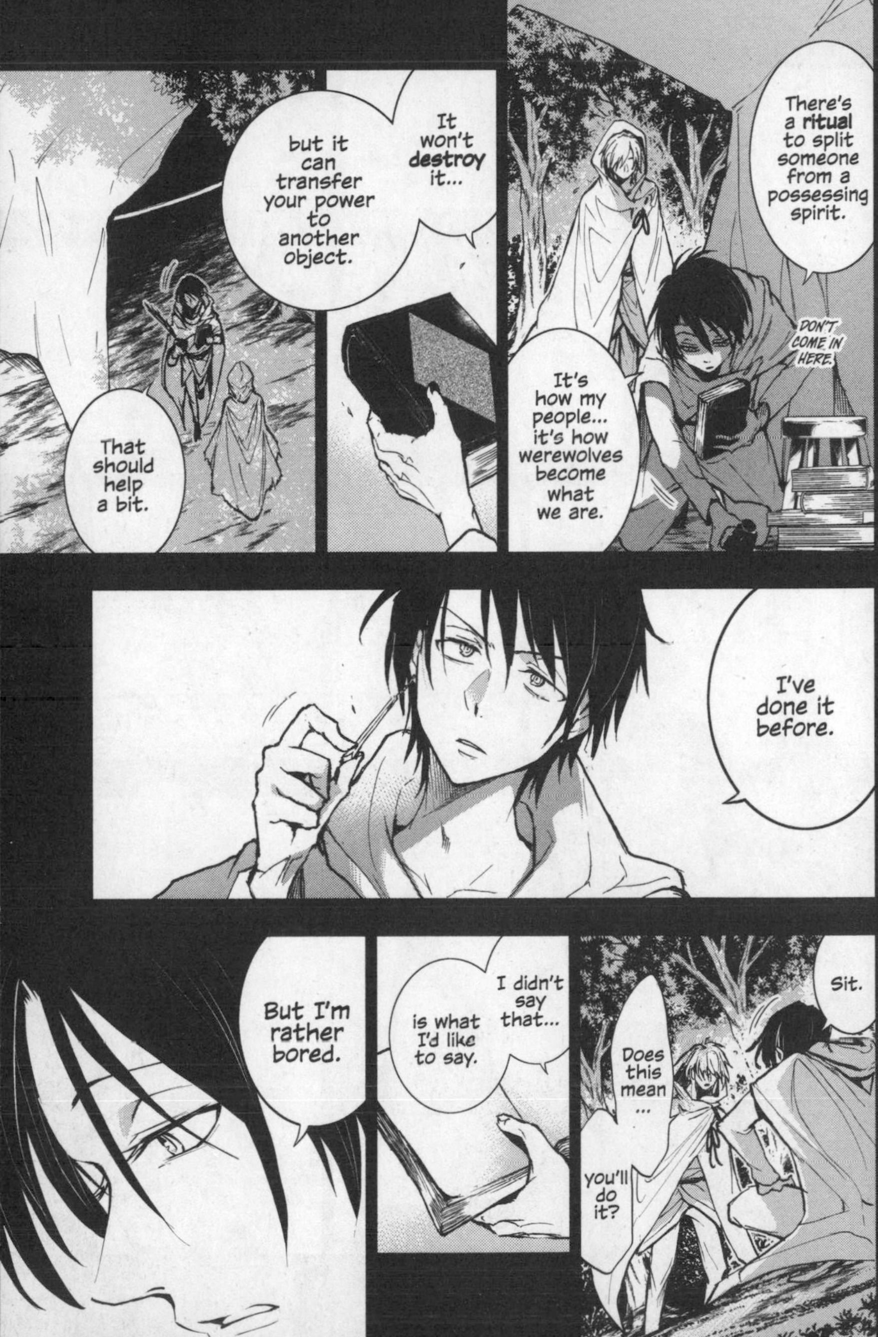

There's a ritual to split someone from a possessing spirit.
DON'T COME IN HERE.
It's how my people... it's how werewolves become what we are.
It won't destroy it...
but it can transfer your power to another object.
That should help a bit.
I've done it before.
Sit.
Does this mean ...
you'll do it?
I didn't say that...
is what I'd like to say.
But I'm rather bored.

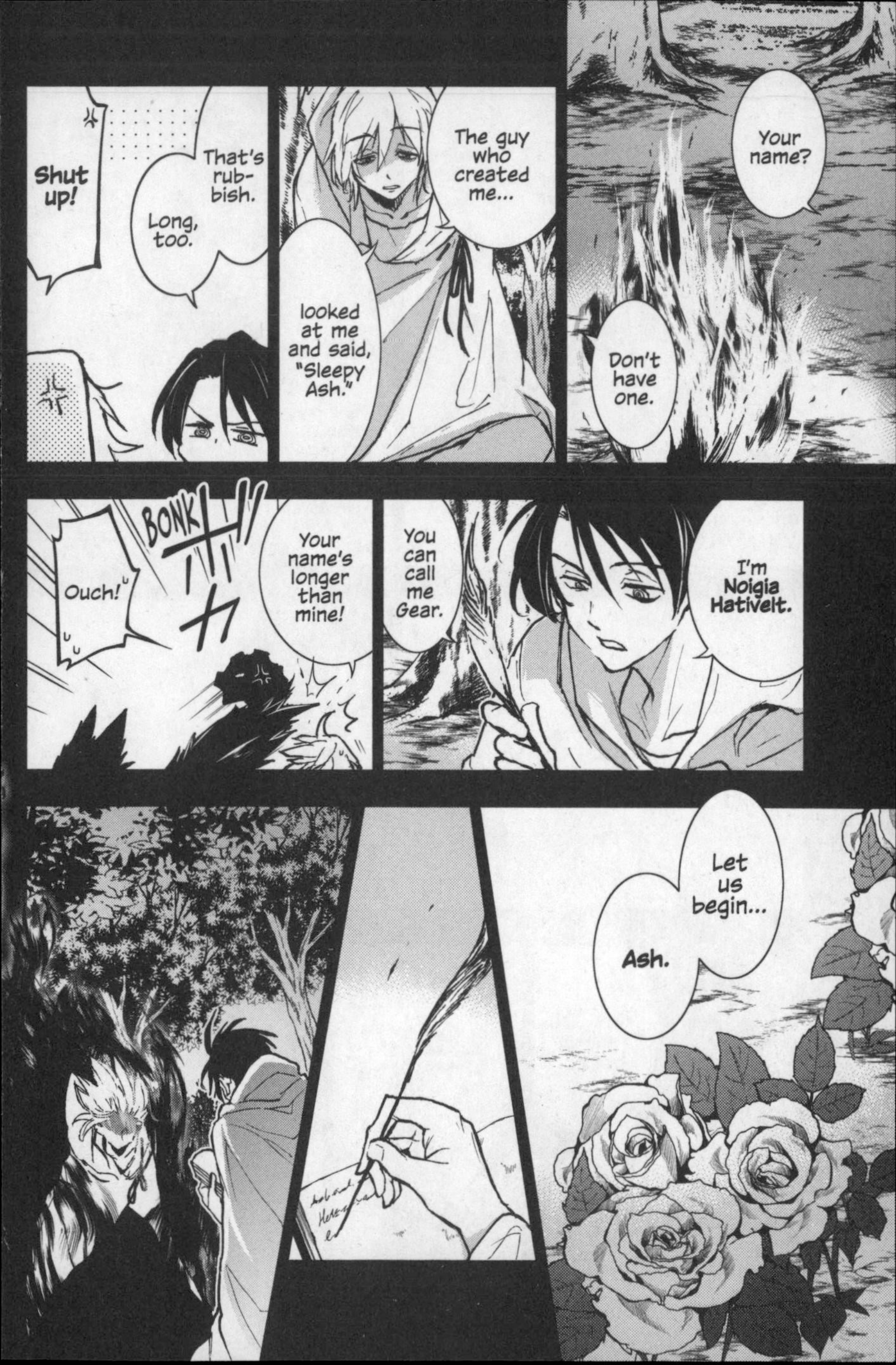
Your name?
Don't have one.
The guy who created me...
looked at me and said, "Sleepy Ash."
That's rub-bish.
Long, too.
Shut up!
I'm Noigia Hativelt.
You can call me Gear.
Your name's longer than mine!
BONK
Ouch!
Let us begin...
Ash.

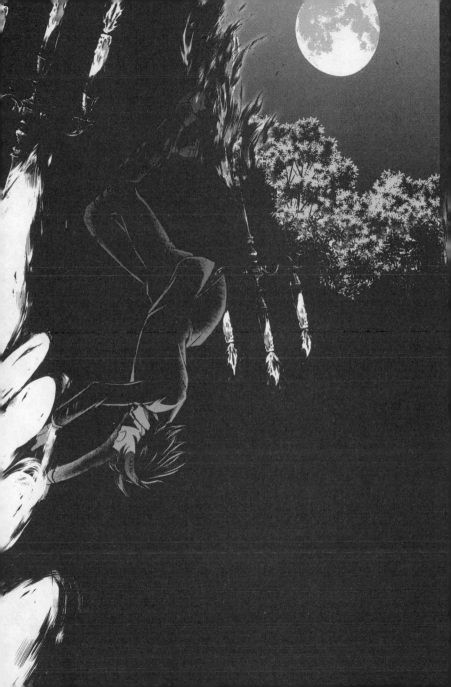

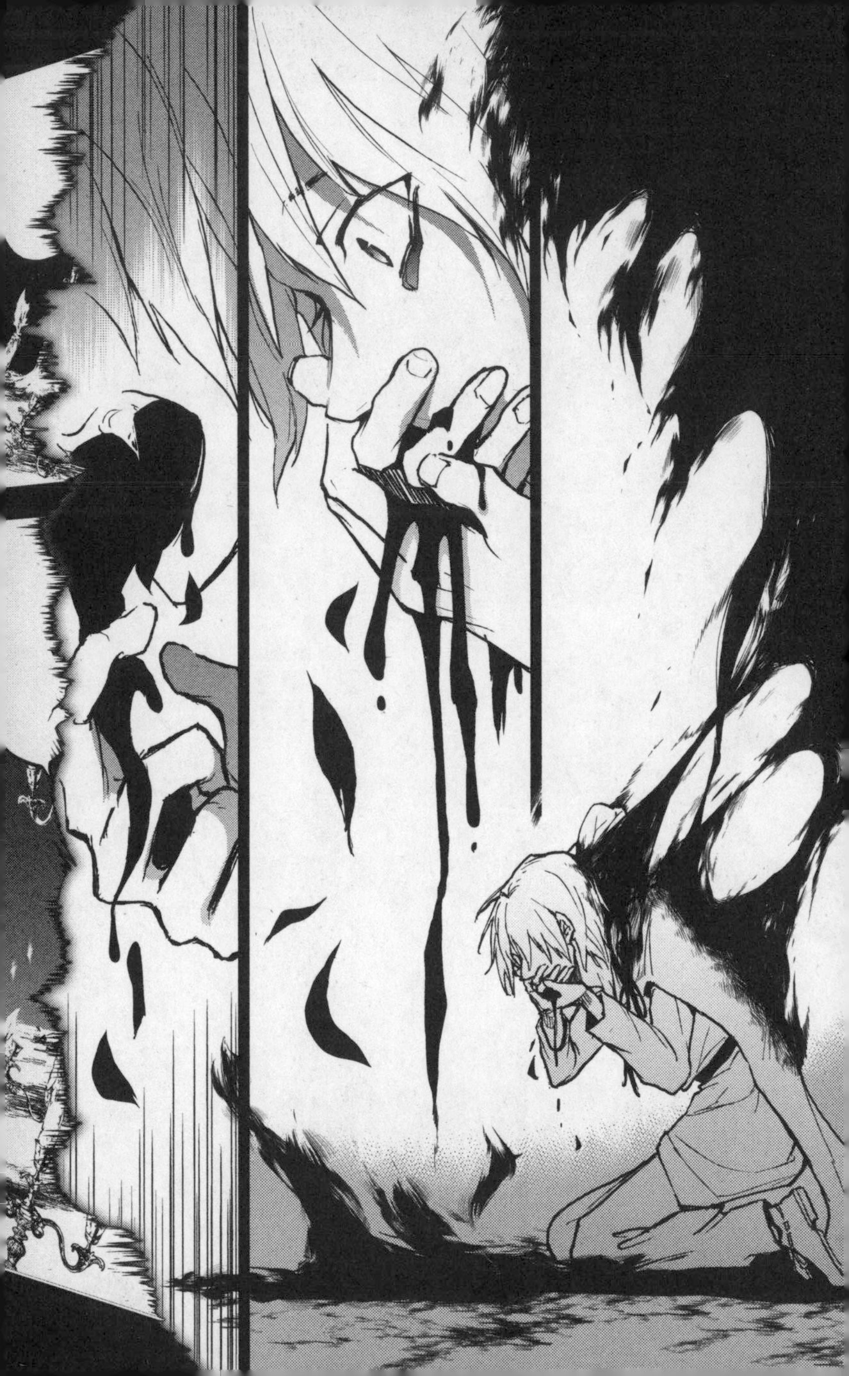

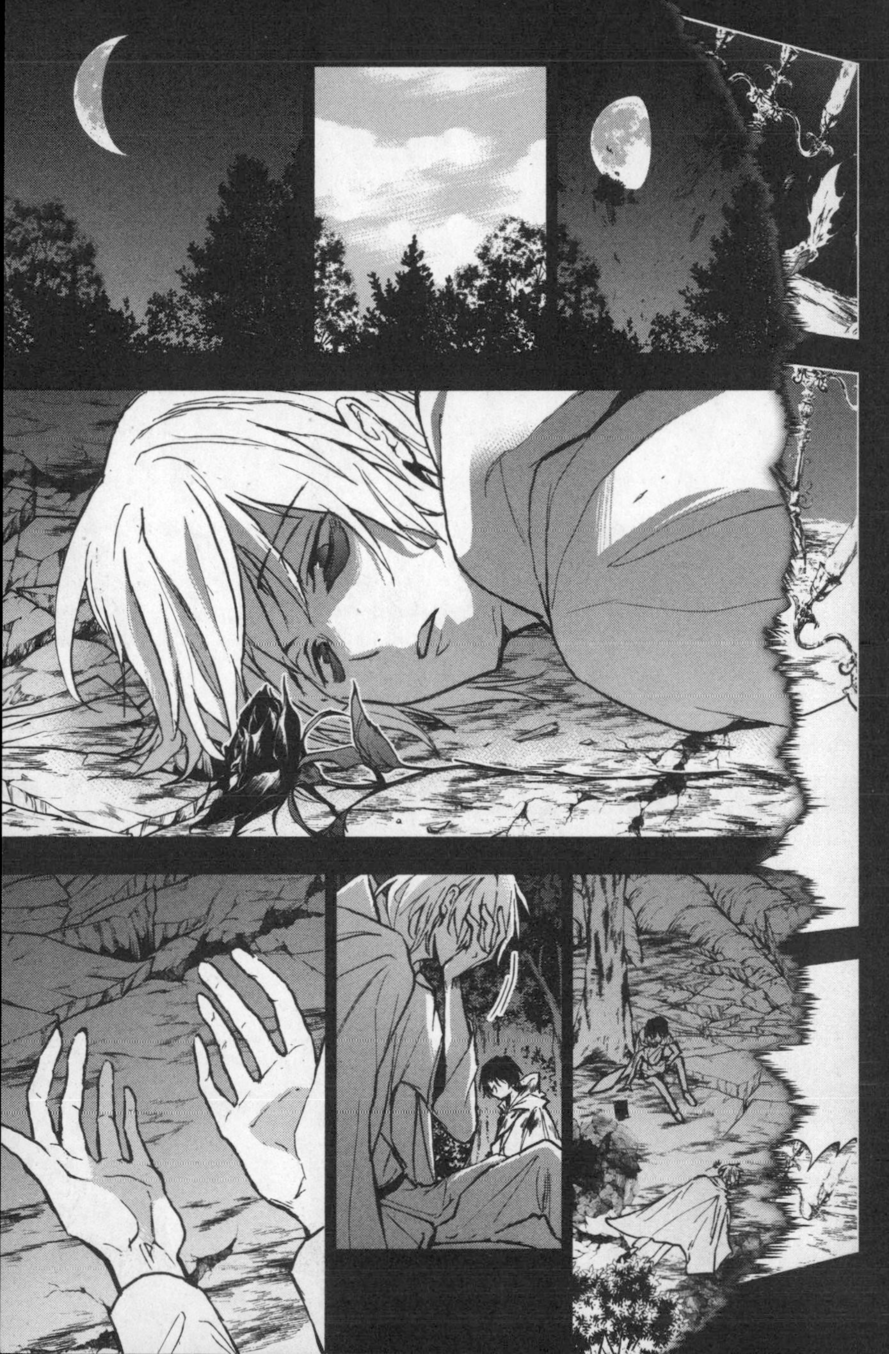

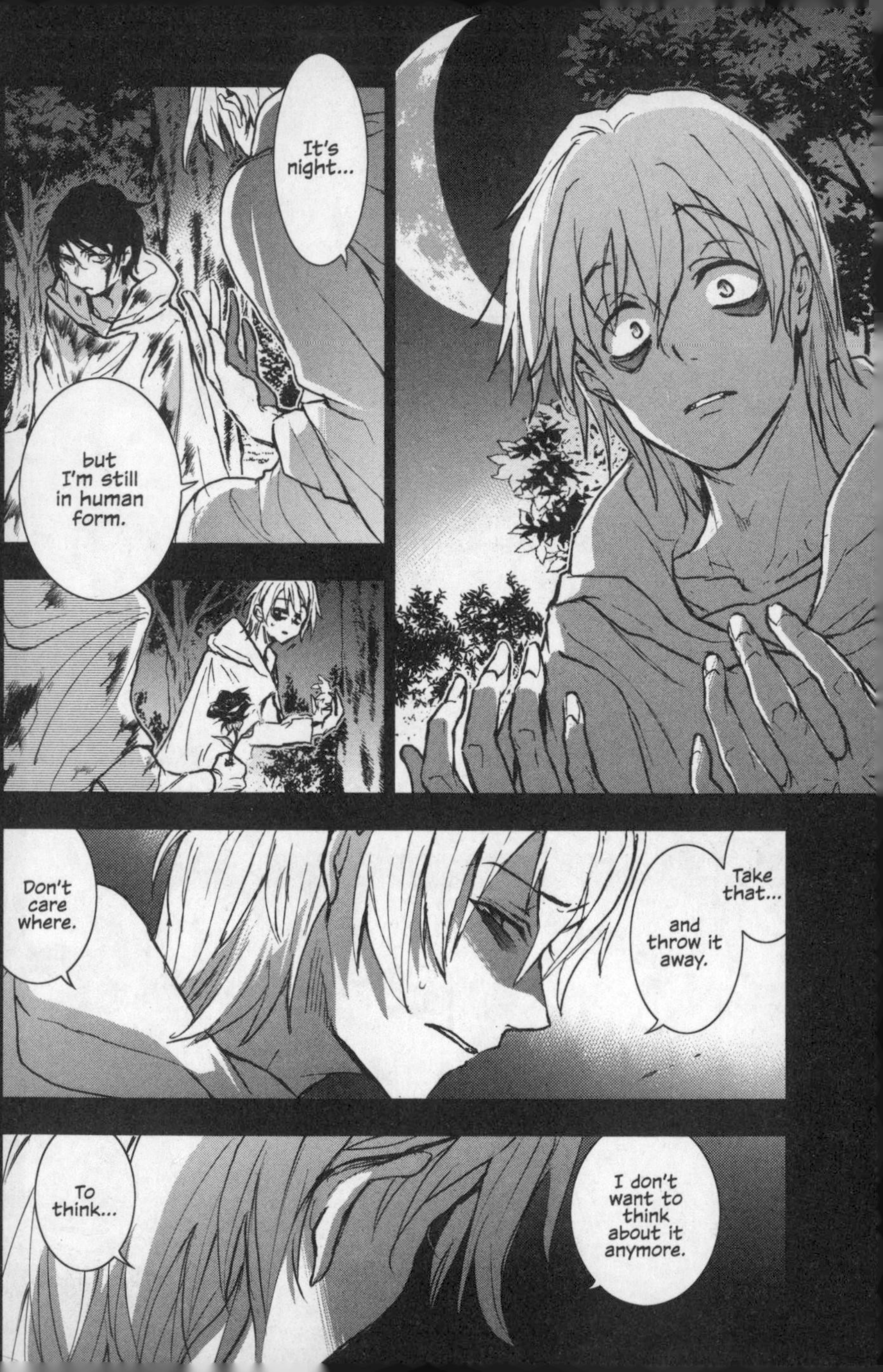
It's night...
but I'm still in human form.
Take that... and throw it away.
Don't care where.
I don't want to think about it anymore.
To think...

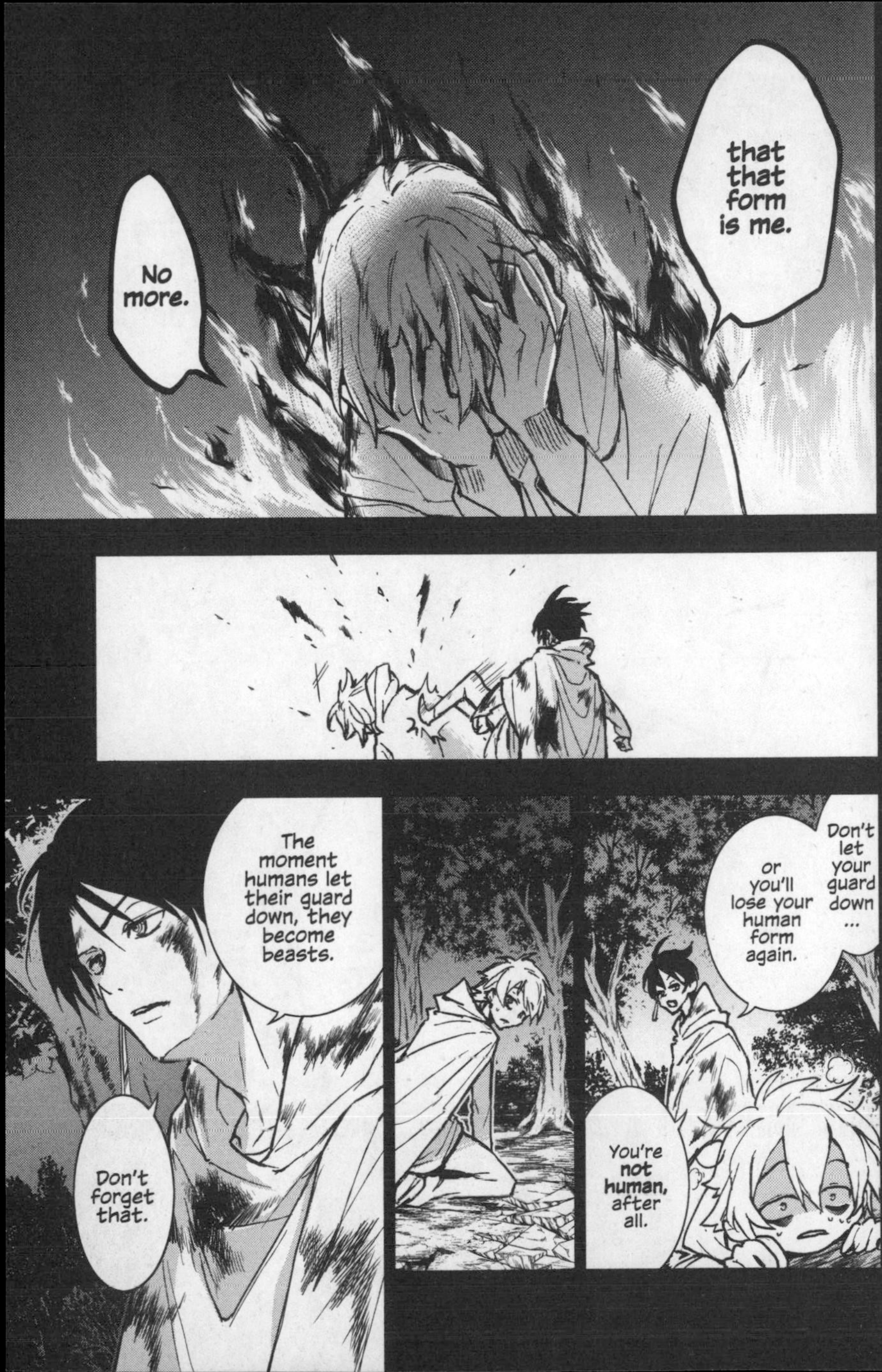
that that form is me.
No more.
Don't let your guard down ...
or you'll lose your human form again.
You're **not human,** after all.
The moment humans let their guard down, they become beasts.
Don't forget that.

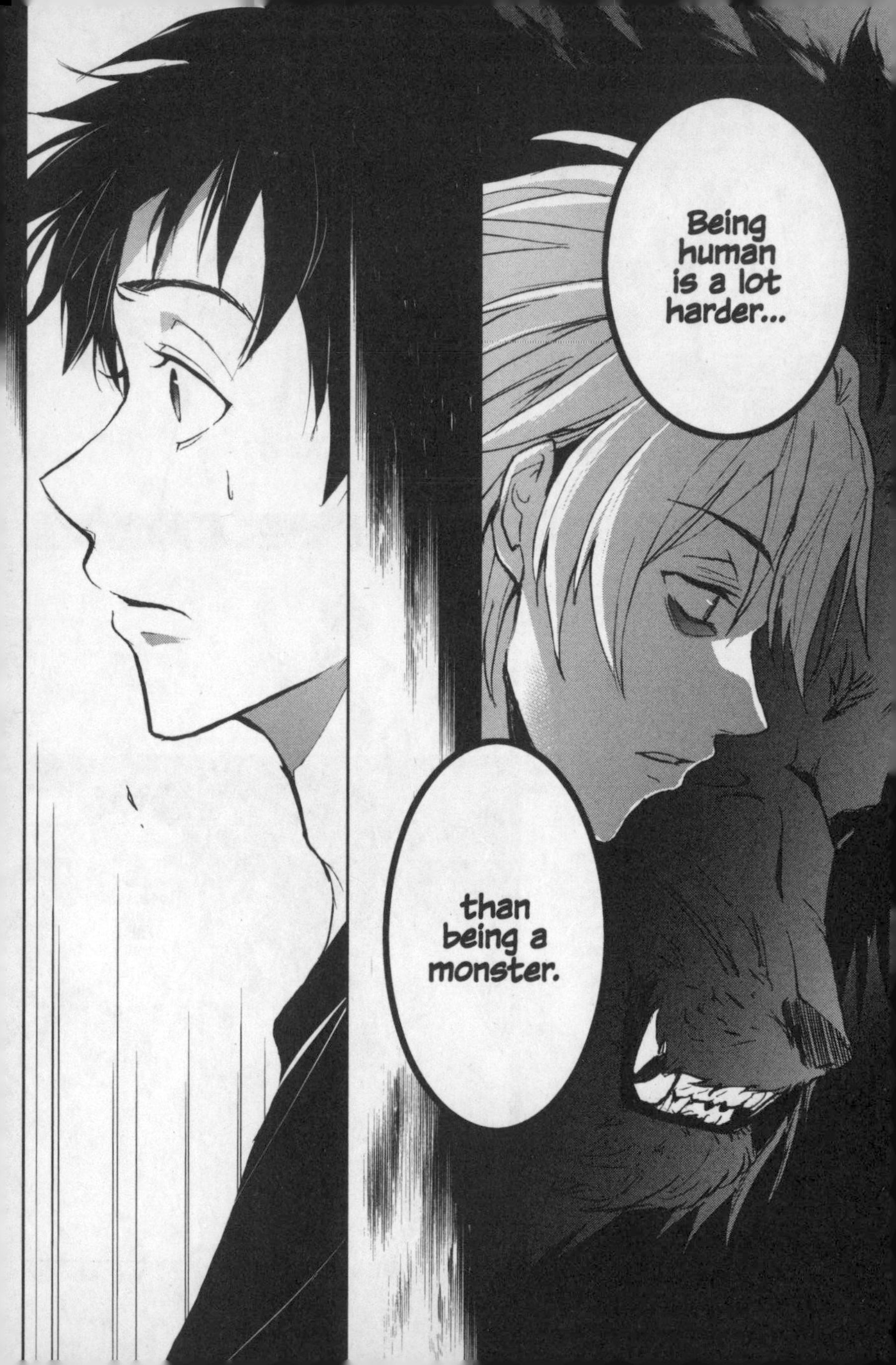
Being human is a lot harder...
than being a monster.

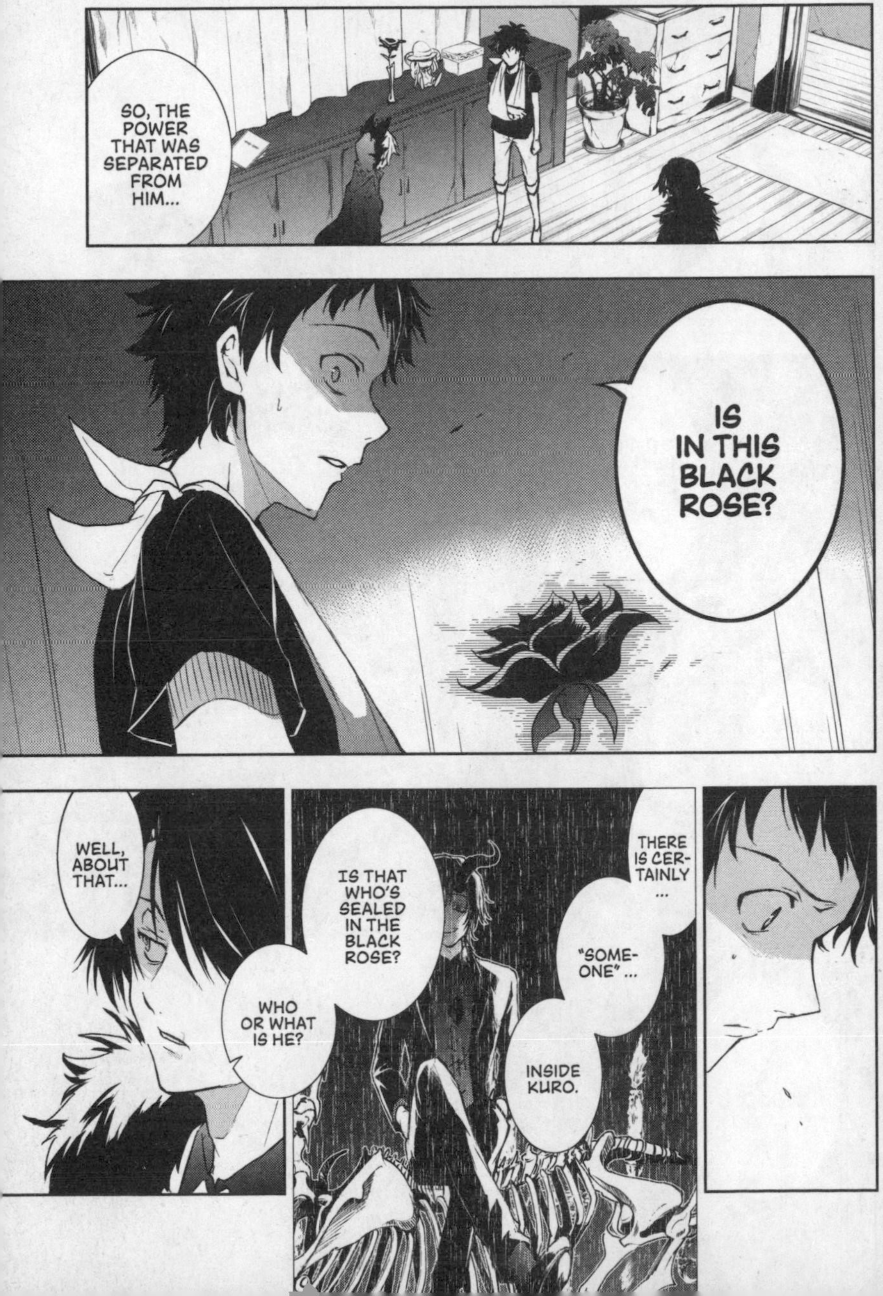
SO, THE POWER THAT WAS SEPARATED FROM HIM...
IS IN THIS BLACK ROSE?
THERE IS CERTAINLY...
"SOMEONE"...
INSIDE KURO.
IS THAT WHO'S SEALED IN THE BLACK ROSE?
WHO OR WHAT IS HE?
WELL, ABOUT THAT...

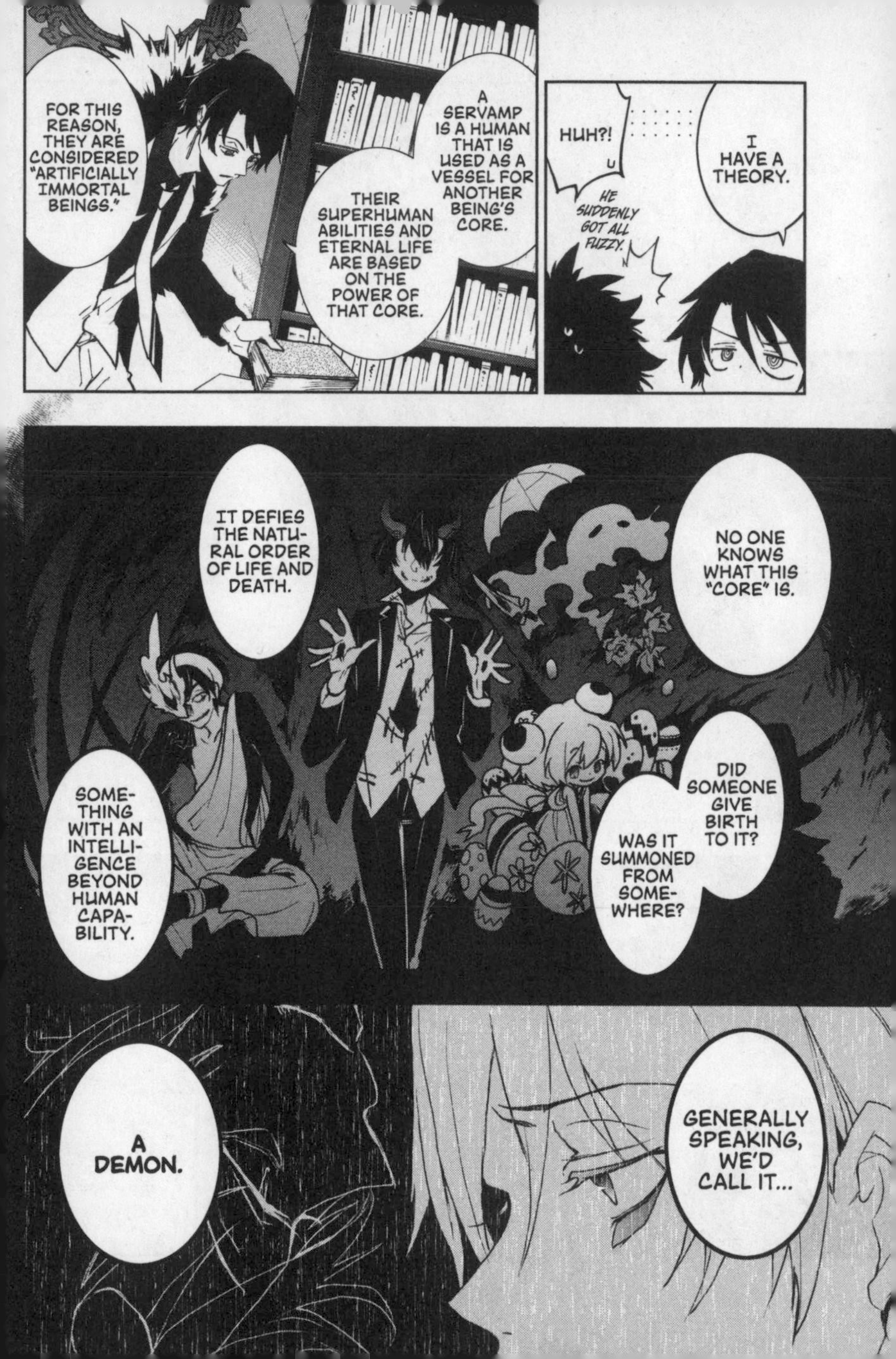
I HAVE A THEORY.
HUH?!
HE SUDDENLY GOT ALL FUZZY.
A SERVAMP IS A HUMAN THAT IS USED AS A VESSEL FOR ANOTHER BEING'S CORE.
THEIR SUPERHUMAN ABILITIES AND ETERNAL LIFE ARE BASED ON THE POWER OF THAT CORE.
FOR THIS REASON, THEY ARE CONSIDERED "ARTIFICIALLY IMMORTAL BEINGS."
NO ONE KNOWS WHAT THIS "CORE" IS.
DID SOMEONE GIVE BIRTH TO IT?
WAS IT SUMMONED FROM SOME-WHERE?
IT DEFIES THE NATU-RAL ORDER OF LIFE AND DEATH.
SOME-THING WITH AN INTELLI-GENCE BEYOND HUMAN CAPA-BILITY.
GENERALLY SPEAKING, WE'D CALL IT...
A DEMON.

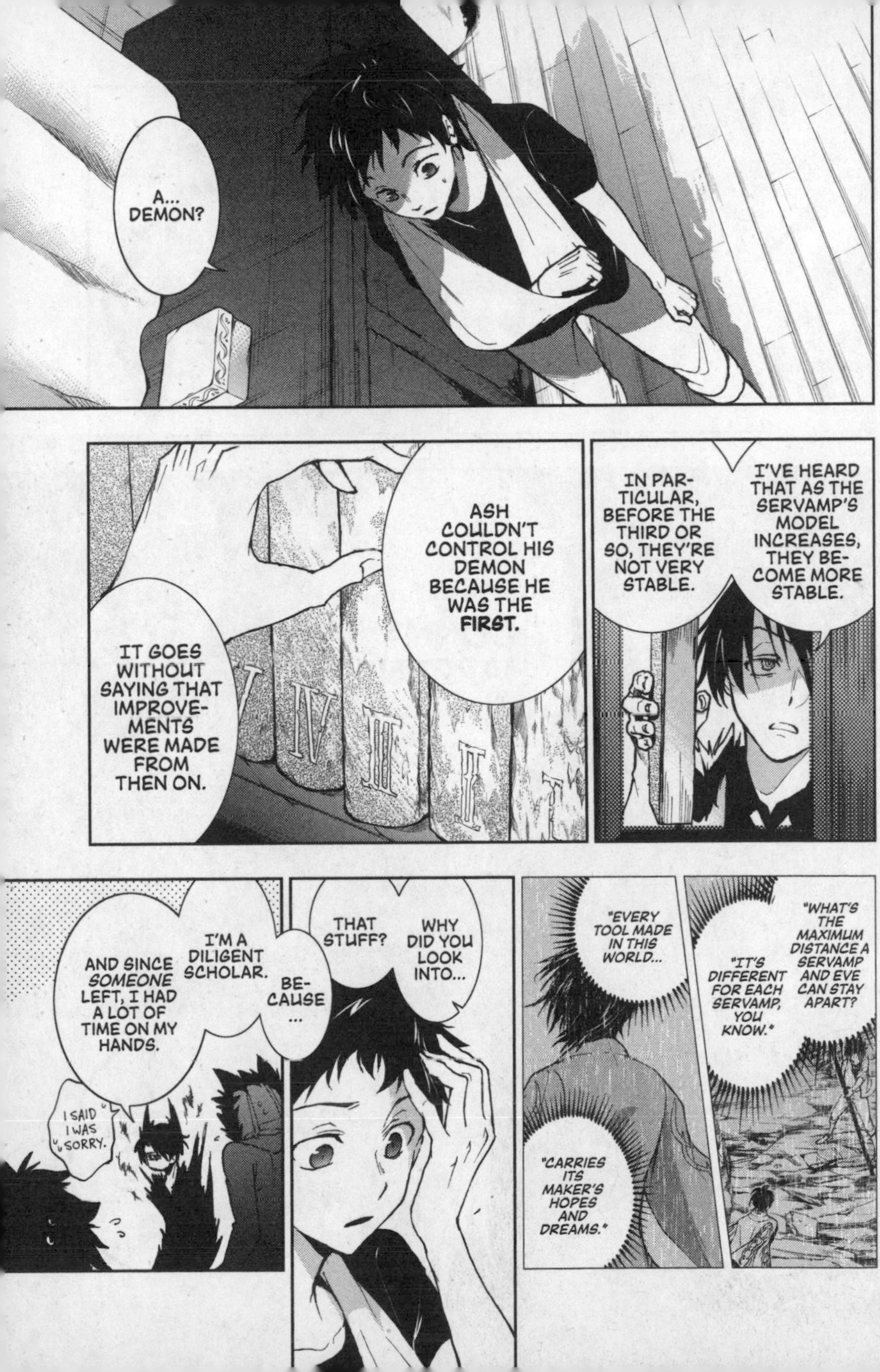
A... DEMON?
I'VE HEARD THAT AS THE SERVAMP'S MODEL INCREASES, THEY BE-COME MORE STABLE.
IN PAR-TICULAR, BEFORE THE THIRD OR SO, THEY'RE NOT VERY STABLE.
ASH COULDN'T CONTROL HIS DEMON BECAUSE HE WAS THE FIRST.
IT GOES WITHOUT SAYING THAT IMPROVE-MENTS WERE MADE FROM THEN ON.
"WHAT'S THE MAXIMUM DISTANCE A SERVAMP AND EVE CAN STAY APART?
"IT'S DIFFERENT FOR EACH SERVAMP, YOU KNOW."
"EVERY TOOL MADE IN THIS WORLD...
"CARRIES ITS MAKER'S HOPES AND DREAMS."
WHY DID YOU LOOK INTO...
THAT STUFF?
BE-CAUSE ...
I'M A DILIGENT SCHOLAR.
AND SINCE SOMEONE LEFT, I HAD A LOT OF TIME ON MY HANDS.
I SAID I WAS SORRY.

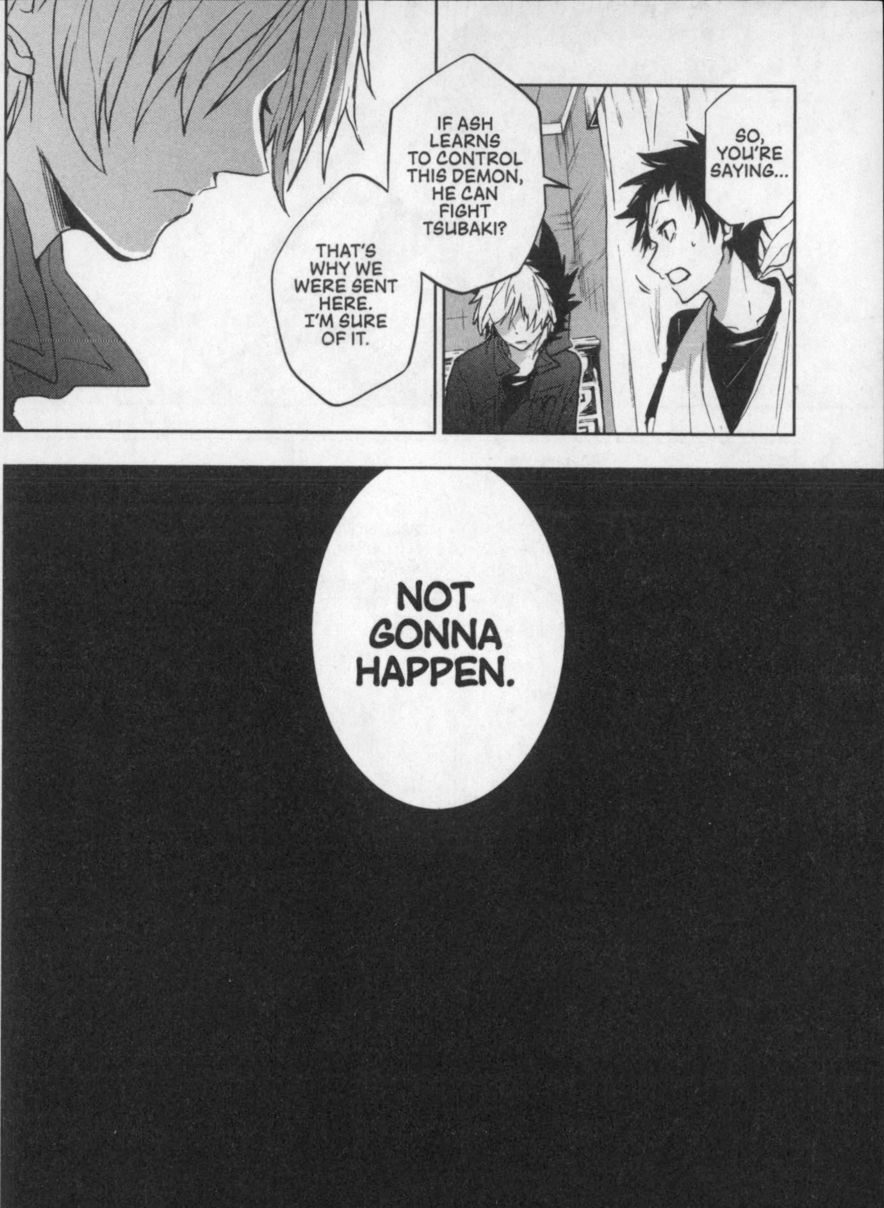
SO, YOU'RE SAYING...
IF ASH LEARNS TO CONTROL THIS DEMON, HE CAN FIGHT TSUBAKI?
THAT'S WHY WE WERE SENT HERE. I'M SURE OF IT.
NOT GONNA HAPPEN.

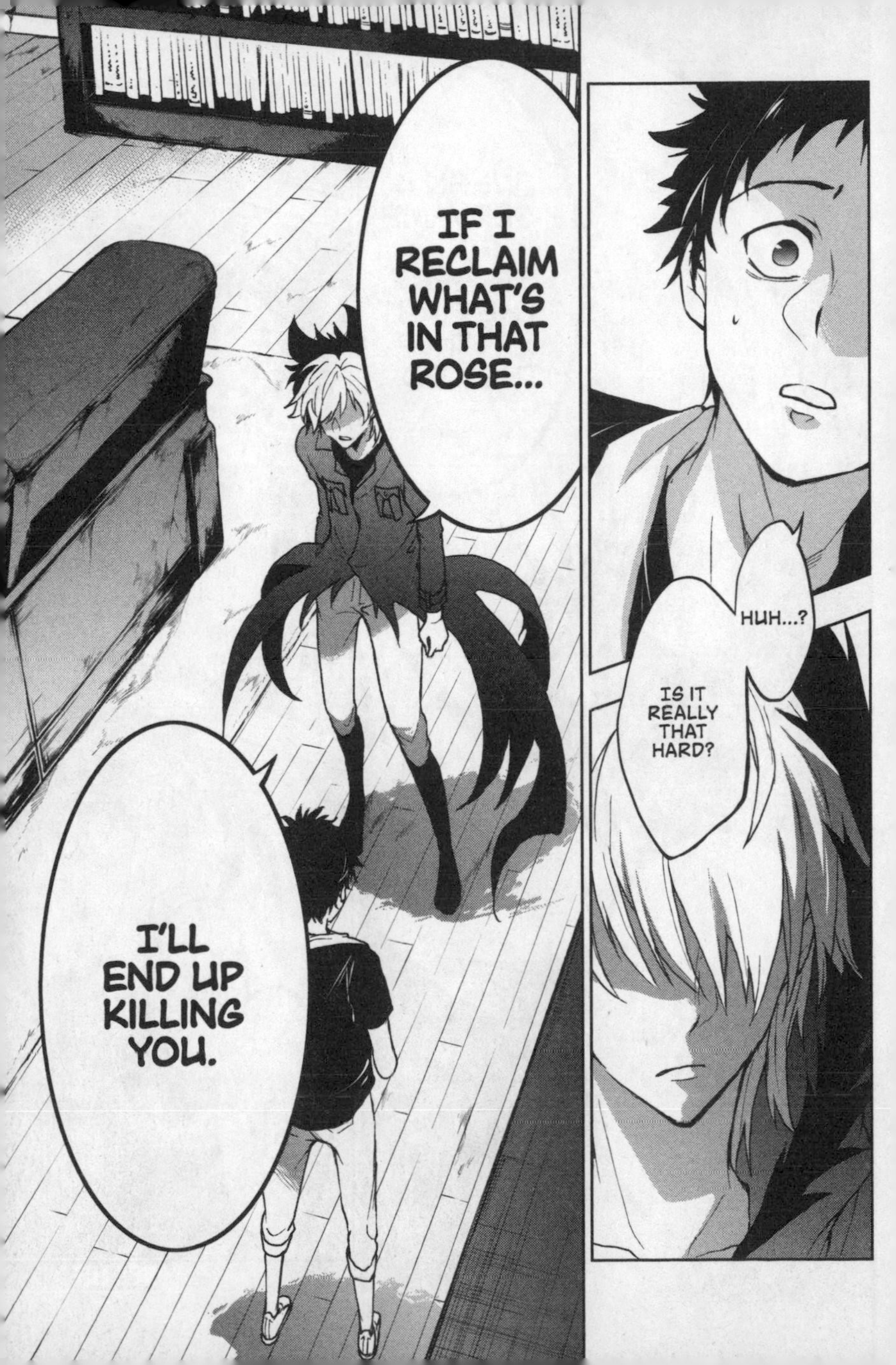
HUH...?
IS IT REALLY THAT HARD?
IF I RECLAIM WHAT'S IN THAT ROSE...
I'LL END UP KILLING YOU.

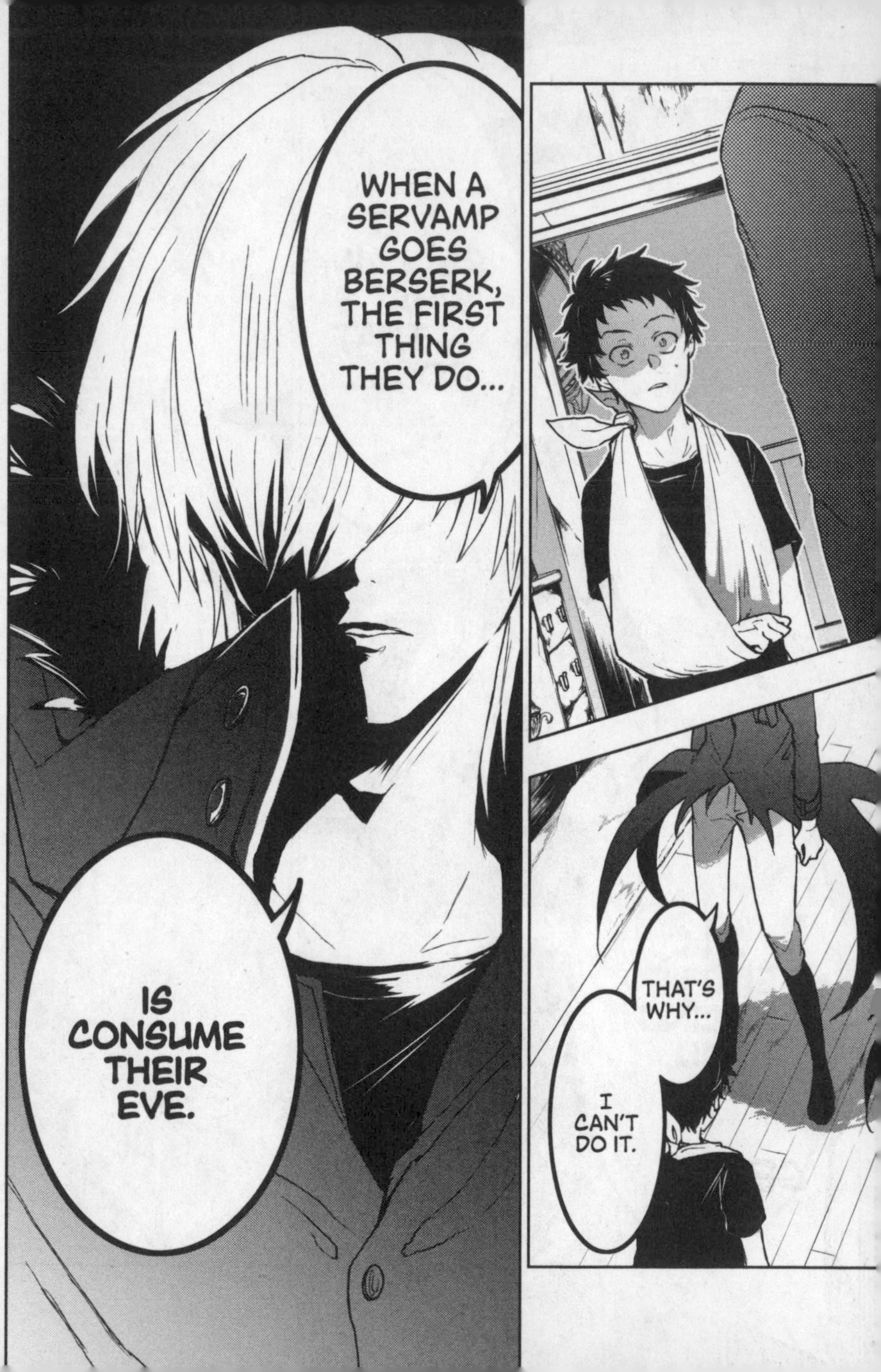
WHEN A SERVAMP GOES BERSERK, THE FIRST THING THEY DO...
IS CONSUME THEIR EVE.
THAT'S WHY...
I CAN'T DO IT.

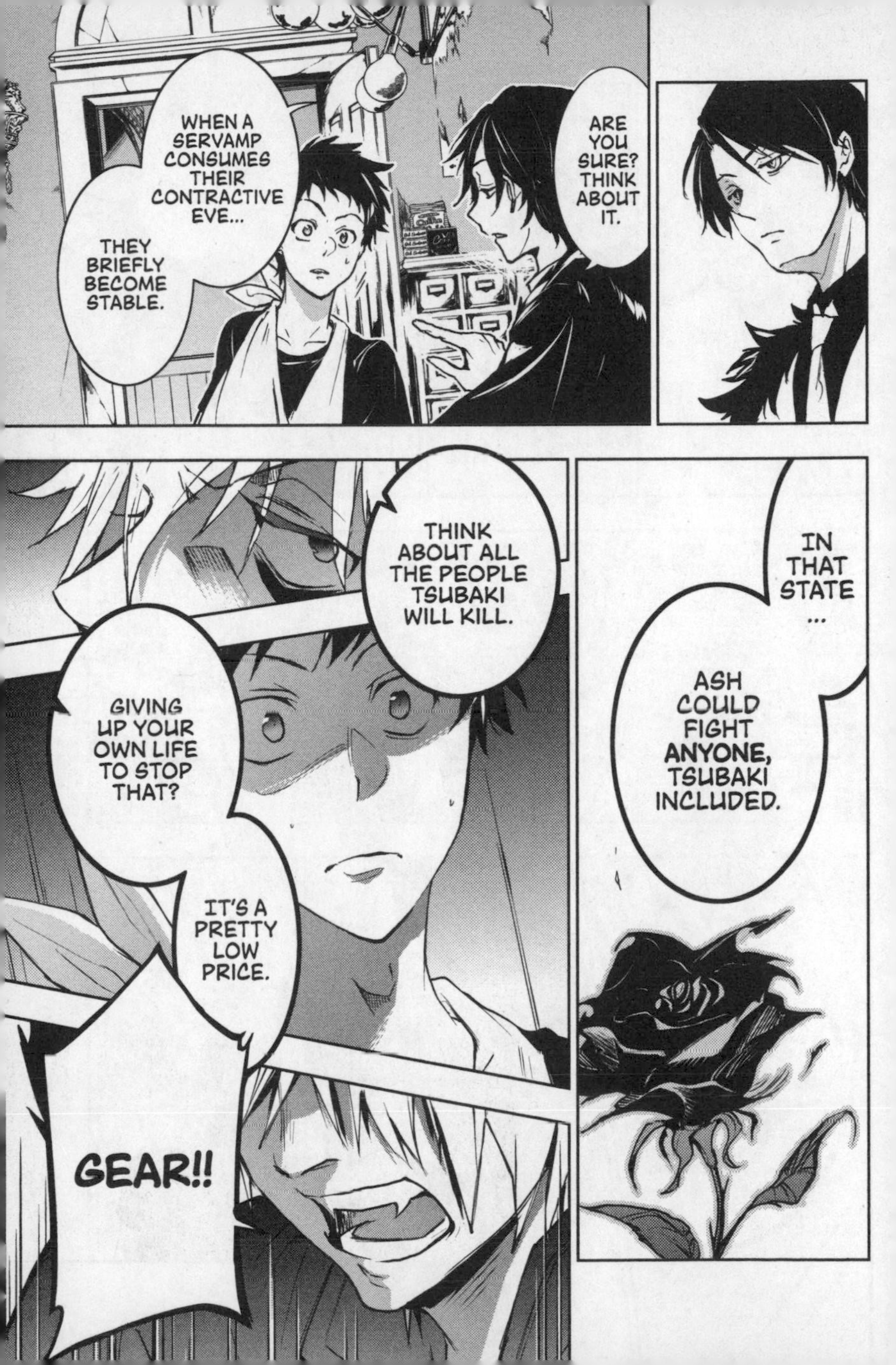
ARE YOU SURE? THINK ABOUT IT.
WHEN A SERVAMP CONSUMES THEIR CONTRACTIVE EVE...
THEY BRIEFLY BECOME STABLE.
IN THAT STATE...
ASH COULD FIGHT ANYONE, TSUBAKI INCLUDED.
THINK ABOUT ALL THE PEOPLE TSUBAKI WILL KILL.
GIVING UP YOUR OWN LIFE TO STOP THAT?
IT'S A PRETTY LOW PRICE.
GEAR!!

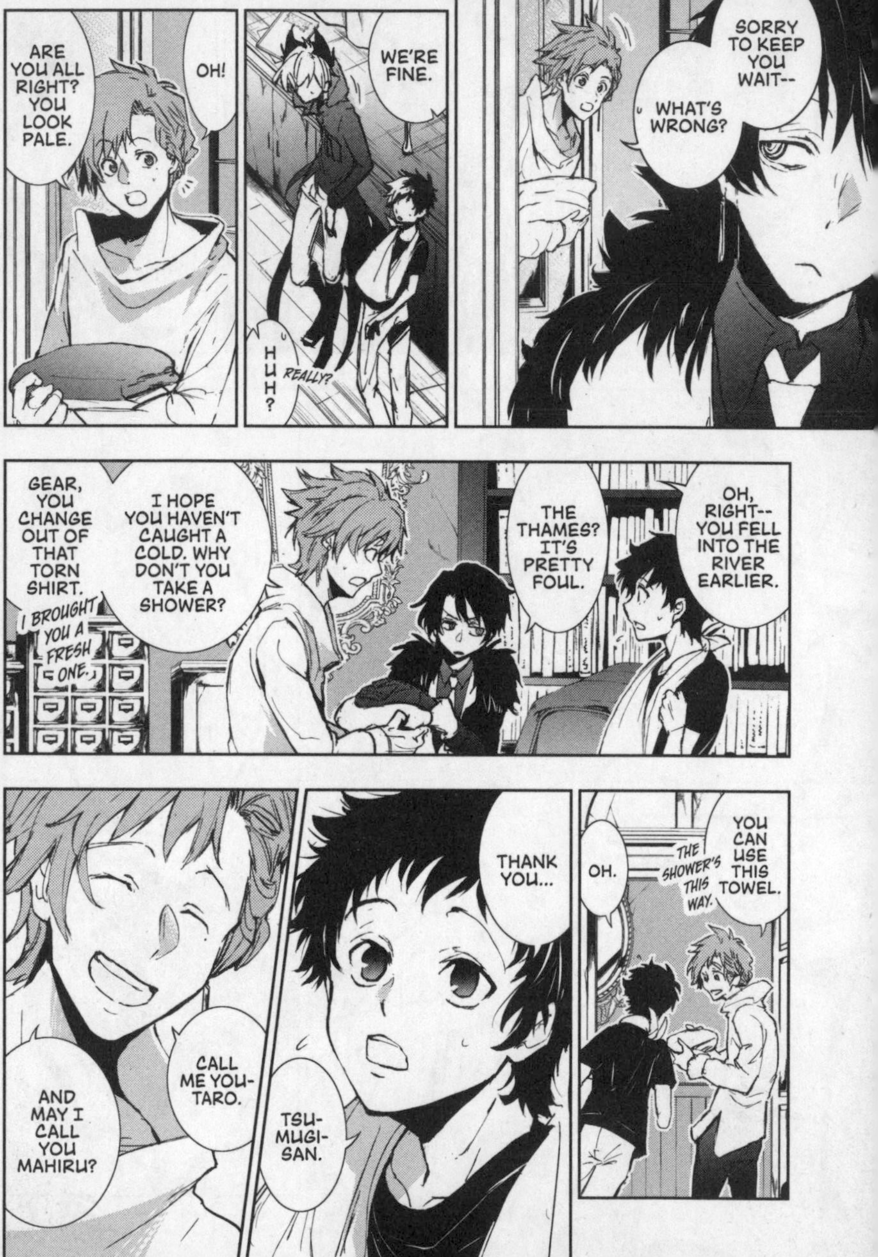
SORRY TO KEEP YOU WAIT--
WHAT'S WRONG?
WE'RE FINE.
REALLY?
HUH?
OH!
ARE YOU ALL RIGHT? YOU LOOK PALE.
OH, RIGHT--YOU FELL INTO THE RIVER EARLIER.
THE THAMES? IT'S PRETTY FOUL.
I HOPE YOU HAVEN'T CAUGHT A COLD. WHY DON'T YOU TAKE A SHOWER?
GEAR, YOU CHANGE OUT OF THAT TORN SHIRT.
I BROUGHT YOU A FRESH ONE.
YOU CAN USE THIS TOWEL.
THE SHOWER'S THIS WAY.
OH.
THANK YOU...
TSU-MUGI-SAN.
CALL ME YOU-TARO.
AND MAY I CALL YOU MAHIRU?

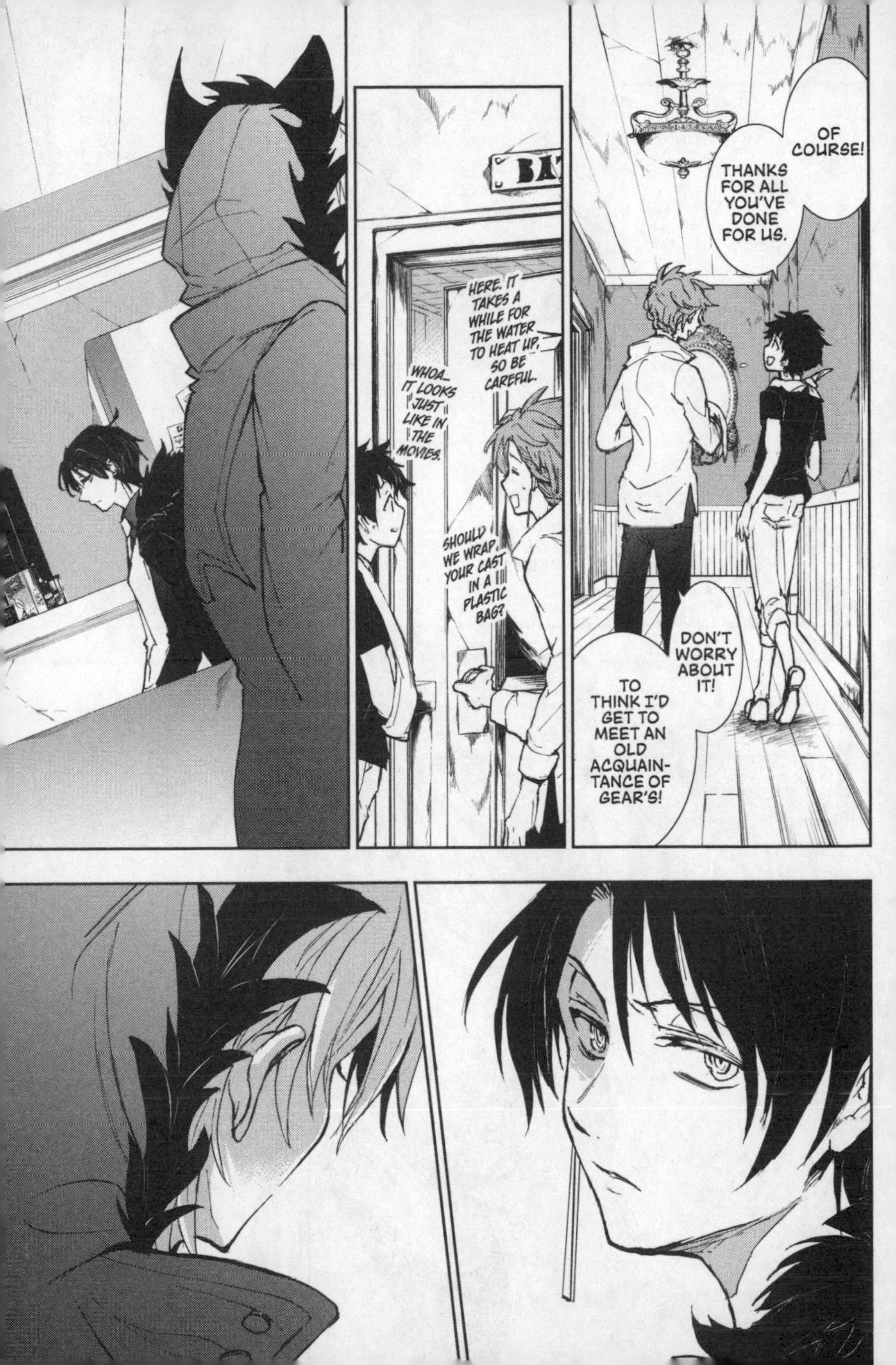
OF COURSE! THANKS FOR ALL YOU'VE DONE FOR US.
DON'T WORRY ABOUT IT!
TO THINK I'D GET TO MEET AN OLD ACQUAINTANCE OF GEAR'S!
HERE. IT TAKES A WHILE FOR THE WATER TO HEAT UP, SO BE CAREFUL.
WHOA... IT LOOKS JUST LIKE IN THE MOVIES.
SHOULD WE WRAP YOUR CAST IN A PLASTIC BAG?

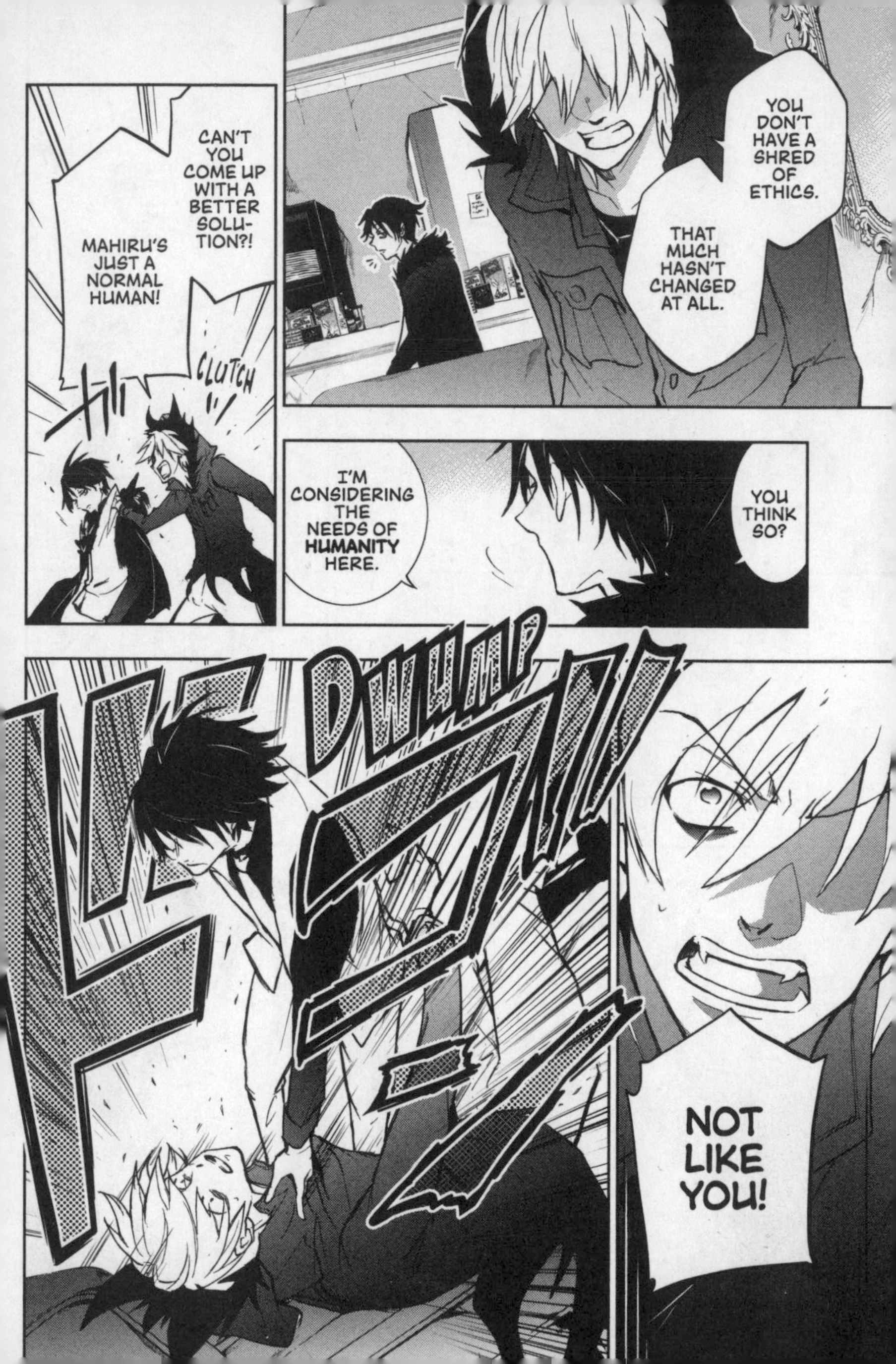
YOU DON'T HAVE A SHRED OF ETHICS.
THAT MUCH HASN'T CHANGED AT ALL.
CAN'T YOU COME UP WITH A BETTER SOLU-TION?!
MAHIRU'S JUST A NORMAL HUMAN!
CLUTCH
YOU THINK SO?
I'M CONSIDERING THE NEEDS OF **HUMANITY** HERE.
NOT LIKE YOU!
DWUMP

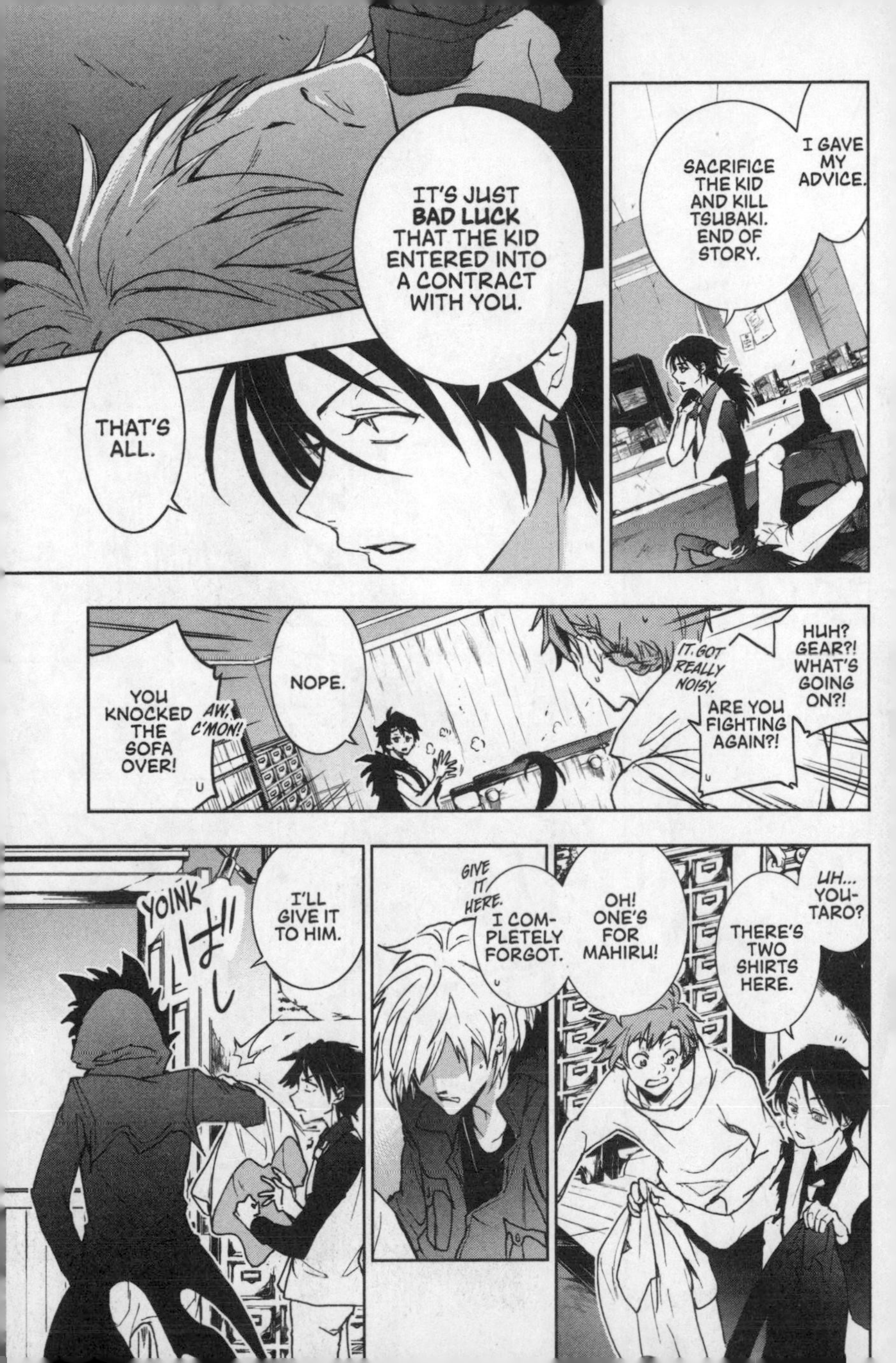
I GAVE MY ADVICE.
SACRIFICE THE KID AND KILL TSUBAKI. END OF STORY.
IT'S JUST **BAD LUCK** THAT THE KID ENTERED INTO A CONTRACT WITH YOU.
THAT'S ALL.
HUH? GEAR?! WHAT'S GOING ON?!
IT GOT REALLY NOISY.
ARE YOU FIGHTING AGAIN?!
NOPE.
AW, C'MON!
YOU KNOCKED THE SOFA OVER!
UH... YOU-TARO?
THERE'S TWO SHIRTS HERE.
OH! ONE'S FOR MAHIRU!
I COM-PLETELY FORGOT.
GIVE IT HERE.
I'LL GIVE IT TO HIM.
YOINK
ぱし

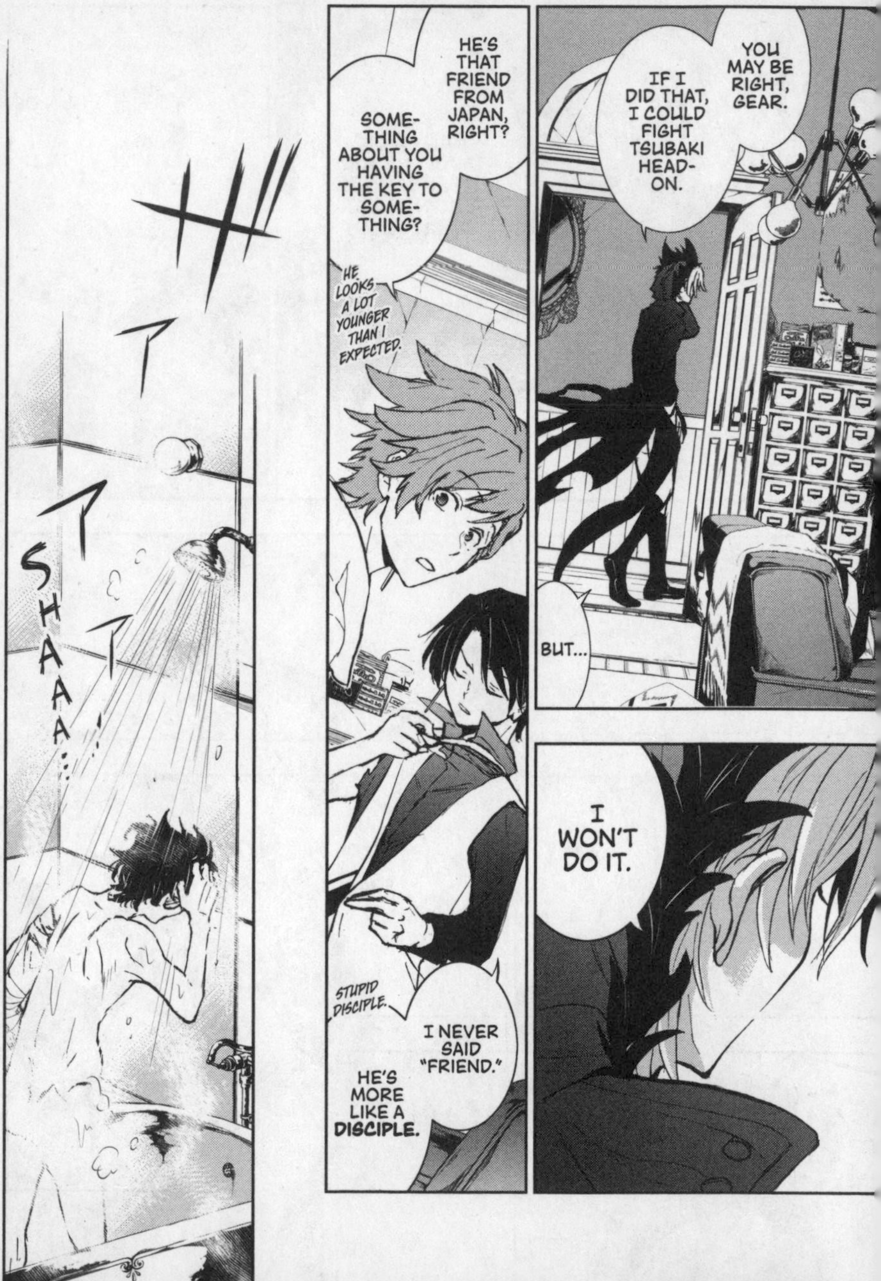
YOU MAY BE RIGHT, GEAR.
IF I DID THAT, I COULD FIGHT TSUBAKI HEAD-ON.
BUT...
I WON'T DO IT.
HE'S THAT FRIEND FROM JAPAN, RIGHT?
SOMETHING ABOUT YOU HAVING THE KEY TO SOMETHING?
HE LOOKS A LOT YOUNGER THAN I EXPECTED.
I NEVER SAID "FRIEND."
HE'S MORE LIKE A DISCIPLE.
STUPID DISCIPLE.
SHAAA...

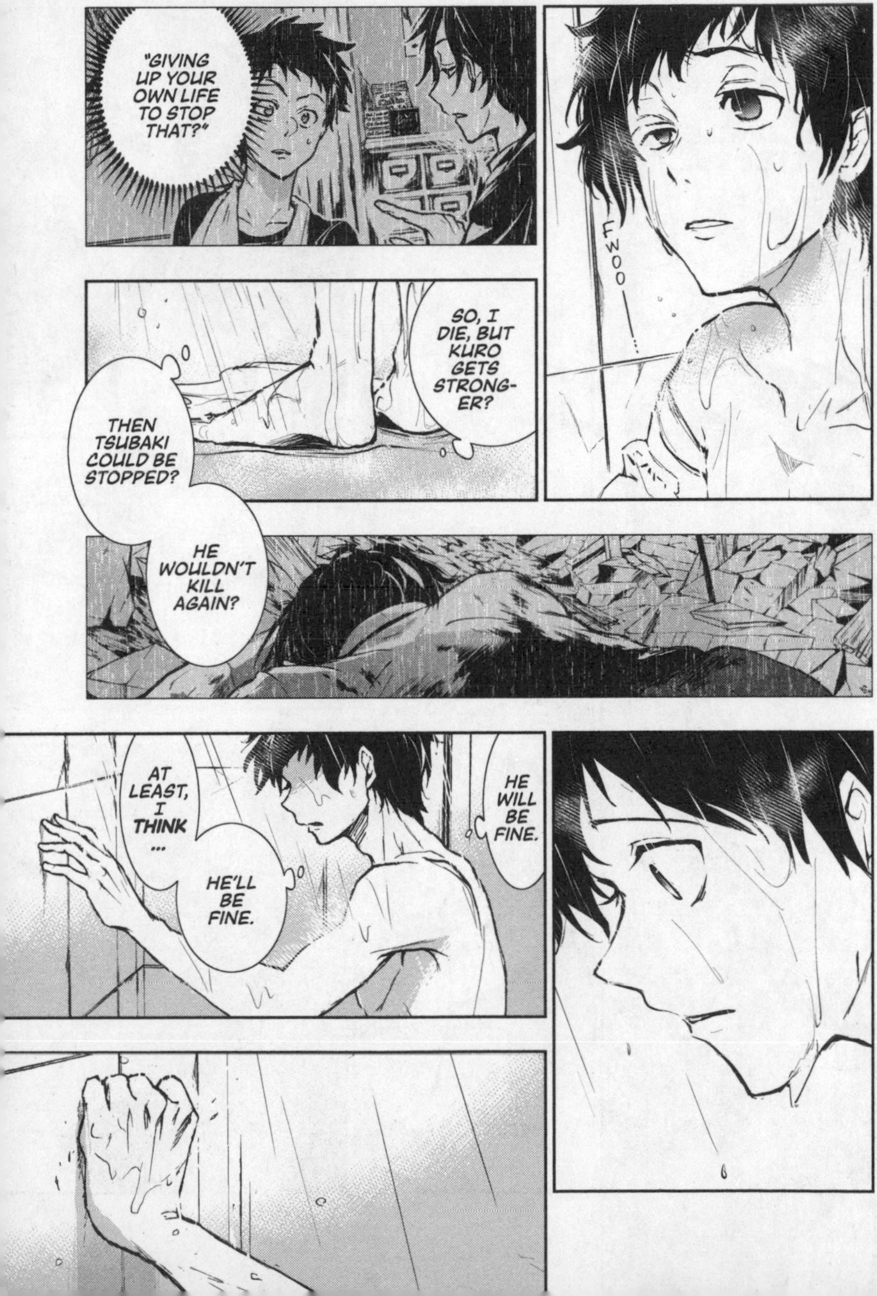
FWOO
"GIVING UP YOUR OWN LIFE TO STOP THAT?"
SO, I DIE, BUT KURO GETS STRONGER?
THEN TSUBAKI COULD BE STOPPED?
HE WOULDN'T KILL AGAIN?
HE WILL BE FINE.
AT LEAST, I THINK ...
HE'LL BE FINE.

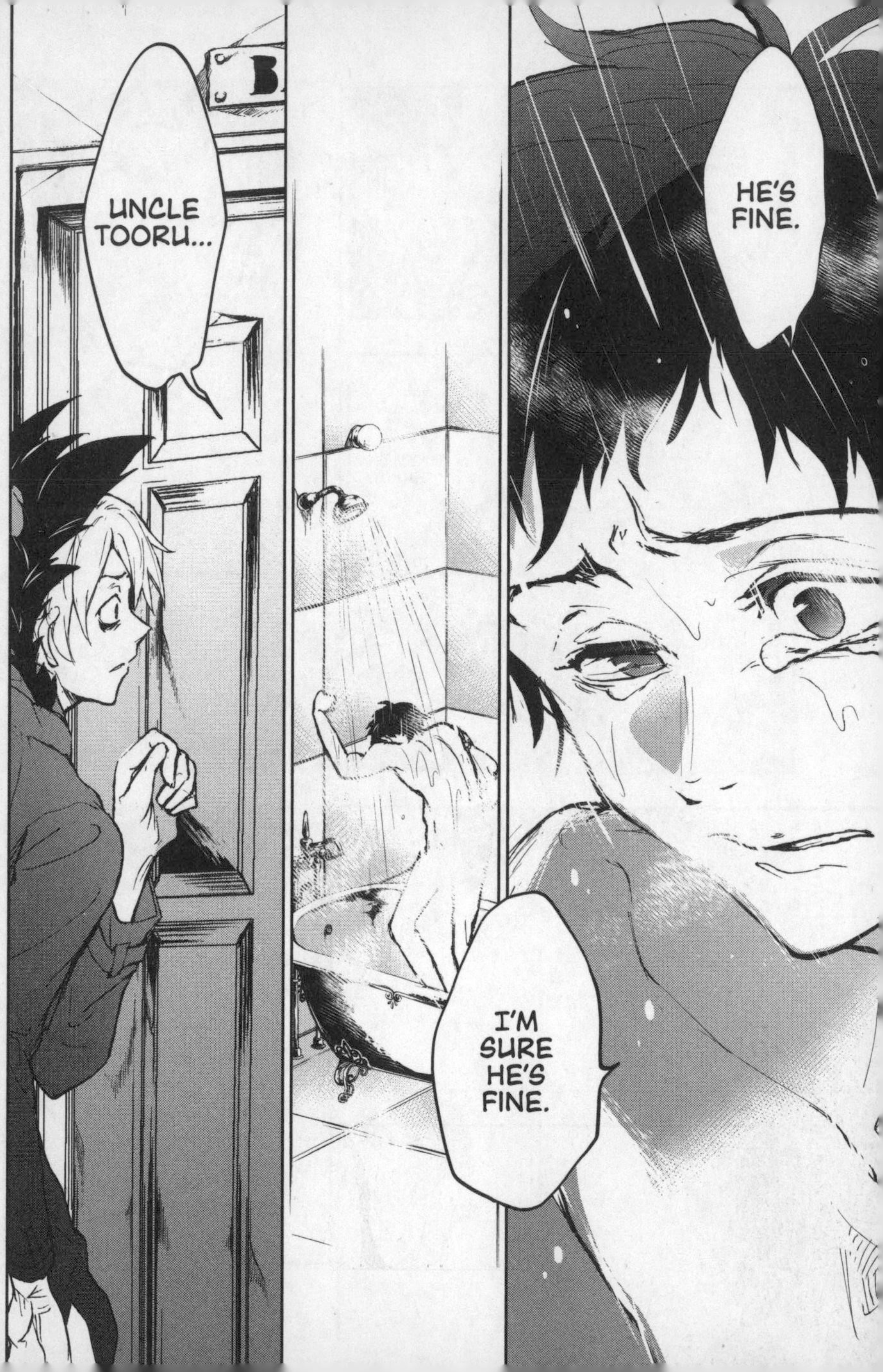
HE'S FINE.
I'M SURE HE'S FINE.
UNCLE TOORU...

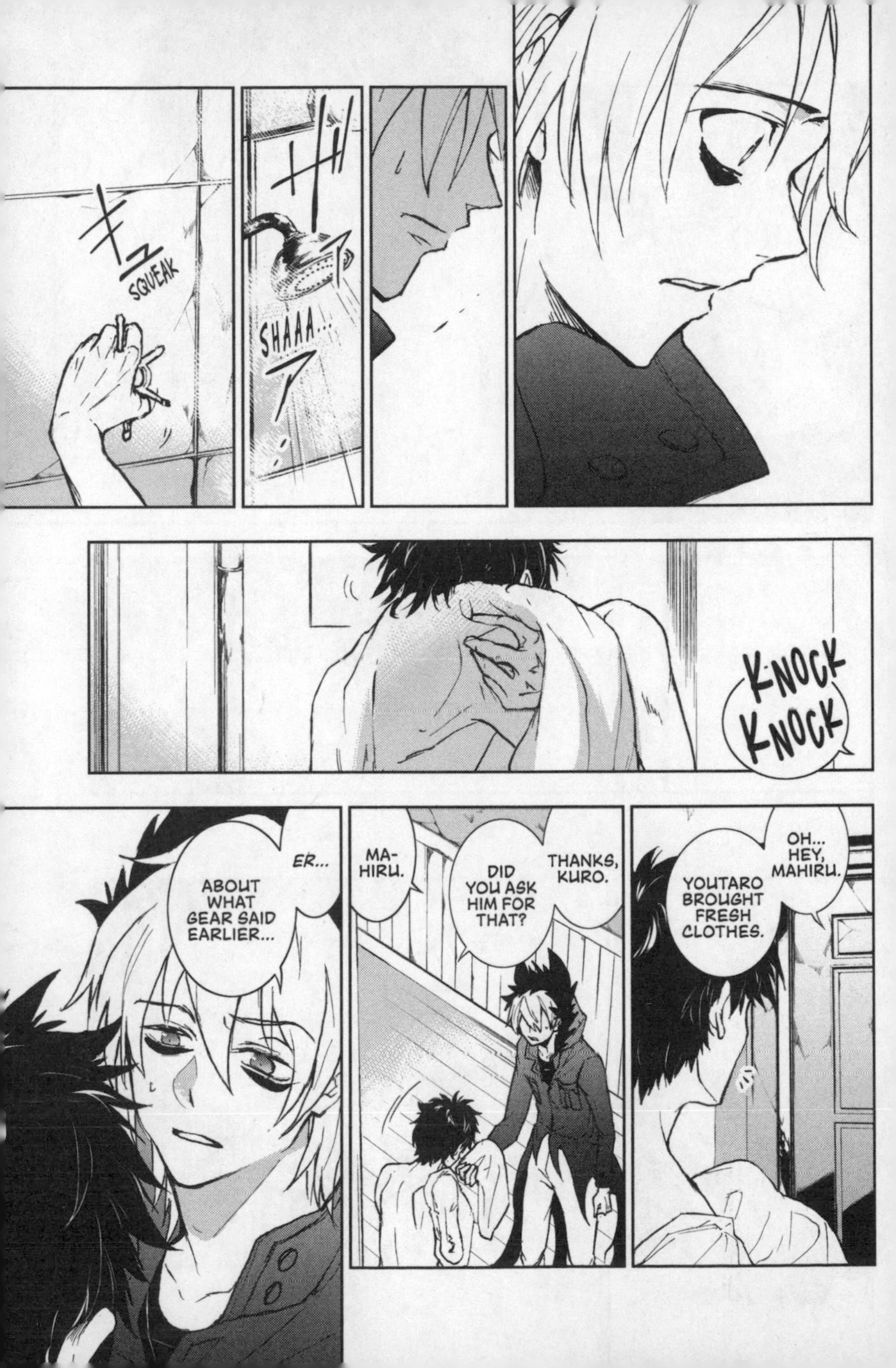
SHAAA...
SQUEAK
KNOCK KNOCK
OH... HEY, MAHIRU.
YOUTARO BROUGHT FRESH CLOTHES.
THANKS, KURO.
DID YOU ASK HIM FOR THAT?
MA-HIRU.
ER...
ABOUT WHAT GEAR SAID EARLIER...

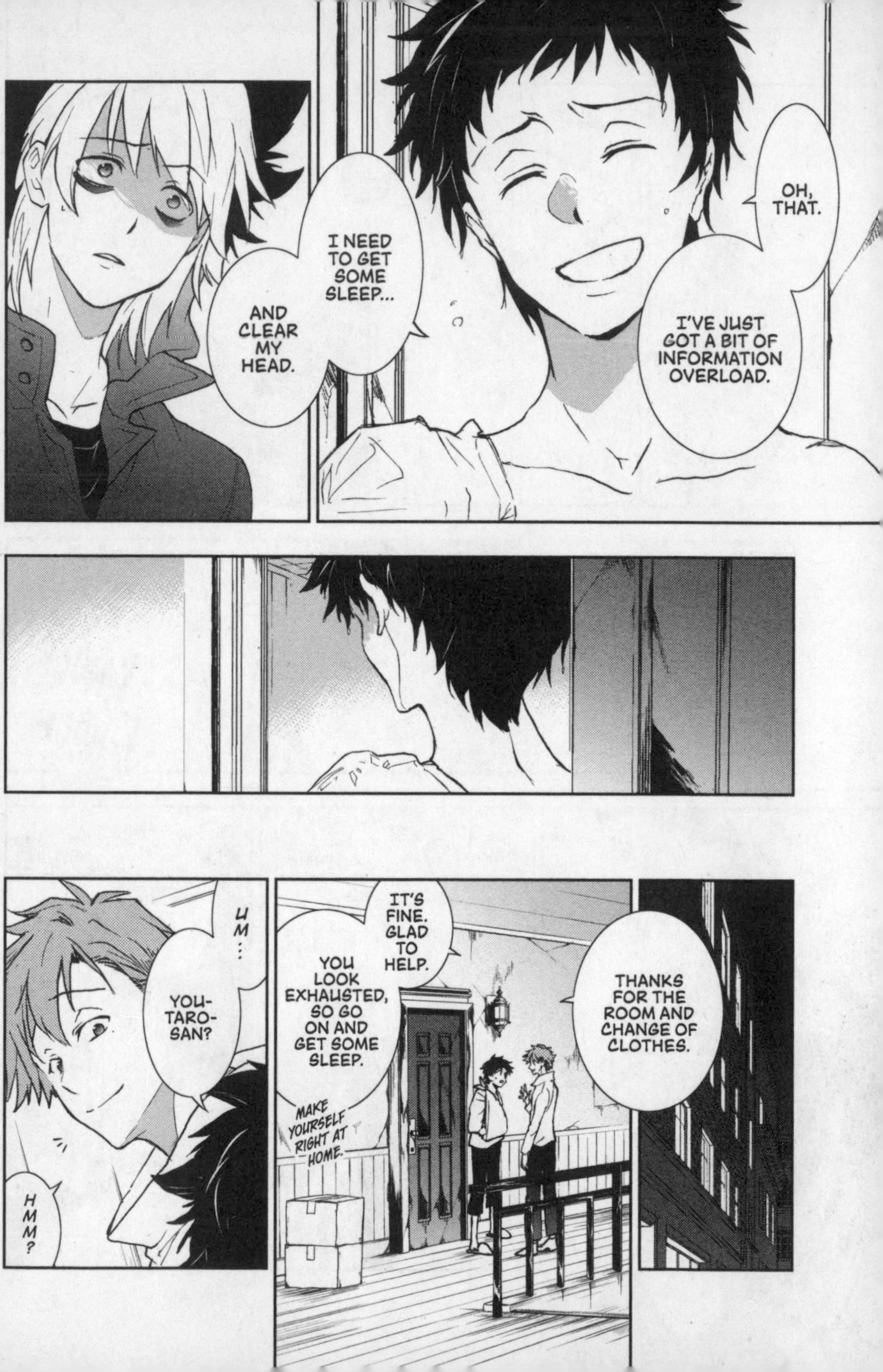
OH, THAT.
I'VE JUST GOT A BIT OF INFORMATION OVERLOAD.
I NEED TO GET SOME SLEEP...
AND CLEAR MY HEAD.
THANKS FOR THE ROOM AND CHANGE OF CLOTHES.
IT'S FINE. GLAD TO HELP.
YOU LOOK EXHAUSTED, SO GO ON AND GET SOME SLEEP.
MAKE YOURSELF RIGHT AT HOME.
UM...
YOU-TARO-SAN?
HMM?

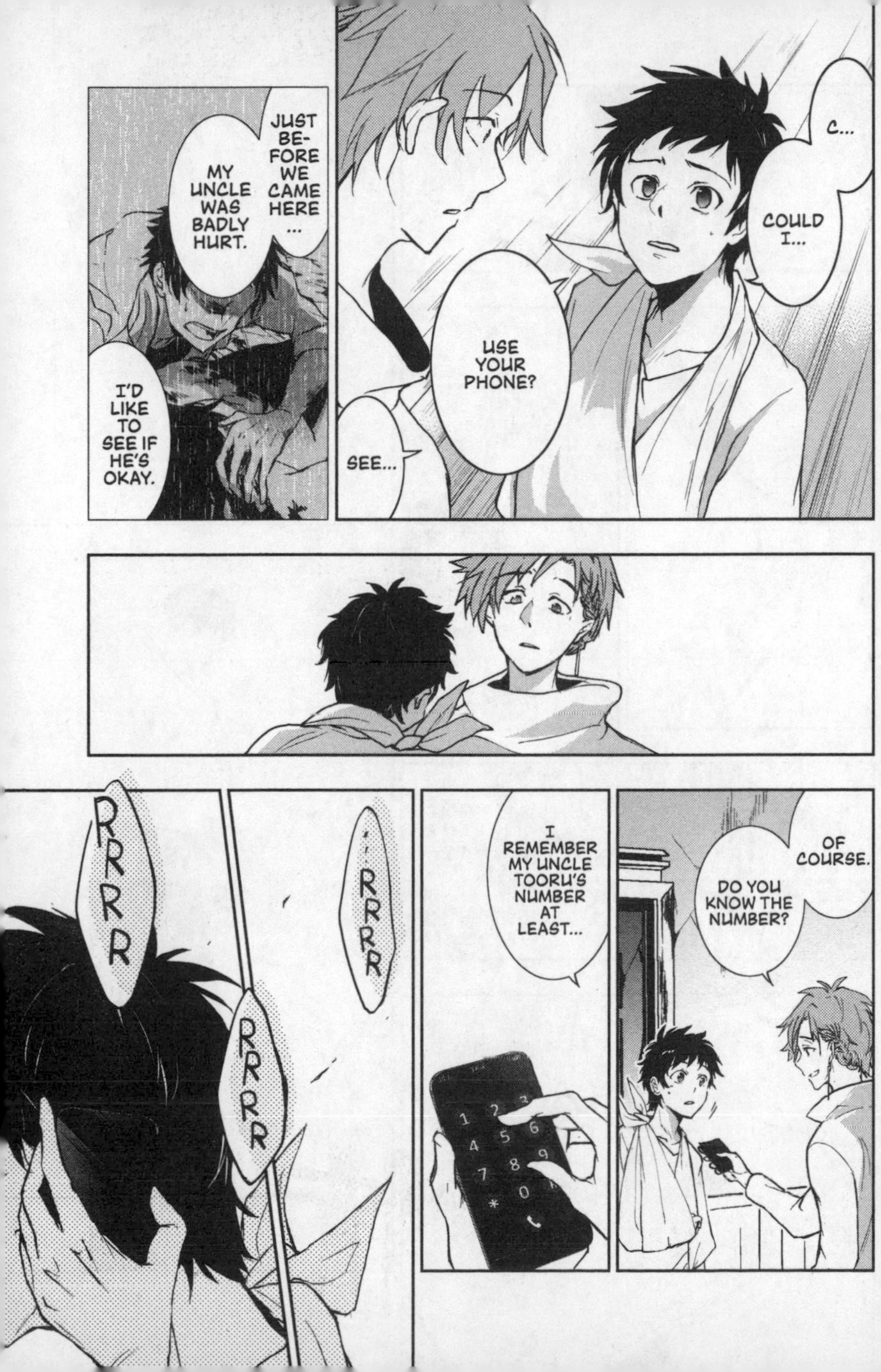
C...
COULD I...
USE YOUR PHONE?
SEE...
JUST BEFORE WE CAME HERE...
MY UNCLE WAS BADLY HURT.
I'D LIKE TO SEE IF HE'S OKAY.
OF COURSE.
DO YOU KNOW THE NUMBER?
I REMEMBER MY UNCLE TOORU'S NUMBER AT LEAST...
...RRRR
RRRR
RRRR

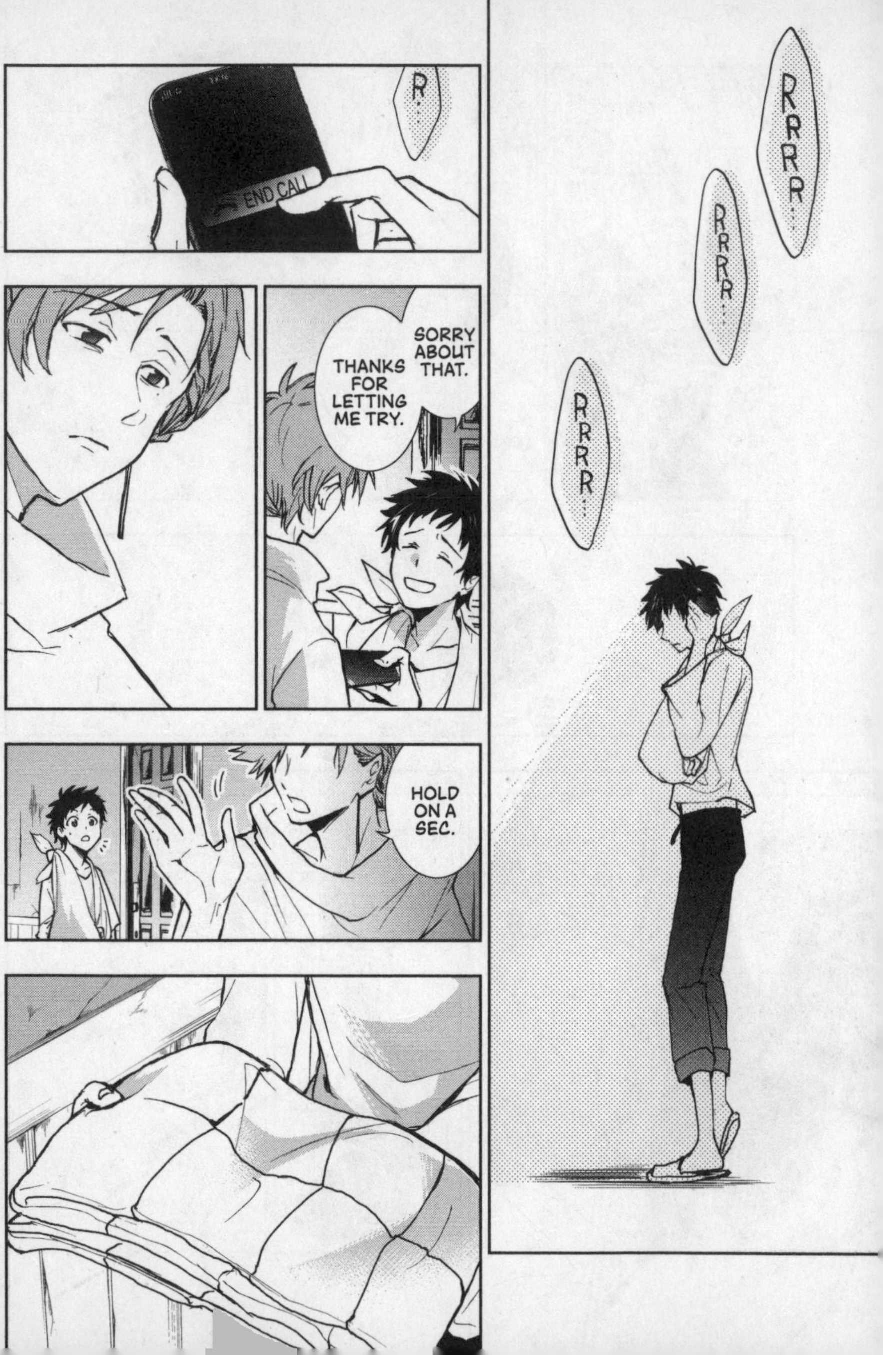
RRRR...
RRRR...
RRRR...
R...
END CALL
SORRY ABOUT THAT.
THANKS FOR LETTING ME TRY.
HOLD ON A SEC.

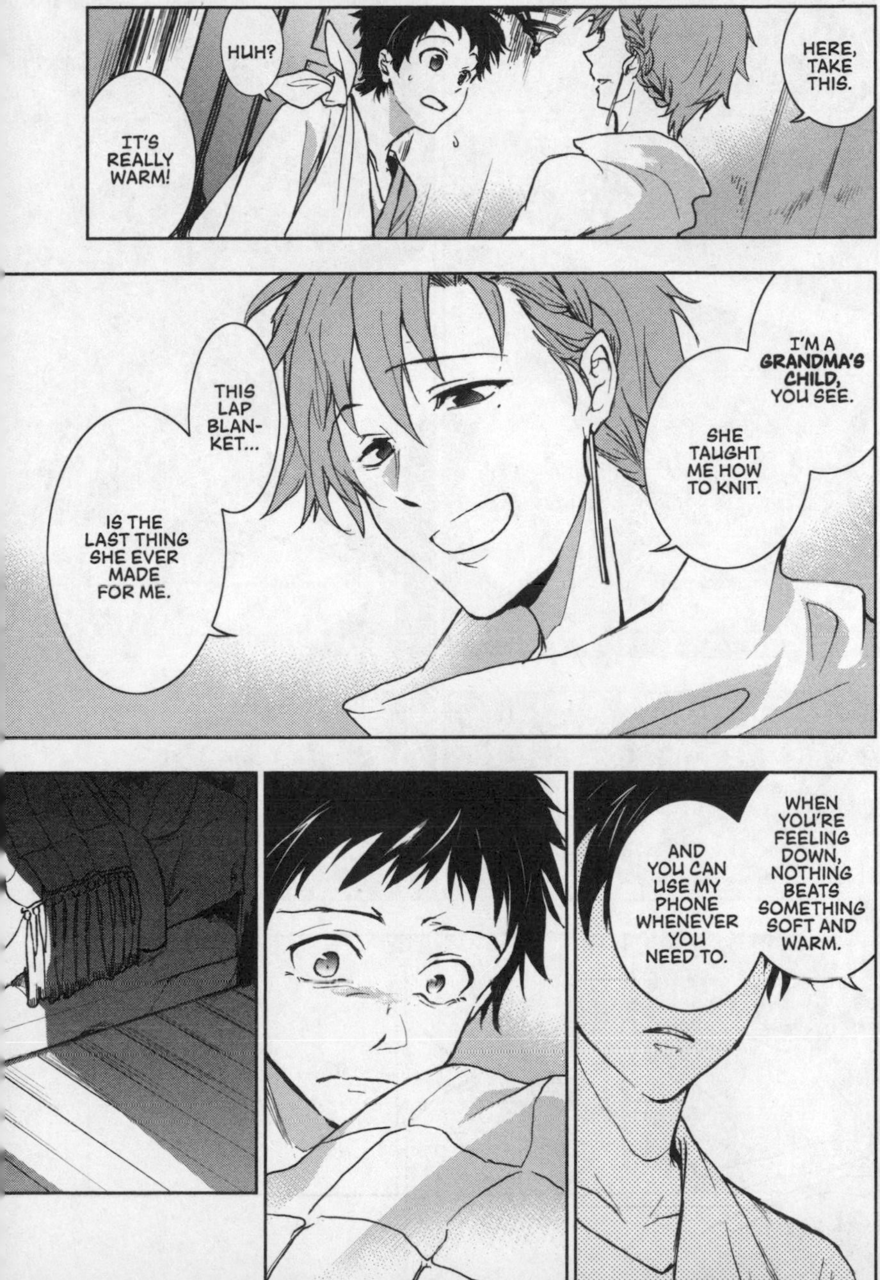
HERE, TAKE THIS.
HUH?
IT'S REALLY WARM!
I'M A GRANDMA'S CHILD, YOU SEE.
SHE TAUGHT ME HOW TO KNIT.
THIS LAP BLAN-KET...
IS THE LAST THING SHE EVER MADE FOR ME.
WHEN YOU'RE FEELING DOWN, NOTHING BEATS SOMETHING SOFT AND WARM.
AND YOU CAN USE MY PHONE WHENEVER YOU NEED TO.

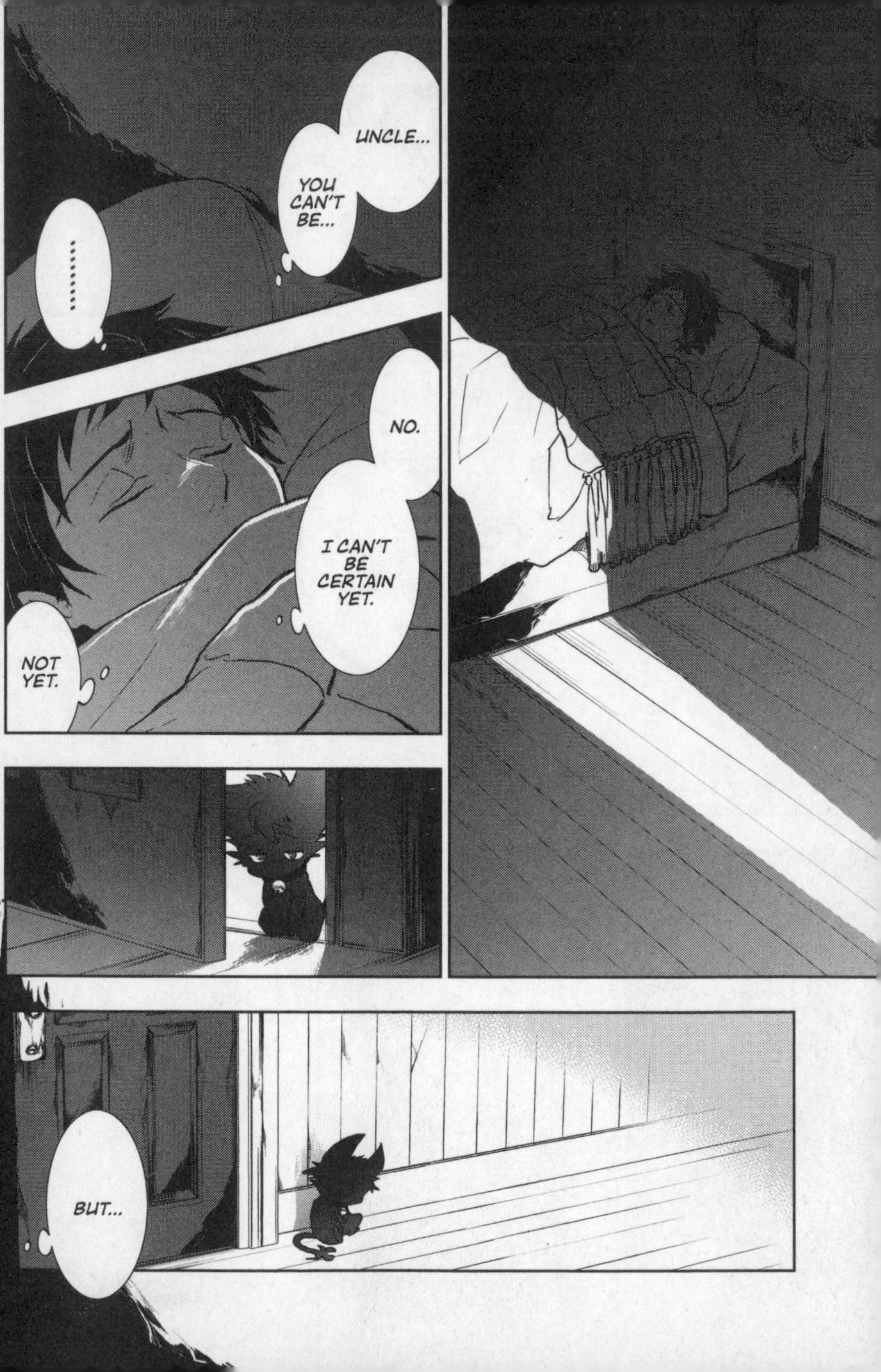
UNCLE...
YOU CAN'T BE...
......
NO.
I CAN'T BE CERTAIN YET.
NOT YET.
BUT...

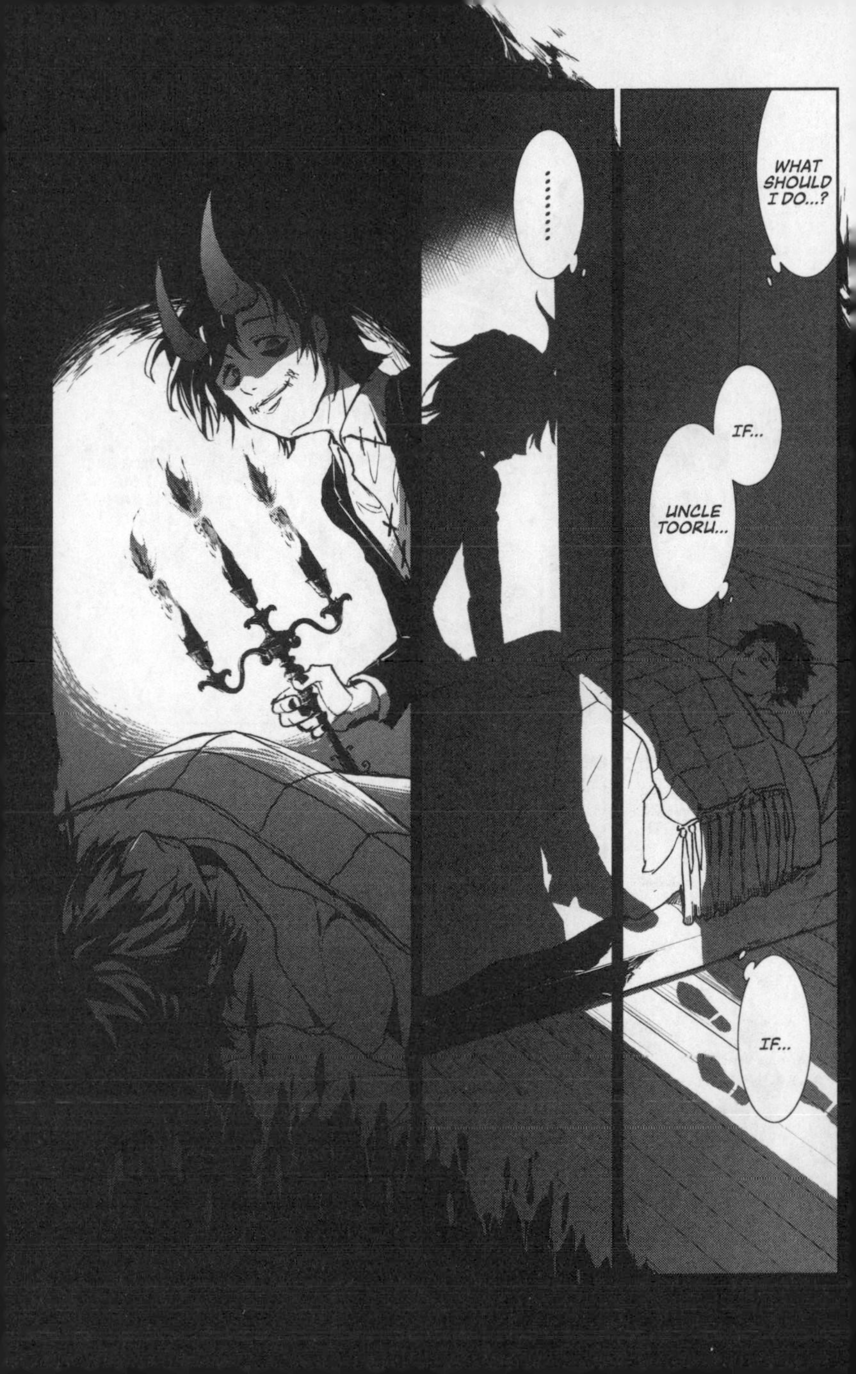
WHAT SHOULD I DO...?
IF...
UNCLE TOORU...
IF...
......

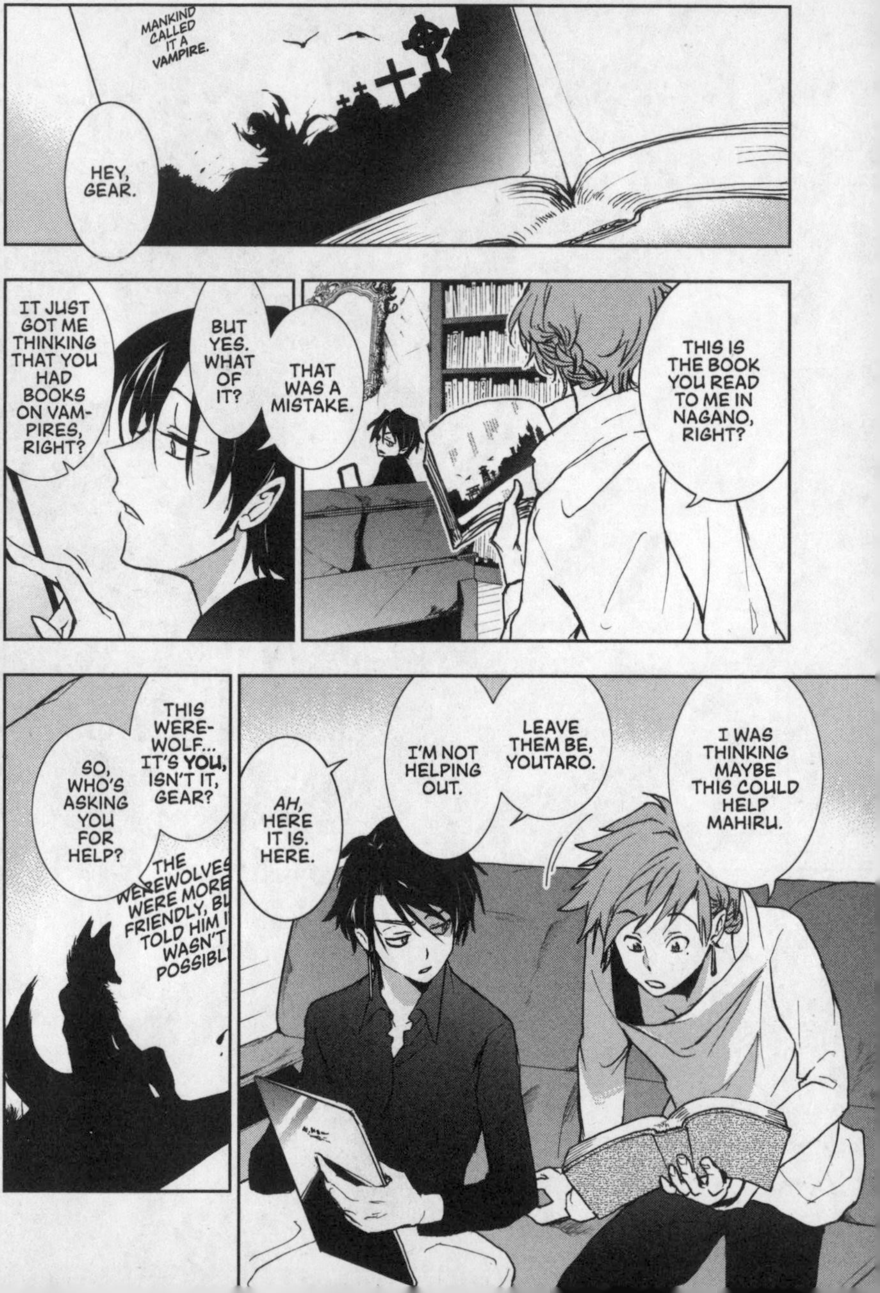
MANKIND CALLED IT A VAMPIRE.
HEY, GEAR.
THIS IS THE BOOK YOU READ TO ME IN NAGANO, RIGHT?
THAT WAS A MISTAKE.
BUT YES. WHAT OF IT?
IT JUST GOT ME THINKING THAT YOU HAD BOOKS ON VAMPIRES, RIGHT?
I WAS THINKING MAYBE THIS COULD HELP MAHIRU.
LEAVE THEM BE, YOUTARO.
I'M NOT HELPING OUT.
AH, HERE IT IS. HERE.
THIS WEREWOLF... IT'S **YOU**, ISN'T IT, GEAR?
SO, WHO'S ASKING YOU FOR HELP?
THE WEREWOLVES WERE MORE FRIENDLY, BU TOLD HIM I WASN'T POSSIBL

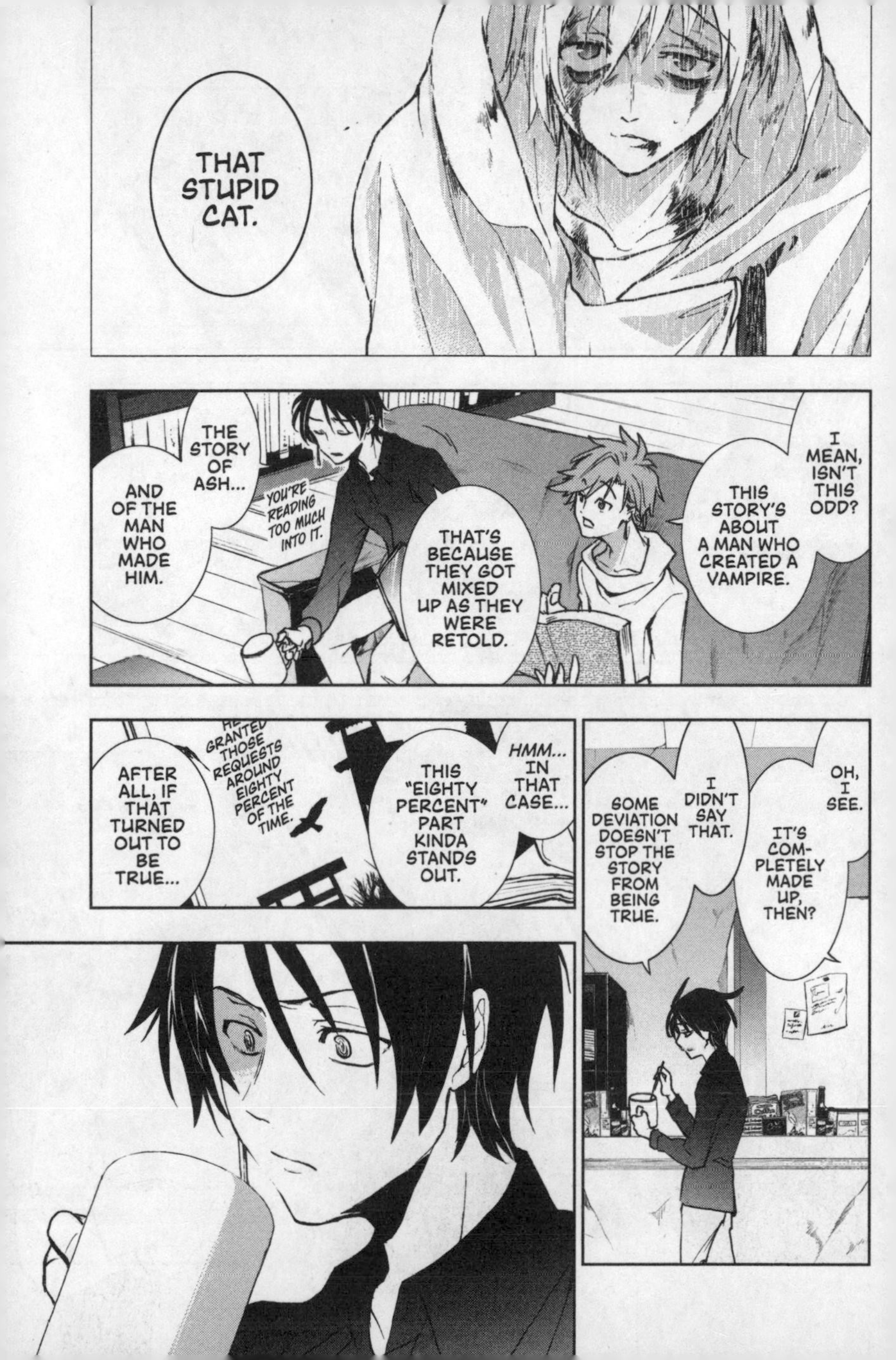
THAT STUPID CAT.
I MEAN, ISN'T THIS ODD?
THIS STORY'S ABOUT A MAN WHO CREATED A VAMPIRE.
THAT'S BECAUSE THEY GOT MIXED UP AS THEY WERE RETOLD.
YOU'RE READING TOO MUCH INTO IT.
THE STORY OF ASH...
AND OF THE MAN WHO MADE HIM.
OH, I SEE.
IT'S COMPLETELY MADE UP, THEN?
I DIDN'T SAY THAT.
SOME DEVIATION DOESN'T STOP THE STORY FROM BEING TRUE.
HMM... IN THAT CASE...
THIS "EIGHTY PERCENT" PART KINDA STANDS OUT.
HE GRANTED THOSE REQUESTS AROUND EIGHTY PERCENT OF THE TIME.
AFTER ALL, IF THAT TURNED OUT TO BE TRUE...

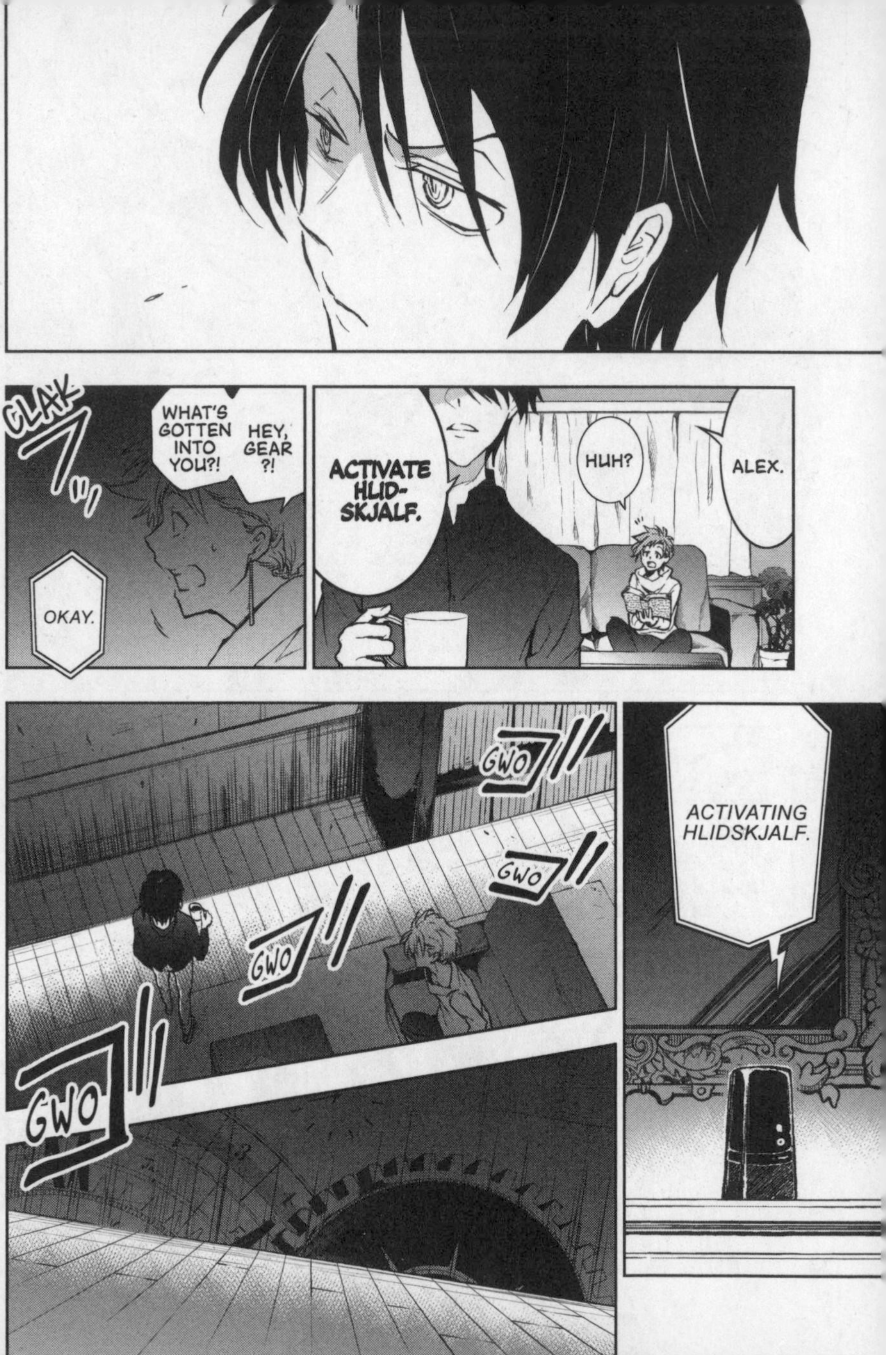
ALEX.
HUH?
ACTIVATE HLID-SKJALF.
HEY, GEAR ?!
WHAT'S GOTTEN INTO YOU?!
CLAK
OKAY.
ACTIVATING HLIDSKJALF.
GWO
GWO
GWO
GWO

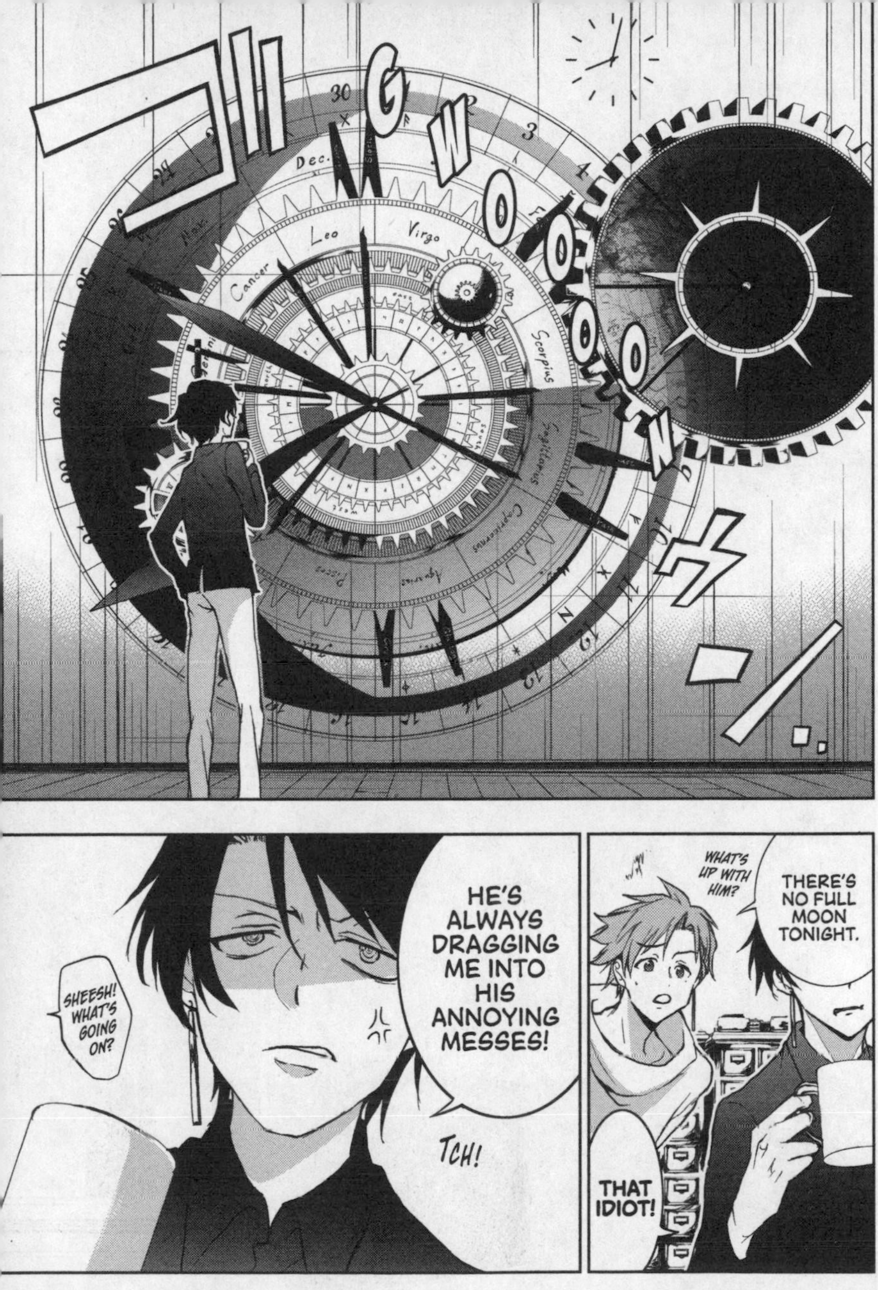
GWOOOON
THERE'S NO FULL MOON TONIGHT.
WHAT'S UP WITH HIM?
THAT IDIOT!
HE'S ALWAYS DRAGGING ME INTO HIS ANNOYING MESSES!
SHEESH! WHAT'S GOING ON?
TCH!

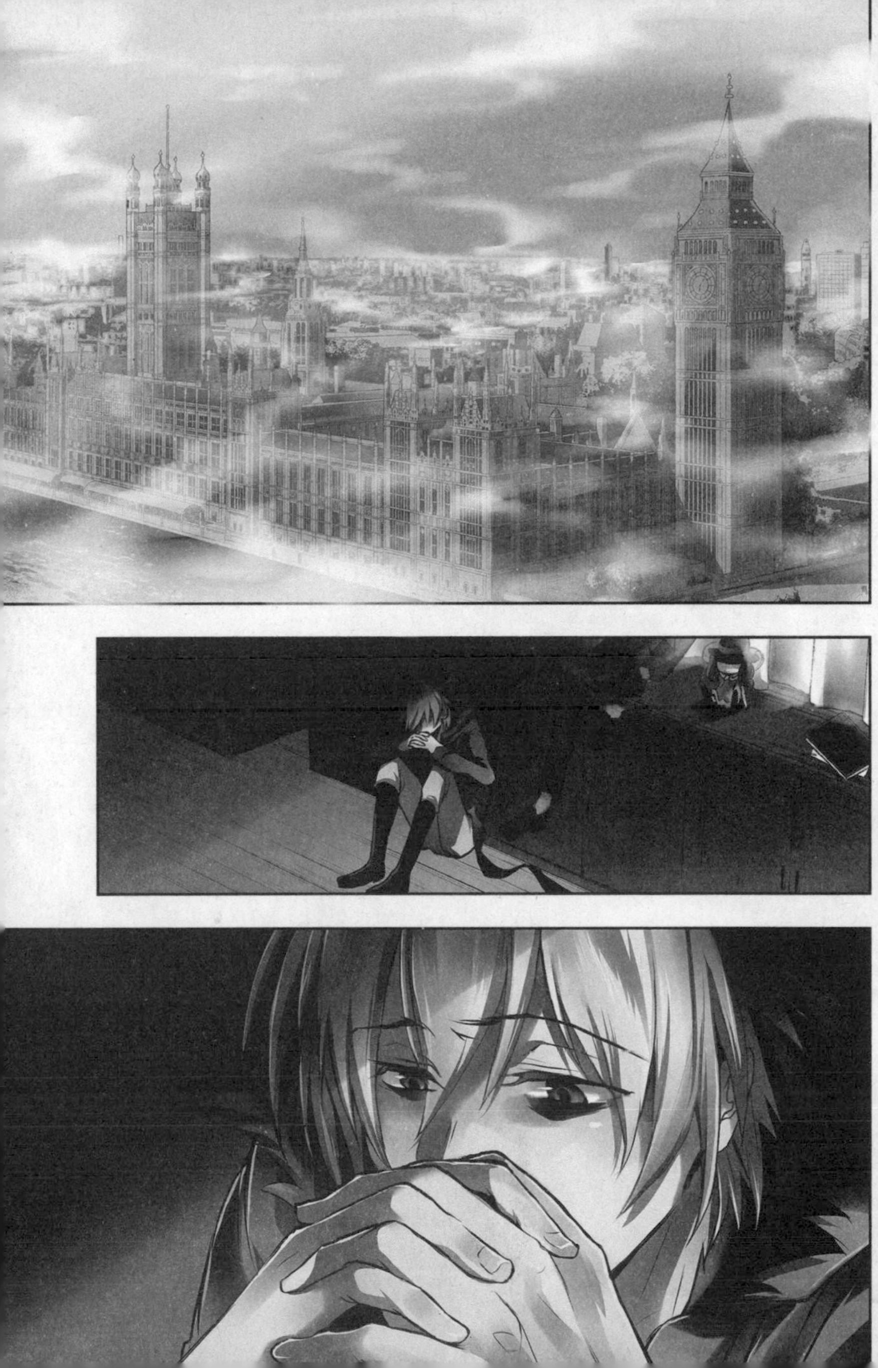

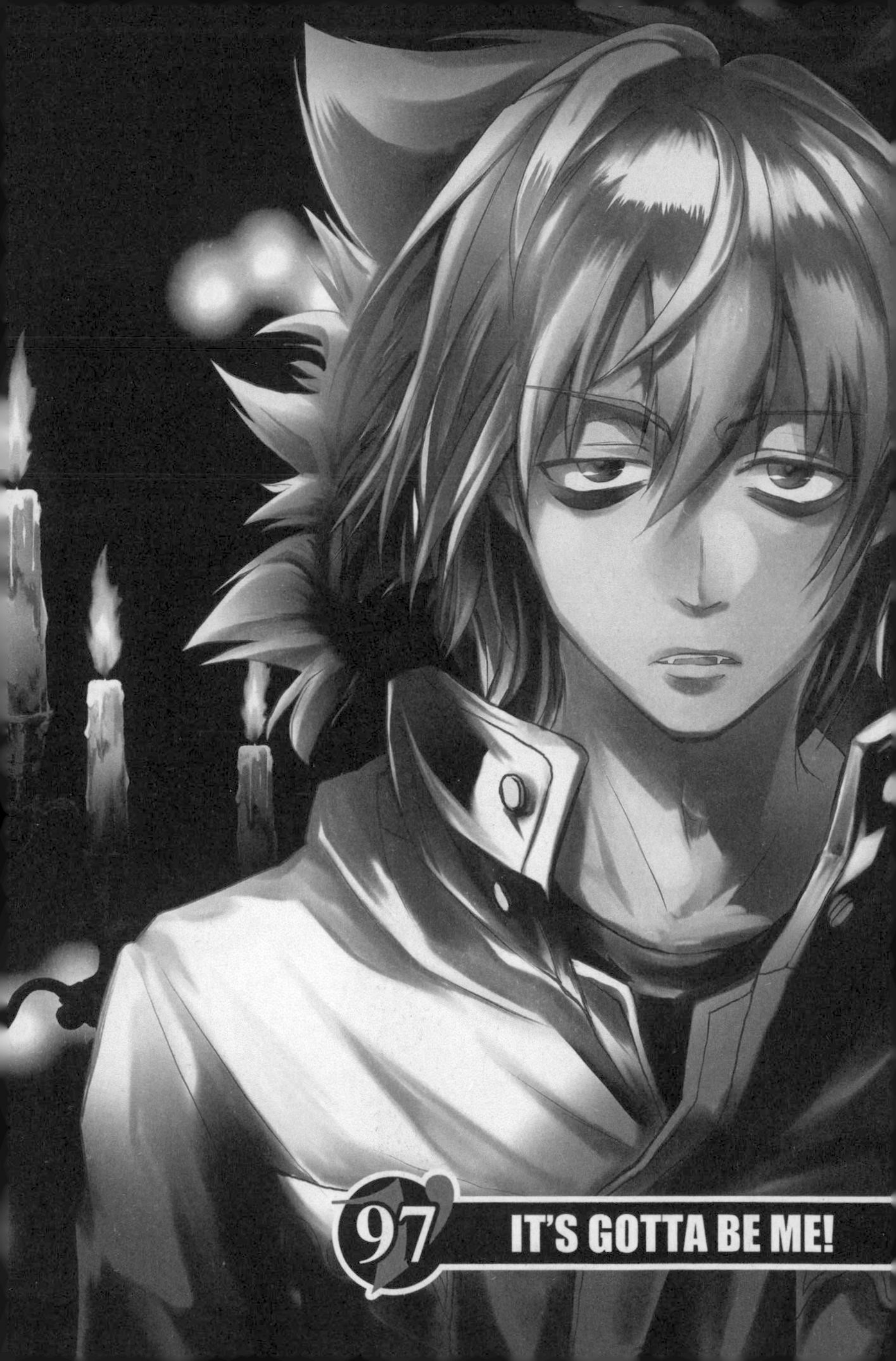
97
IT'S GOTTA BE ME!

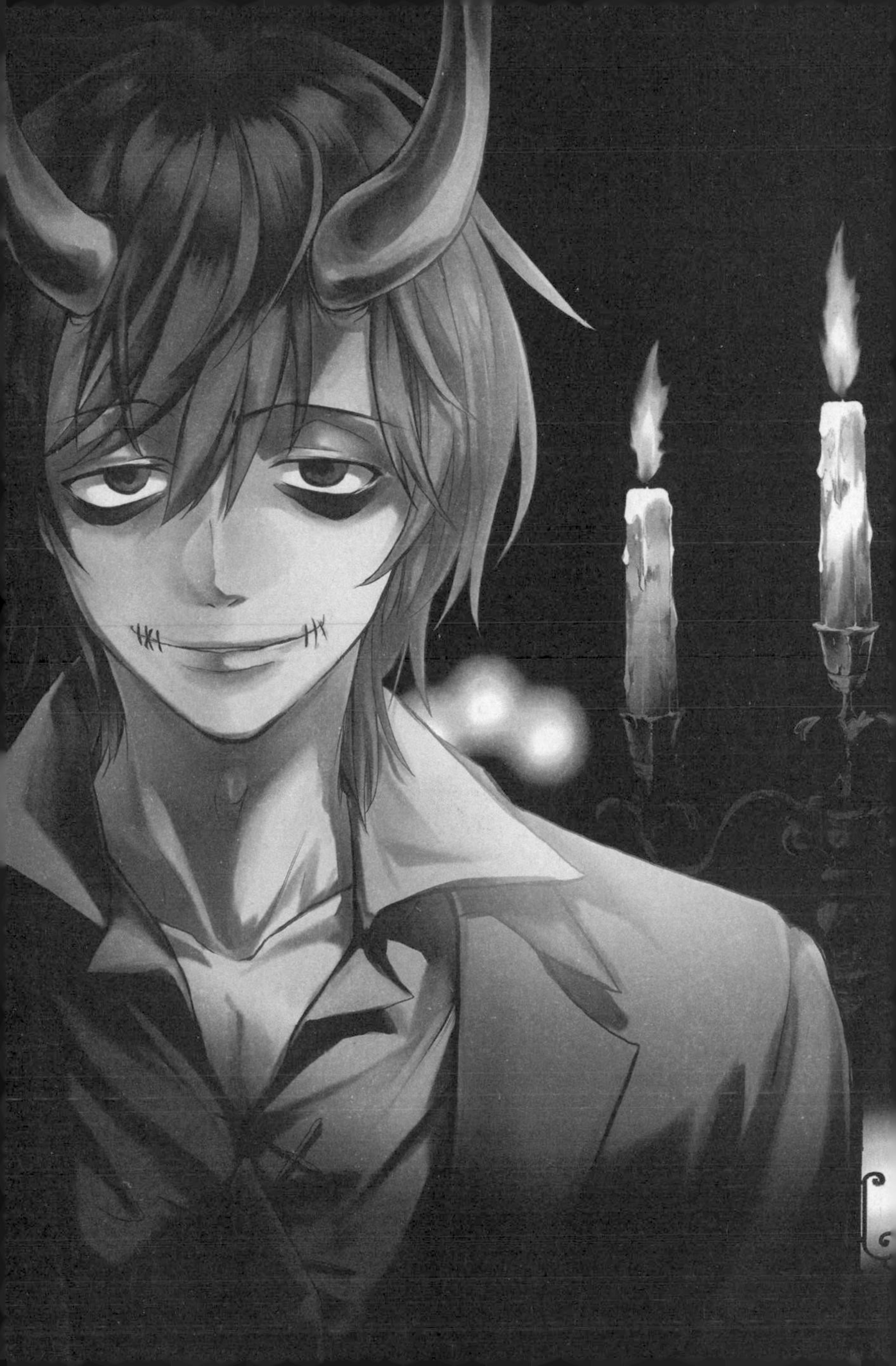

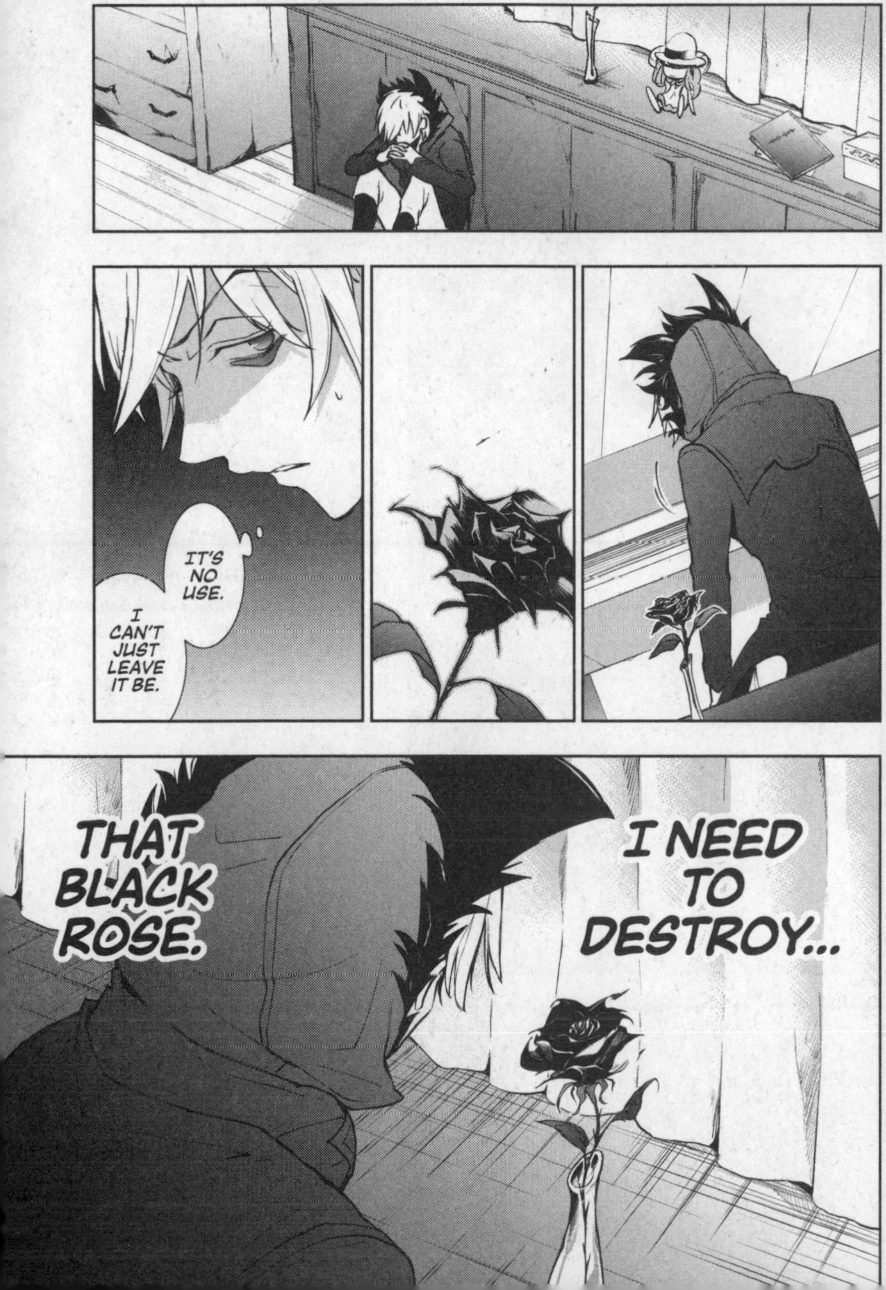
IT'S NO USE.
I CAN'T JUST LEAVE IT BE.
I NEED TO DESTROY...
THAT BLACK ROSE.

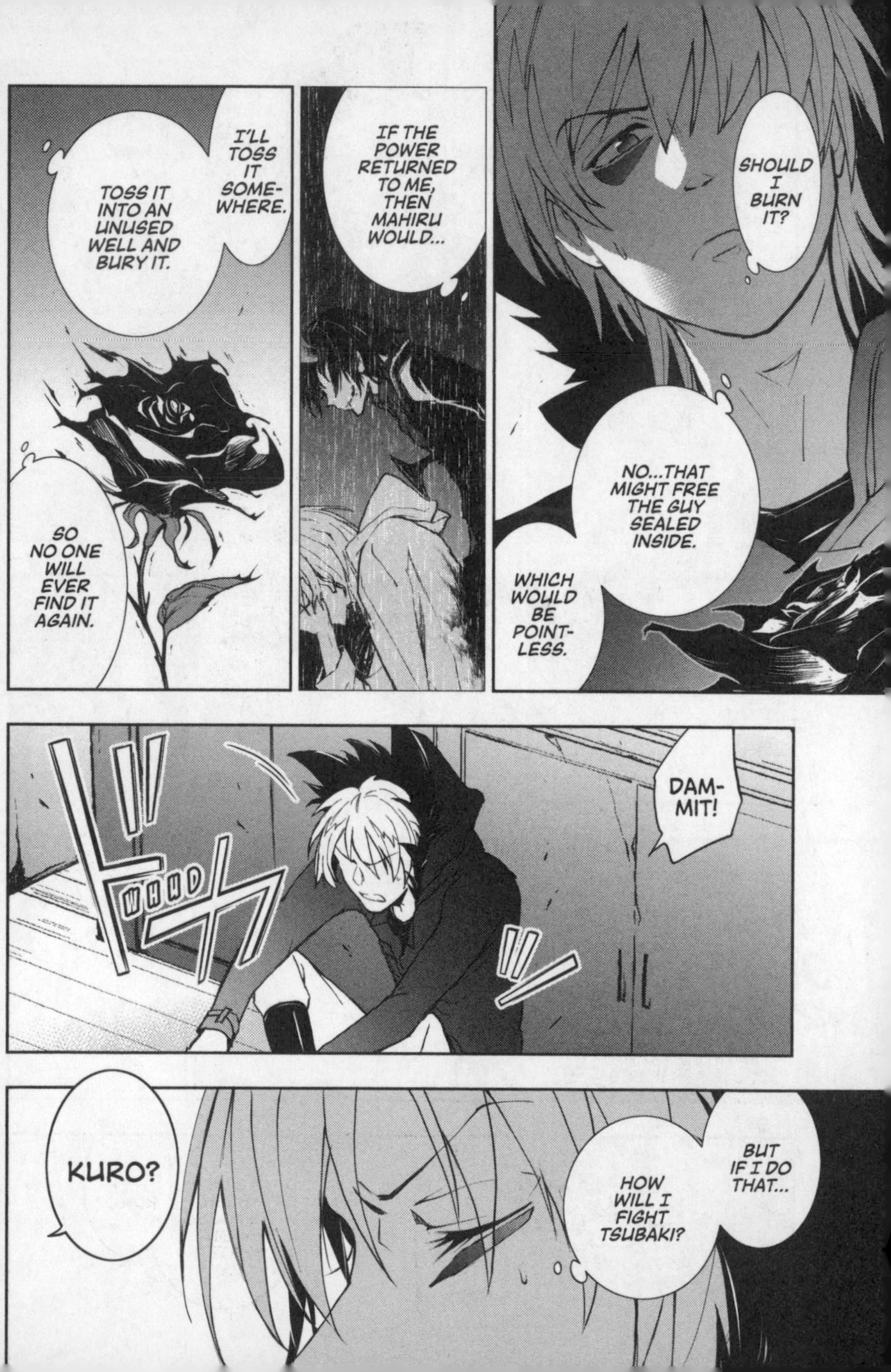
SHOULD I BURN IT?
NO...THAT MIGHT FREE THE GUY SEALED INSIDE.
WHICH WOULD BE POINTLESS.
IF THE POWER RETURNED TO ME, THEN MAHIRU WOULD...
I'LL TOSS IT SOMEWHERE.
TOSS IT INTO AN UNUSED WELL AND BURY IT.
SO NO ONE WILL EVER FIND IT AGAIN.
DAM-MIT!
WHUD
BUT IF I DO THAT...
HOW WILL I FIGHT TSUBAKI?
KURO?

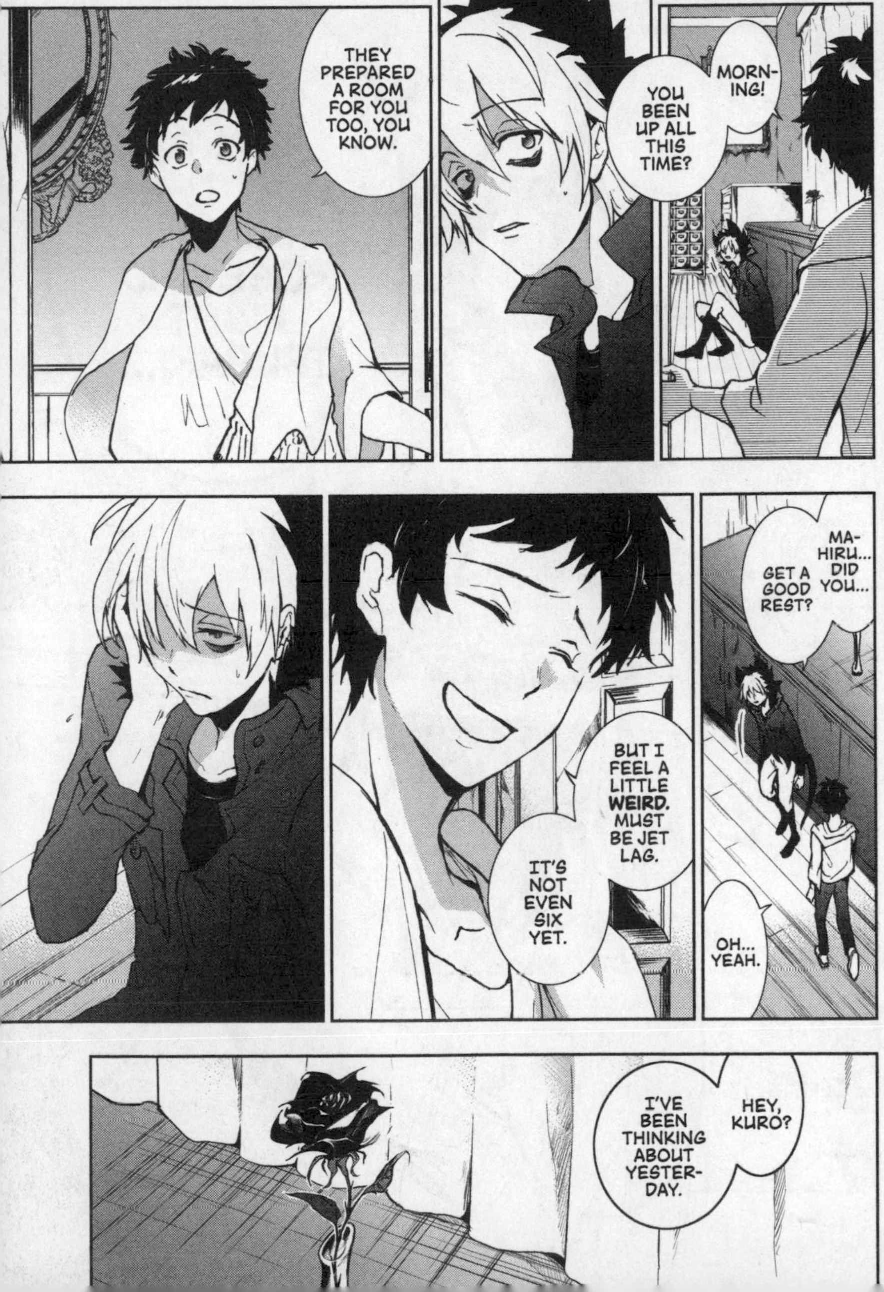
MORN-ING!
YOU BEEN UP ALL THIS TIME?
THEY PREPARED A ROOM FOR YOU TOO, YOU KNOW.
MA-HIRU... DID YOU...
GET A GOOD REST?
OH... YEAH.
BUT I FEEL A LITTLE WEIRD. MUST BE JET LAG.
IT'S NOT EVEN SIX YET.
HEY, KURO?
I'VE BEEN THINKING ABOUT YESTER-DAY.

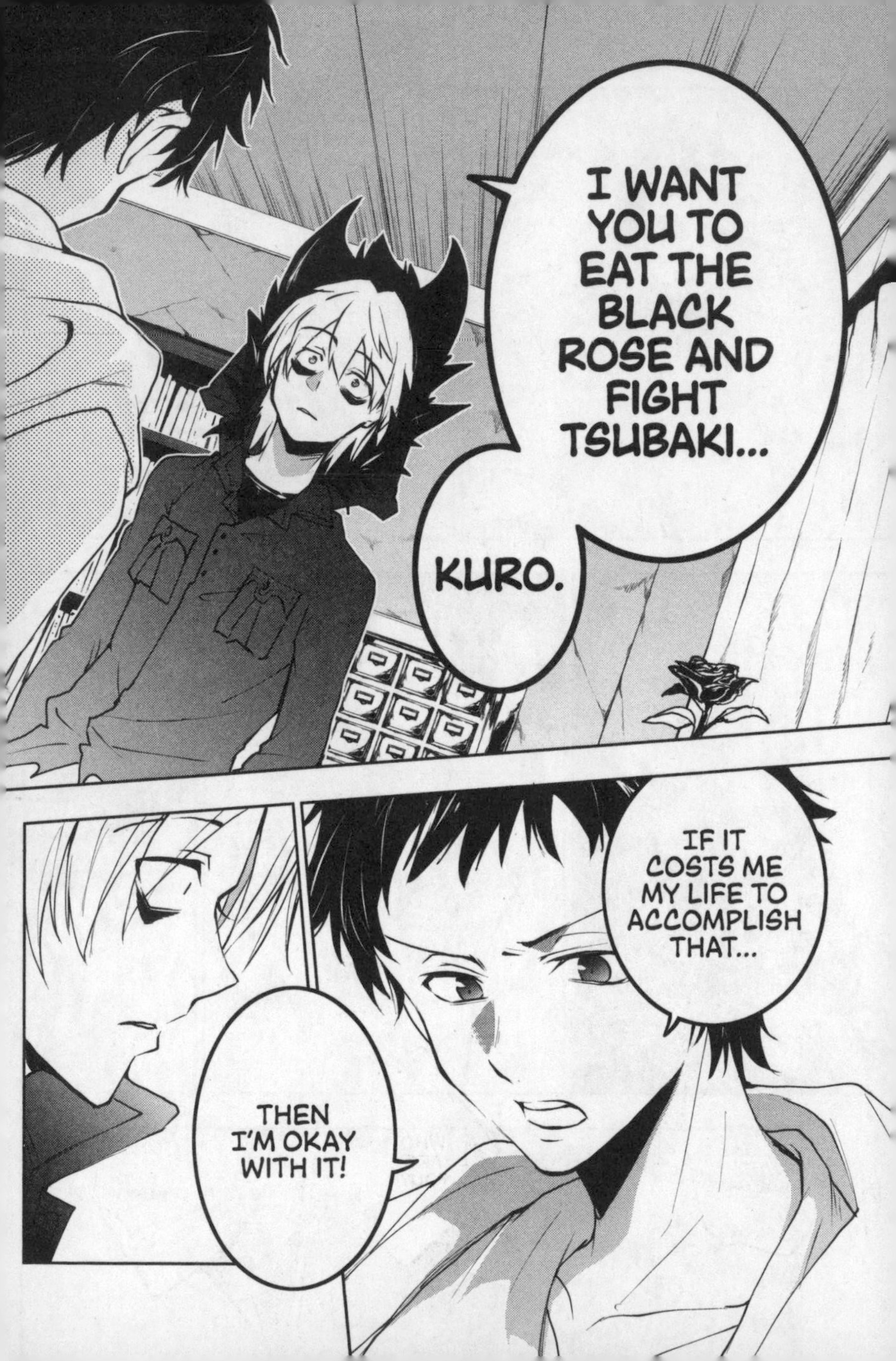
I WANT YOU TO EAT THE BLACK ROSE AND FIGHT TSUBAKI...
KURO.
IF IT COSTS ME MY LIFE TO ACCOMPLISH THAT...
THEN I'M OKAY WITH IT!

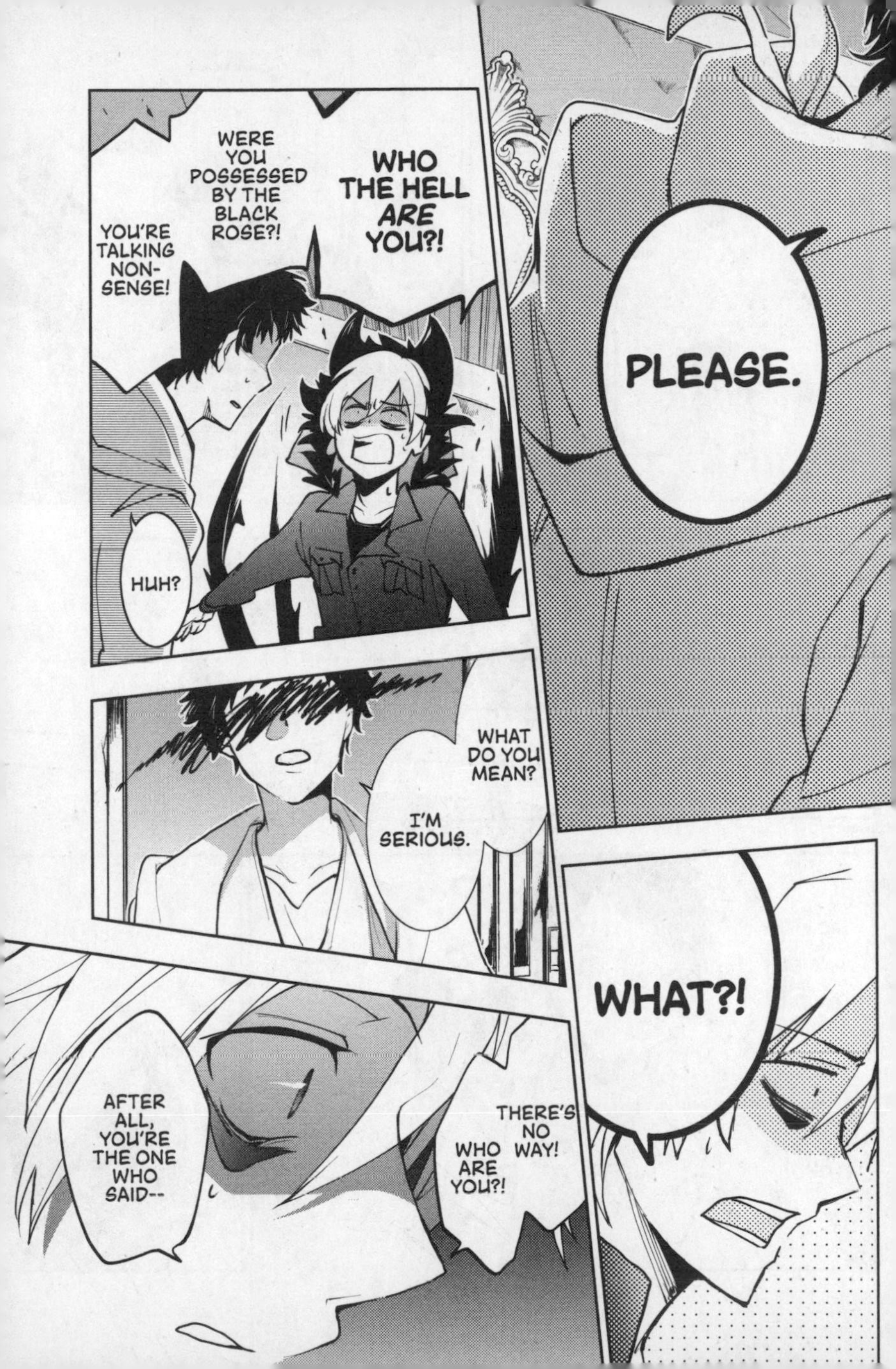
PLEASE.
WHO THE HELL ARE YOU?!
WERE YOU POSSESSED BY THE BLACK ROSE?!
YOU'RE TALKING NON-SENSE!
HUH?
WHAT DO YOU MEAN?
I'M SERIOUS.
WHAT?!
THERE'S NO WAY!
WHO ARE YOU?!
AFTER ALL, YOU'RE THE ONE WHO SAID--

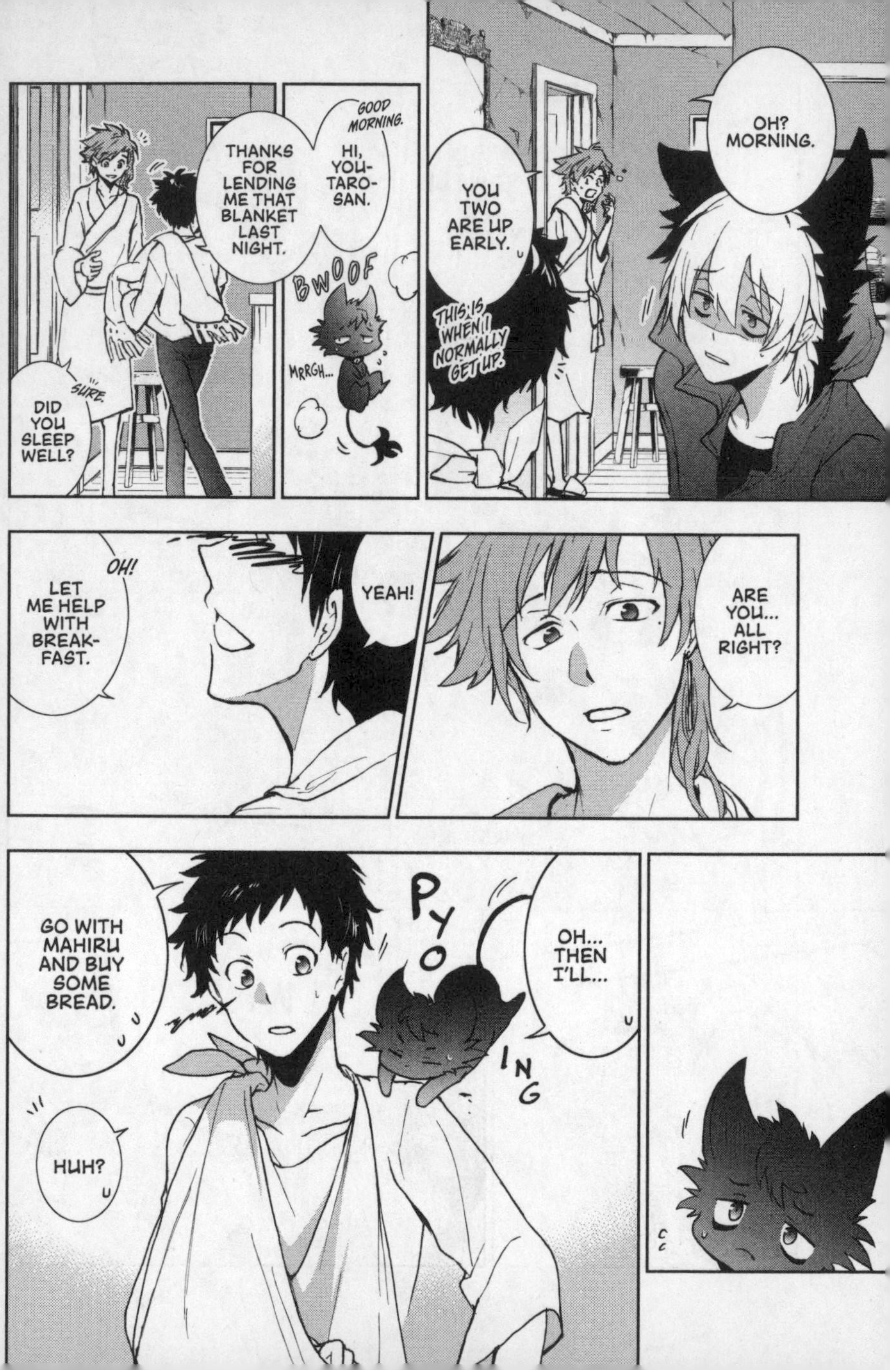
OH? MORNING.
YOU TWO ARE UP EARLY.
THIS IS WHEN I NORMALLY GET UP.
GOOD MORNING.
HI, YOU-TARO-SAN.
BWOOF
MRRGH...
THANKS FOR LENDING ME THAT BLANKET LAST NIGHT.
SURE.
DID YOU SLEEP WELL?
ARE YOU... ALL RIGHT?
YEAH!
OH!
LET ME HELP WITH BREAK-FAST.
OH... THEN I'LL...
PYOING
GO WITH MAHIRU AND BUY SOME BREAD.
HUH?

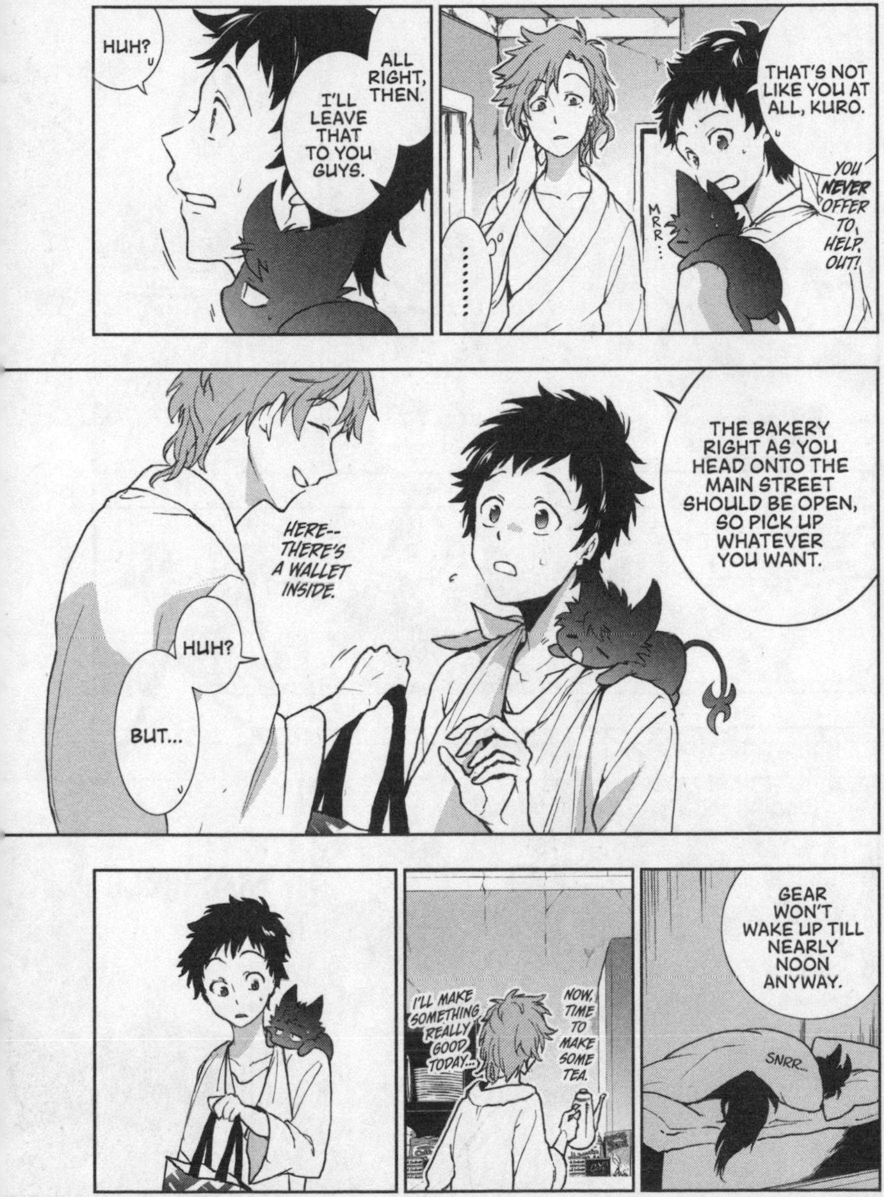
THAT'S NOT LIKE YOU AT ALL, KURO.
YOU NEVER OFFER TO HELP OUT!
MRR...
......
ALL RIGHT, THEN.
I'LL LEAVE THAT TO YOU GUYS.
HUH?
THE BAKERY RIGHT AS YOU HEAD ONTO THE MAIN STREET SHOULD BE OPEN, SO PICK UP WHATEVER YOU WANT.
HERE-- THERE'S A WALLET INSIDE.
HUH?
BUT...
GEAR WON'T WAKE UP TILL NEARLY NOON ANYWAY.
SNRR...
NOW, TIME TO MAKE SOME TEA.
I'LL MAKE SOMETHING REALLY GOOD TODAY...

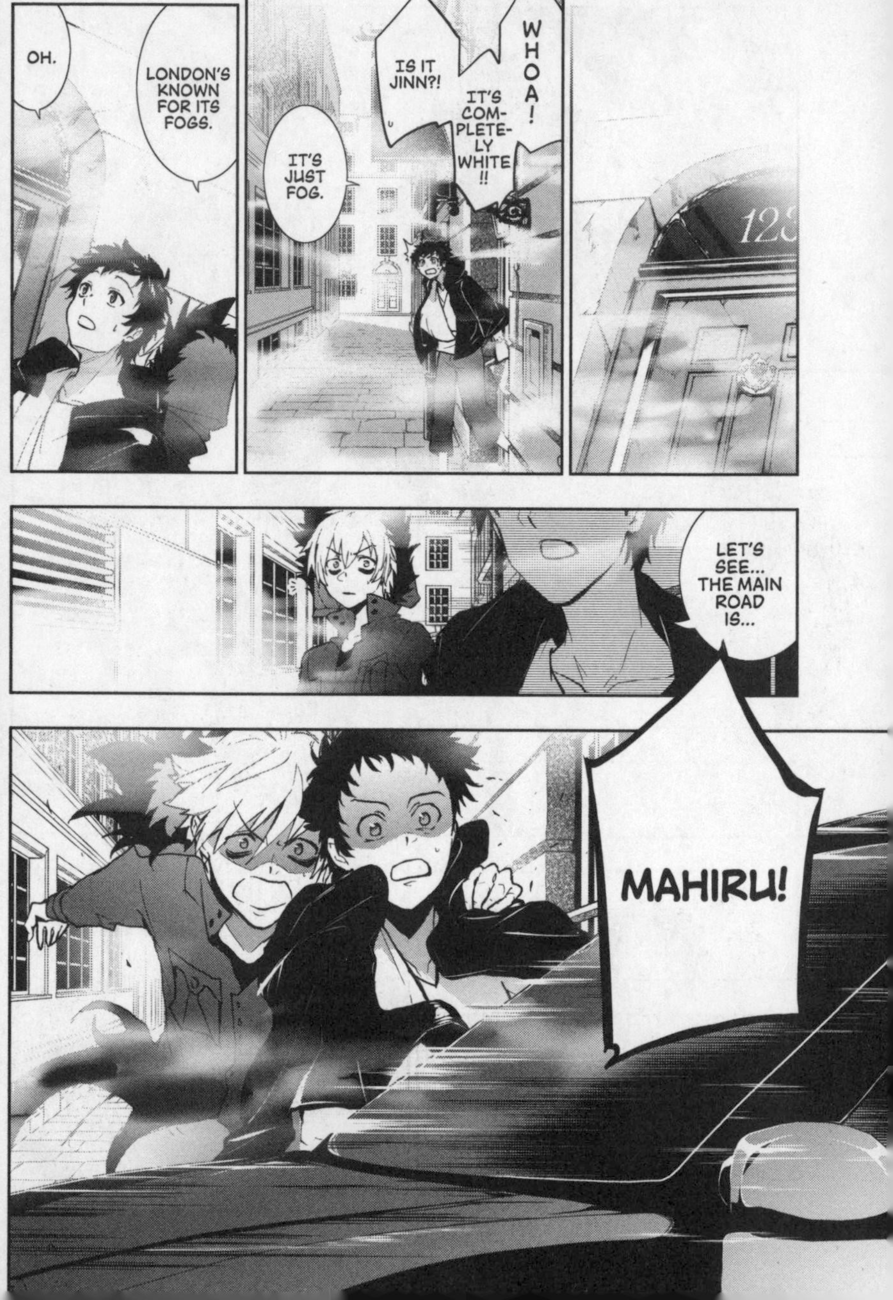
WHOA!
IT'S COMPLETELY WHITE!!
IS IT JINN?!
IT'S JUST FOG.
LONDON'S KNOWN FOR ITS FOGS.
OH.
LET'S SEE... THE MAIN ROAD IS...
MAHIRU!

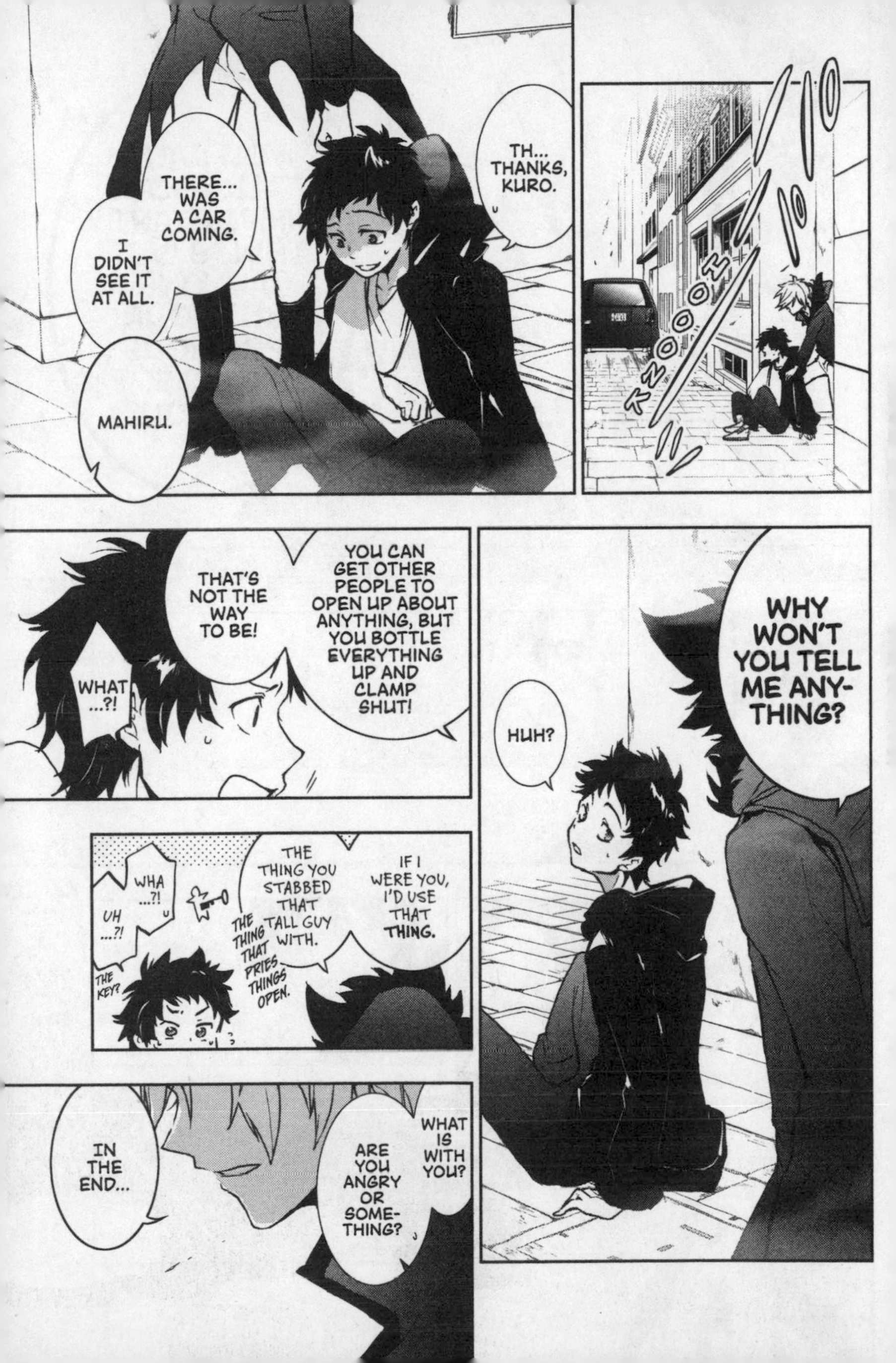
TH... THANKS, KURO.
THERE... WAS A CAR COMING.
I DIDN'T SEE IT AT ALL.
MAHIRU.
WHY WON'T YOU TELL ME ANYTHING?
HUH?
YOU CAN GET OTHER PEOPLE TO OPEN UP ABOUT ANYTHING, BUT YOU BOTTLE EVERYTHING UP AND CLAMP SHUT!
THAT'S NOT THE WAY TO BE!
WHAT ...?!
IF I WERE YOU, I'D USE THAT THING.
THE THING YOU STABBED THAT TALL GUY WITH.
THE THING THAT PRIES THINGS OPEN.
WHA ...?!
UH ...?!
THE KEY?
WHAT IS WITH YOU?
ARE YOU ANGRY OR SOMETHING?
IN THE END...

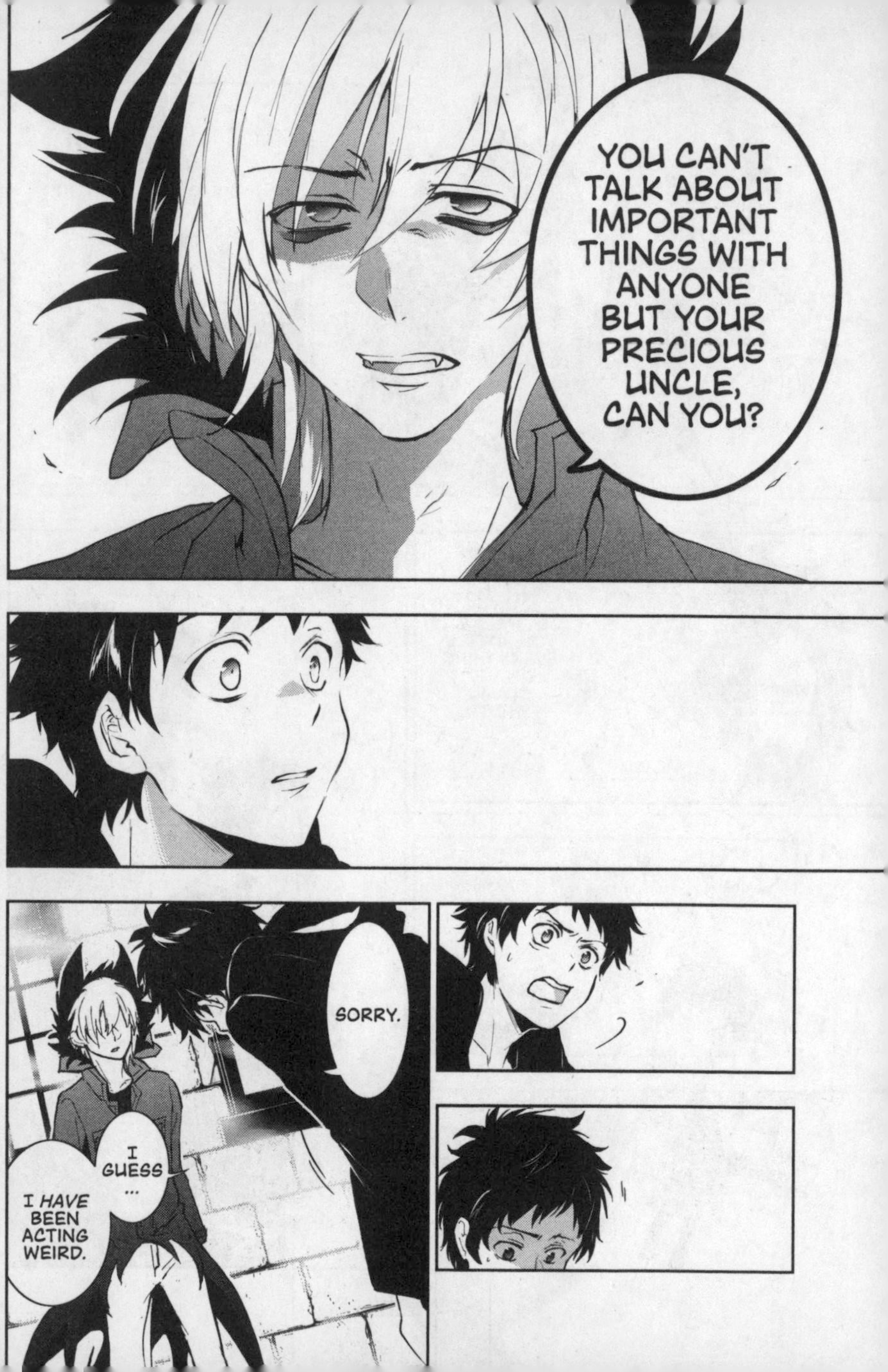
YOU CAN'T TALK ABOUT IMPORTANT THINGS WITH ANYONE BUT YOUR PRECIOUS UNCLE, CAN YOU?
SORRY.
I GUESS... I *HAVE* BEEN ACTING WEIRD.

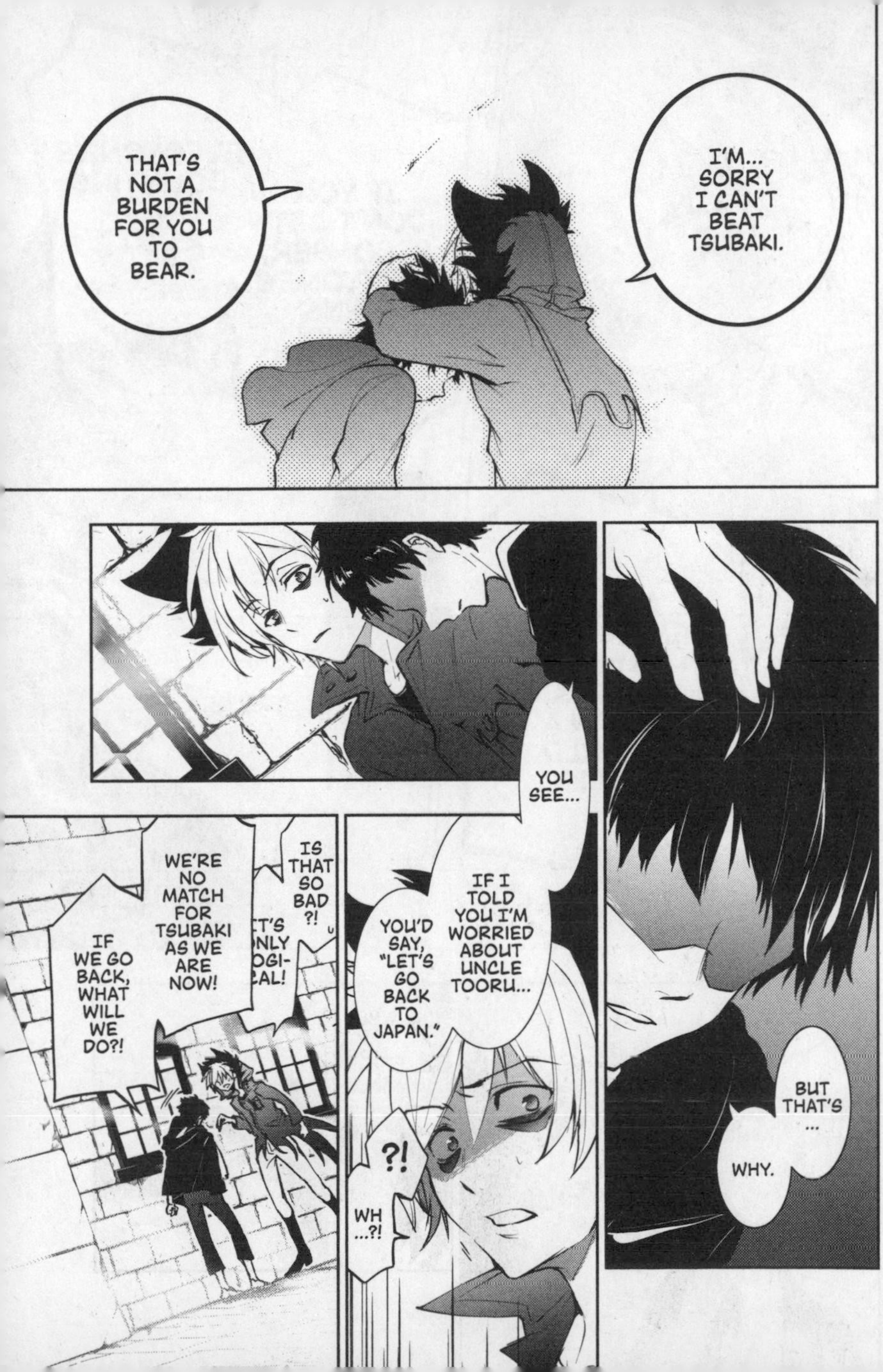
I'M... SORRY I CAN'T BEAT TSUBAKI.
THAT'S NOT A BURDEN FOR YOU TO BEAR.
YOU SEE...
IF I TOLD YOU I'M WORRIED ABOUT UNCLE TOORU...
YOU'D SAY, "LET'S GO BACK TO JAPAN."
BUT THAT'S ...
WHY.
?!
WH ...?!
IS THAT SO BAD ?!
T'S NLY OGI- CAL!
WE'RE NO MATCH FOR TSUBAKI AS WE ARE NOW!
IF WE GO BACK, WHAT WILL WE DO?!

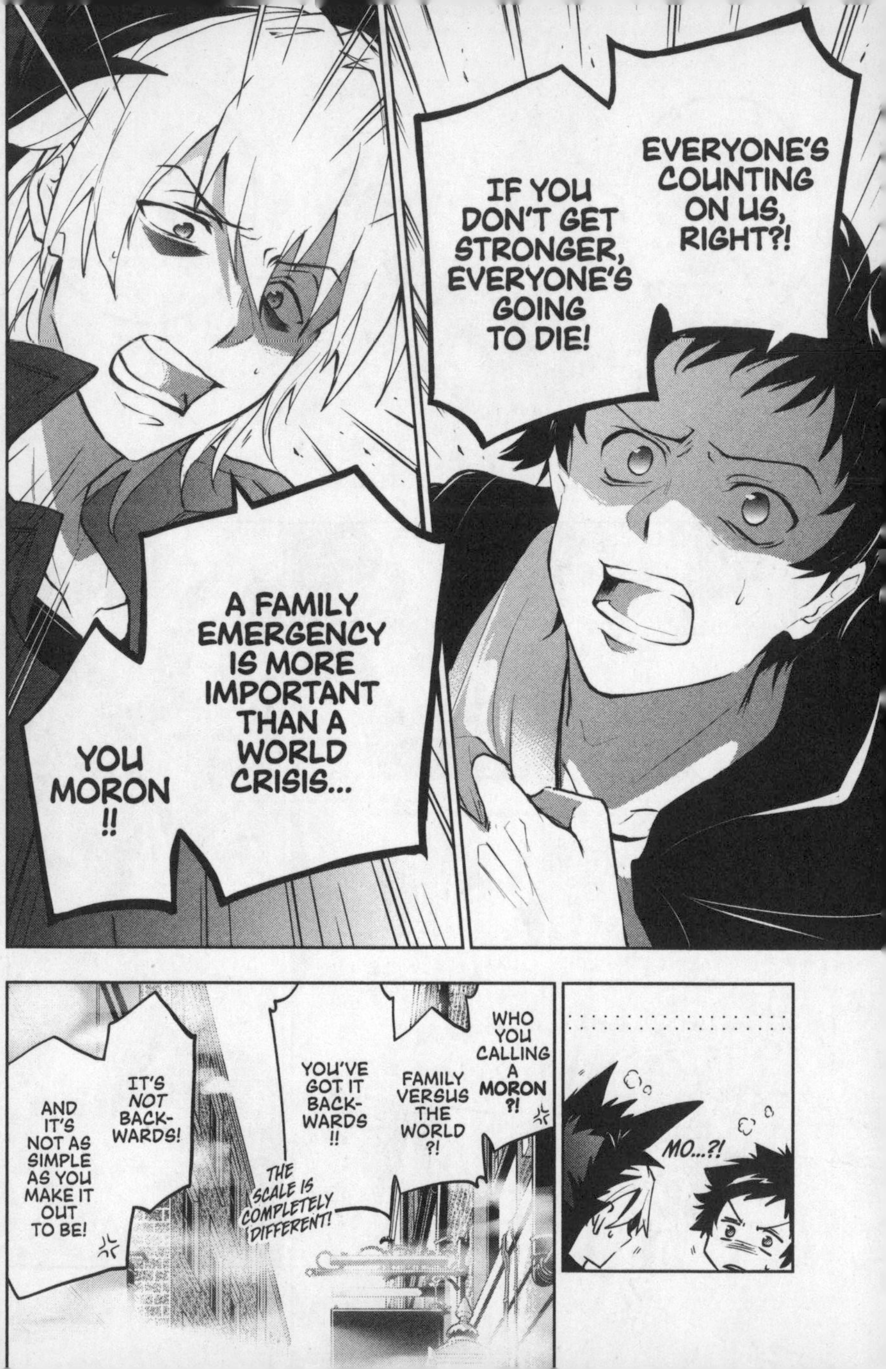
EVERYONE'S COUNTING ON US, RIGHT?!
IF YOU DON'T GET STRONGER, EVERYONE'S GOING TO DIE!
A FAMILY EMERGENCY IS MORE IMPORTANT THAN A WORLD CRISIS...
YOU MORON !!
MO...?!
WHO YOU CALLING A MORON ?!
FAMILY VERSUS THE WORLD ?!
YOU'VE GOT IT BACK-WARDS !!
THE SCALE IS COMPLETELY DIFFERENT!
IT'S NOT BACK-WARDS!
AND IT'S NOT AS SIMPLE AS YOU MAKE IT OUT TO BE!

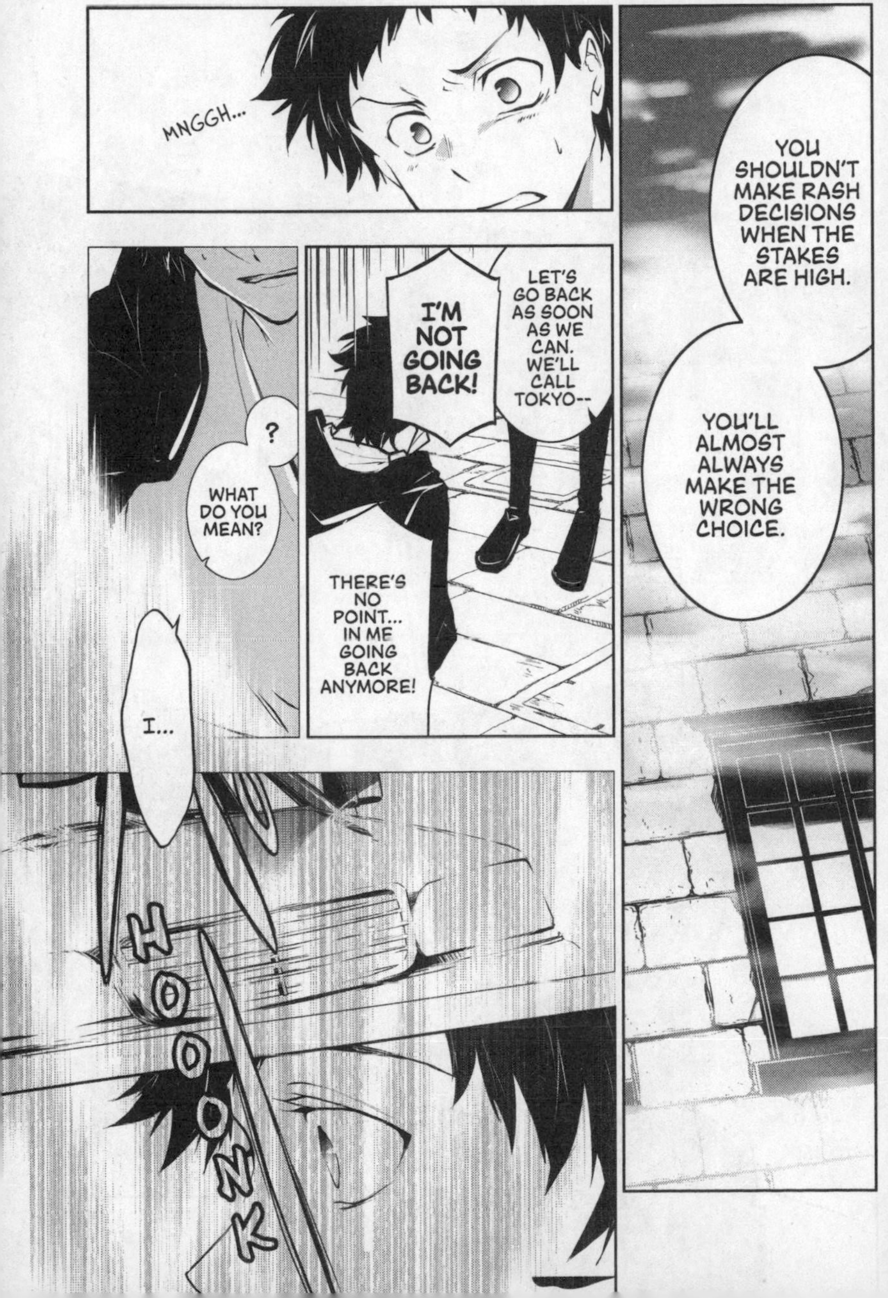

YOU SHOULDN'T MAKE RASH DECISIONS WHEN THE STAKES ARE HIGH.
YOU'LL ALMOST ALWAYS MAKE THE WRONG CHOICE.
MNGGH...
LET'S GO BACK AS SOON AS WE CAN. WE'LL CALL TOKYO--
I'M NOT GOING BACK!
THERE'S NO POINT... IN ME GOING BACK ANYMORE!
?
WHAT DO YOU MEAN?
I...
HOONK

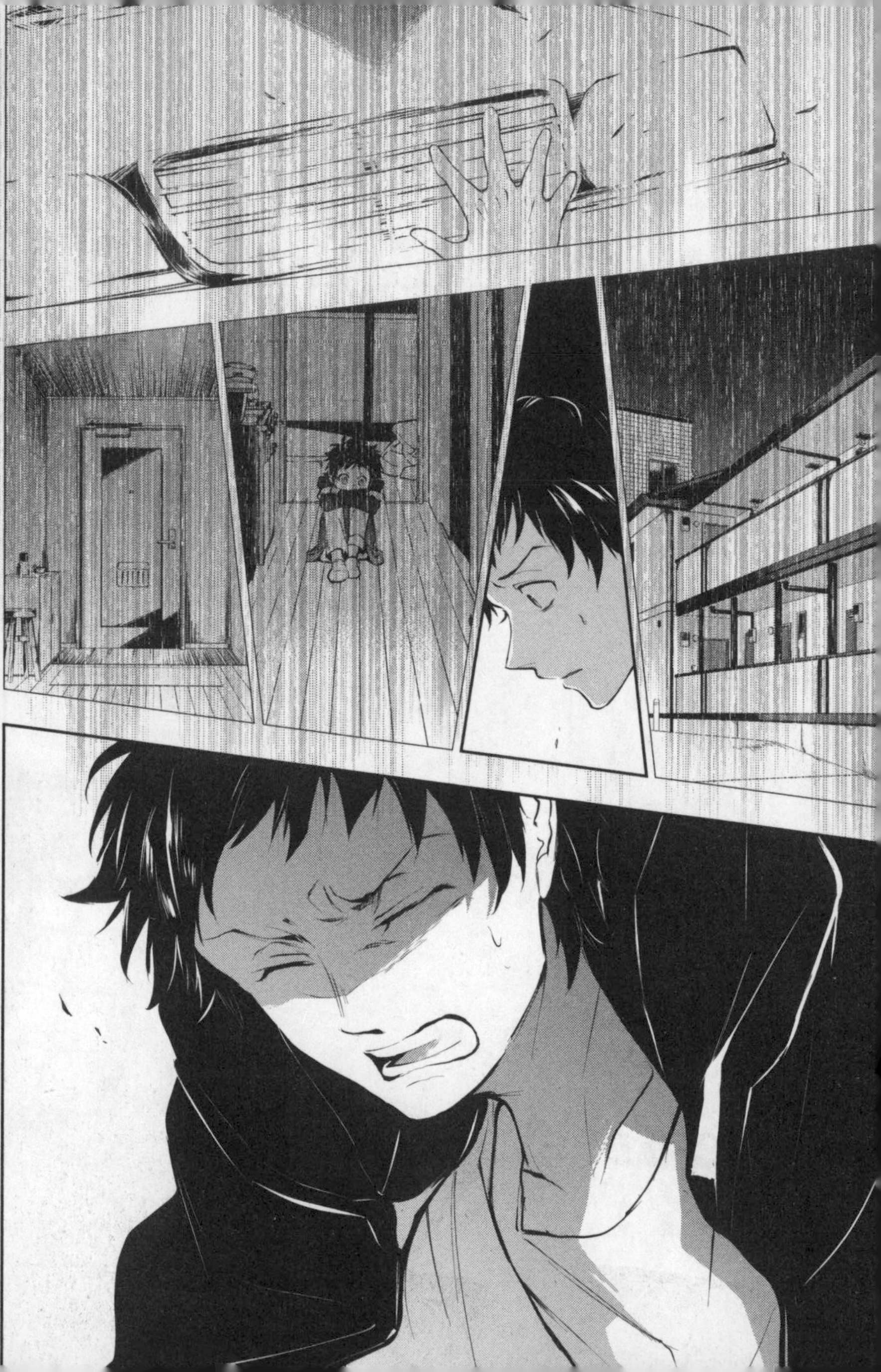

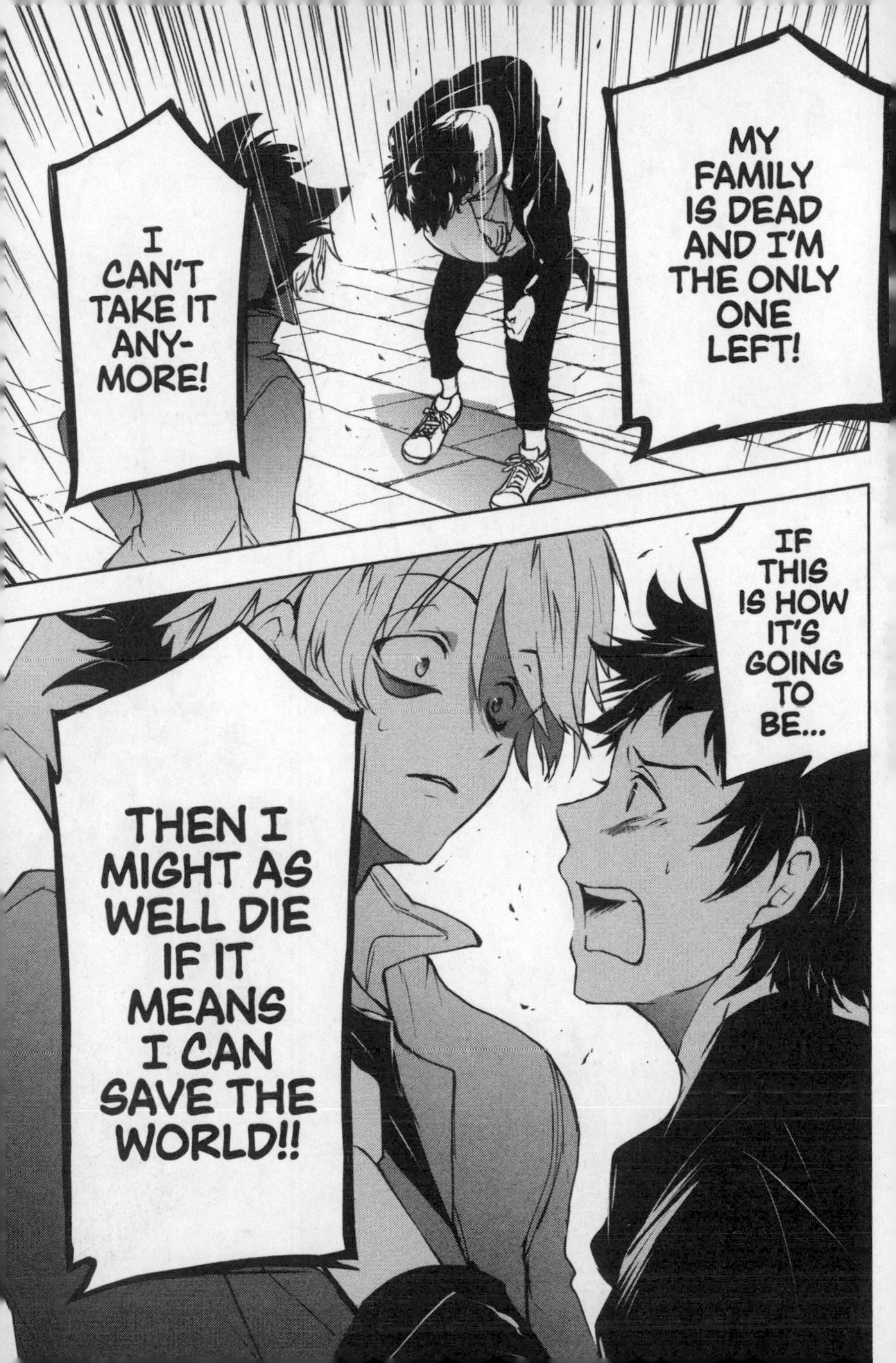
MY FAMILY IS DEAD AND I'M THE ONLY ONE LEFT!
I CAN'T TAKE IT ANY-MORE!
IF THIS IS HOW IT'S GOING TO BE...
THEN I MIGHT AS WELL DIE IF IT MEANS I CAN SAVE THE WORLD!!

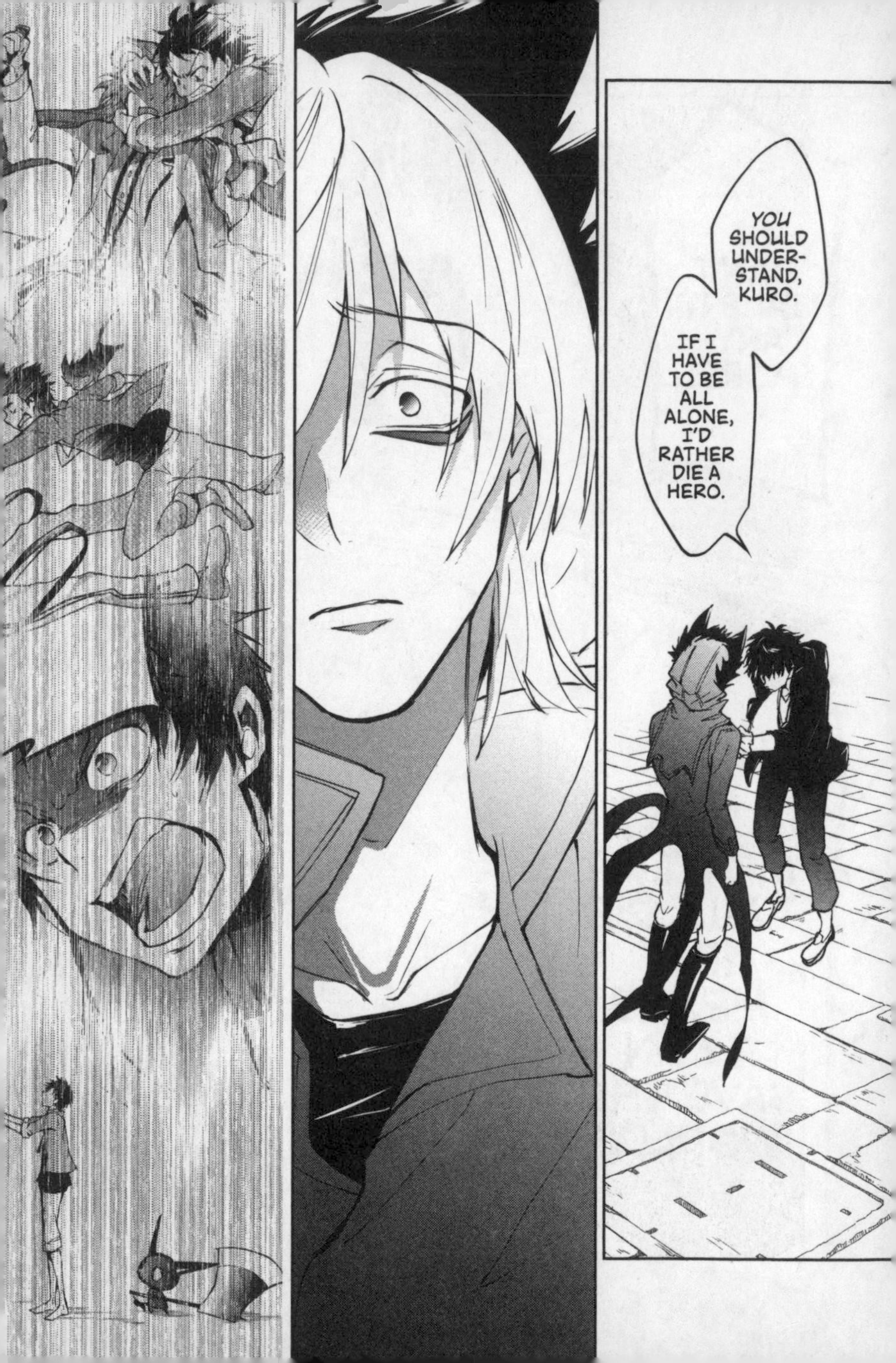
YOU SHOULD UNDER-STAND, KURO.
IF I HAVE TO BE ALL ALONE, I'D RATHER DIE A HERO.

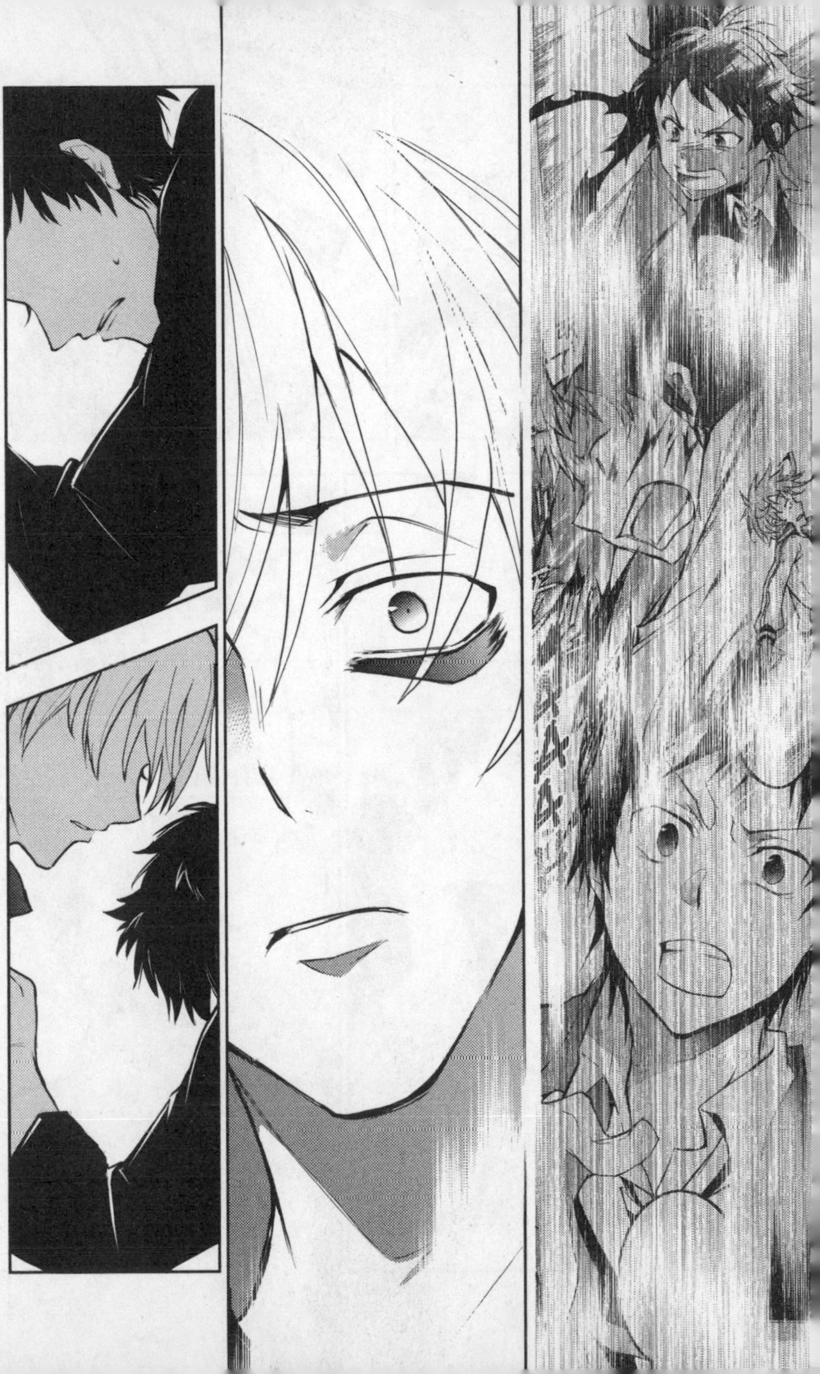

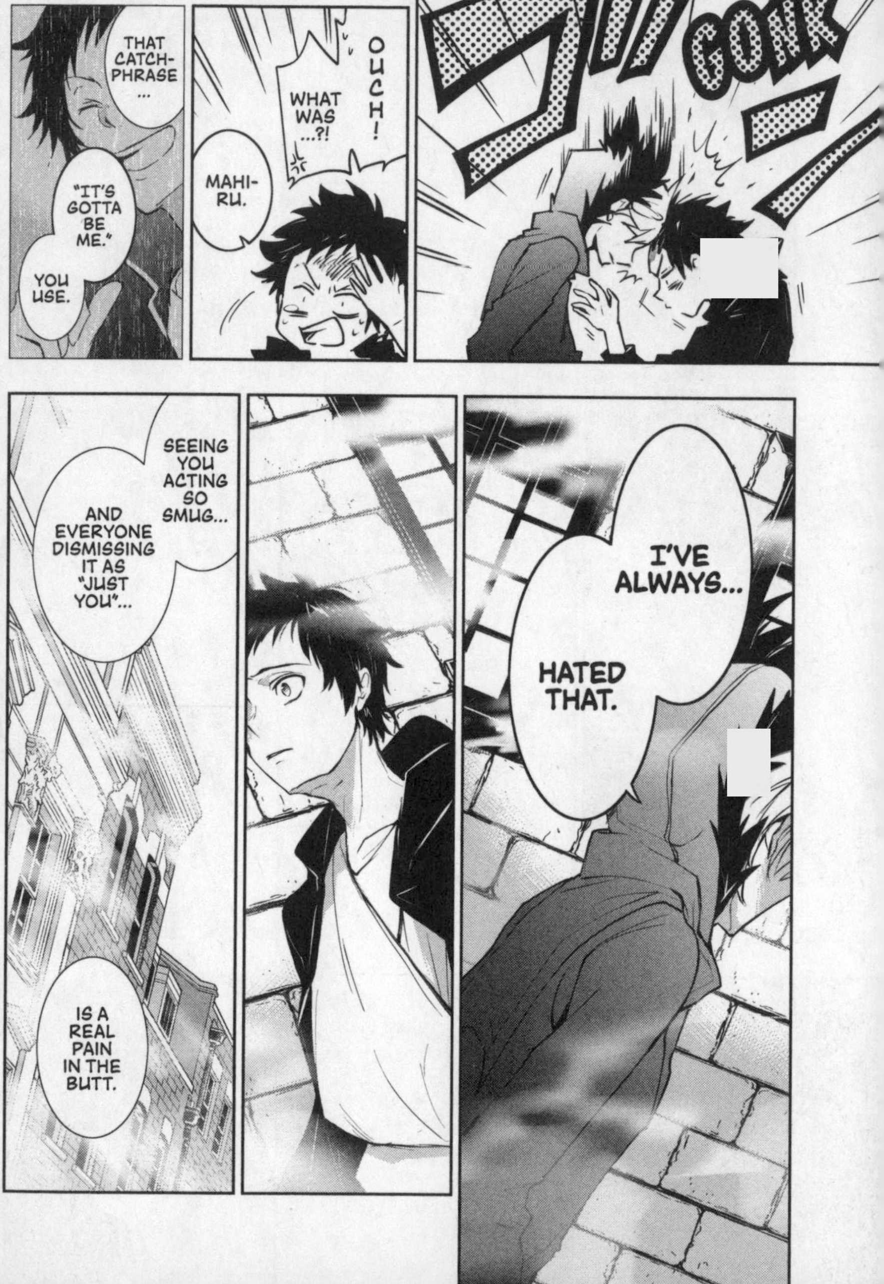
GONK
OUCH!
WHAT WAS ...?!
MAHIRU.
THAT CATCHPHRASE ...
"IT'S GOTTA BE ME."
YOU USE.
I'VE ALWAYS...
HATED THAT.
SEEING YOU ACTING SO SMUG...
AND EVERYONE DISMISSING IT AS "JUST YOU"...
IS A REAL PAIN IN THE BUTT.

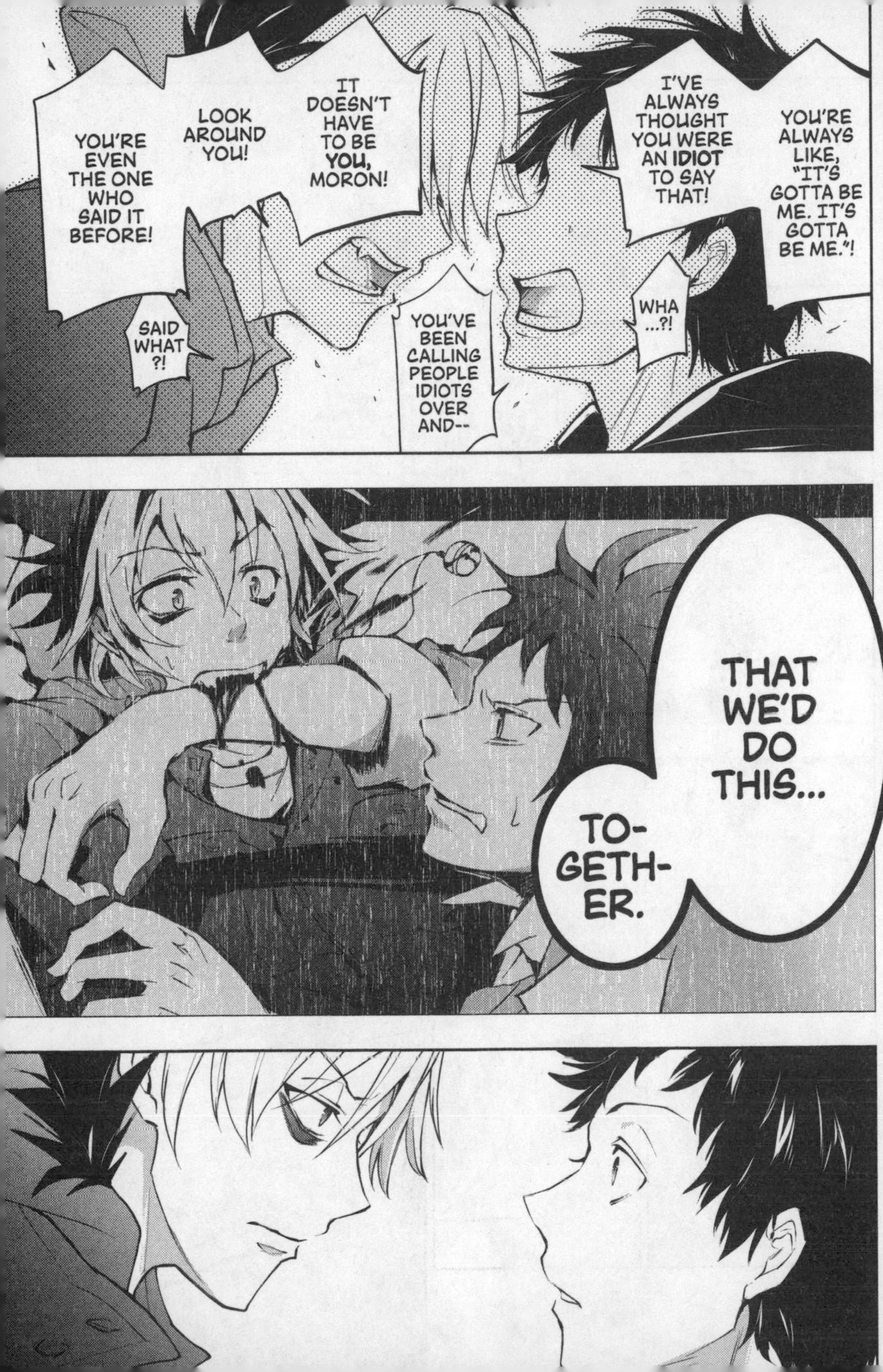
YOU'RE ALWAYS LIKE, "IT'S GOTTA BE ME. IT'S GOTTA BE ME."!
I'VE ALWAYS THOUGHT YOU WERE AN **IDIOT** TO SAY THAT!
WHA ...?!
IT DOESN'T HAVE TO BE **YOU,** MORON!
YOU'VE BEEN CALLING PEOPLE IDIOTS OVER AND--
LOOK AROUND YOU!
YOU'RE EVEN THE ONE WHO SAID IT BEFORE!
SAID WHAT ?!
THAT WE'D DO THIS...
TO-GETH-ER.

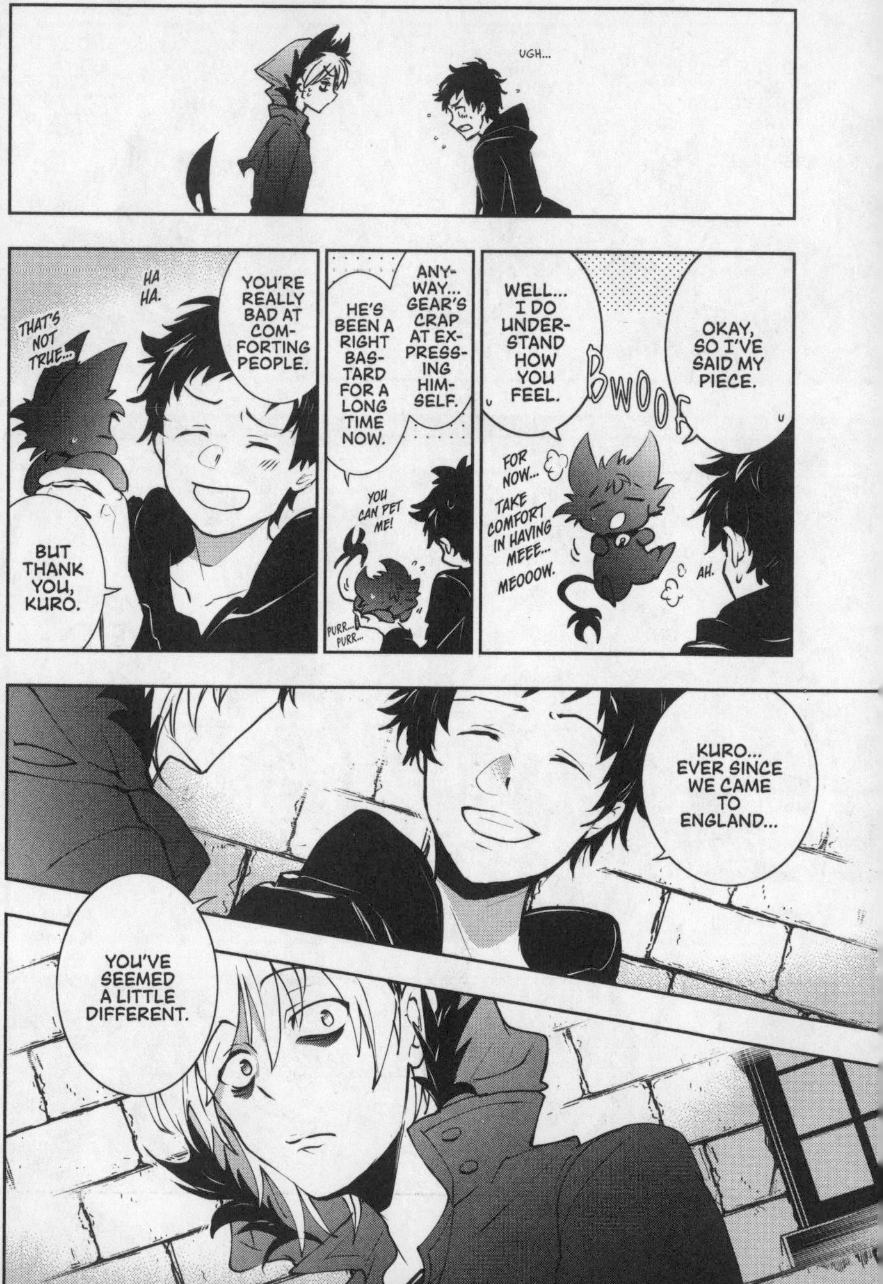
UGH...
OKAY, SO I'VE SAID MY PIECE.
AH.
BWOOF
WELL... I DO UNDERSTAND HOW YOU FEEL.
FOR NOW... TAKE COMFORT IN HAVING MEEE... MEOOOW.
ANYWAY... GEAR'S CRAP AT EXPRESSING HIMSELF.
HE'S BEEN A RIGHT BASTARD FOR A LONG TIME NOW.
YOU CAN PET ME!
PURR... PURR...
YOU'RE REALLY BAD AT COMFORTING PEOPLE.
HA HA.
THAT'S NOT TRUE...
BUT THANK YOU, KURO.
KURO... EVER SINCE WE CAME TO ENGLAND...
YOU'VE SEEMED A LITTLE DIFFERENT.

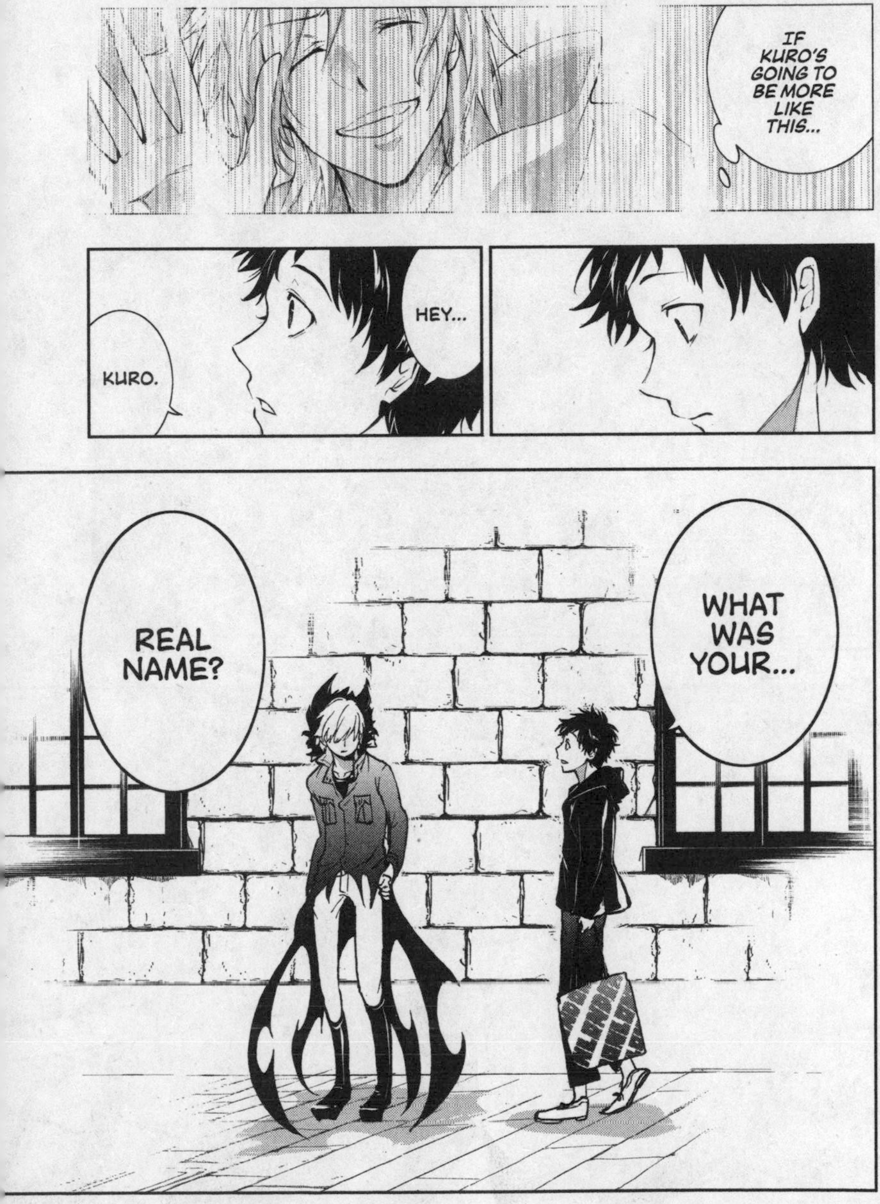

IF KURO'S GOING TO BE MORE LIKE THIS...
HEY...
KURO.
WHAT WAS YOUR...
REAL NAME?

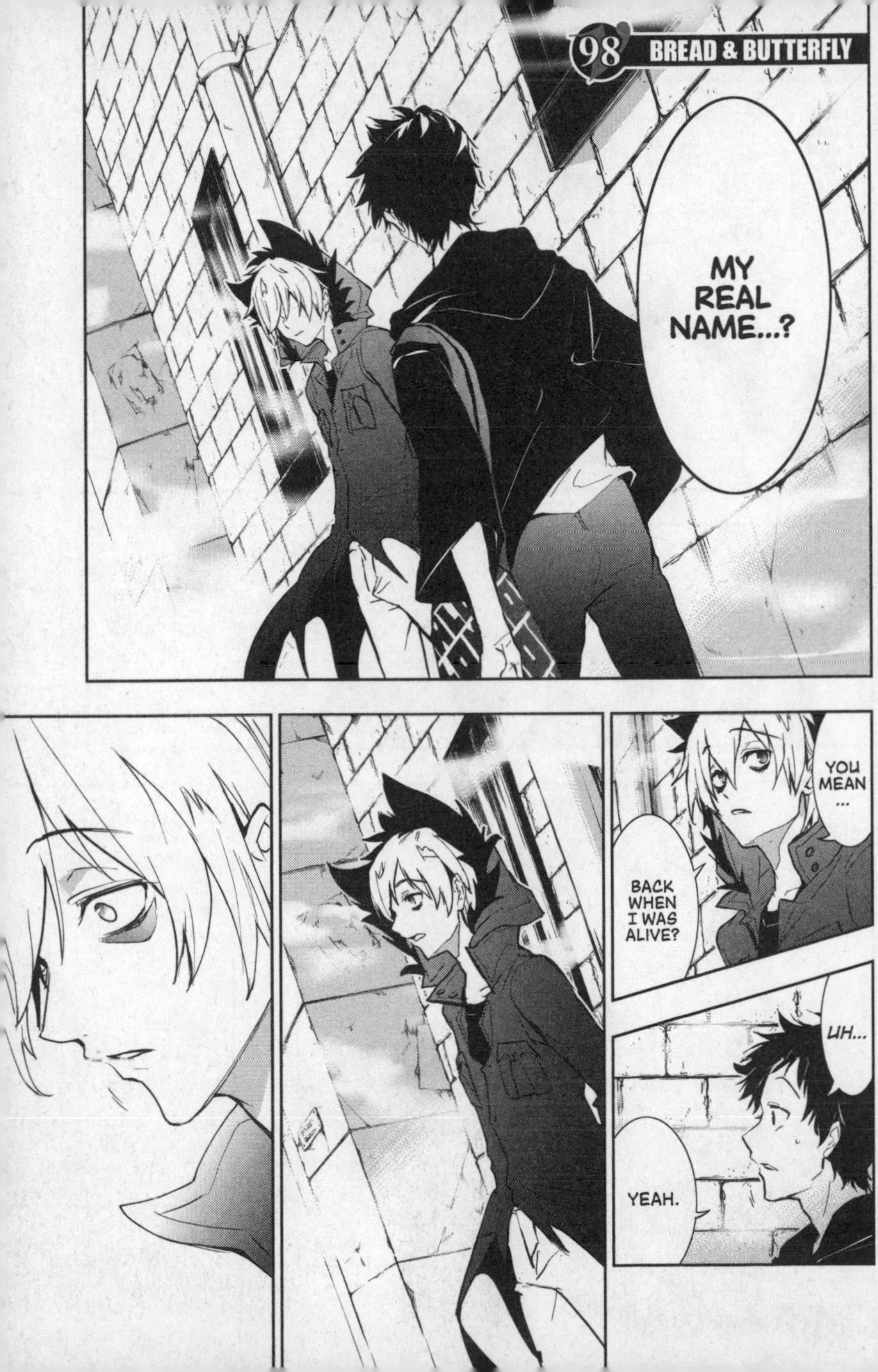
MY REAL NAME...?
YOU MEAN ...
BACK WHEN I WAS ALIVE?
UH...
YEAH.

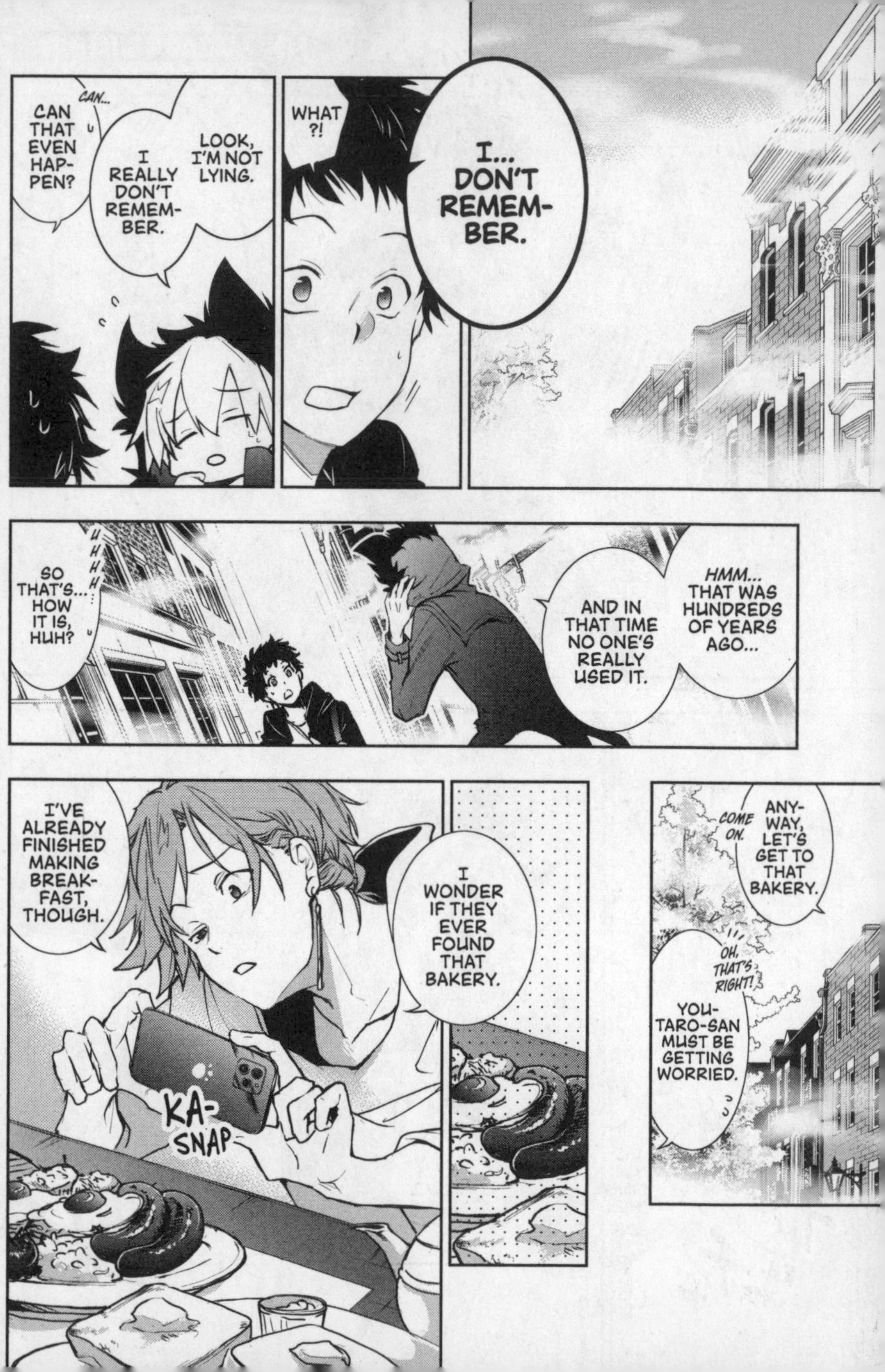
I... DON'T REMEM-BER.
WHAT ?!
LOOK, I'M NOT LYING.
I REALLY DON'T REMEM-BER.
CAN...
CAN THAT EVEN HAP-PEN?
HMM... THAT WAS HUNDREDS OF YEARS AGO...
AND IN THAT TIME NO ONE'S REALLY USED IT.
UHHHH...
SO THAT'S... HOW IT IS, HUH?
ANY-WAY, LET'S GET TO THAT BAKERY.
COME ON.
OH, THAT'S RIGHT!
YOU-TARO-SAN MUST BE GETTING WORRIED.
I WONDER IF THEY EVER FOUND THAT BAKERY.
I'VE ALREADY FINISHED MAKING BREAK-FAST, THOUGH.
KA-SNAP

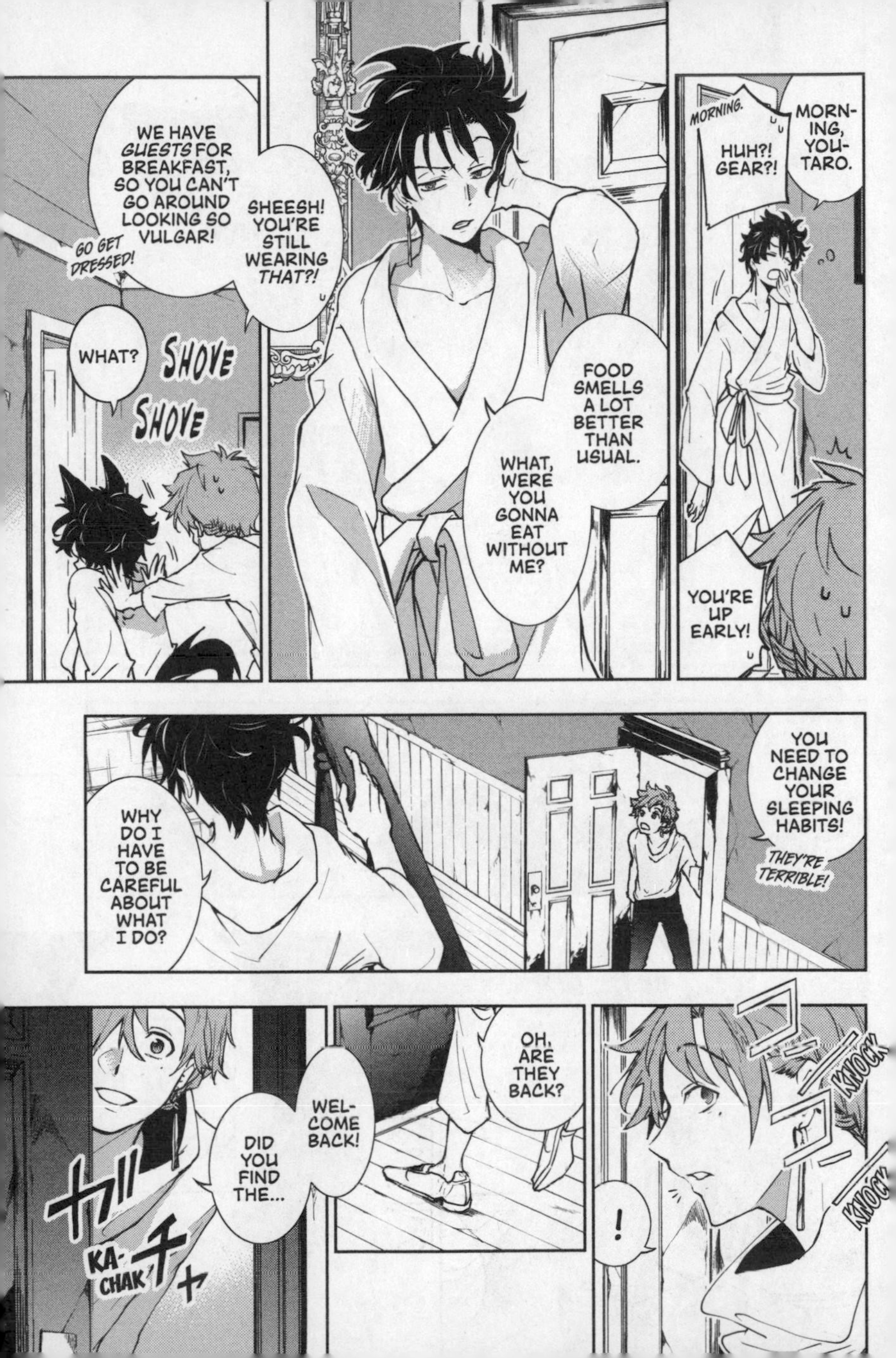
MORN-ING, YOU-TARO.
MORNING.
HUH?! GEAR?!
YOU'RE UP EARLY!
FOOD SMELLS A LOT BETTER THAN USUAL.
WHAT, WERE YOU GONNA EAT WITHOUT ME?
SHEESH! YOU'RE STILL WEARING THAT?!
WE HAVE GUESTS FOR BREAKFAST, SO YOU CAN'T GO AROUND LOOKING SO VULGAR!
GO GET DRESSED!
WHAT?
SHOVE
SHOVE
YOU NEED TO CHANGE YOUR SLEEPING HABITS!
THEY'RE TERRIBLE!
WHY DO I HAVE TO BE CAREFUL ABOUT WHAT I DO?
KNOCK
KNOCK
!
OH, ARE THEY BACK?
WEL-COME BACK!
DID YOU FIND THE...
KA-CHAK

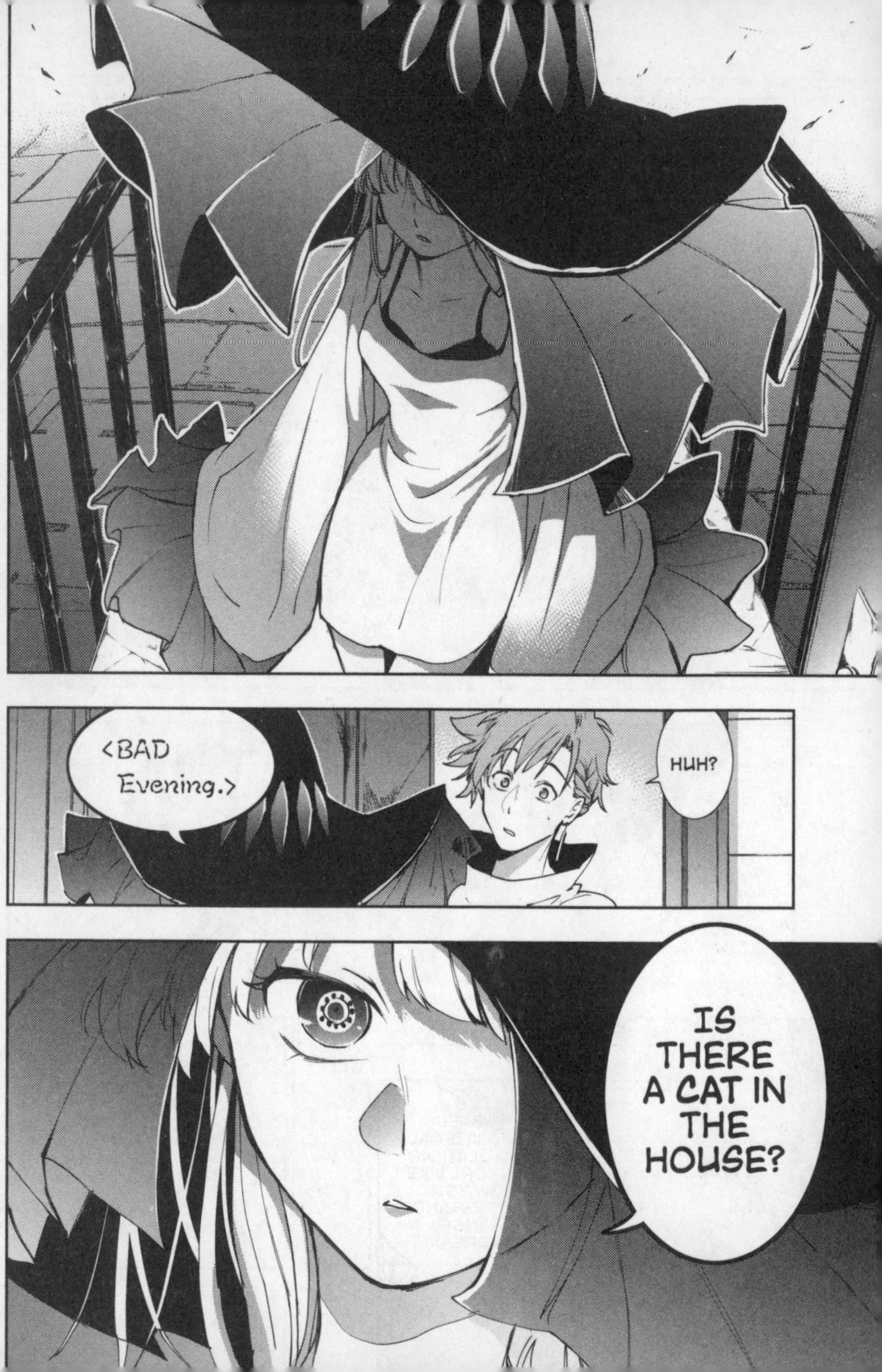
HUH?
<BAD Evening.>
IS THERE A CAT IN THE HOUSE?

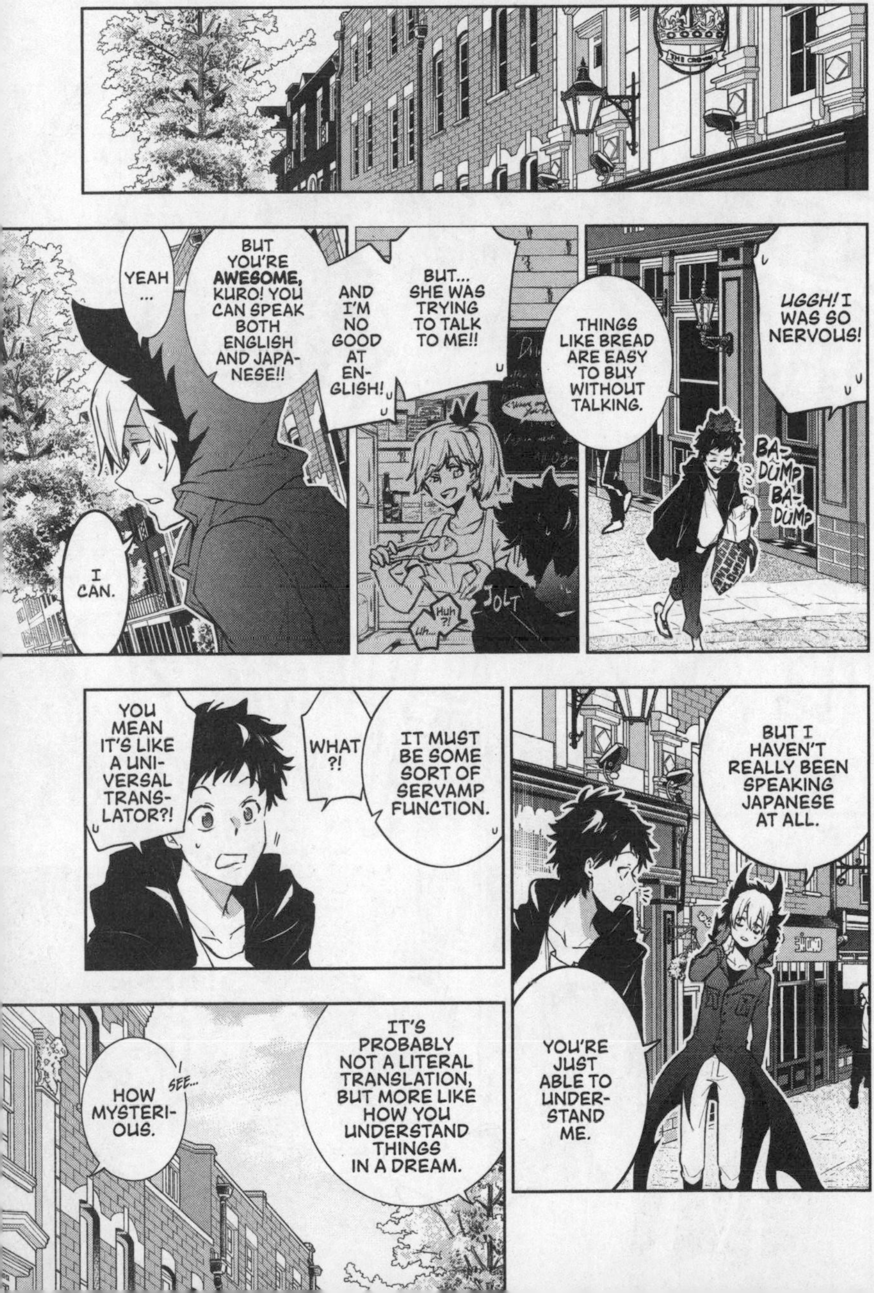
UGGH! I WAS SO NERVOUS!
BA-DUMP BA-DUMP
THINGS LIKE BREAD ARE EASY TO BUY WITHOUT TALKING.
BUT... SHE WAS TRYING TO TALK TO ME!!
AND I'M NO GOOD AT ENGLISH!
Huh?!
Uh...
JOLT
BUT YOU'RE **AWESOME,** KURO! YOU CAN SPEAK BOTH ENGLISH AND JAPANESE!!
YEAH...
I CAN.
BUT I HAVEN'T REALLY BEEN SPEAKING JAPANESE AT ALL.
YOU'RE JUST ABLE TO UNDERSTAND ME.
IT MUST BE SOME SORT OF SERVAMP FUNCTION.
WHAT?!
YOU MEAN IT'S LIKE A UNIVERSAL TRANSLATOR?!
IT'S PROBABLY NOT A LITERAL TRANSLATION, BUT MORE LIKE HOW YOU UNDERSTAND THINGS IN A DREAM.
I SEE...
HOW MYSTERIOUS.

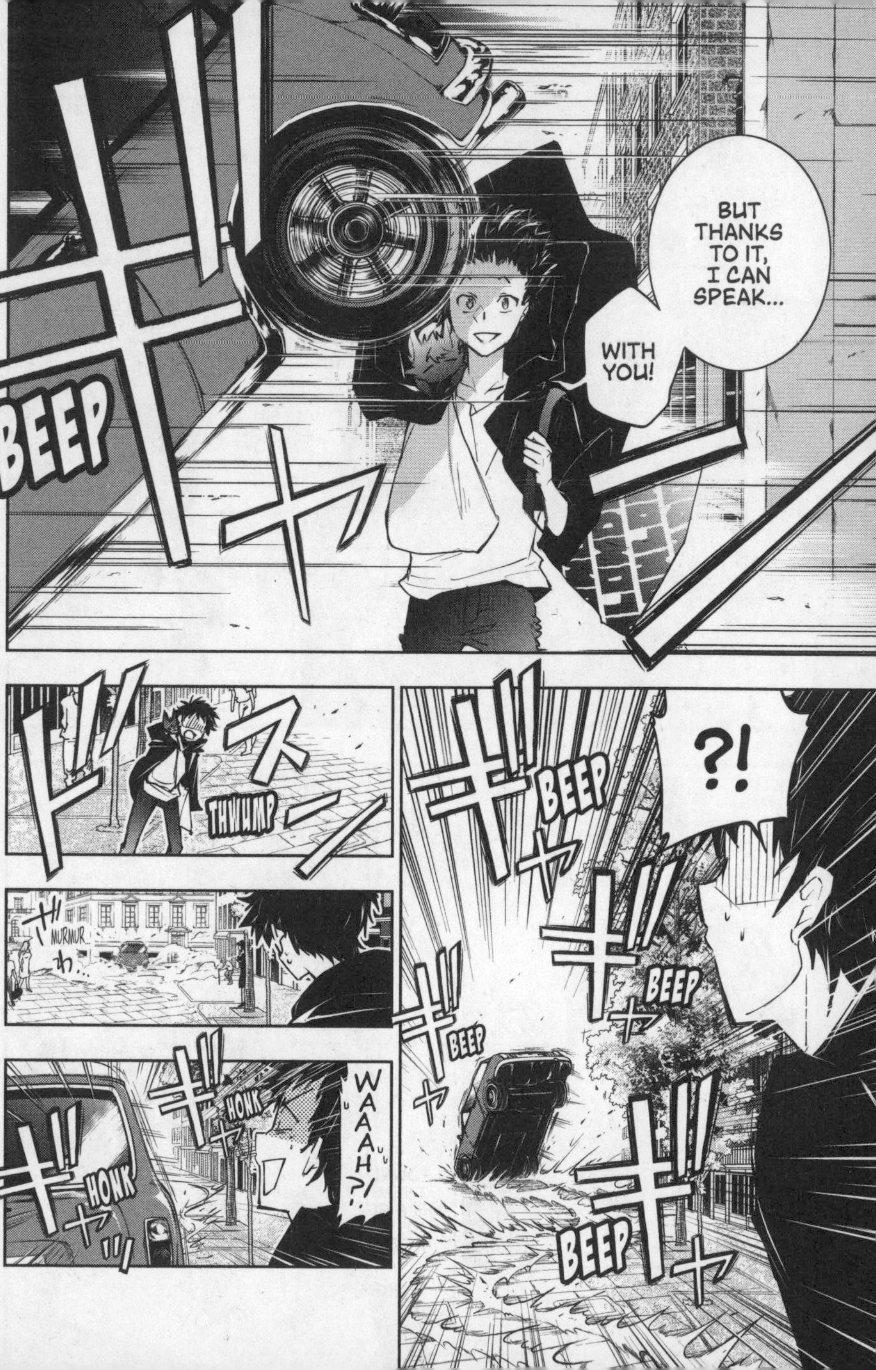
BUT THANKS TO IT, I CAN SPEAK...
WITH YOU!
BEEP
?!
BEEP
BEEP
BEEP
BEEP
THWUMP
MURMUR...
WAAAAH?!
HONK
HONK

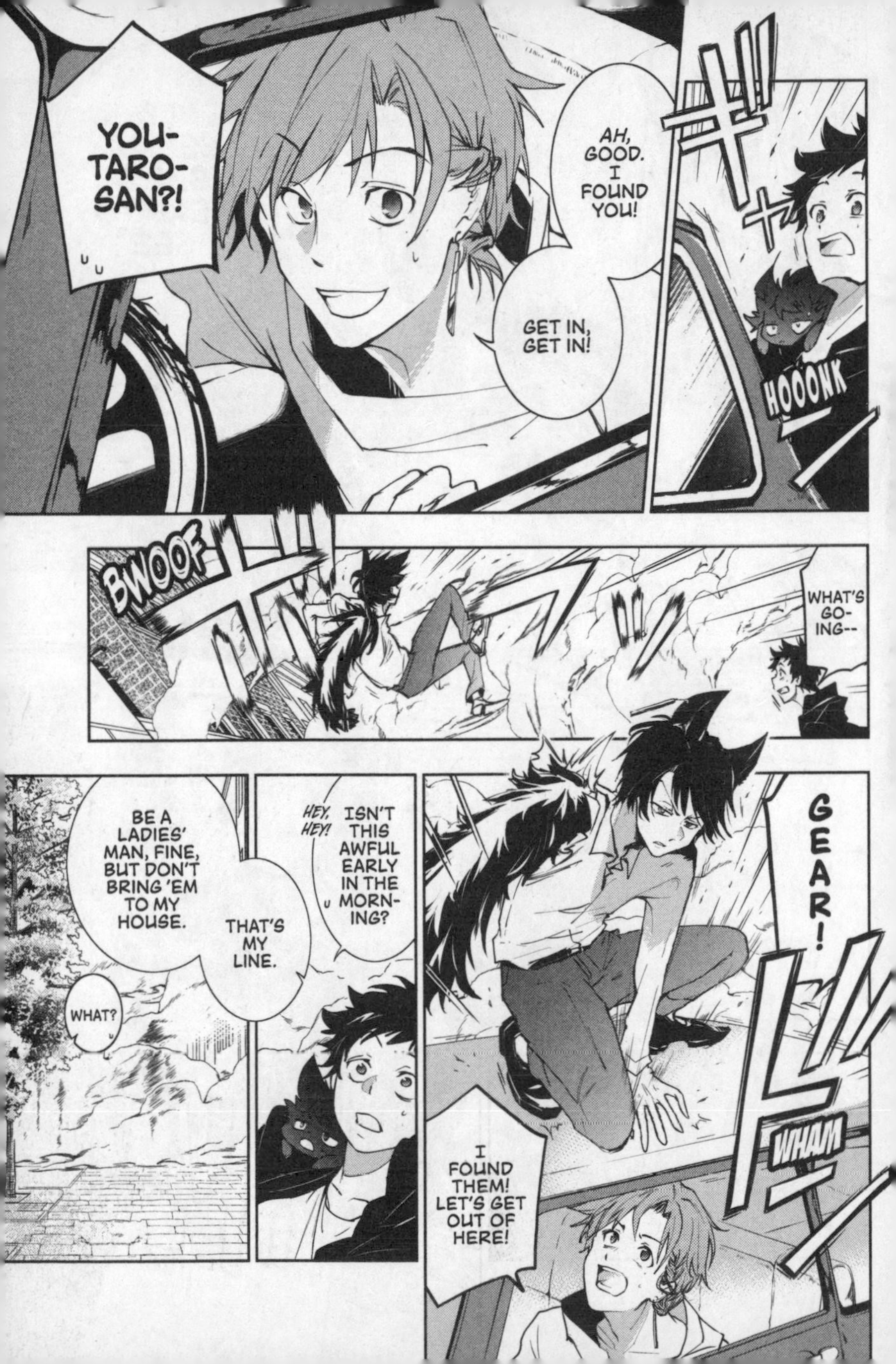
AH, GOOD. I FOUND YOU!
GET IN, GET IN!
HOOONK
YOU-TARO-SAN?!
WHAT'S GO-ING--
BWOOF
GEAR!
WHAM
I FOUND THEM! LET'S GET OUT OF HERE!
HEY, HEY!
ISN'T THIS AWFUL EARLY IN THE MORNING?
THAT'S MY LINE.
BE A LADIES' MAN, FINE, BUT DON'T BRING 'EM TO MY HOUSE.
WHAT?

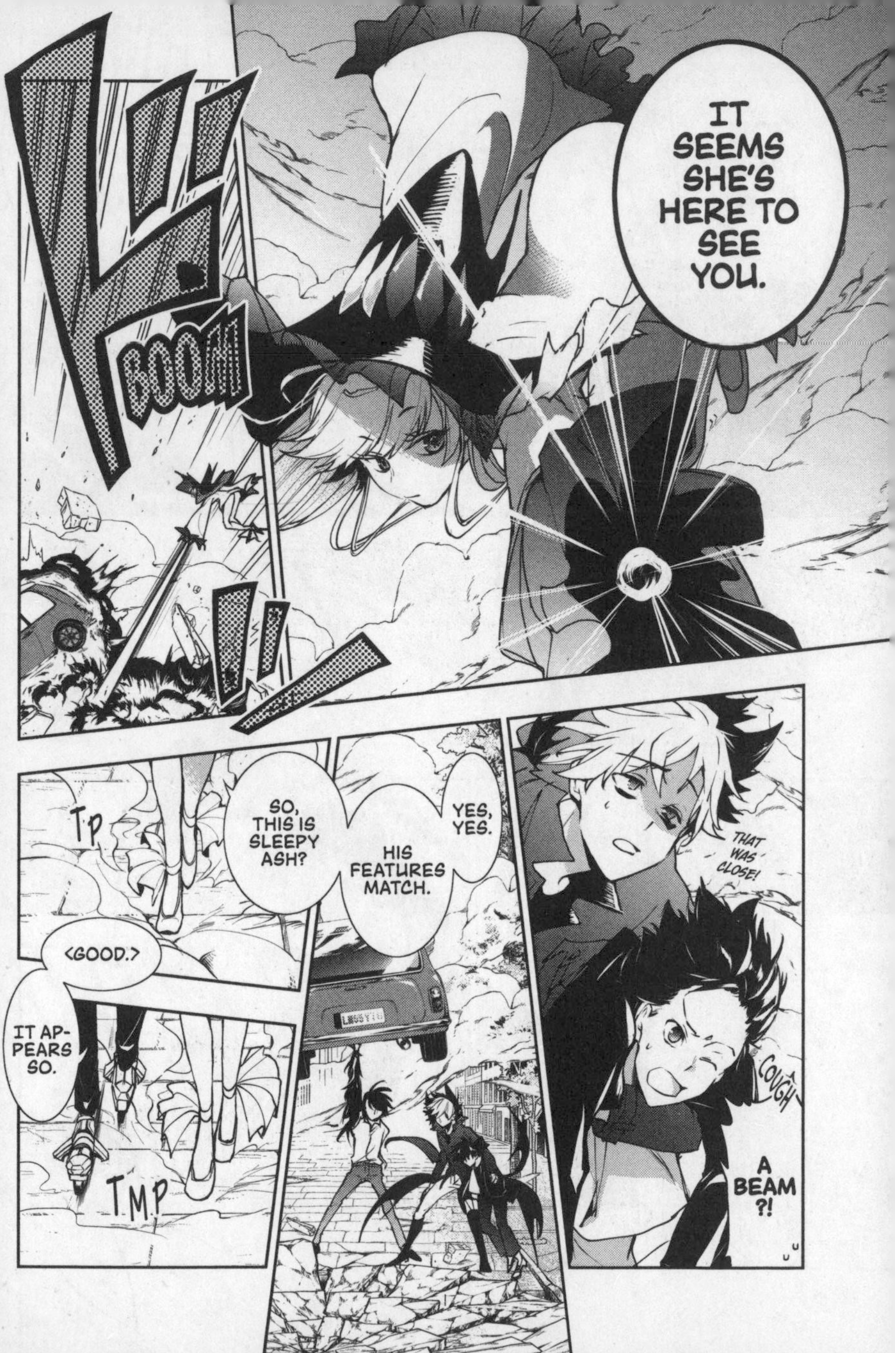
IT SEEMS SHE'S HERE TO SEE YOU.
BOOM!!
THAT WAS CLOSE!
COUGH
A BEAM ?!
SO, THIS IS SLEEPY ASH?
YES, YES.
HIS FEATURES MATCH.
Tp
<GOOD.>
IT AP-PEARS SO.
TMP

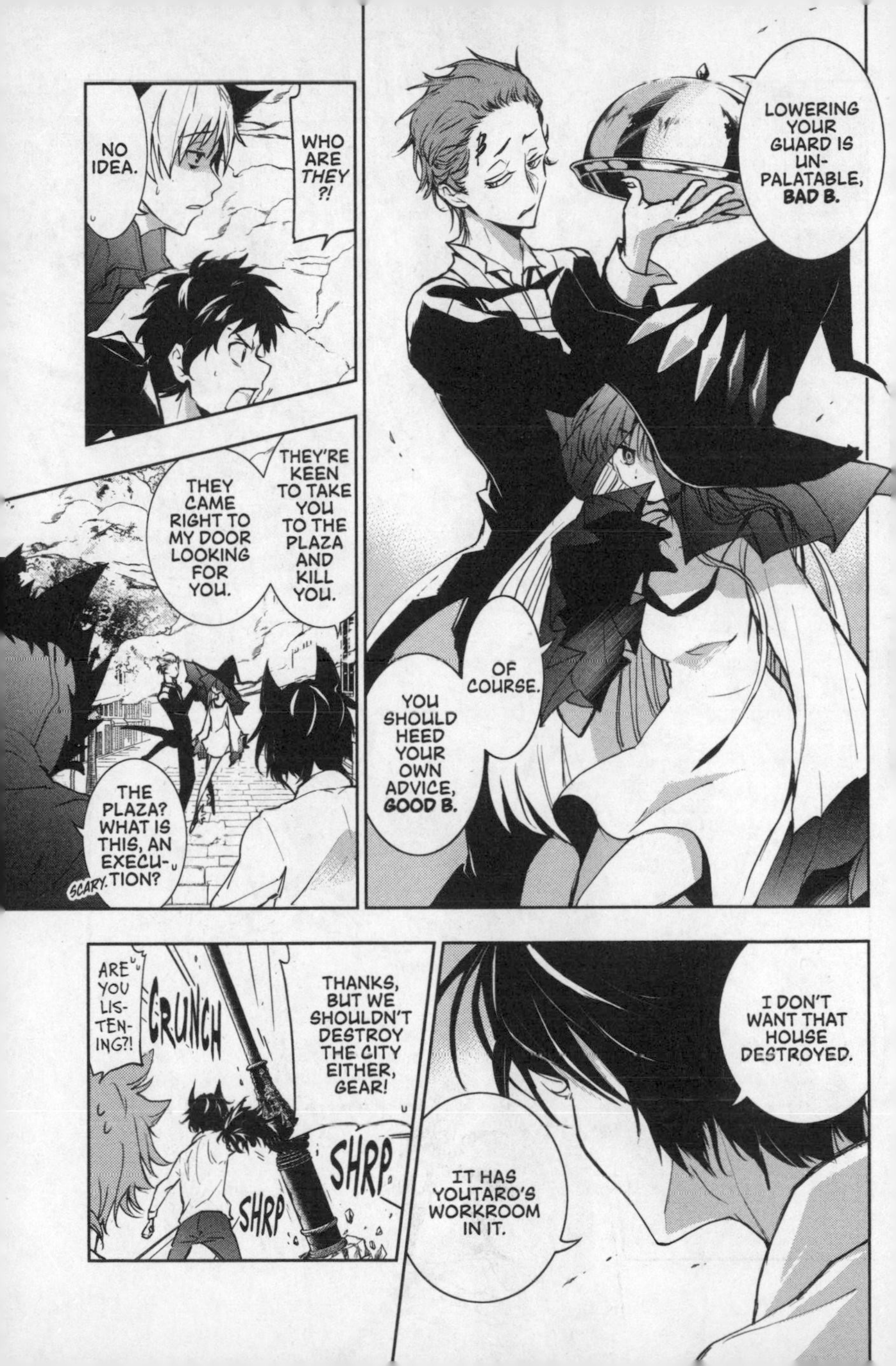

LOWERING YOUR GUARD IS UN-PALATABLE, BAD B.
OF COURSE.
YOU SHOULD HEED YOUR OWN ADVICE, GOOD B.
WHO ARE THEY?!
NO IDEA.
THEY'RE KEEN TO TAKE YOU TO THE PLAZA AND KILL YOU.
THEY CAME RIGHT TO MY DOOR LOOKING FOR YOU.
THE PLAZA? WHAT IS THIS, AN EXECU-TION?
SCARY.
I DON'T WANT THAT HOUSE DESTROYED.
IT HAS YOUTARO'S WORKROOM IN IT.
THANKS, BUT WE SHOULDN'T DESTROY THE CITY EITHER, GEAR!
ARE YOU LIS-TEN-ING?!
CRUNCH
SHRP
SHRP

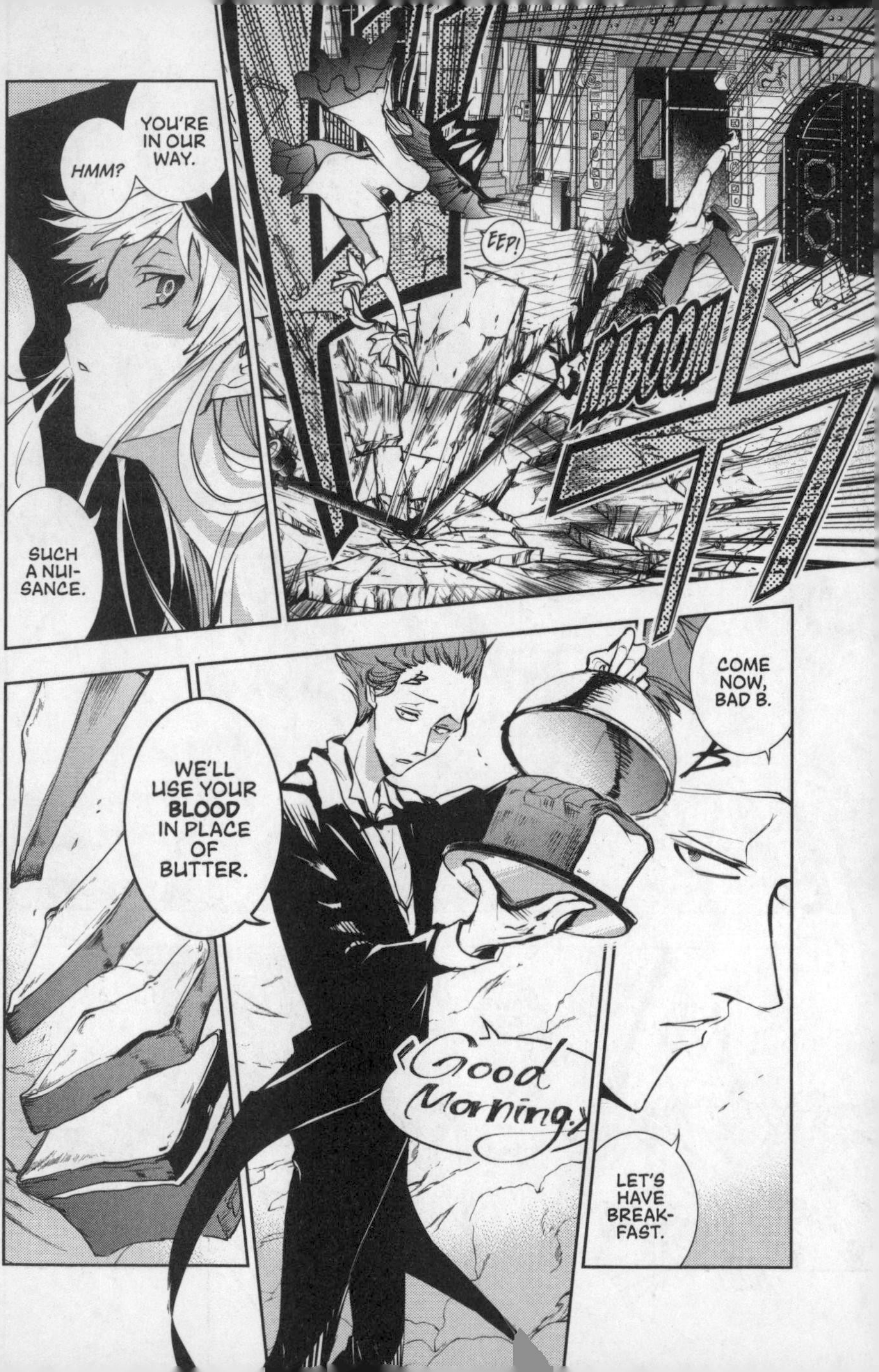
EEP!
HMM?
YOU'RE IN OUR WAY.
SUCH A NUISANCE.
COME NOW, BAD B.
LET'S HAVE BREAKFAST.
WE'LL USE YOUR BLOOD IN PLACE OF BUTTER.
Good Morning.

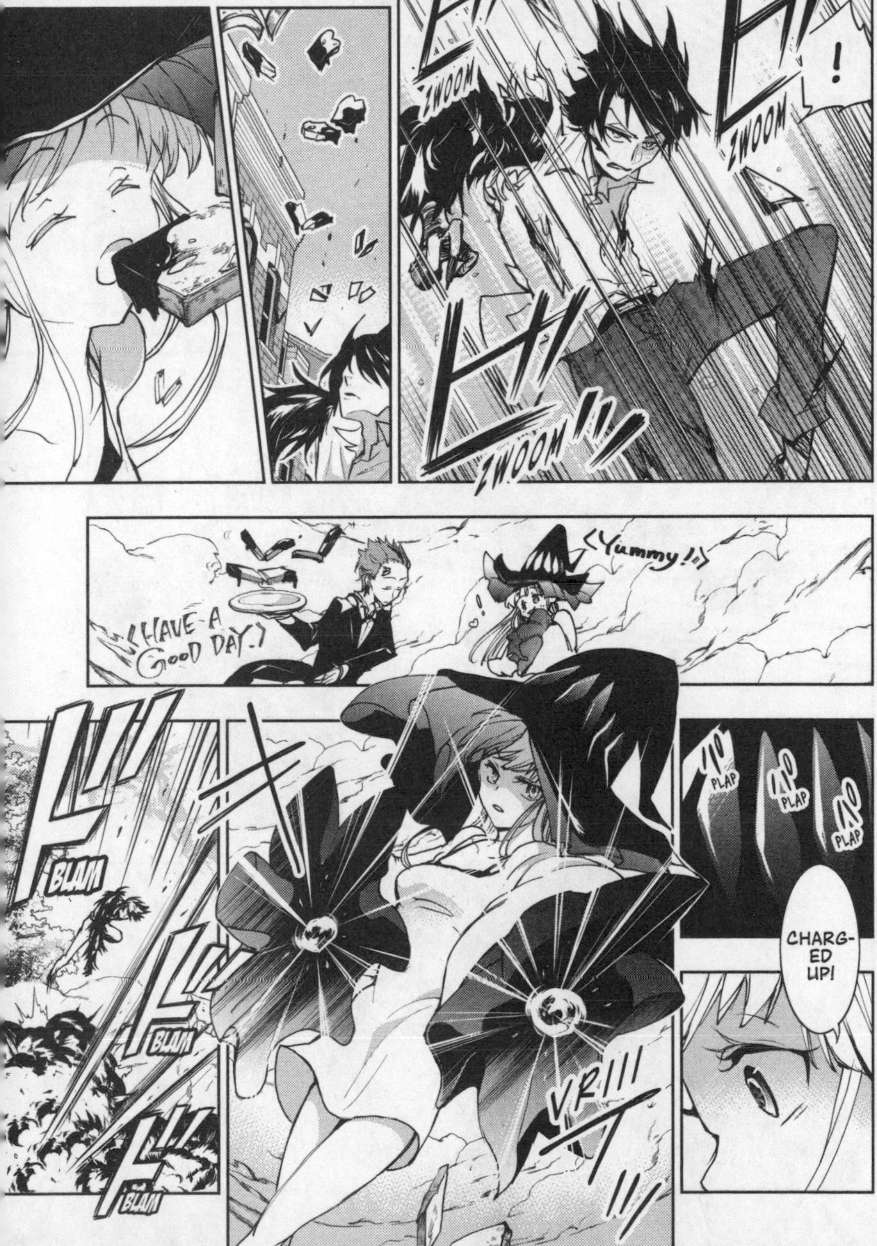

!
ZWOOM
ZWOOM
ZWOOM!!
<Yummy!!>
<HAVE A GOOD DAY.>
PLAP
PLAP
PLAP
CHARG-ED UP!
VRIIII
BLAM
BLAM
BLAM

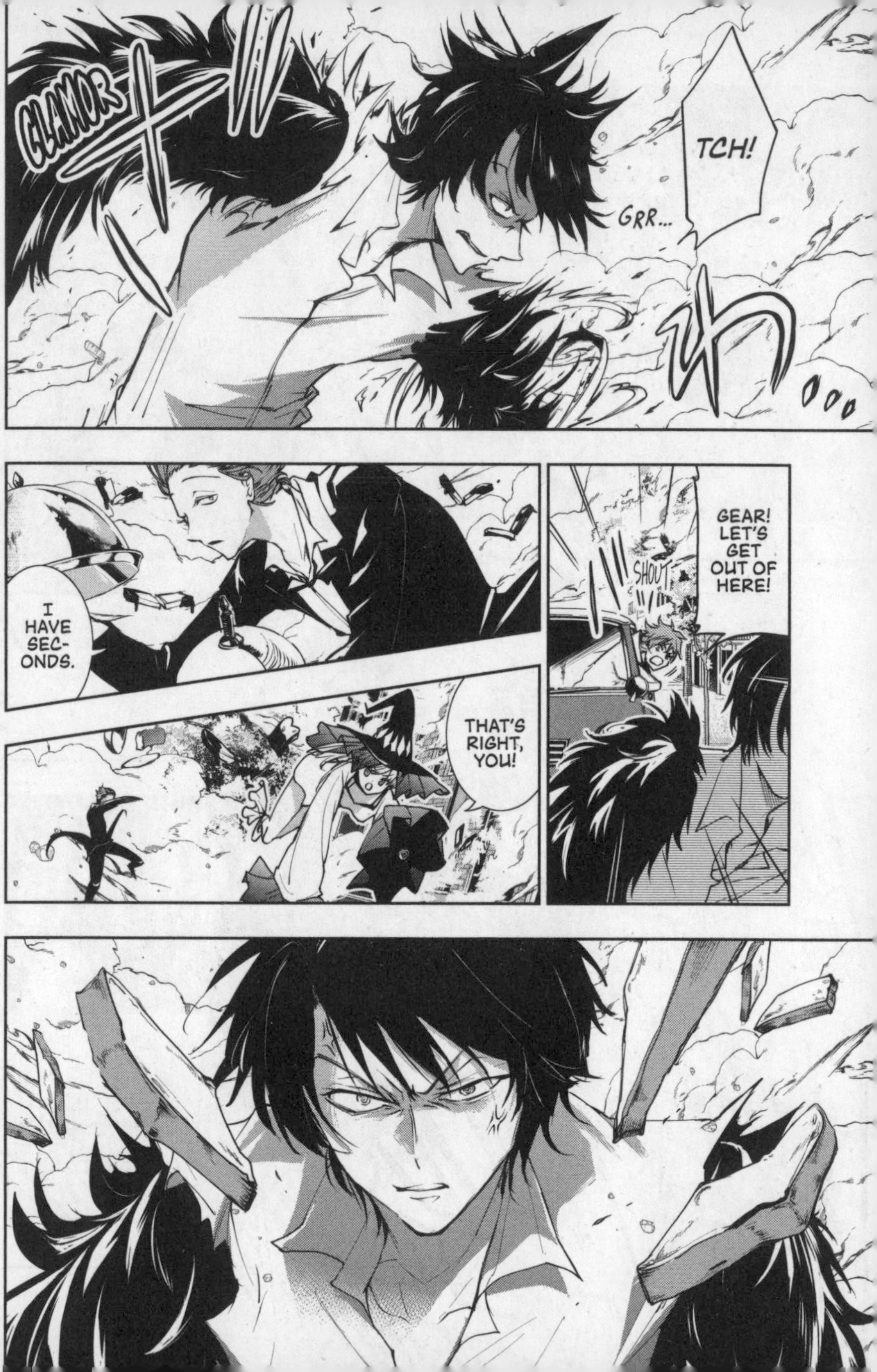

TCH!
GRR...
CLAMOR
GEAR! LET'S GET OUT OF HERE!
SHOUT
I HAVE SEC-ONDS.
THAT'S RIGHT, YOU!

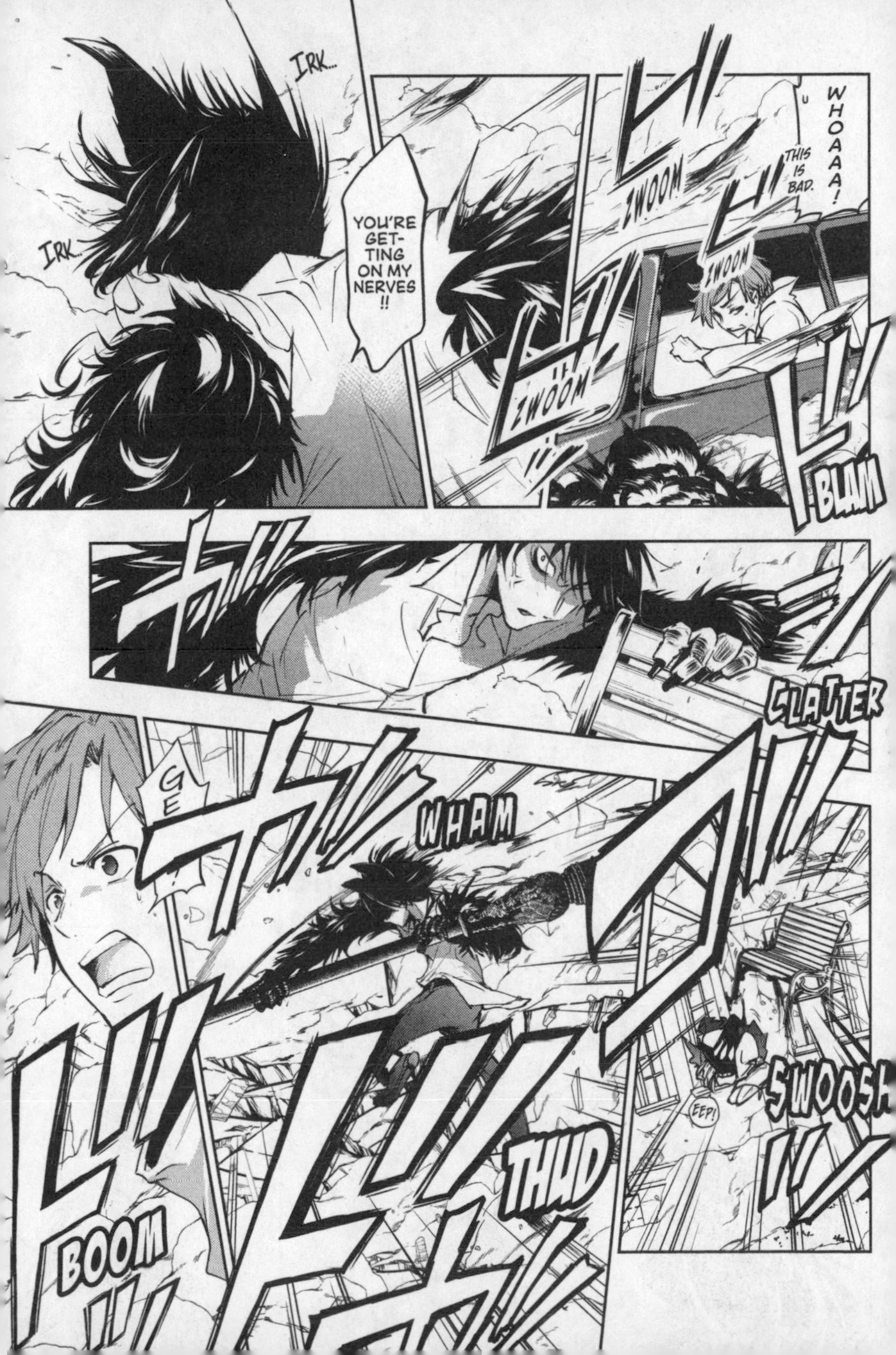
WHOAAAA!
THIS IS BAD.
ZWOOM
ZWOOM
ZWOOM
BLAM
YOU'RE GETTING ON MY NERVES!!
IRK...
IRK...
CLATTER
SWOOSH
EEP!
WHAM
GE
THUD
BOOM

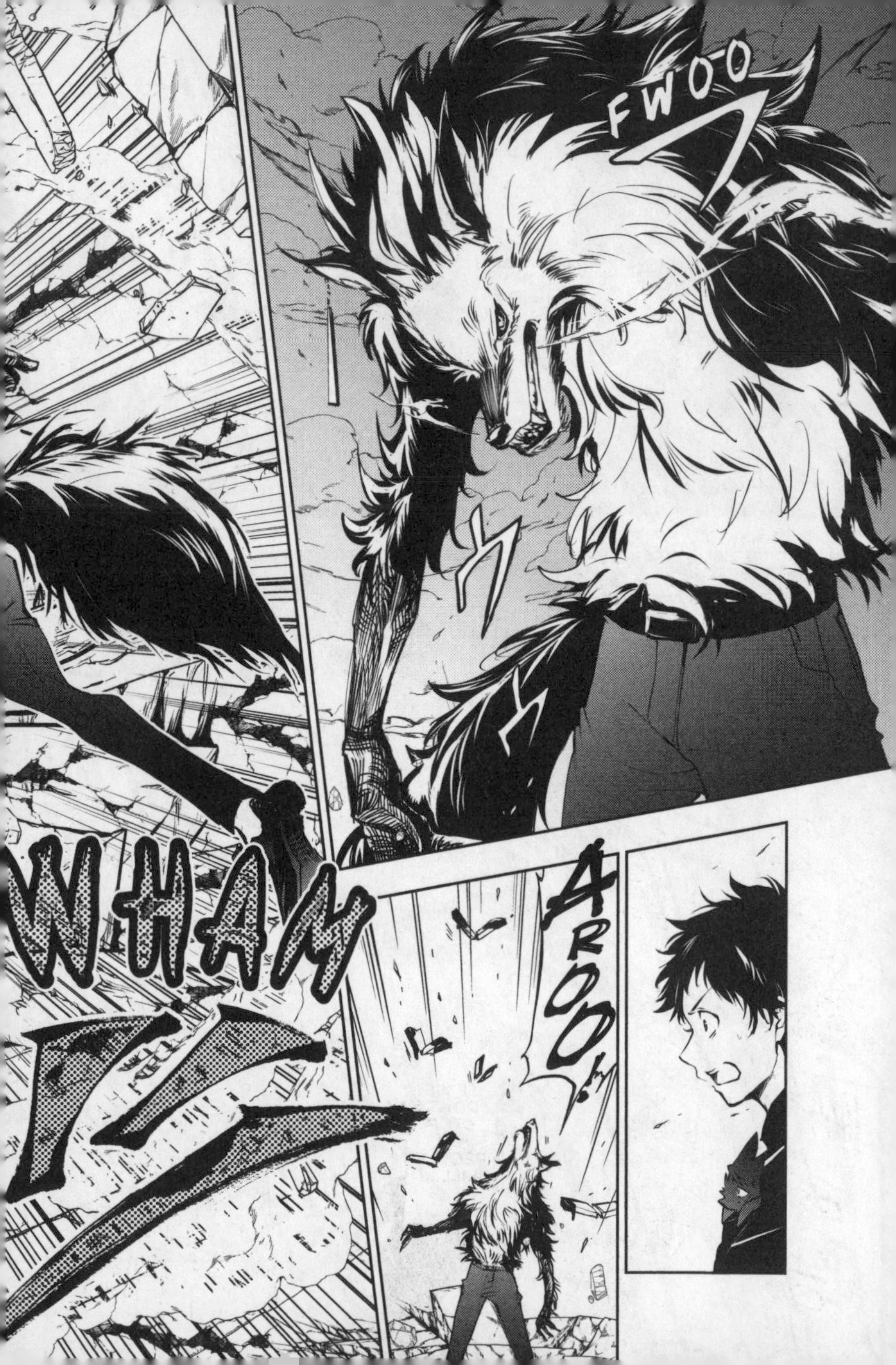
FWOO
WHAM
AROOO!

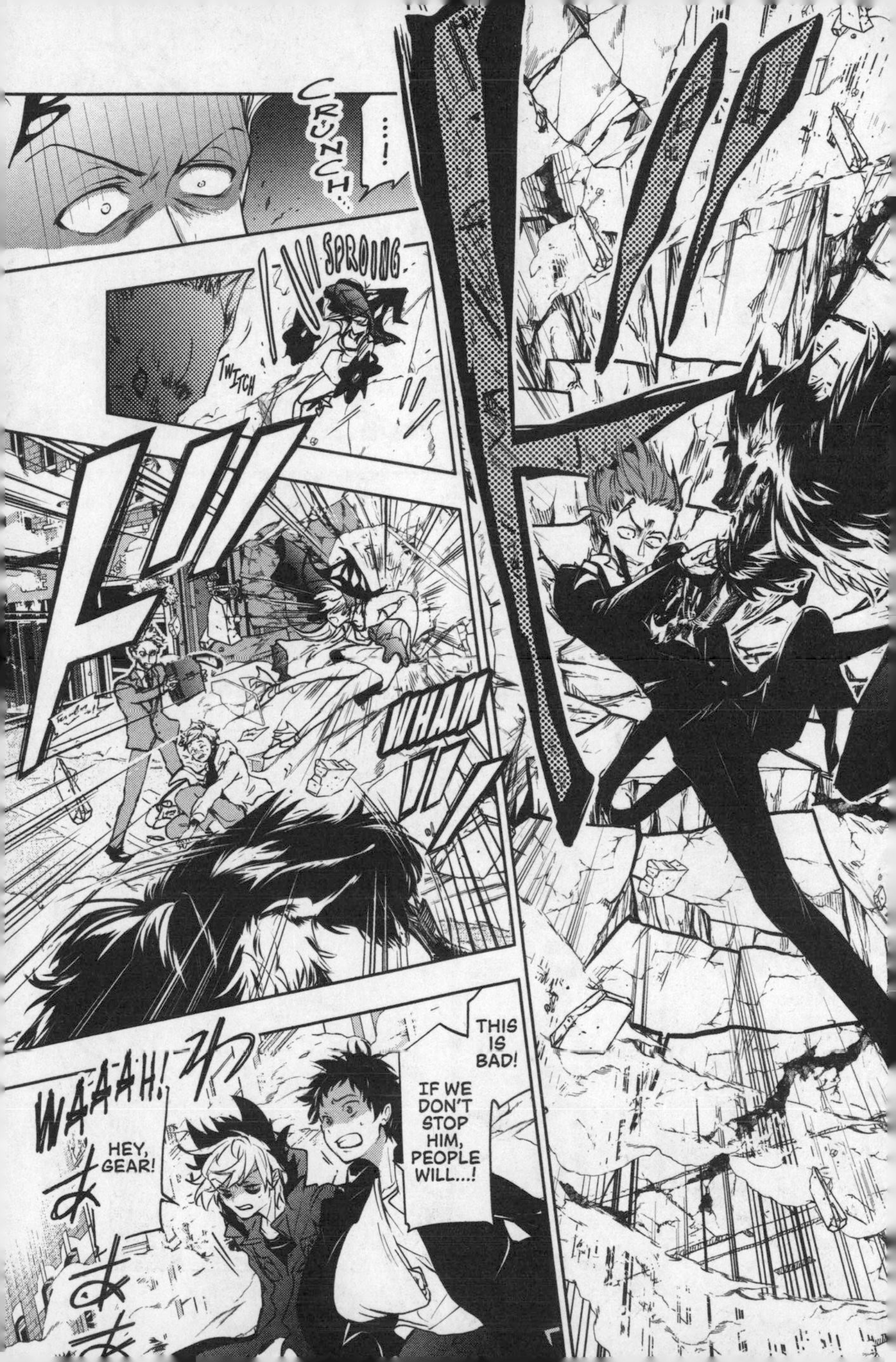
CRUNCH...
...!
SPROING
TWITCH
WHAM
THIS IS BAD!
IF WE DON'T STOP HIM, PEOPLE WILL...!
HEY, GEAR!
WAAAH!

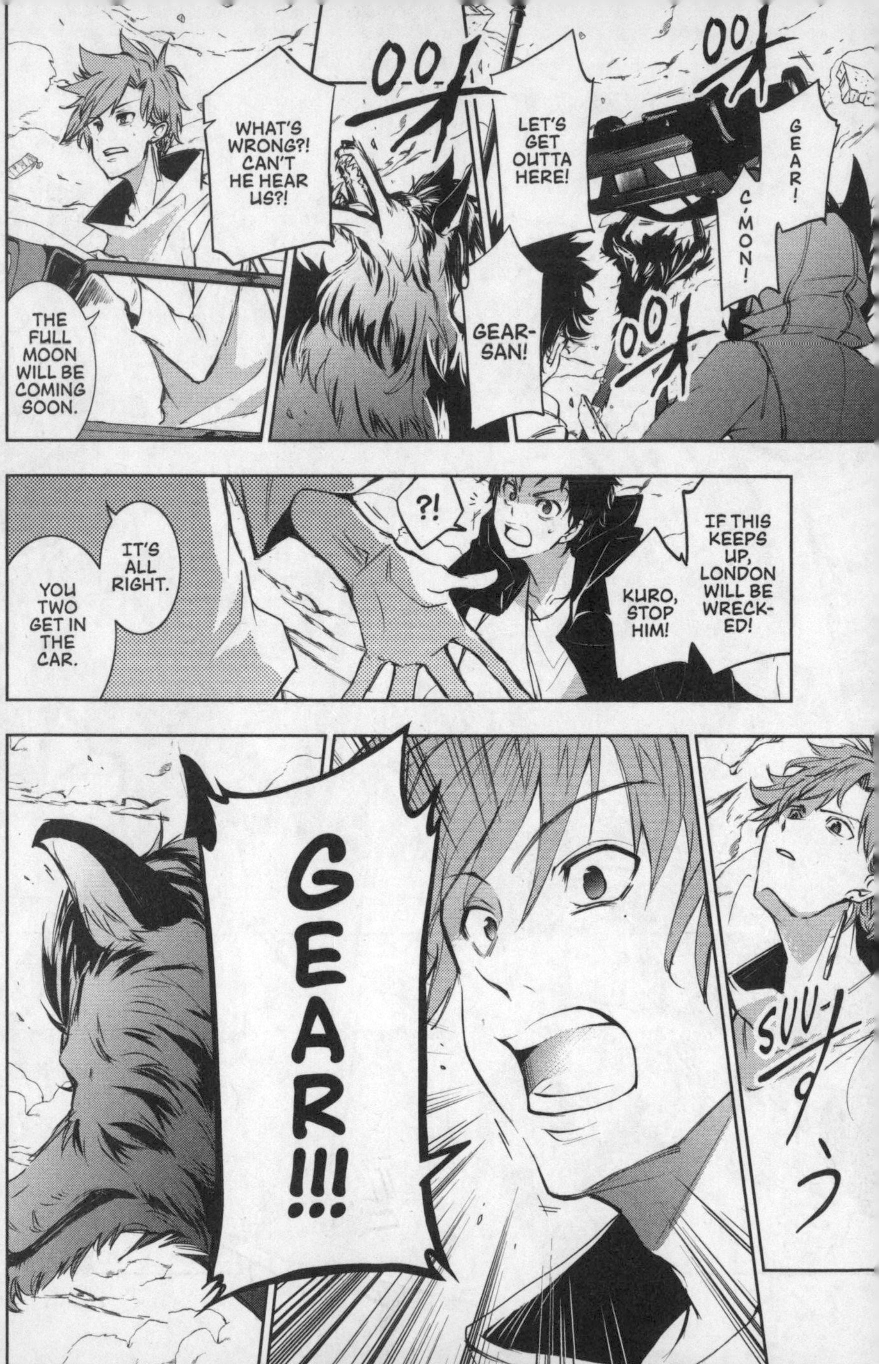
GEAR! C-MON!
LET'S GET OUTTA HERE!
GEAR-SAN!
WHAT'S WRONG?! CAN'T HE HEAR US?!
THE FULL MOON WILL BE COMING SOON.
IF THIS KEEPS UP, LONDON WILL BE WRECKED!
KURO, STOP HIM!
?!
IT'S ALL RIGHT.
YOU TWO GET IN THE CAR.
SUU-
GEAR!!!

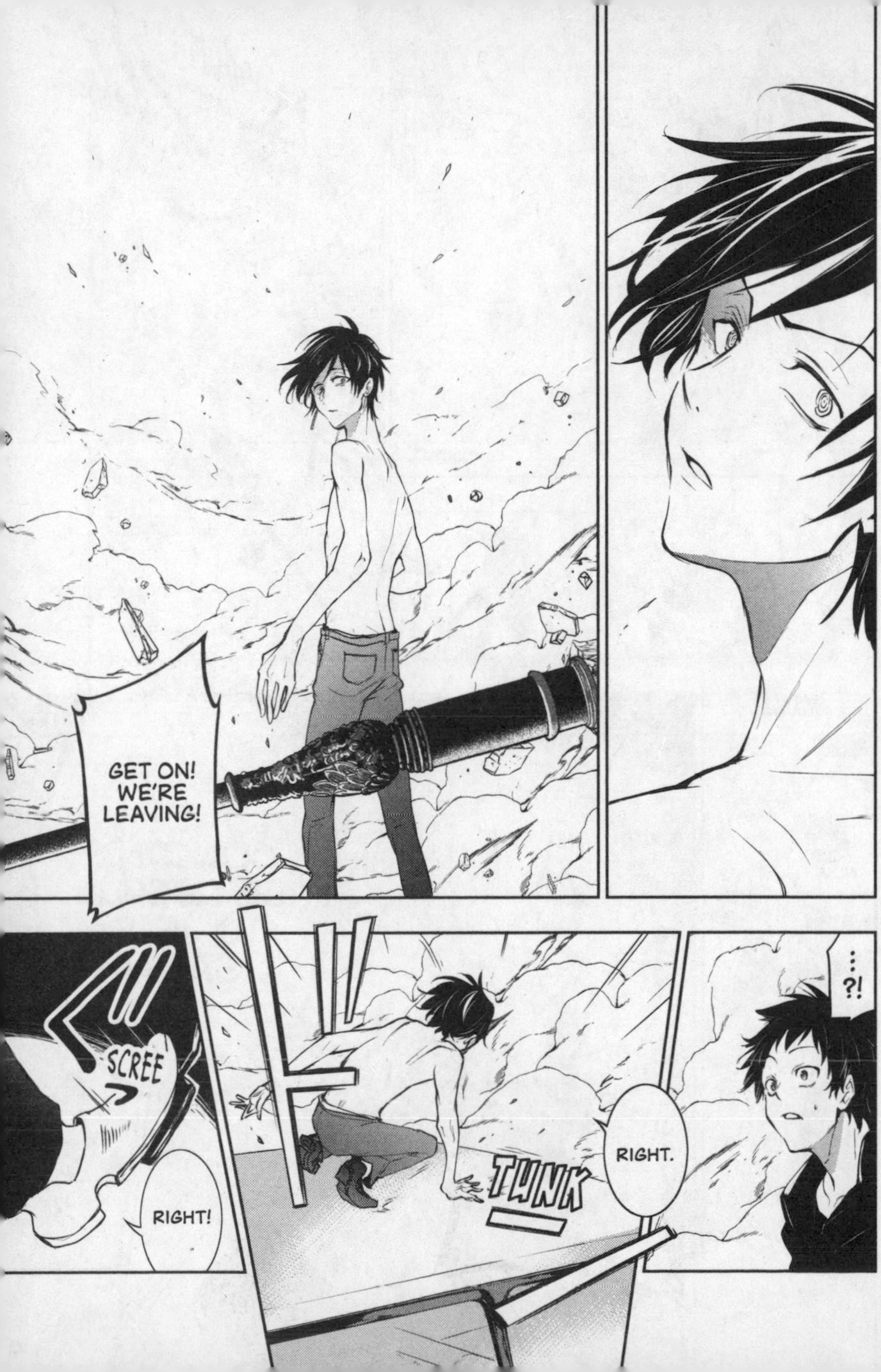
GET ON! WE'RE LEAVING!
...?!
RIGHT.
TUNK
SCREE
RIGHT!

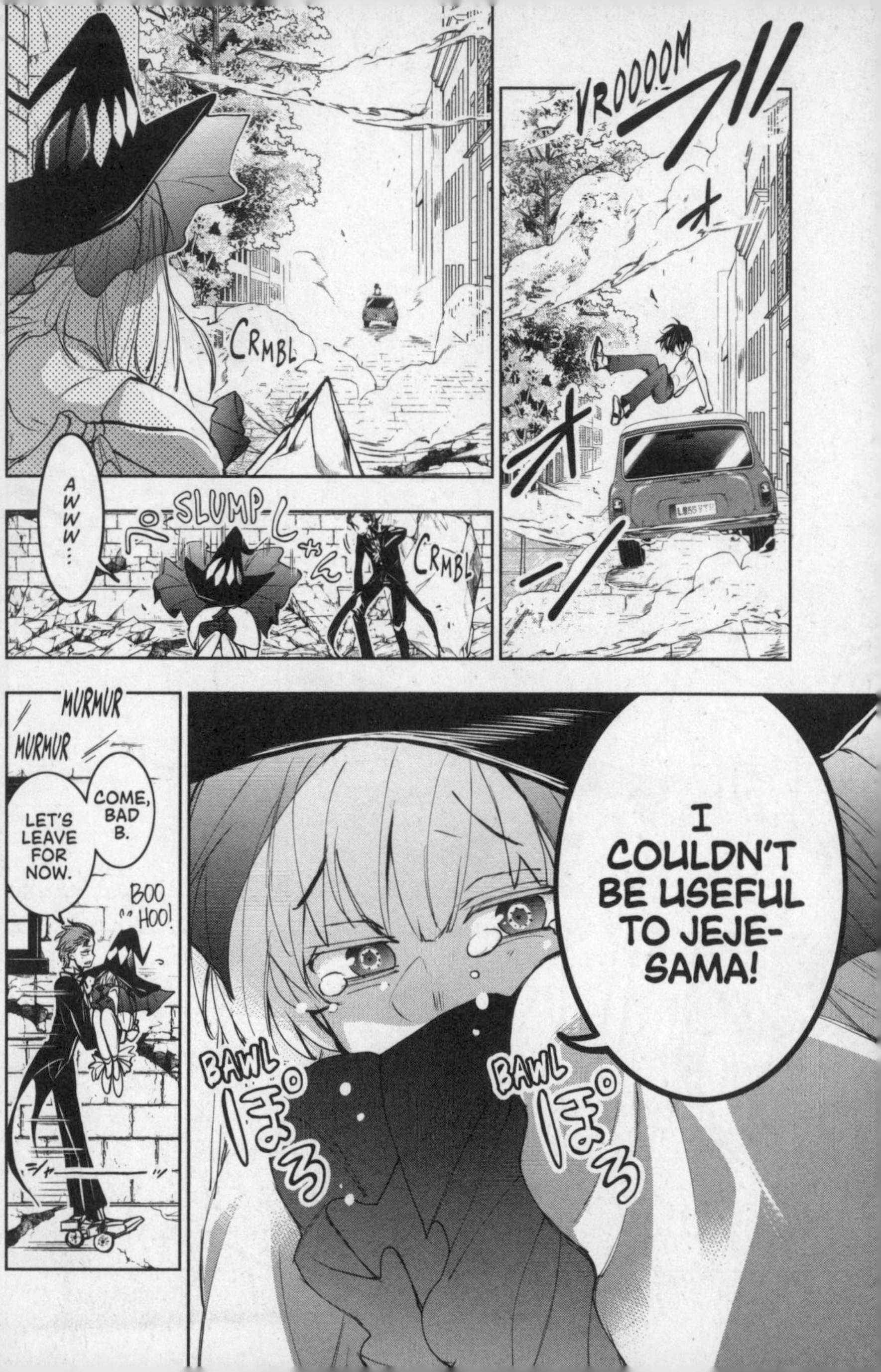
VROOOOM
CRMBL
CRMBL
SLUMP
AWWW...
I COULDN'T BE USEFUL TO JEJE-SAMA!
BAWL
BAWL
MURMUR
MURMUR
COME, BAD B.
LET'S LEAVE FOR NOW.
BOO HOO!

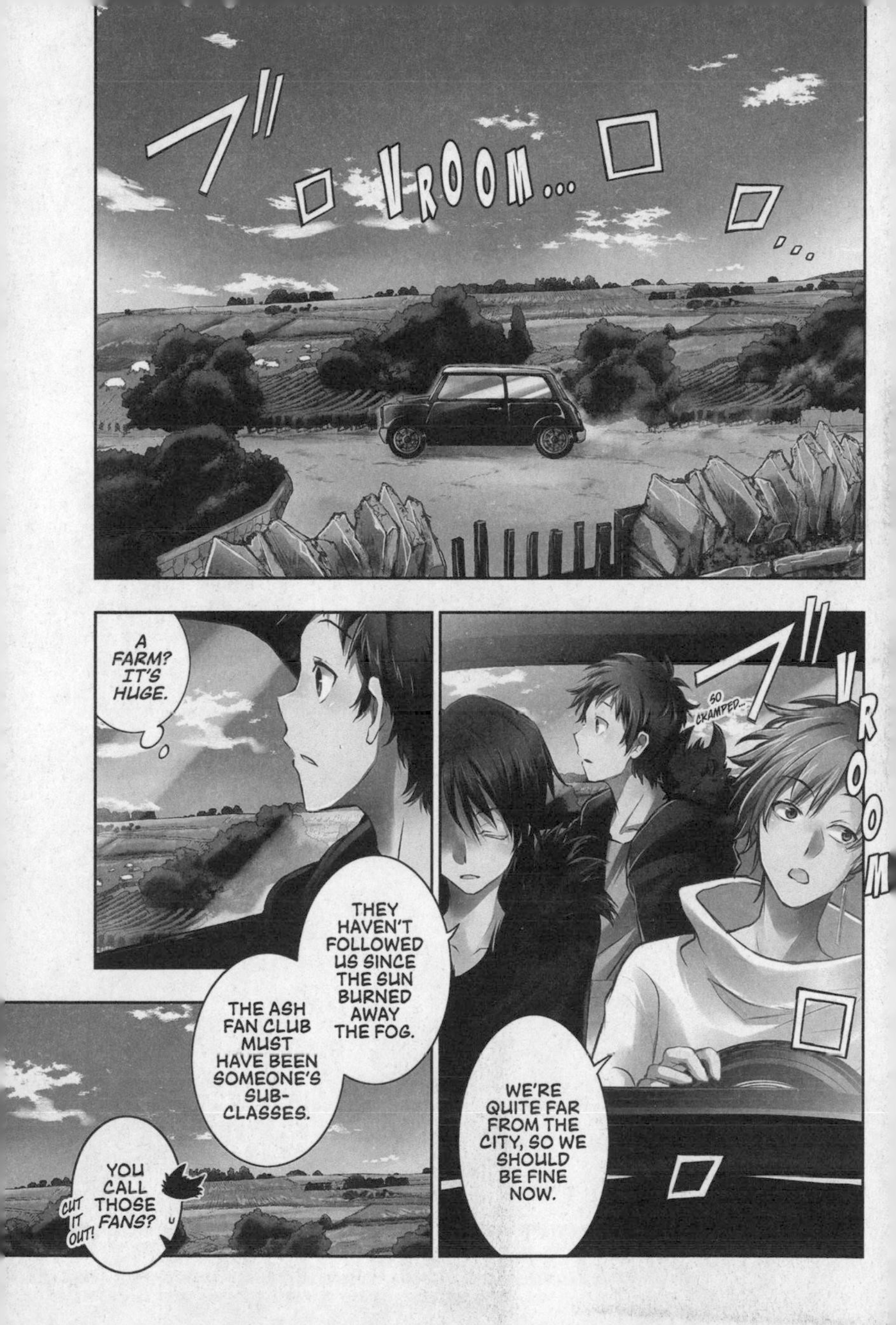
VROOM...
A FARM? IT'S HUGE.
SO CRAMPED...
VROOM
THEY HAVEN'T FOLLOWED US SINCE THE SUN BURNED AWAY THE FOG.
WE'RE QUITE FAR FROM THE CITY, SO WE SHOULD BE FINE NOW.
THE ASH FAN CLUB MUST HAVE BEEN SOMEONE'S SUB-CLASSES.
YOU CALL THOSE FANS?
CUT IT OUT!

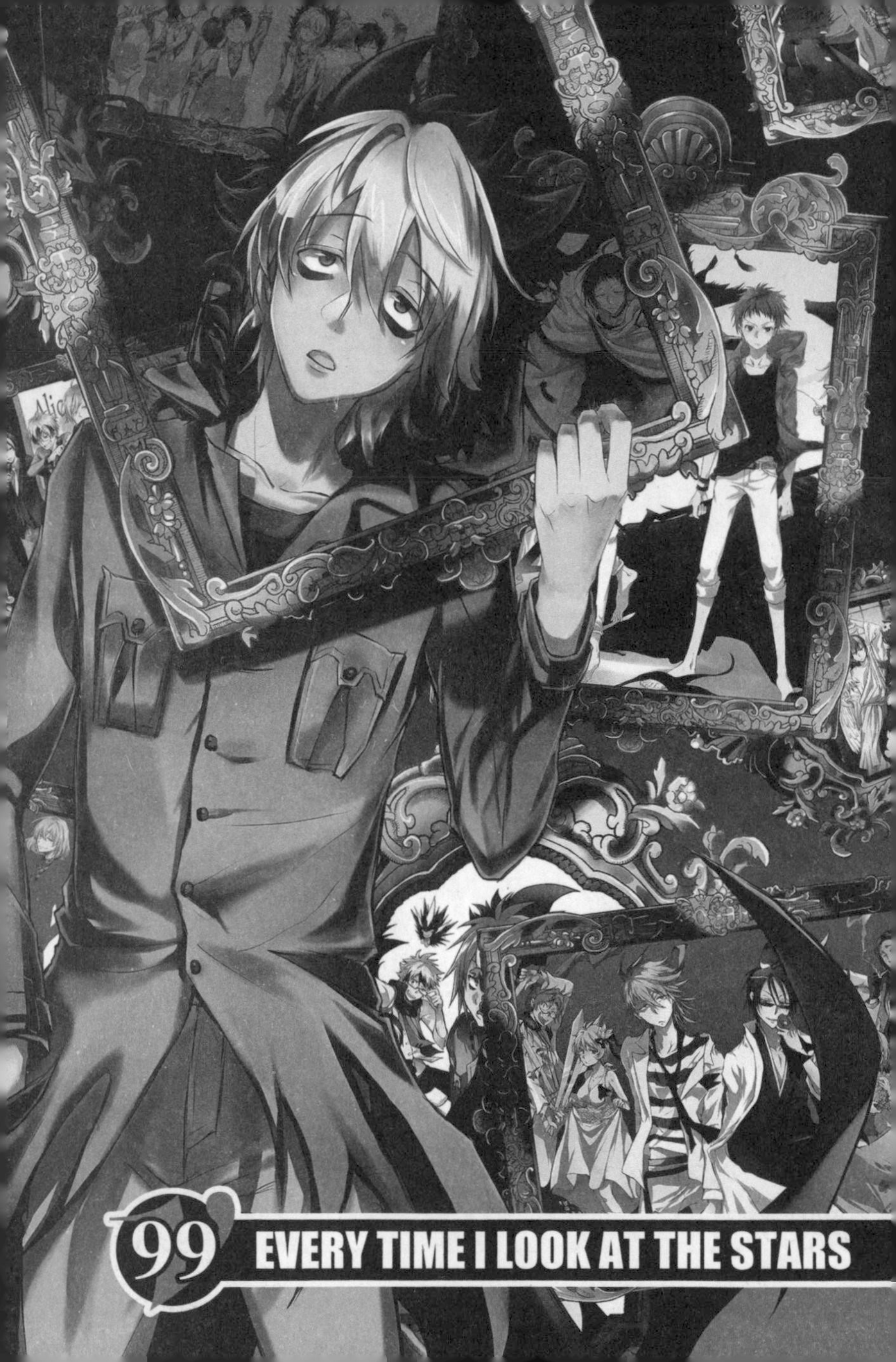
99
EVERY TIME I LOOK AT THE STARS

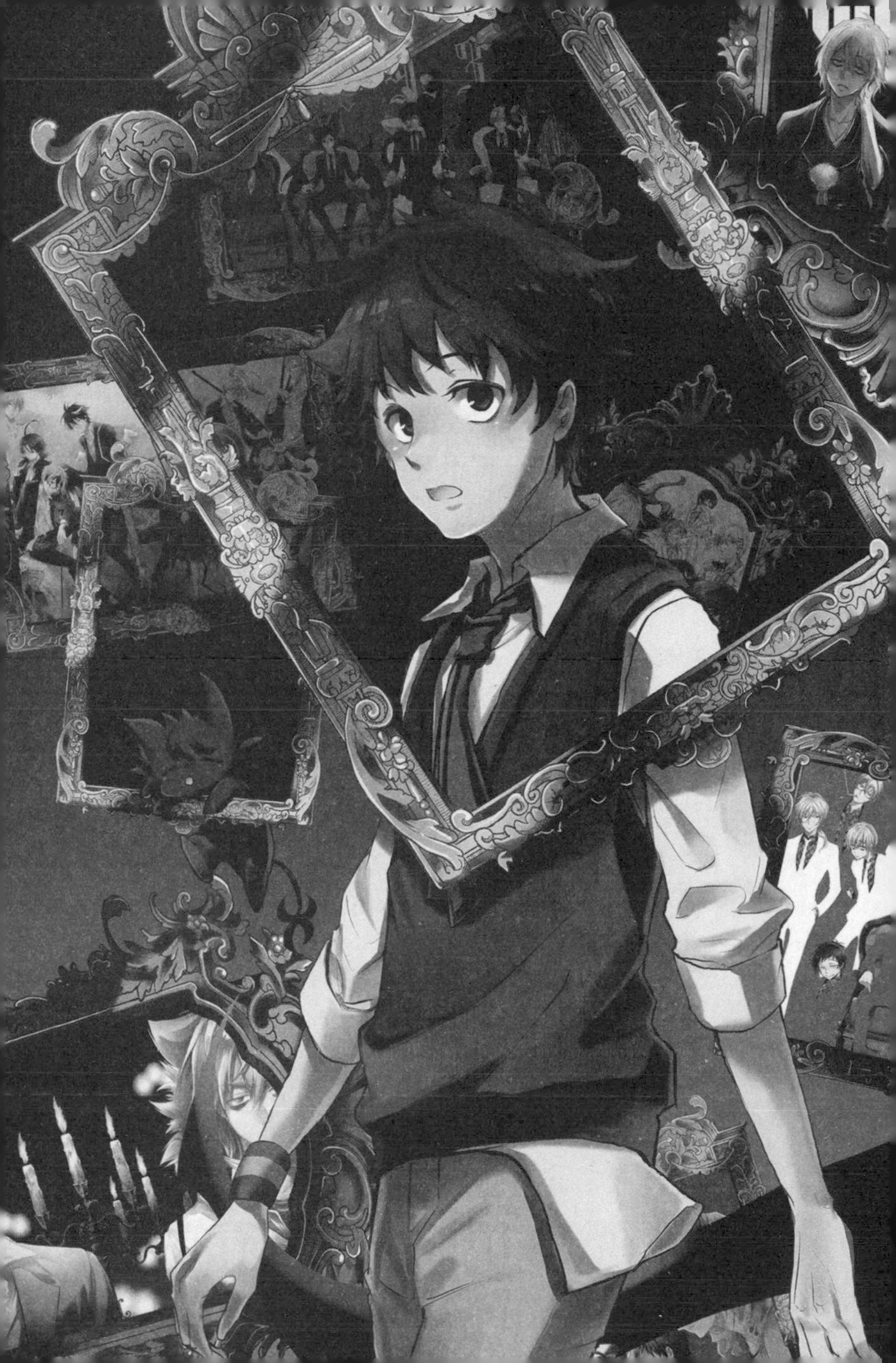

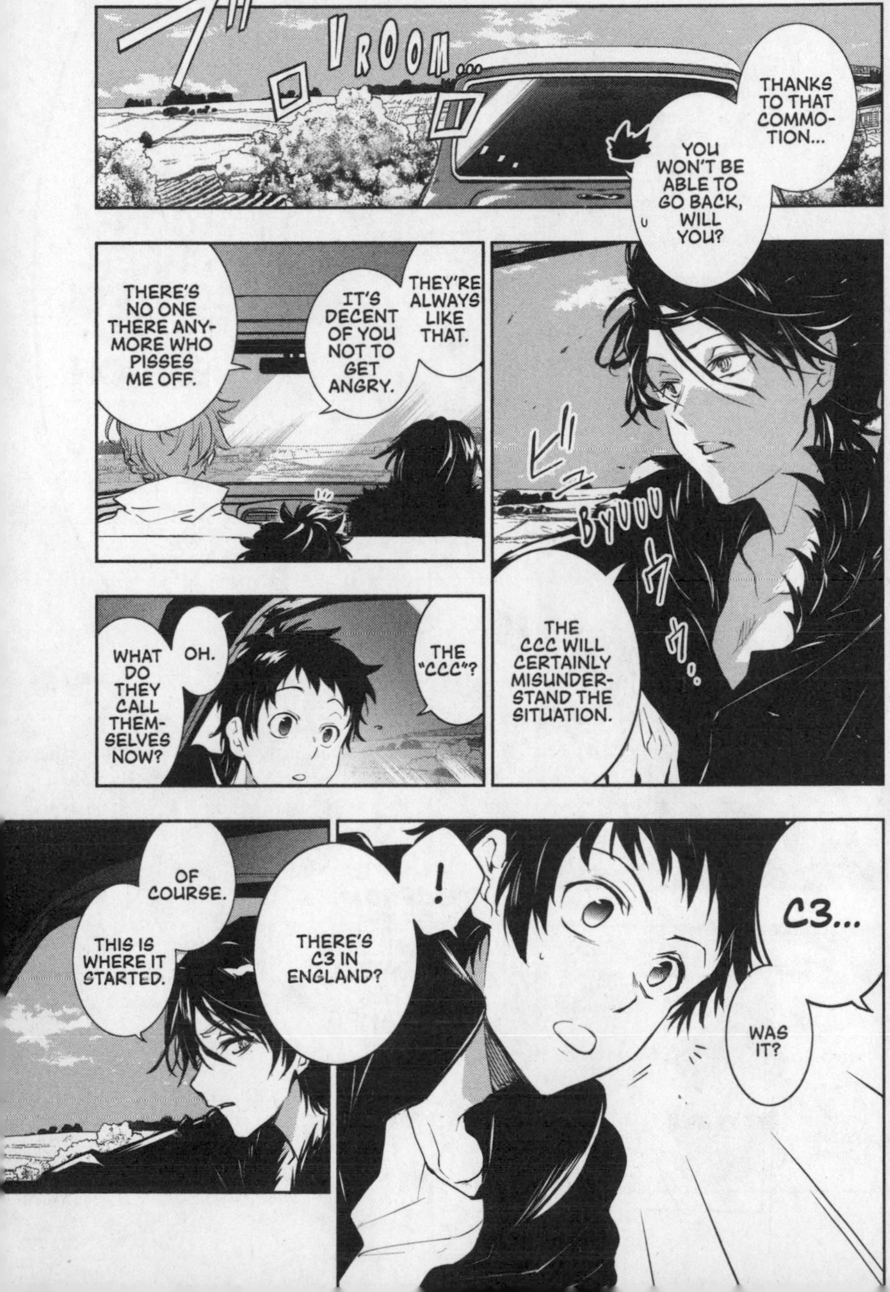
VROOM
THANKS TO THAT COMMOTION...
YOU WON'T BE ABLE TO GO BACK, WILL YOU?
BYUUU
THE CCC WILL CERTAINLY MISUNDERSTAND THE SITUATION.
THEY'RE ALWAYS LIKE THAT.
IT'S DECENT OF YOU NOT TO GET ANGRY.
THERE'S NO ONE THERE ANYMORE WHO PISSES ME OFF.
THE "CCC"?
OH.
WHAT DO THEY CALL THEMSELVES NOW?
C3...
WAS IT?
!
THERE'S C3 IN ENGLAND?
OF COURSE.
THIS IS WHERE IT STARTED.

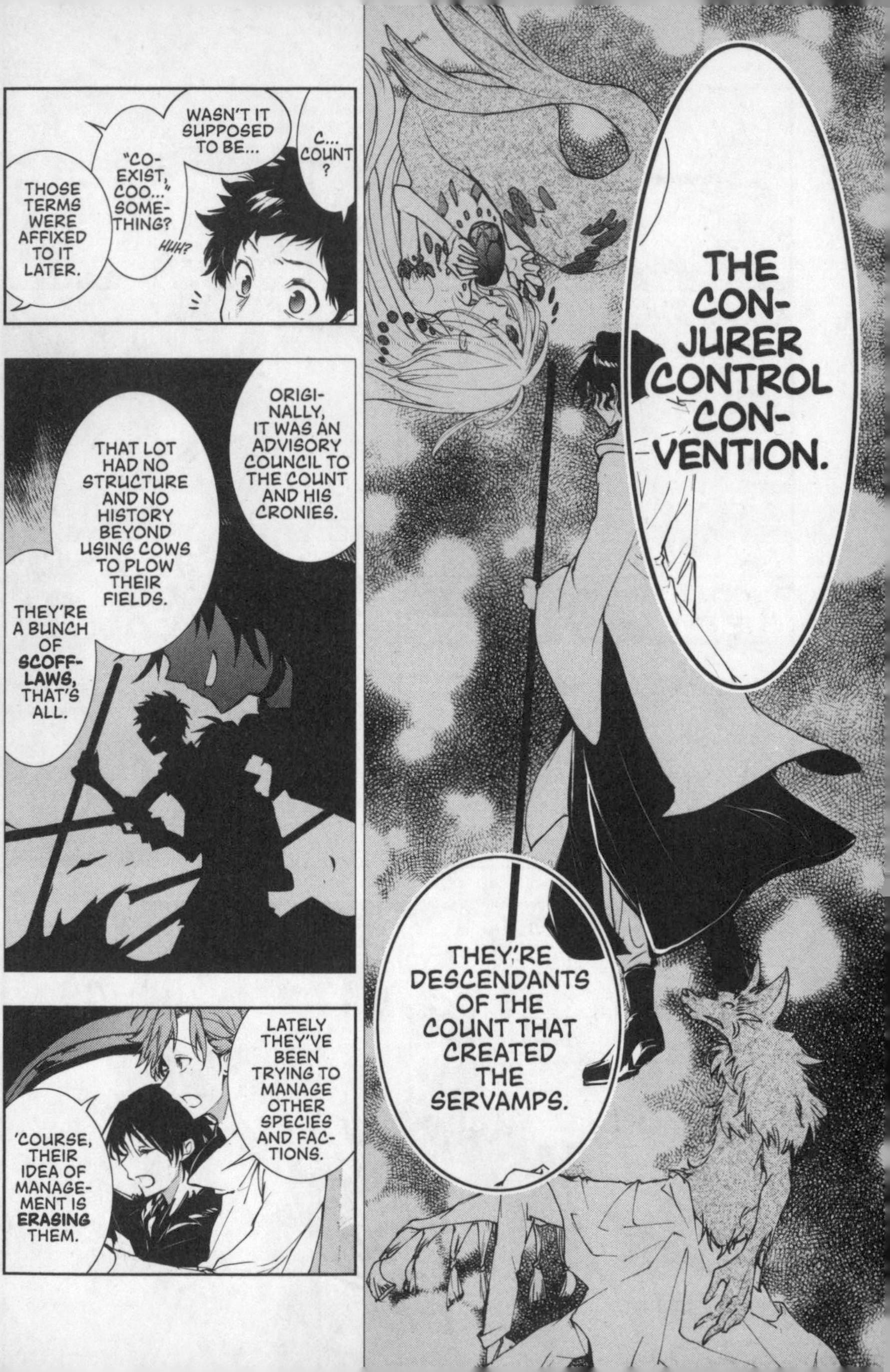
THE CONJURER CONTROL CONVENTION.
THEY'RE DESCENDANTS OF THE COUNT THAT CREATED THE SERVAMPS.
C... COUNT?
WASN'T IT SUPPOSED TO BE...
"CO-EXIST, COO..." SOMETHING?
HUH?
THOSE TERMS WERE AFFIXED TO IT LATER.
ORIGINALLY, IT WAS AN ADVISORY COUNCIL TO THE COUNT AND HIS CRONIES.
THAT LOT HAD NO STRUCTURE AND NO HISTORY BEYOND USING COWS TO PLOW THEIR FIELDS.
THEY'RE A BUNCH OF **SCOFFLAWS**, THAT'S ALL.
LATELY THEY'VE BEEN TRYING TO MANAGE OTHER SPECIES AND FACTIONS.
'COURSE, THEIR IDEA OF MANAGEMENT IS **ERASING** THEM.

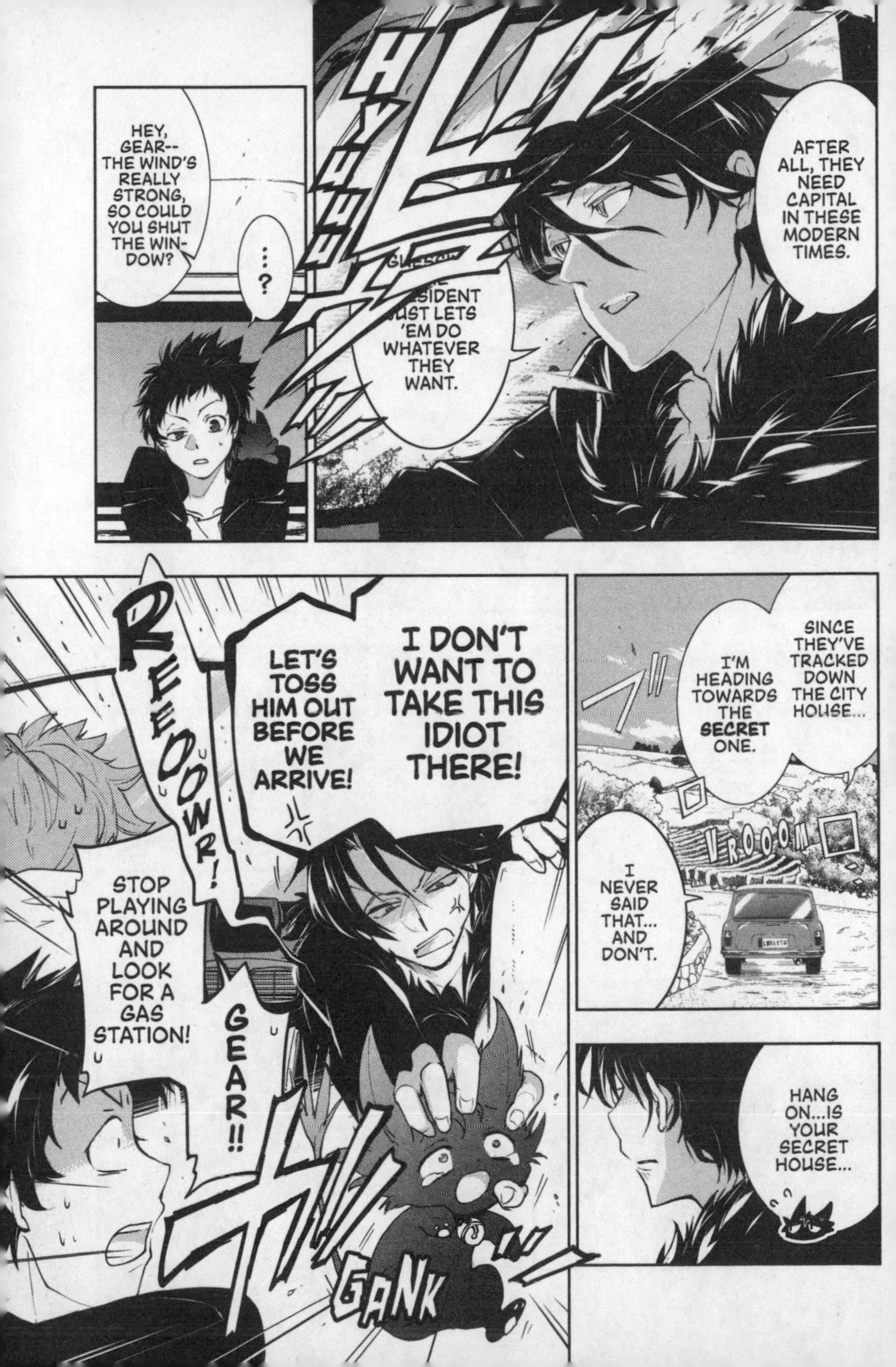
AFTER ALL, THEY NEED CAPITAL IN THESE MODERN TIMES.
JUST LETS 'EM DO WHATEVER THEY WANT.
HEY, GEAR-- THE WIND'S REALLY STRONG, SO COULD YOU SHUT THE WIN-DOW?
...?
SINCE THEY'VE TRACKED DOWN THE CITY HOUSE...
I'M HEADING TOWARDS THE **SECRET** ONE.
VROOOM
I NEVER SAID THAT... AND DON'T.
I DON'T WANT TO TAKE THIS IDIOT THERE!
LET'S TOSS HIM OUT BEFORE WE ARRIVE!
REOOOWR!
STOP PLAYING AROUND AND LOOK FOR A GAS STATION!
GEAR!!
GANK
HANG ON...IS YOUR SECRET HOUSE...

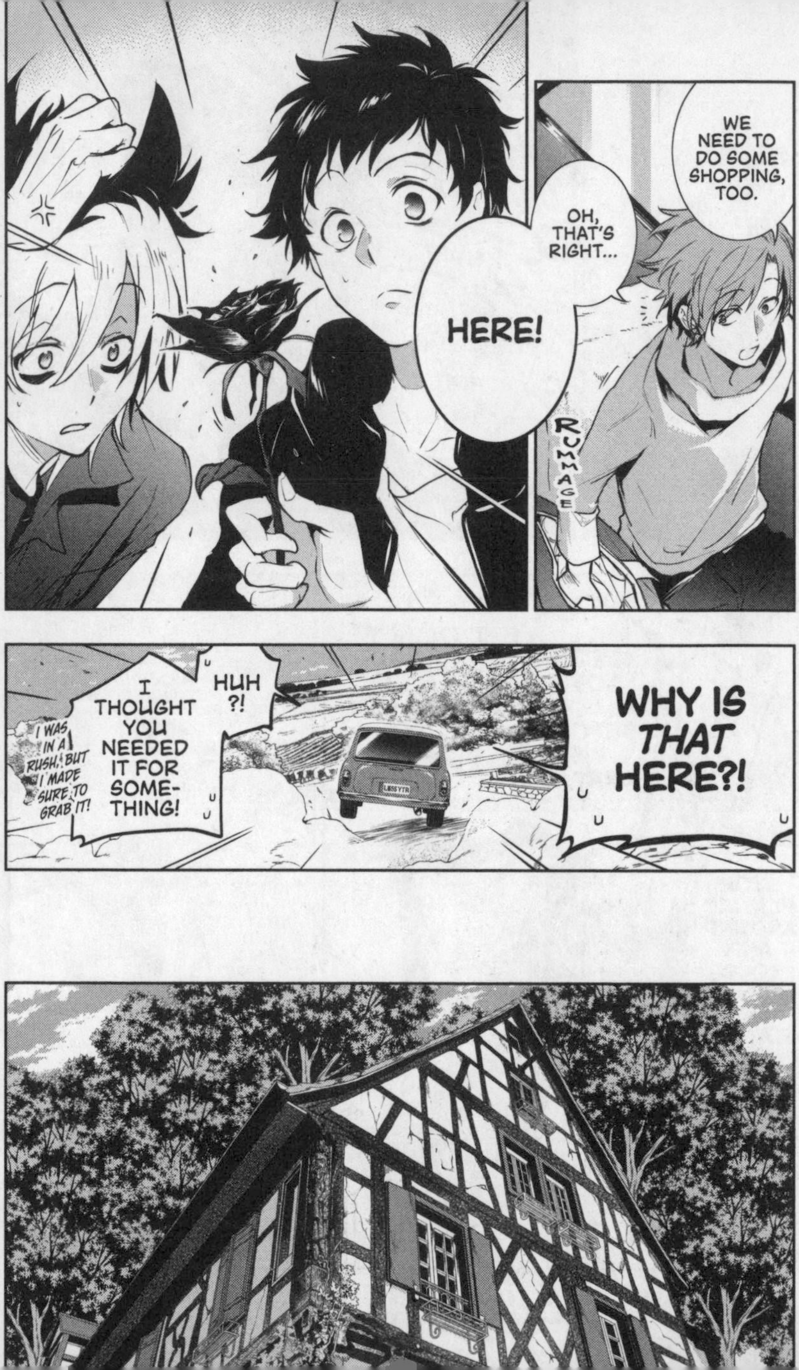
WE NEED TO DO SOME SHOPPING, TOO.
OH, THAT'S RIGHT...
RUMMAGE
HERE!
WHY IS THAT HERE?!
HUH ?!
I THOUGHT YOU NEEDED IT FOR SOME-THING!
I WAS IN A RUSH, BUT I MADE SURE TO GRAB IT!

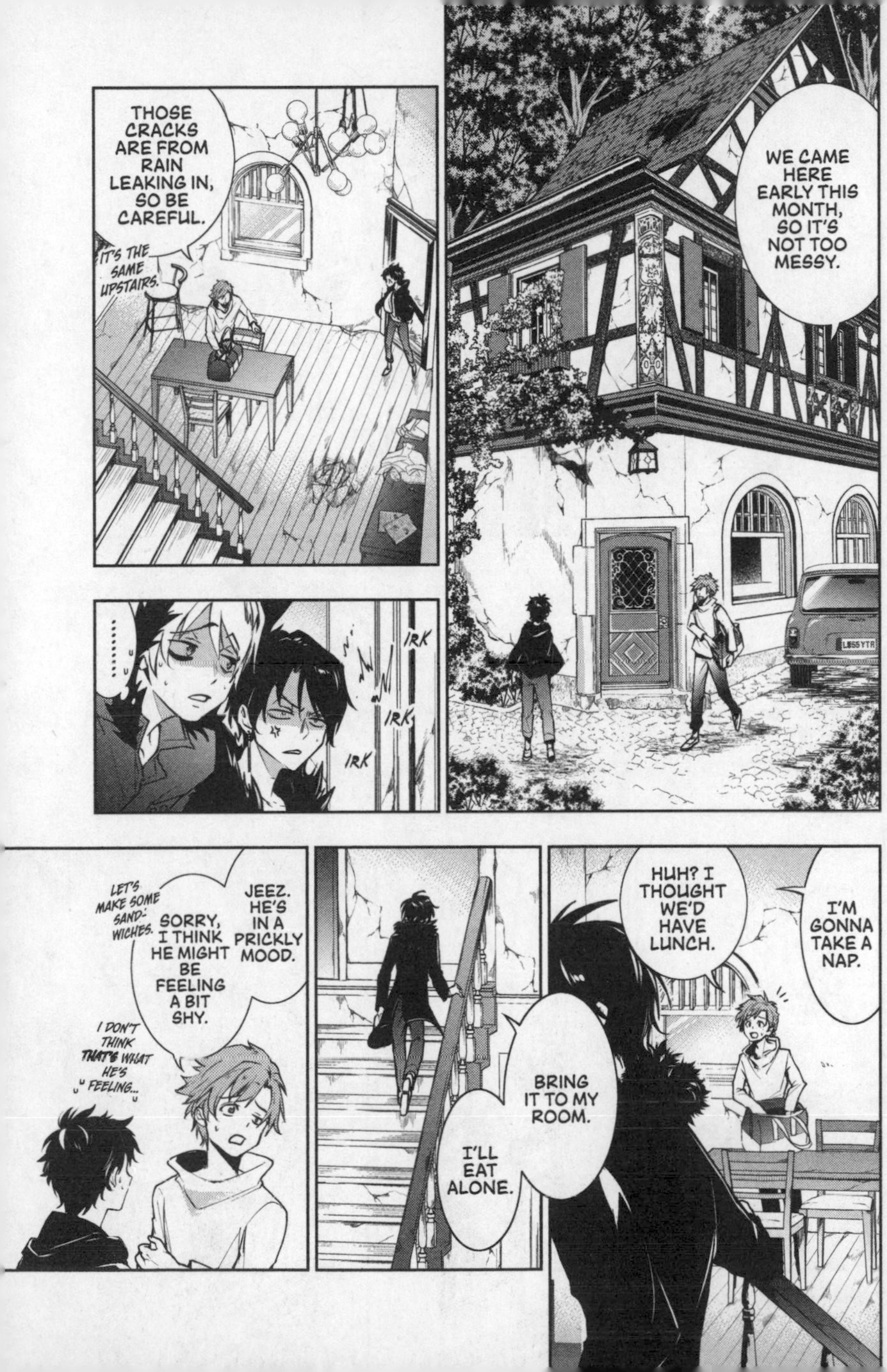
WE CAME HERE EARLY THIS MONTH, SO IT'S NOT TOO MESSY.
THOSE CRACKS ARE FROM RAIN LEAKING IN, SO BE CAREFUL.
IT'S THE SAME UPSTAIRS.
......
IRK
IRK
IRK
I'M GONNA TAKE A NAP.
HUH? I THOUGHT WE'D HAVE LUNCH.
BRING IT TO MY ROOM.
I'LL EAT ALONE.
JEEZ. HE'S IN A PRICKLY MOOD.
SORRY, I THINK HE MIGHT BE FEELING A BIT SHY.
LET'S MAKE SOME SAND-WICHES.
I DON'T THINK THAT'S WHAT HE'S FEELING...

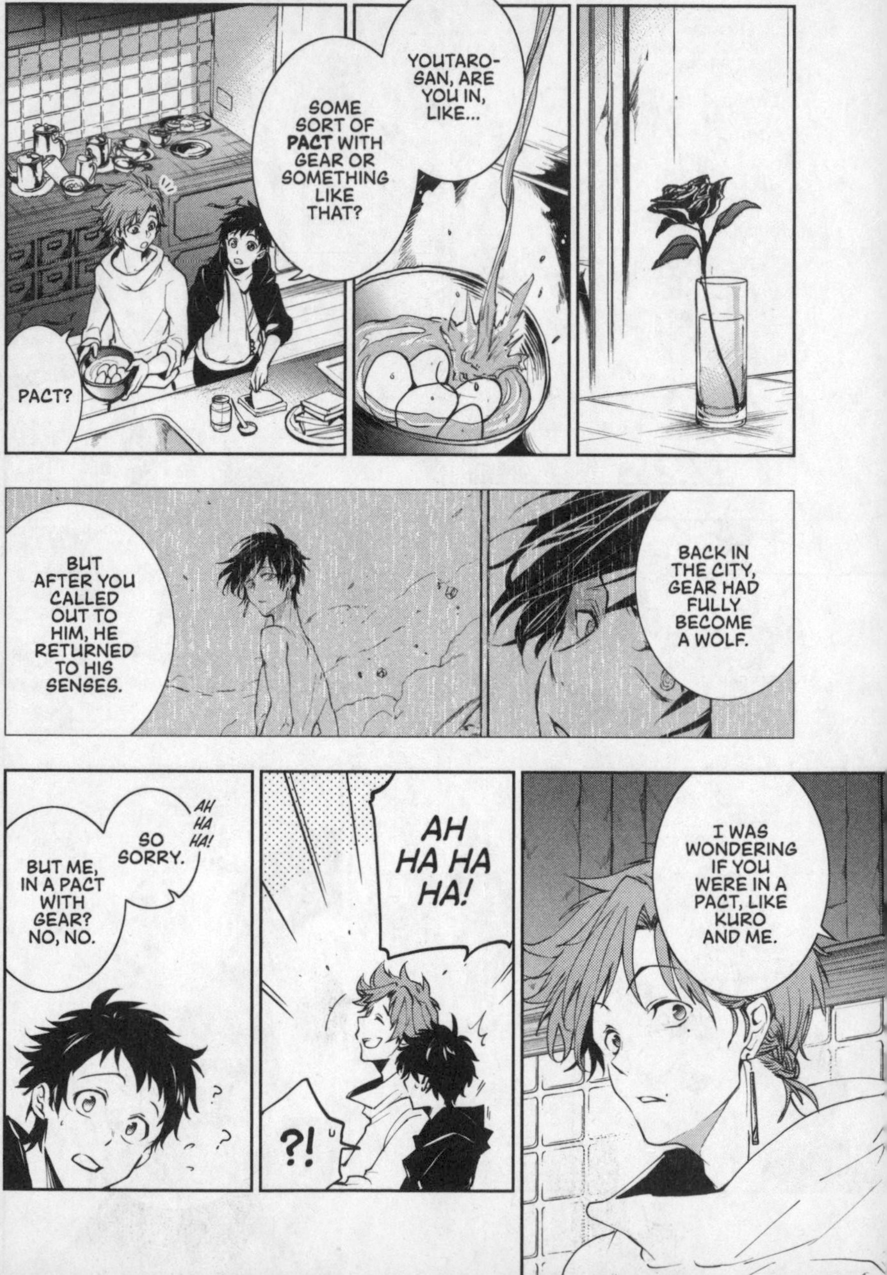
YOUTARO-SAN, ARE YOU IN, LIKE...
SOME SORT OF PACT WITH GEAR OR SOMETHING LIKE THAT?
PACT?
BACK IN THE CITY, GEAR HAD FULLY BECOME A WOLF.
BUT AFTER YOU CALLED OUT TO HIM, HE RETURNED TO HIS SENSES.
I WAS WONDERING IF YOU WERE IN A PACT, LIKE KURO AND ME.
AH HA HA HA!
?!
AH HA HA!
SO SORRY.
BUT ME, IN A PACT WITH GEAR? NO, NO.

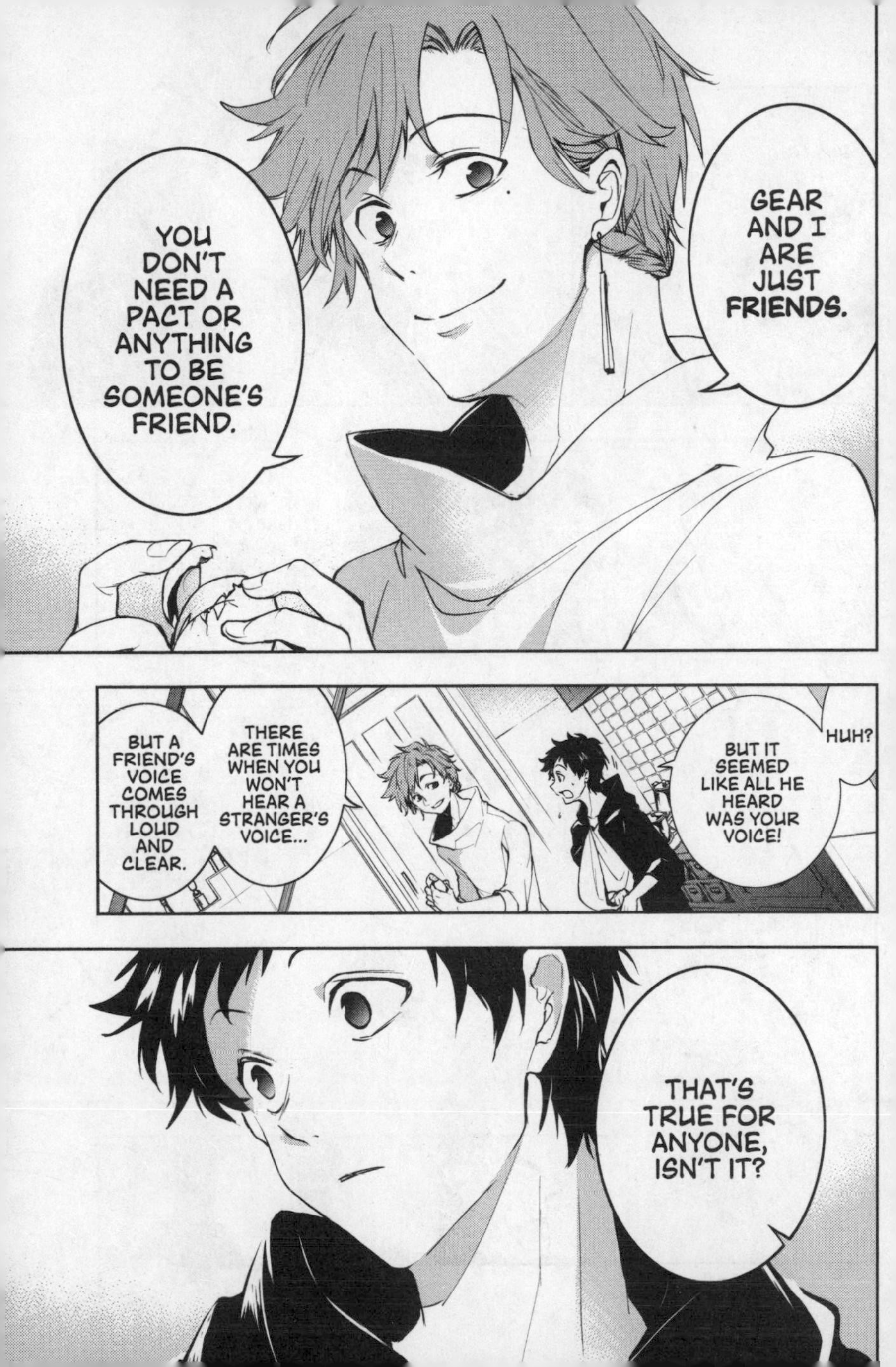
GEAR AND I ARE JUST FRIENDS.
YOU DON'T NEED A PACT OR ANYTHING TO BE SOMEONE'S FRIEND.
HUH?
BUT IT SEEMED LIKE ALL HE HEARD WAS YOUR VOICE!
THERE ARE TIMES WHEN YOU WON'T HEAR A STRANGER'S VOICE...
BUT A FRIEND'S VOICE COMES THROUGH LOUD AND CLEAR.
THAT'S TRUE FOR ANYONE, ISN'T IT?

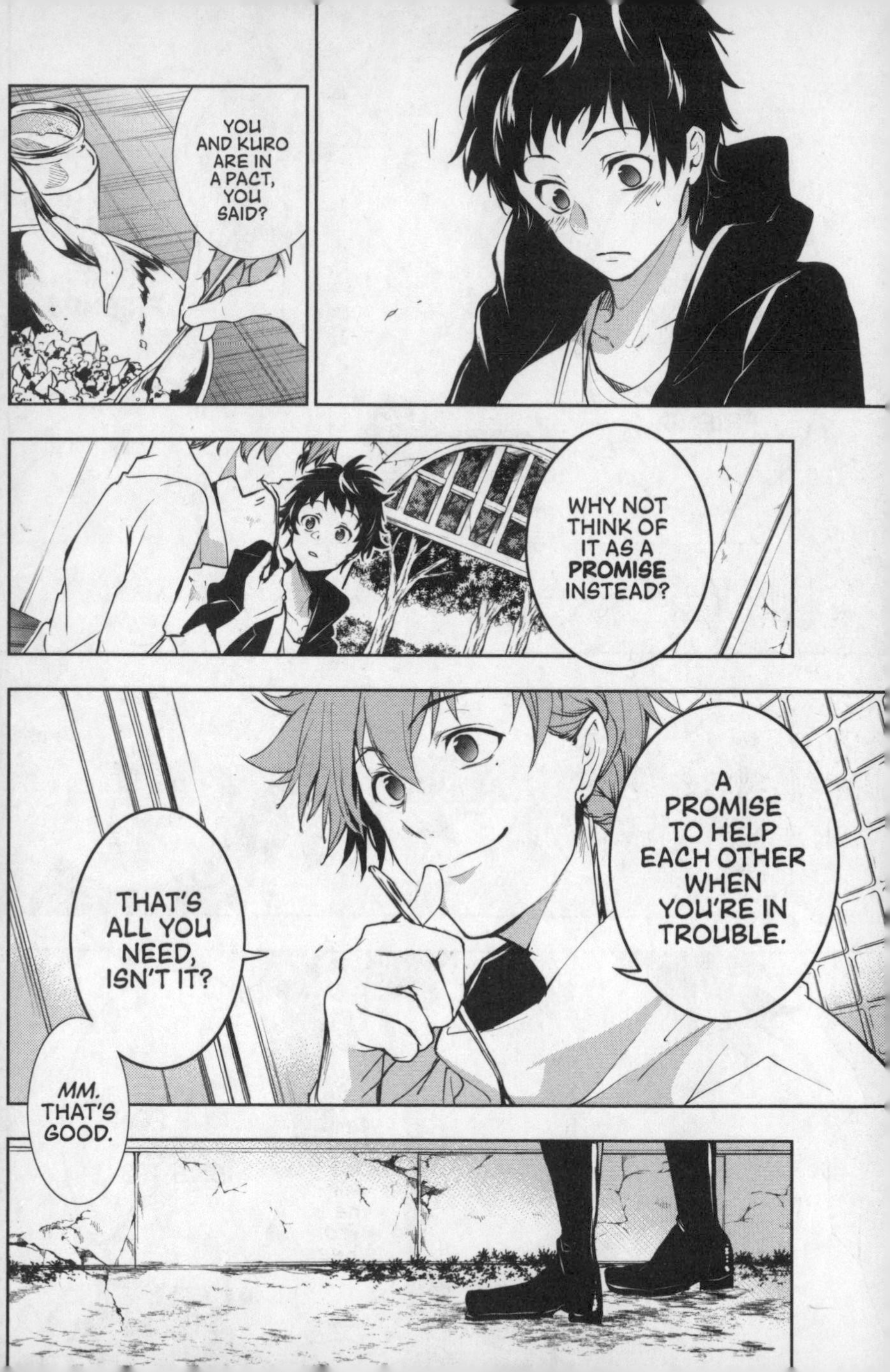
YOU AND KURO ARE IN A PACT, YOU SAID?
WHY NOT THINK OF IT AS A PROMISE INSTEAD?
A PROMISE TO HELP EACH OTHER WHEN YOU'RE IN TROUBLE.
THAT'S ALL YOU NEED, ISN'T IT?
MM. THAT'S GOOD.

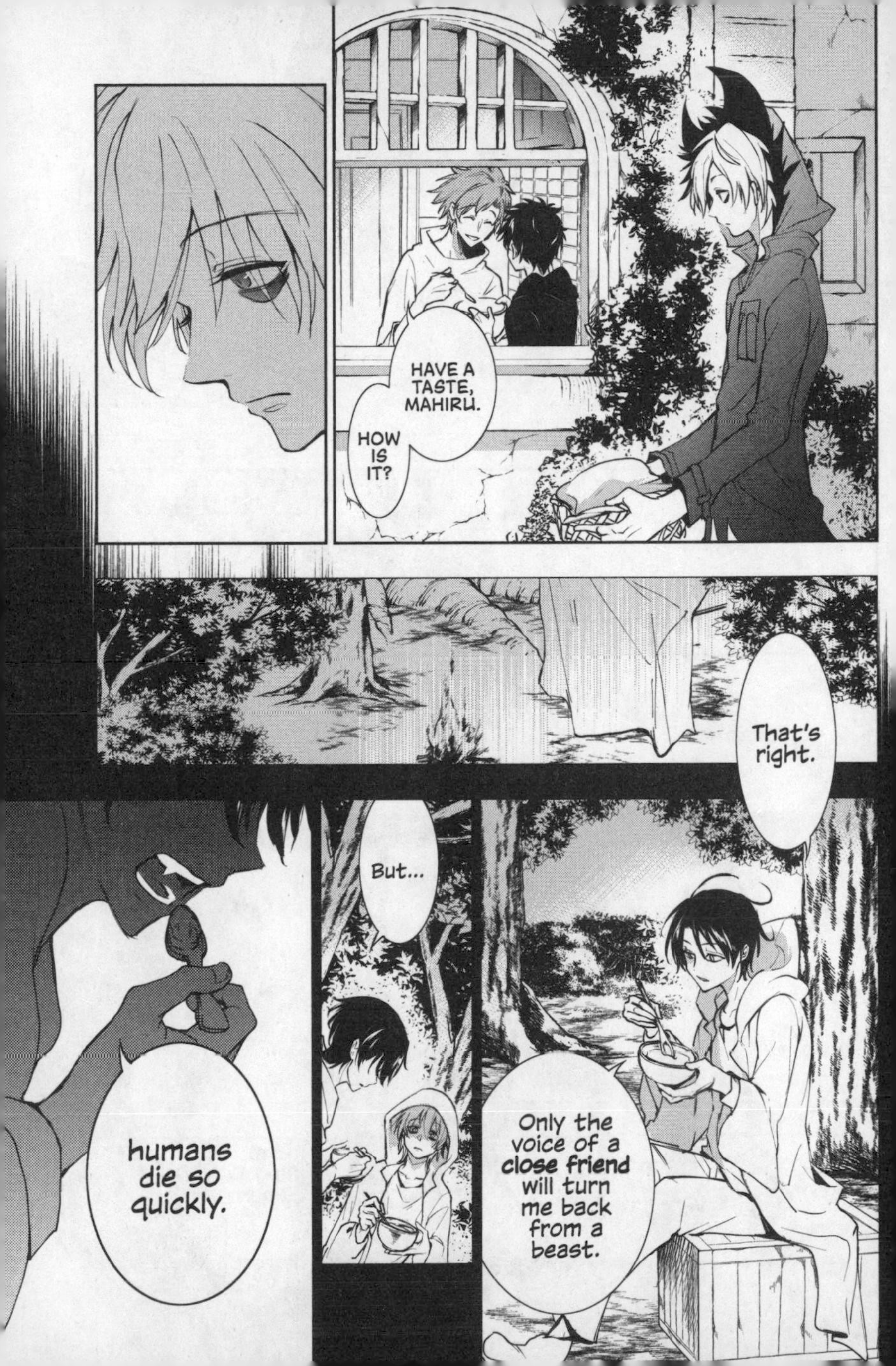

HAVE A TASTE, MAHIRU.
HOW IS IT?
That's right.
But...
Only the voice of a close friend will turn me back from a beast.
humans die so quickly.

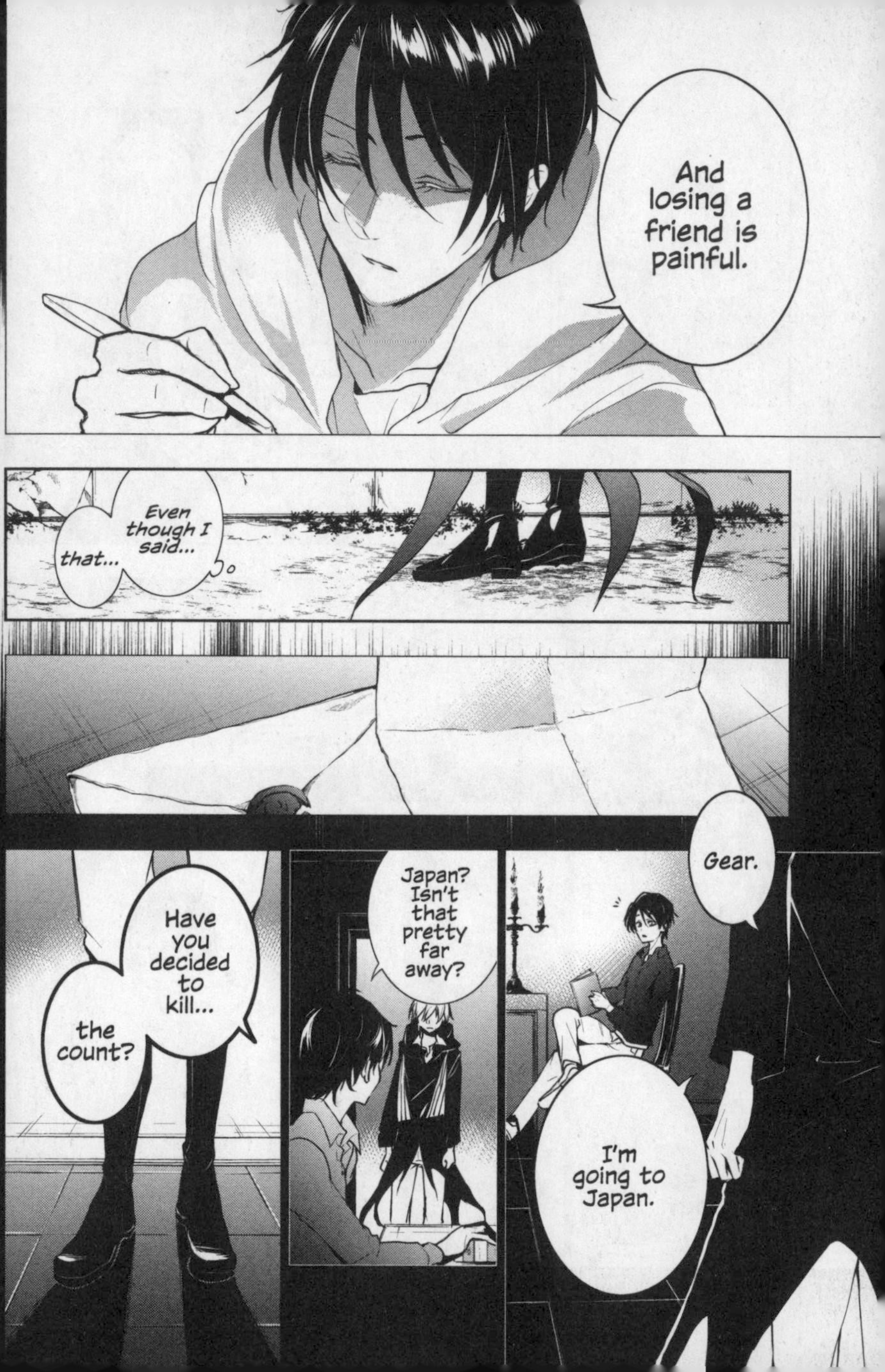
And losing a friend is painful.
Even though I said...
that...
Gear.
I'm going to Japan.
Japan? Isn't that pretty far away?
Have you decided to kill...
the count?

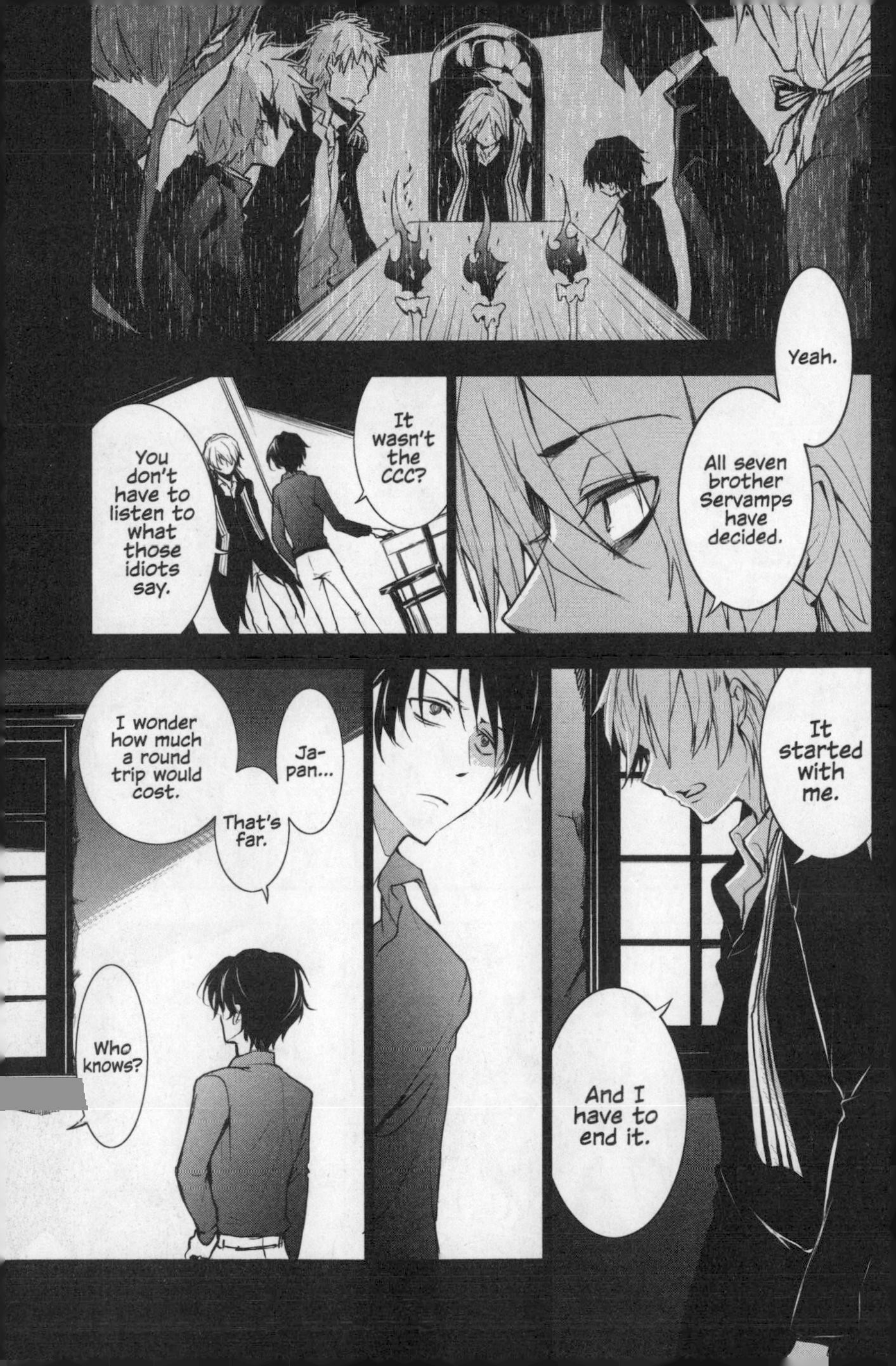
Yeah.
All seven brother Servamps have decided.
It wasn't the CCC?
You don't have to listen to what those idiots say.
It started with me.
And I have to end it.
Ja-pan...
That's far.
I wonder how much a round trip would cost.
Who knows?

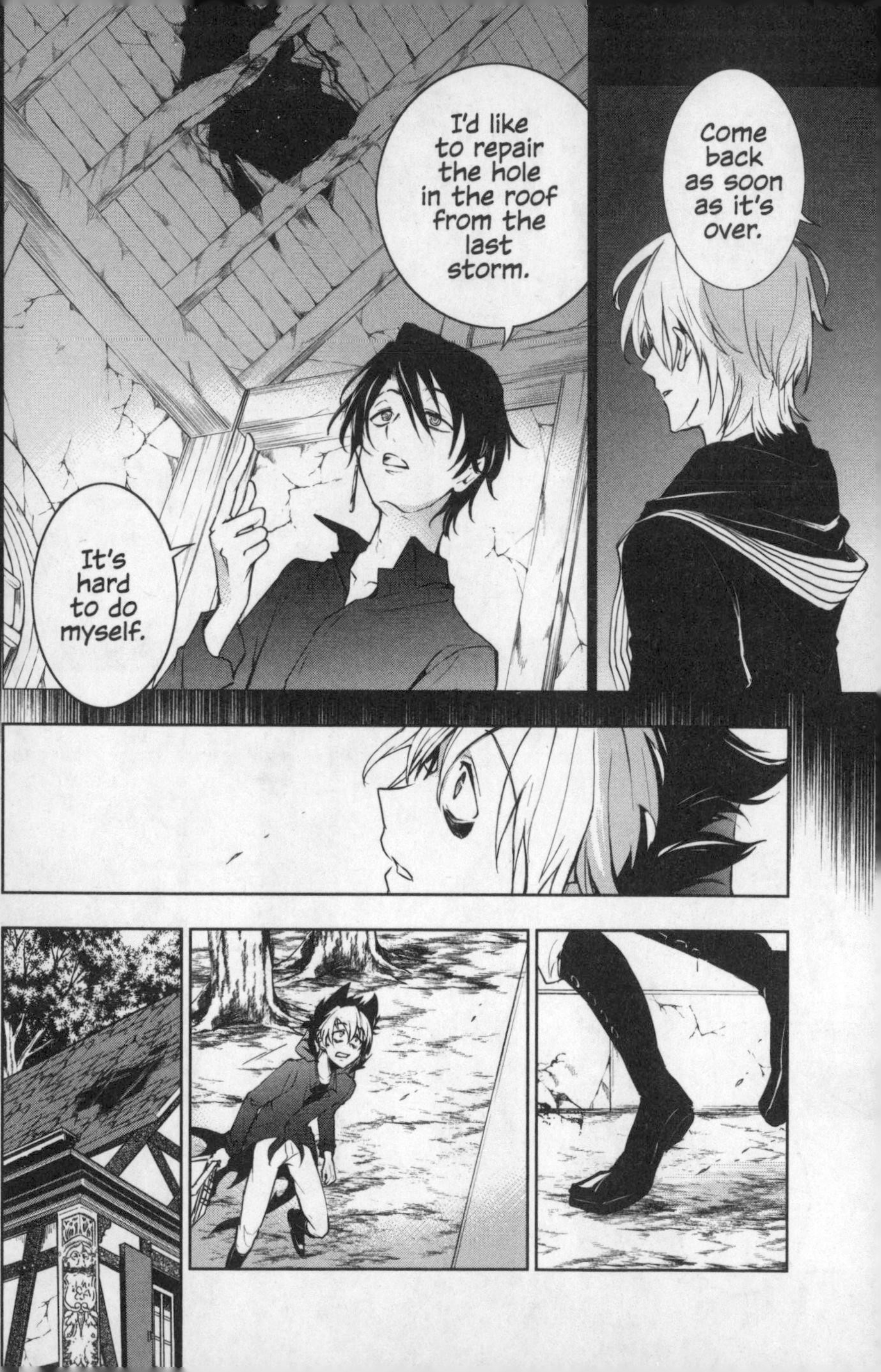
Come back as soon as it's over.
I'd like to repair the hole in the roof from the last storm.
It's hard to do myself.

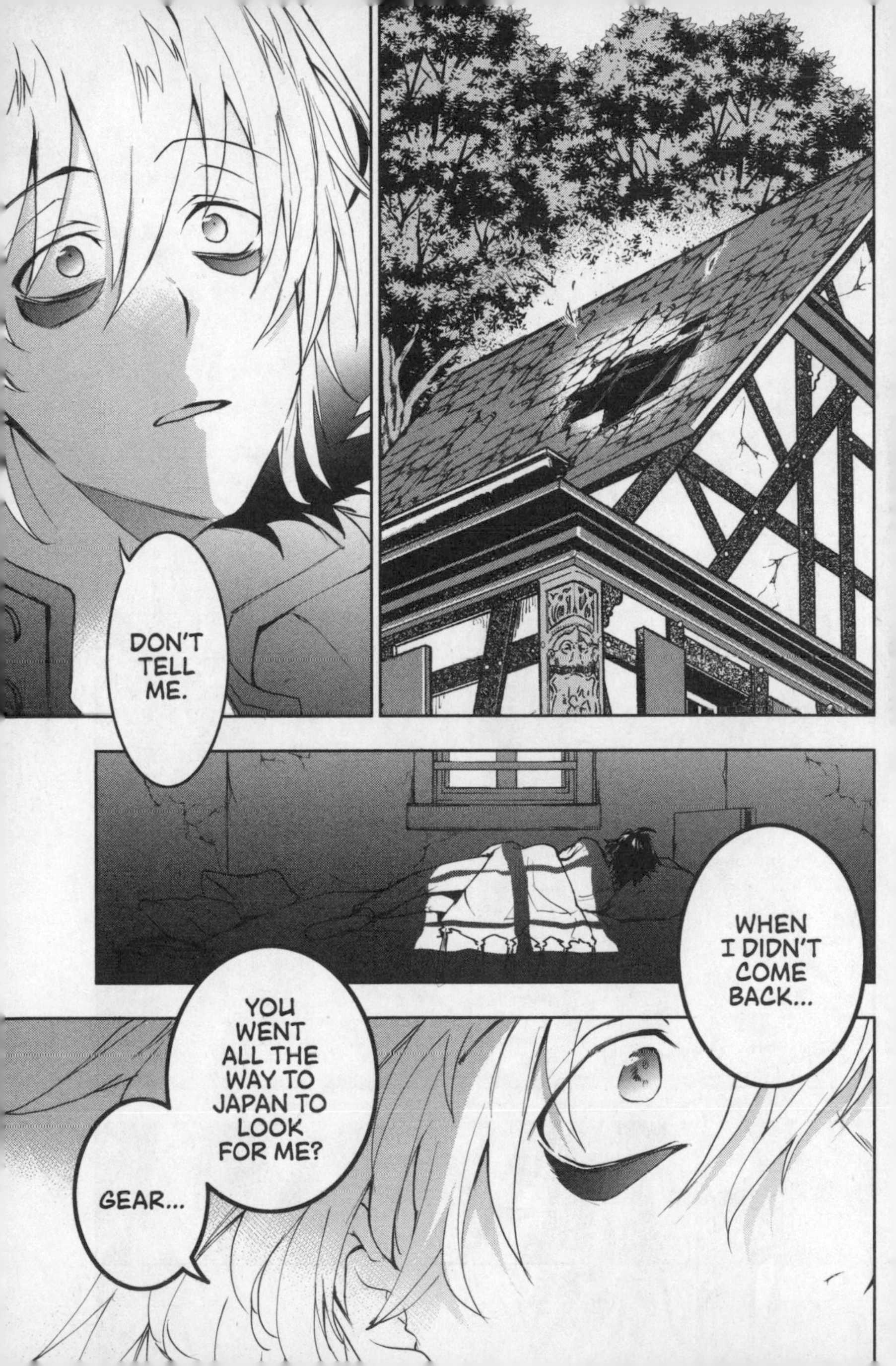
DON'T TELL ME.
WHEN I DIDN'T COME BACK...
YOU WENT ALL THE WAY TO JAPAN TO LOOK FOR ME?
GEAR...

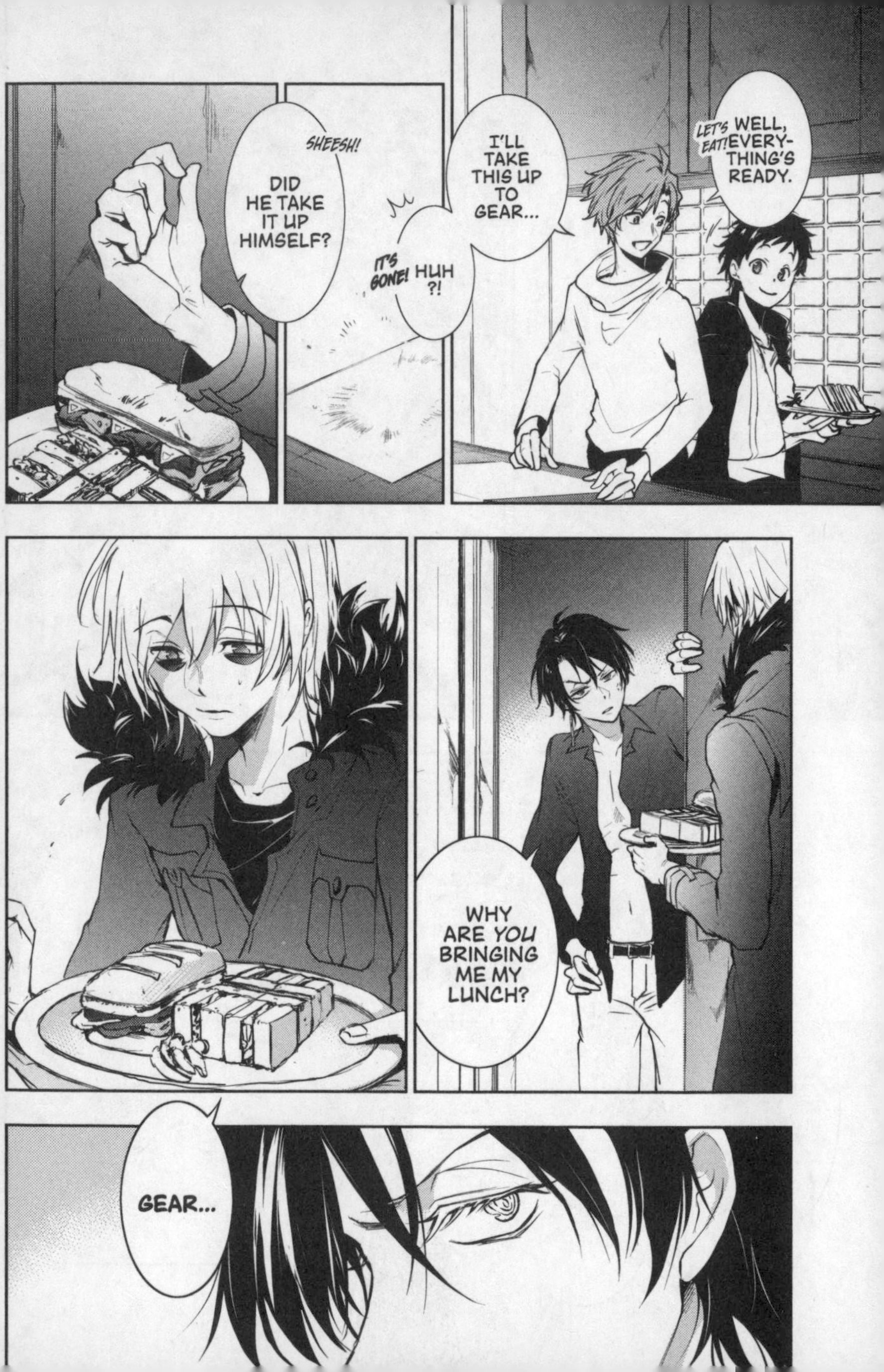
WELL, EVERY-THING'S READY.
LET'S EAT!
I'LL TAKE THIS UP TO GEAR...
HUH ?!
IT'S GONE!
SHEESH!
DID HE TAKE IT UP HIMSELF?
WHY ARE *YOU* BRINGING ME MY LUNCH?
GEAR...

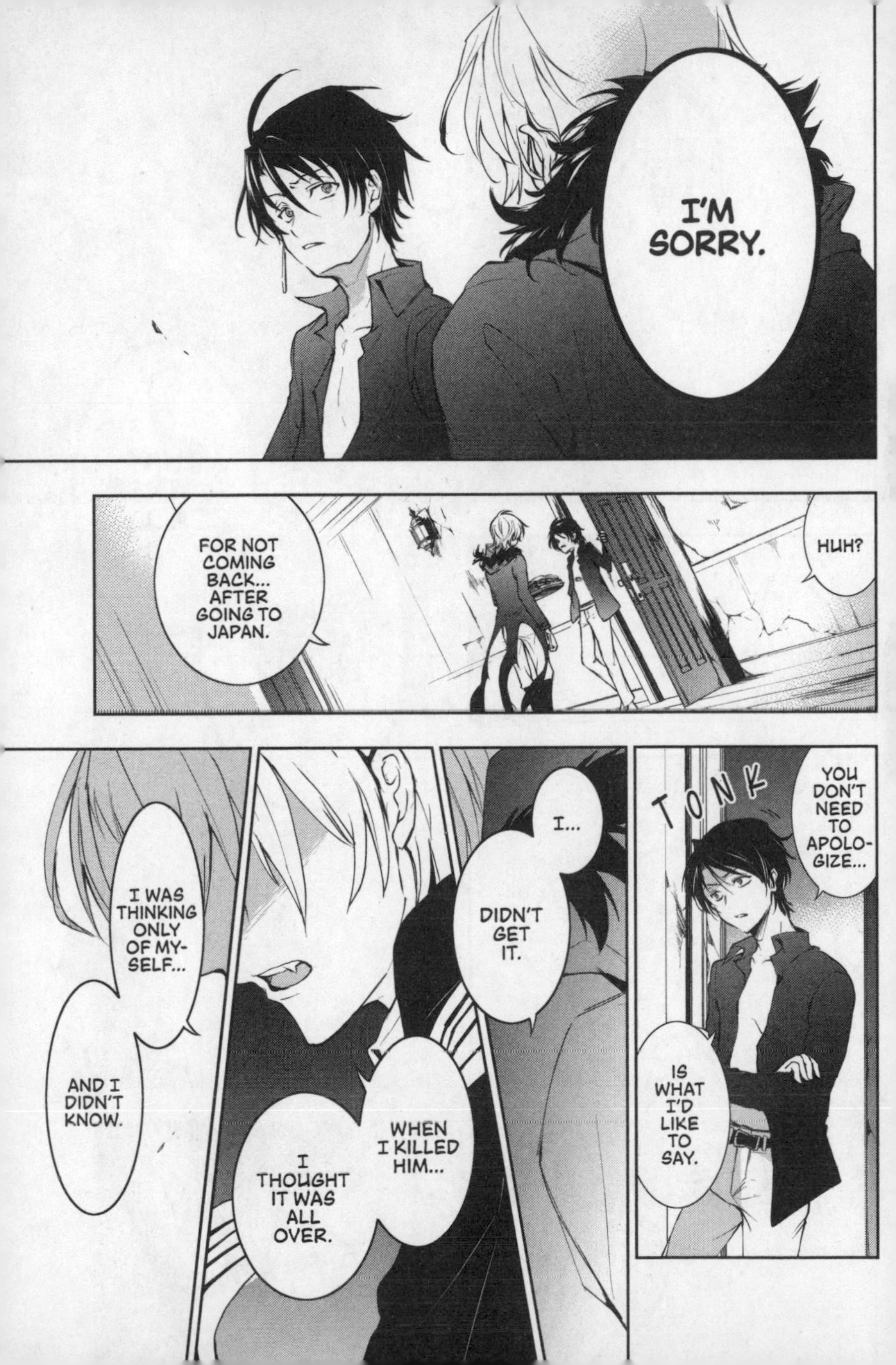
I'M SORRY.
HUH?
FOR NOT COMING BACK... AFTER GOING TO JAPAN.
TONK
YOU DON'T NEED TO APOLOGIZE...
IS WHAT I'D LIKE TO SAY.
I...
DIDN'T GET IT.
WHEN I KILLED HIM...
I THOUGHT IT WAS ALL OVER.
I WAS THINKING ONLY OF MYSELF...
AND I DIDN'T KNOW.

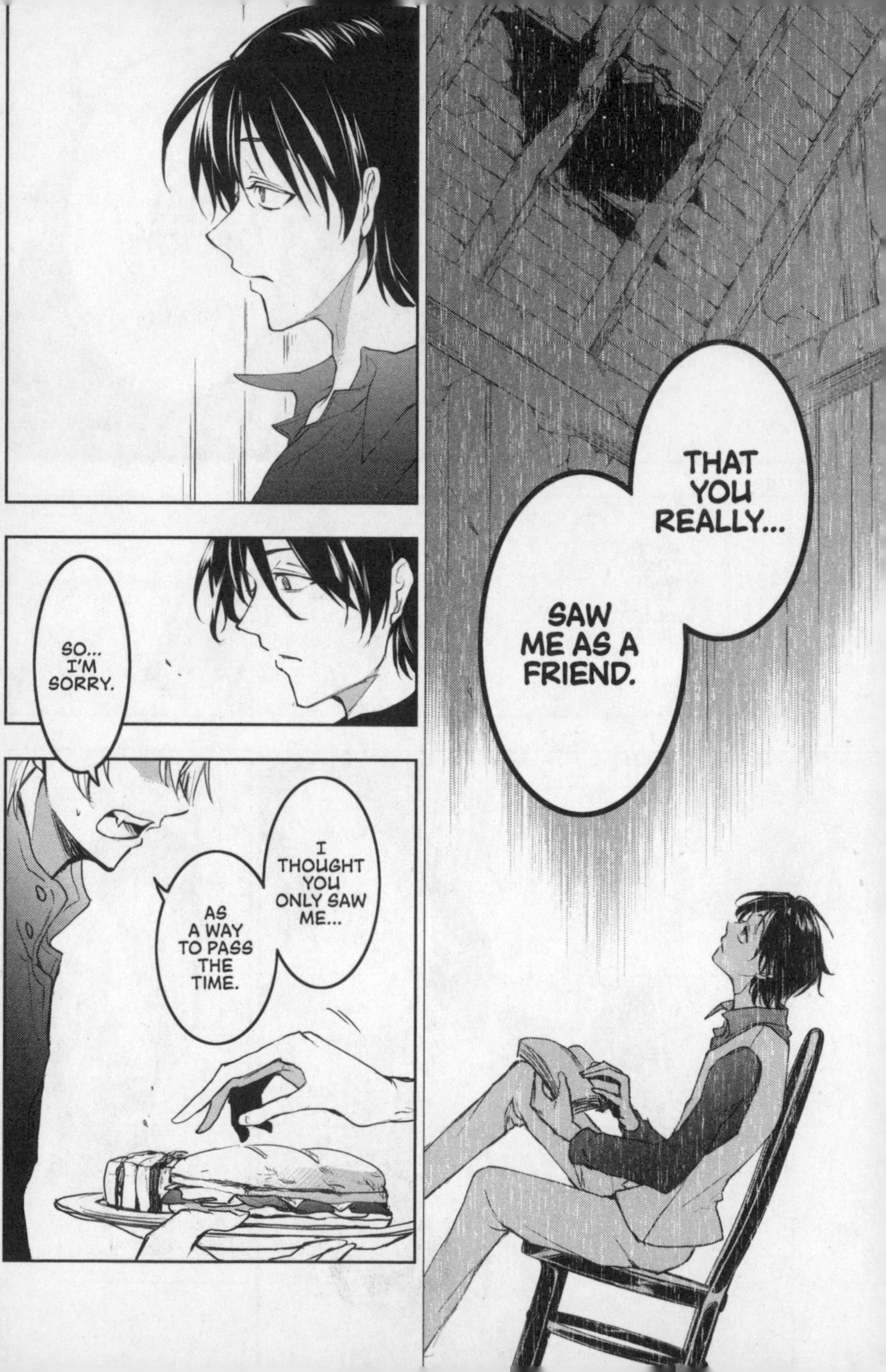
THAT YOU REALLY...
SAW ME AS A FRIEND.
SO... I'M SORRY.
I THOUGHT YOU ONLY SAW ME...
AS A WAY TO PASS THE TIME.

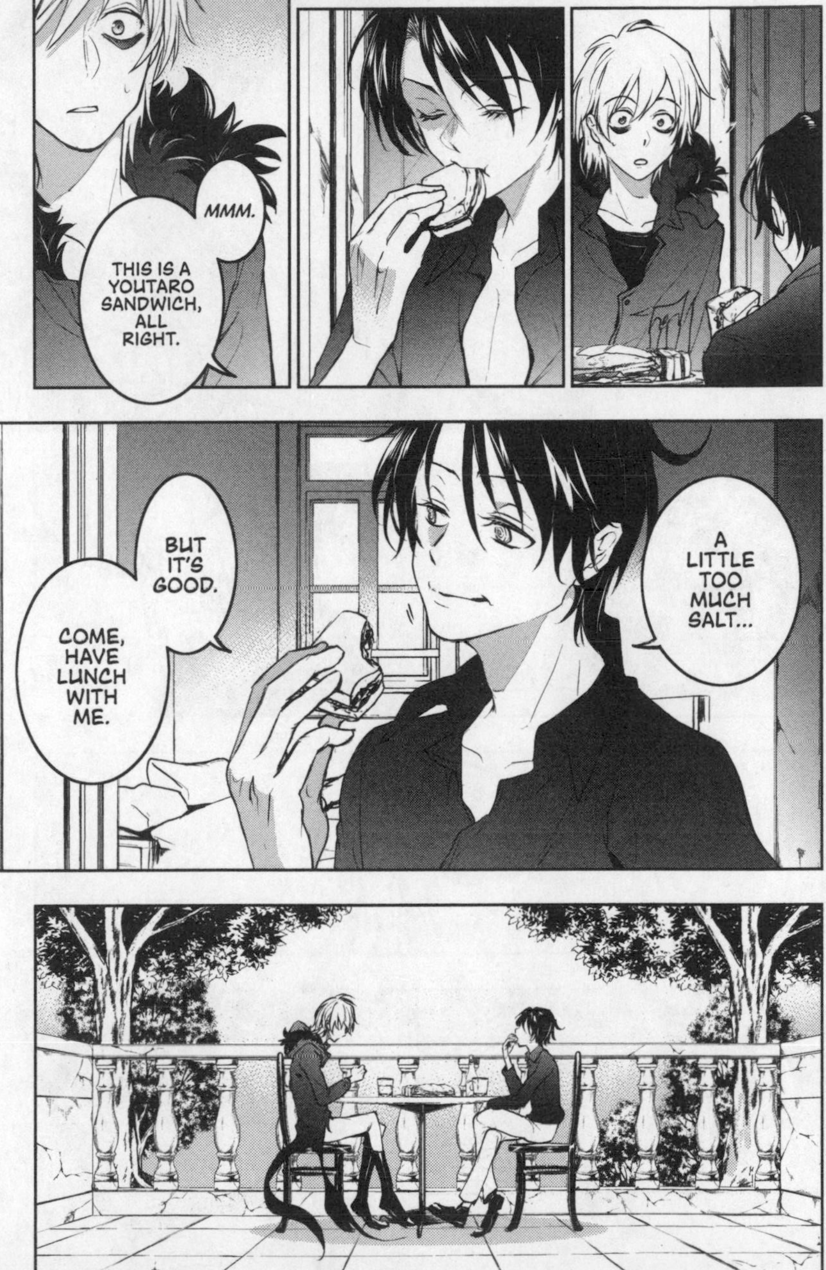
MMM.
THIS IS A YOUTARO SANDWICH, ALL RIGHT.
A LITTLE TOO MUCH SALT...
BUT IT'S GOOD.
COME, HAVE LUNCH WITH ME.

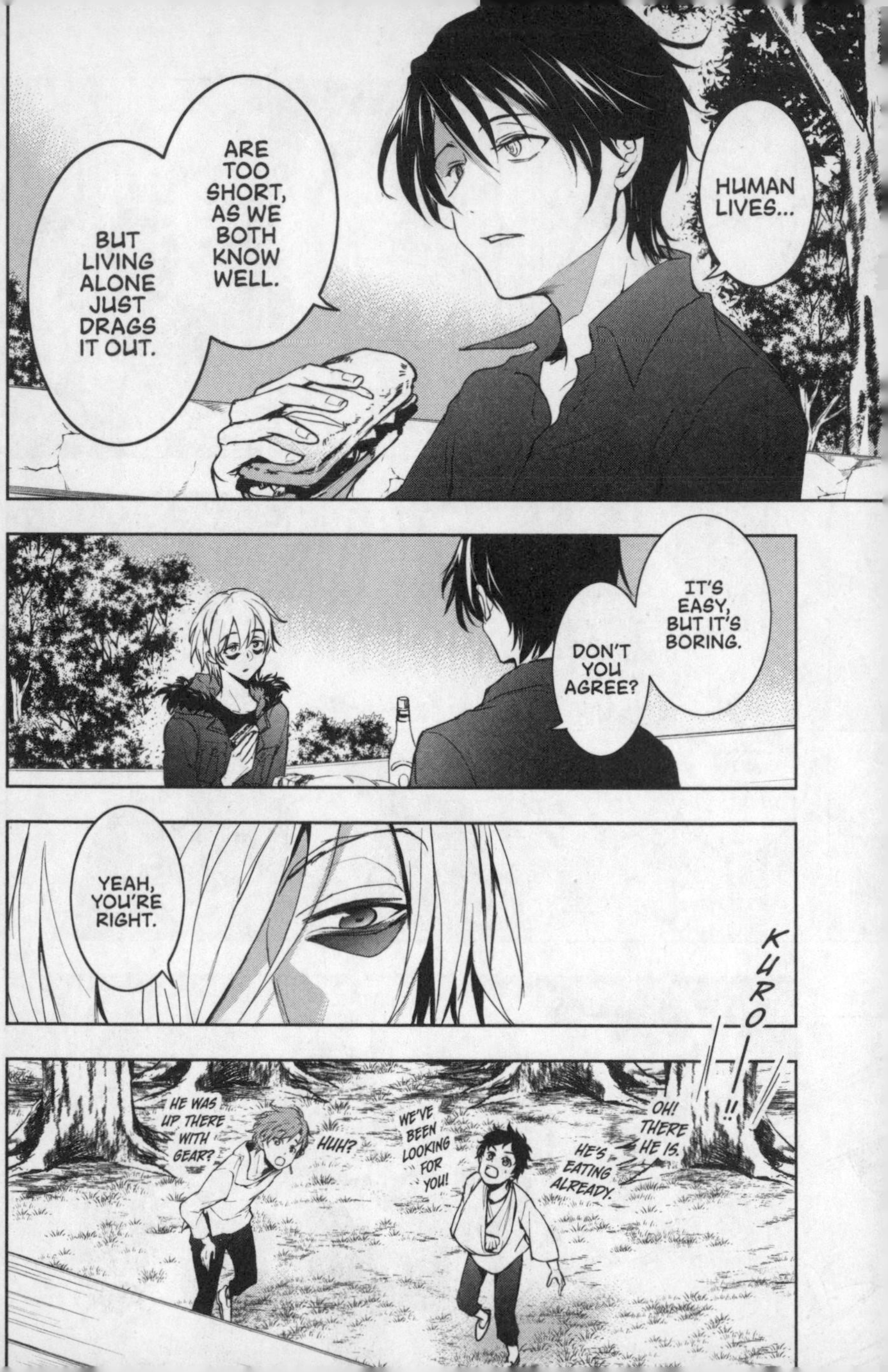
HUMAN LIVES...
ARE TOO SHORT, AS WE BOTH KNOW WELL.
BUT LIVING ALONE JUST DRAGS IT OUT.
IT'S EASY, BUT IT'S BORING.
DON'T YOU AGREE?
YEAH, YOU'RE RIGHT.
KURO—!!
OH! THERE HE IS.
HE'S EATING ALREADY.
WE'VE BEEN LOOKING FOR YOU!
HUH?
HE WAS UP THERE WITH GEAR?

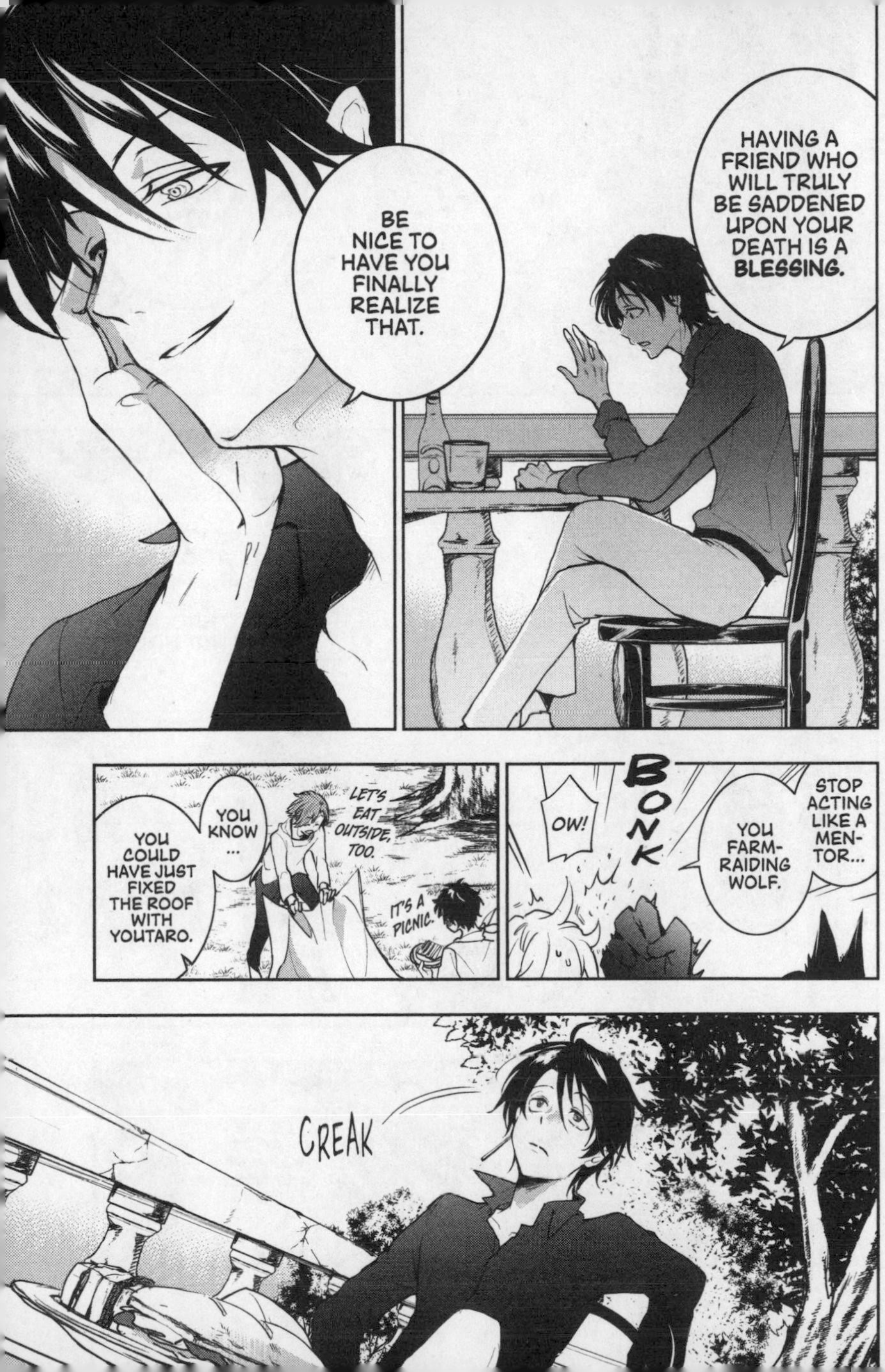
HAVING A FRIEND WHO WILL TRULY BE SADDENED UPON YOUR DEATH IS A BLESSING.
BE NICE TO HAVE YOU FINALLY REALIZE THAT.
YOU KNOW ...
YOU COULD HAVE JUST FIXED THE ROOF WITH YOUTARO.
LET'S EAT OUTSIDE, TOO.
IT'S A PICNIC.
STOP ACTING LIKE A MEN-TOR...
YOU FARM-RAIDING WOLF.
BONK
OW!
CREAK

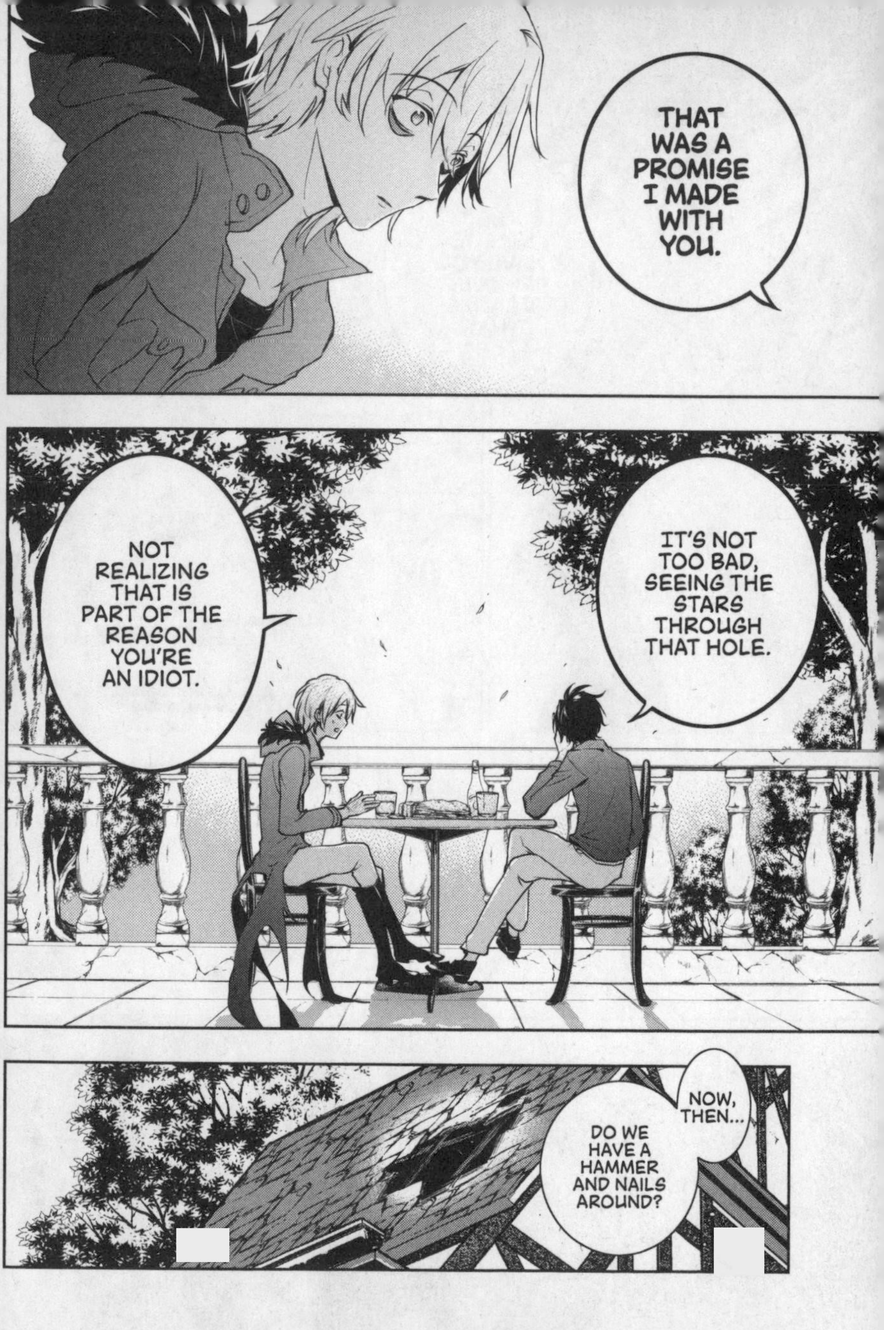
THAT WAS A PROMISE I MADE WITH YOU.
IT'S NOT TOO BAD, SEEING THE STARS THROUGH THAT HOLE.
NOT REALIZING THAT IS PART OF THE REASON YOU'RE AN IDIOT.
NOW, THEN...
DO WE HAVE A HAMMER AND NAILS AROUND?

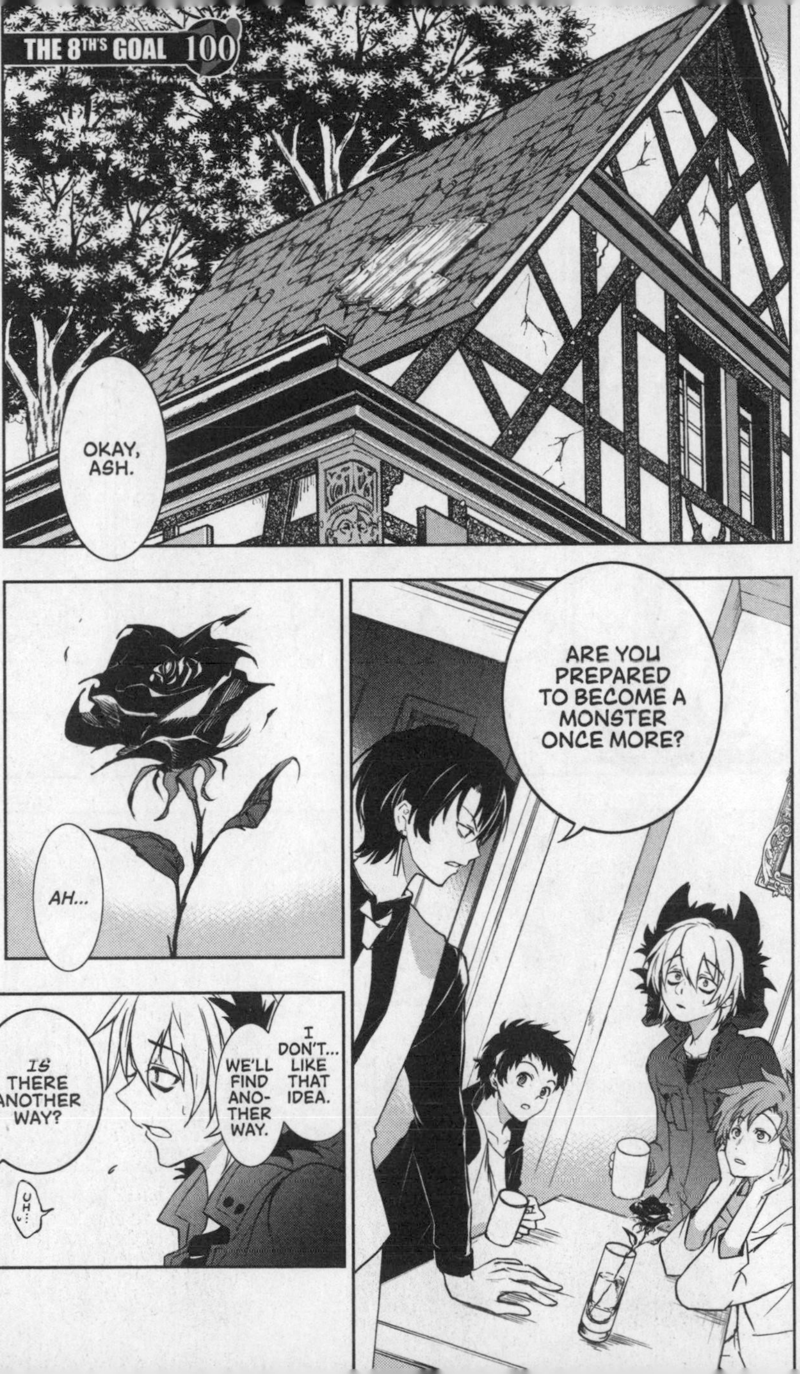
THE 8TH'S GOAL 100
OKAY, ASH.
ARE YOU PREPARED TO BECOME A MONSTER ONCE MORE?
AH...
I DON'T... LIKE THAT IDEA.
WE'LL FIND ANOTHER WAY.
IS THERE ANOTHER WAY?
UH...

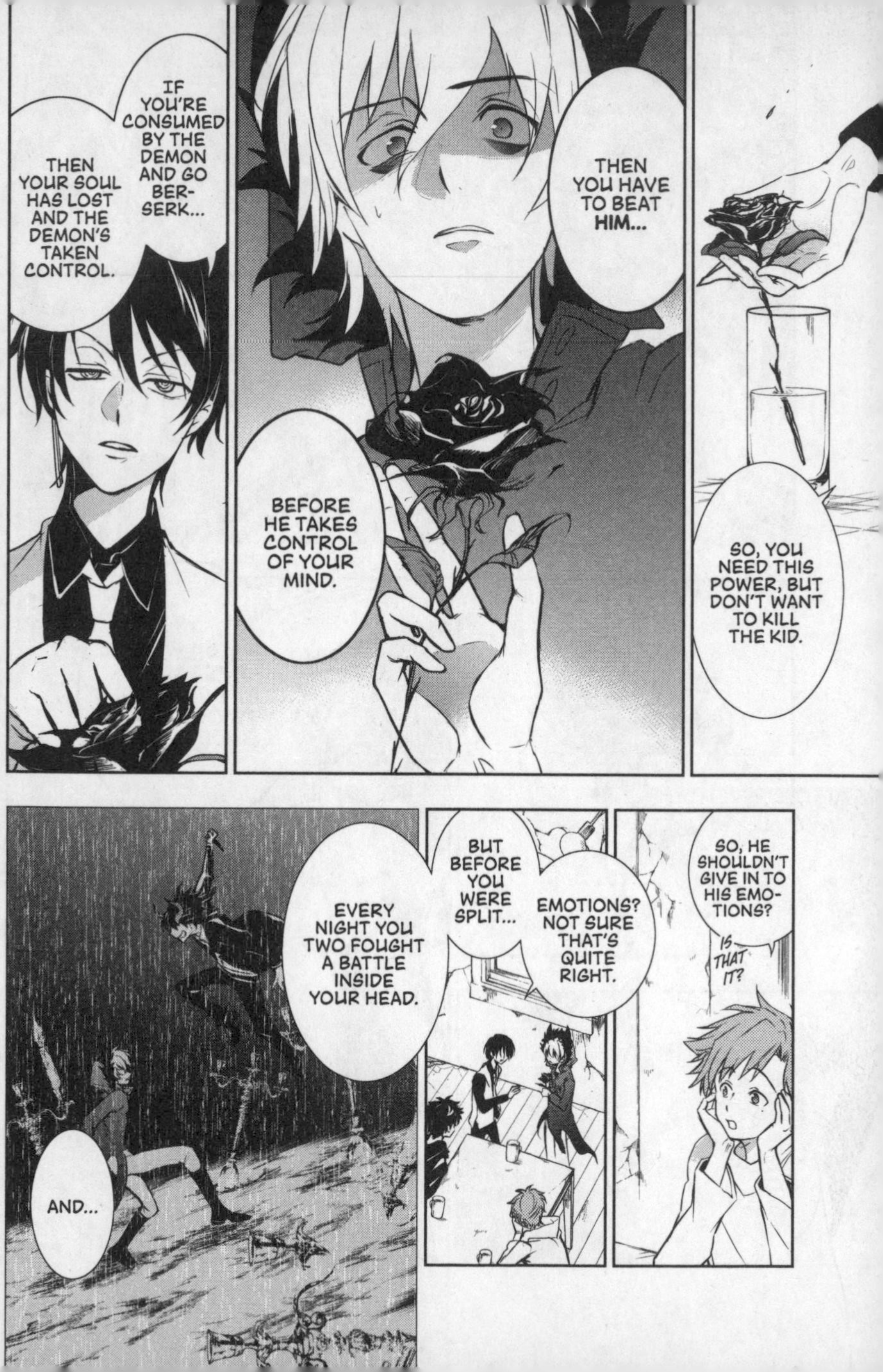
SO, YOU NEED THIS POWER, BUT DON'T WANT TO KILL THE KID.
THEN YOU HAVE TO BEAT HIM...
BEFORE HE TAKES CONTROL OF YOUR MIND.
IF YOU'RE CONSUMED BY THE DEMON AND GO BER-SERK...
THEN YOUR SOUL HAS LOST AND THE DEMON'S TAKEN CONTROL.
SO, HE SHOULDN'T GIVE IN TO HIS EMO-TIONS?
IS THAT IT?
EMOTIONS? NOT SURE THAT'S QUITE RIGHT.
BUT BEFORE YOU WERE SPLIT...
EVERY NIGHT YOU TWO FOUGHT A BATTLE INSIDE YOUR HEAD.
AND...

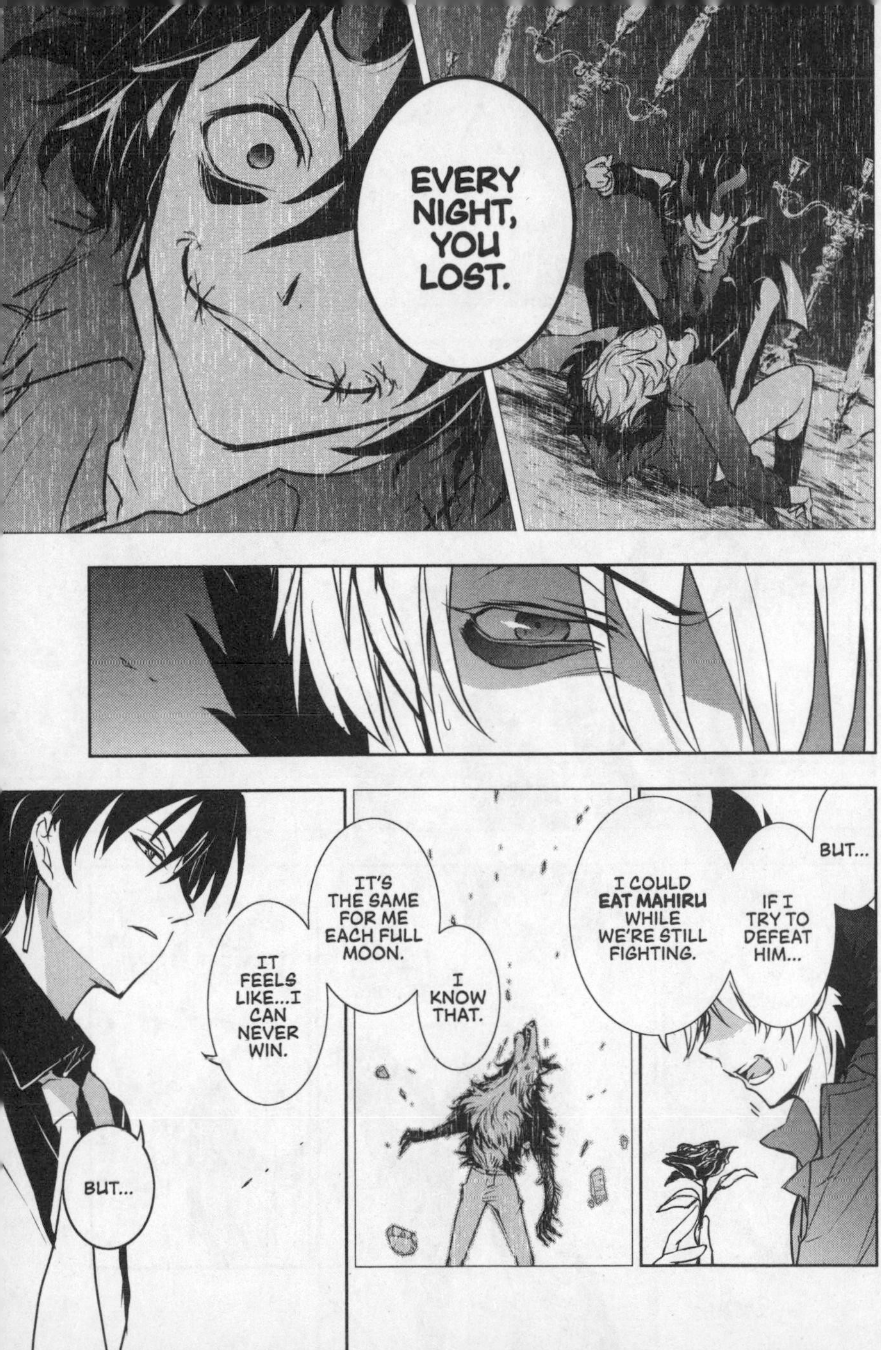
EVERY NIGHT, YOU LOST.
BUT...
IF I TRY TO DEFEAT HIM...
I COULD **EAT MAHIRU** WHILE WE'RE STILL FIGHTING.
I KNOW THAT.
IT'S THE SAME FOR ME EACH FULL MOON.
IT FEELS LIKE...I CAN NEVER WIN.
BUT...

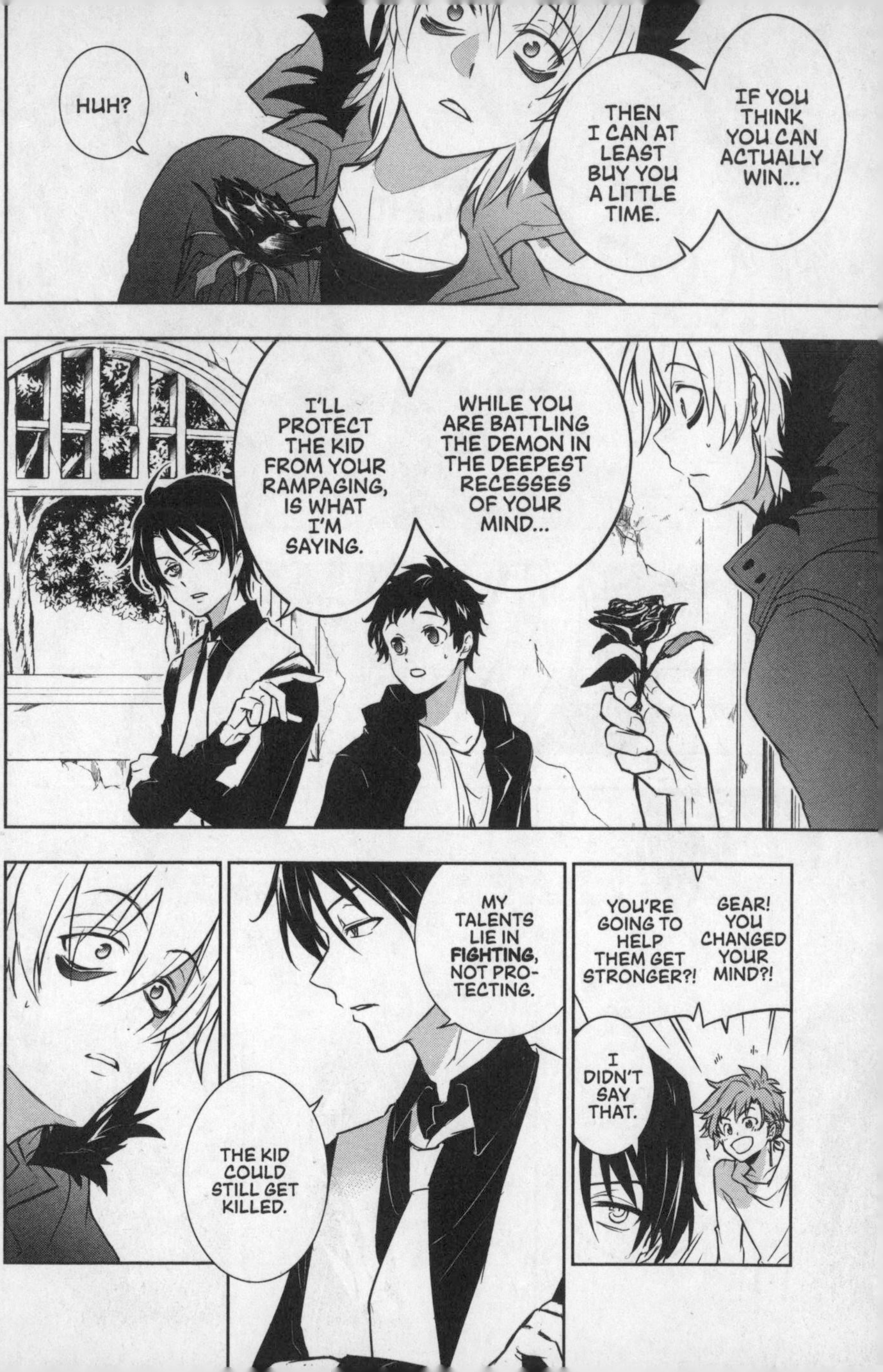
IF YOU THINK YOU CAN ACTUALLY WIN...
THEN I CAN AT LEAST BUY YOU A LITTLE TIME.
HUH?
WHILE YOU ARE BATTLING THE DEMON IN THE DEEPEST RECESSES OF YOUR MIND...
I'LL PROTECT THE KID FROM YOUR RAMPAGING, IS WHAT I'M SAYING.
GEAR! YOU CHANGED YOUR MIND?!
YOU'RE GOING TO HELP THEM GET STRONGER?!
I DIDN'T SAY THAT.
MY TALENTS LIE IN **FIGHTING**, NOT PRO-TECTING.
THE KID COULD STILL GET KILLED.

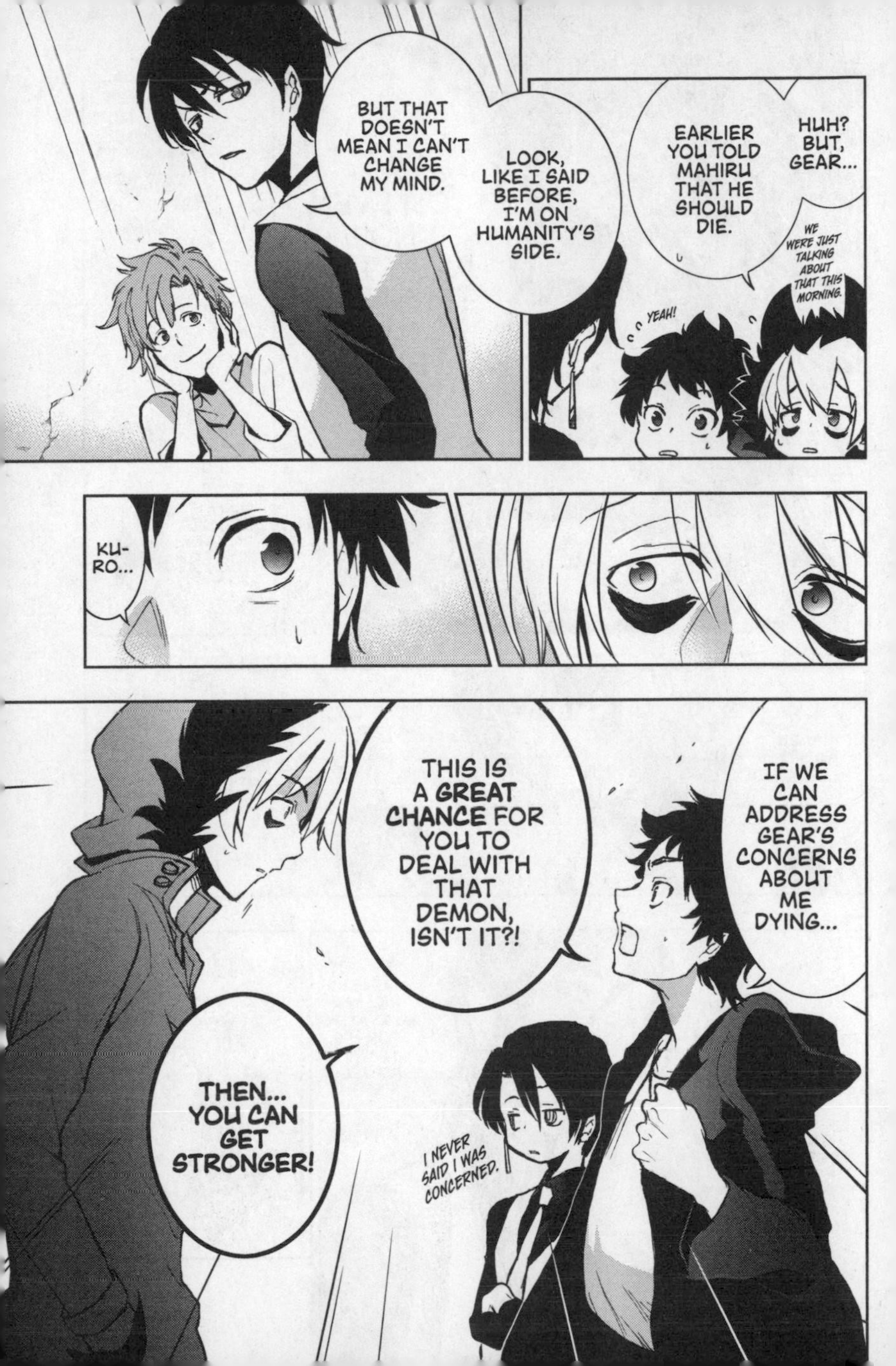
HUH? BUT, GEAR...
EARLIER YOU TOLD MAHIRU THAT HE SHOULD DIE.
WE WERE JUST TALKING ABOUT THAT THIS MORNING.
YEAH!
LOOK, LIKE I SAID BEFORE, I'M ON HUMANITY'S SIDE.
BUT THAT DOESN'T MEAN I CAN'T CHANGE MY MIND.
KU-RO...
IF WE CAN ADDRESS GEAR'S CONCERNS ABOUT ME DYING...
THIS IS A GREAT CHANCE FOR YOU TO DEAL WITH THAT DEMON, ISN'T IT?!
I NEVER SAID I WAS CONCERNED.
THEN... YOU CAN GET STRONGER!

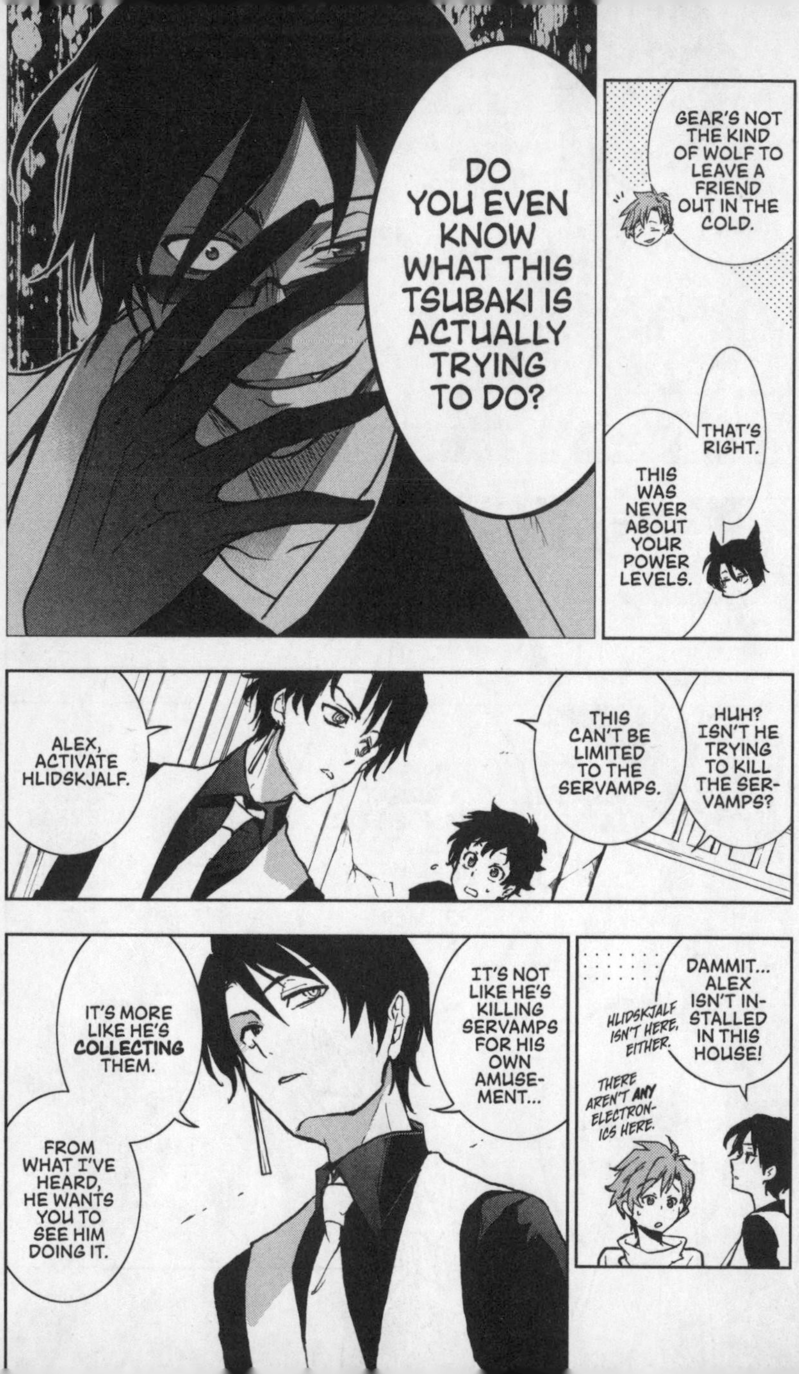
GEAR'S NOT THE KIND OF WOLF TO LEAVE A FRIEND OUT IN THE COLD.
THAT'S RIGHT.
THIS WAS NEVER ABOUT YOUR POWER LEVELS.
DO YOU EVEN KNOW WHAT THIS TSUBAKI IS ACTUALLY TRYING TO DO?
HUH? ISN'T HE TRYING TO KILL THE SER-VAMPS?
THIS CAN'T BE LIMITED TO THE SERVAMPS.
ALEX, ACTIVATE HLIDSKJALF.
DAMMIT... ALEX ISN'T IN-STALLED IN THIS HOUSE!
HLIDSKJALF ISN'T HERE, EITHER.
THERE AREN'T ANY ELECTRON-ICS HERE.
IT'S NOT LIKE HE'S KILLING SERVAMPS FOR HIS OWN AMUSE-MENT...
IT'S MORE LIKE HE'S COLLECTING THEM.
FROM WHAT I'VE HEARD, HE WANTS YOU TO SEE HIM DOING IT.

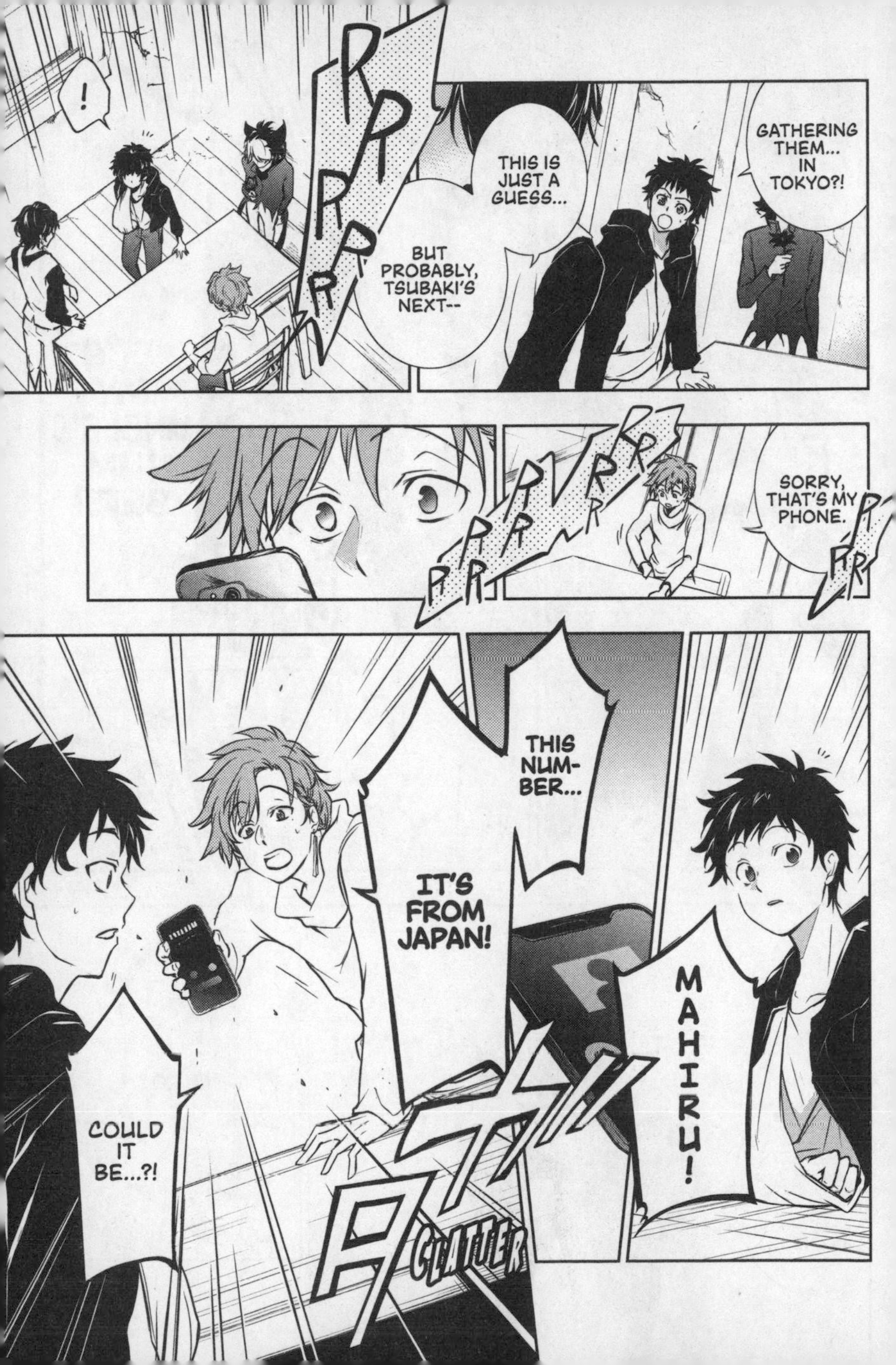
GATHERING THEM... IN TOKYO?!
THIS IS JUST A GUESS...
BUT PROBABLY, TSUBAKI'S NEXT--
RRRRRR
!
SORRY, THAT'S MY PHONE.
PRRR
PRRR
THIS NUMBER...
IT'S FROM JAPAN!
MAHIRU!
COULD IT BE...?!
CLATTER

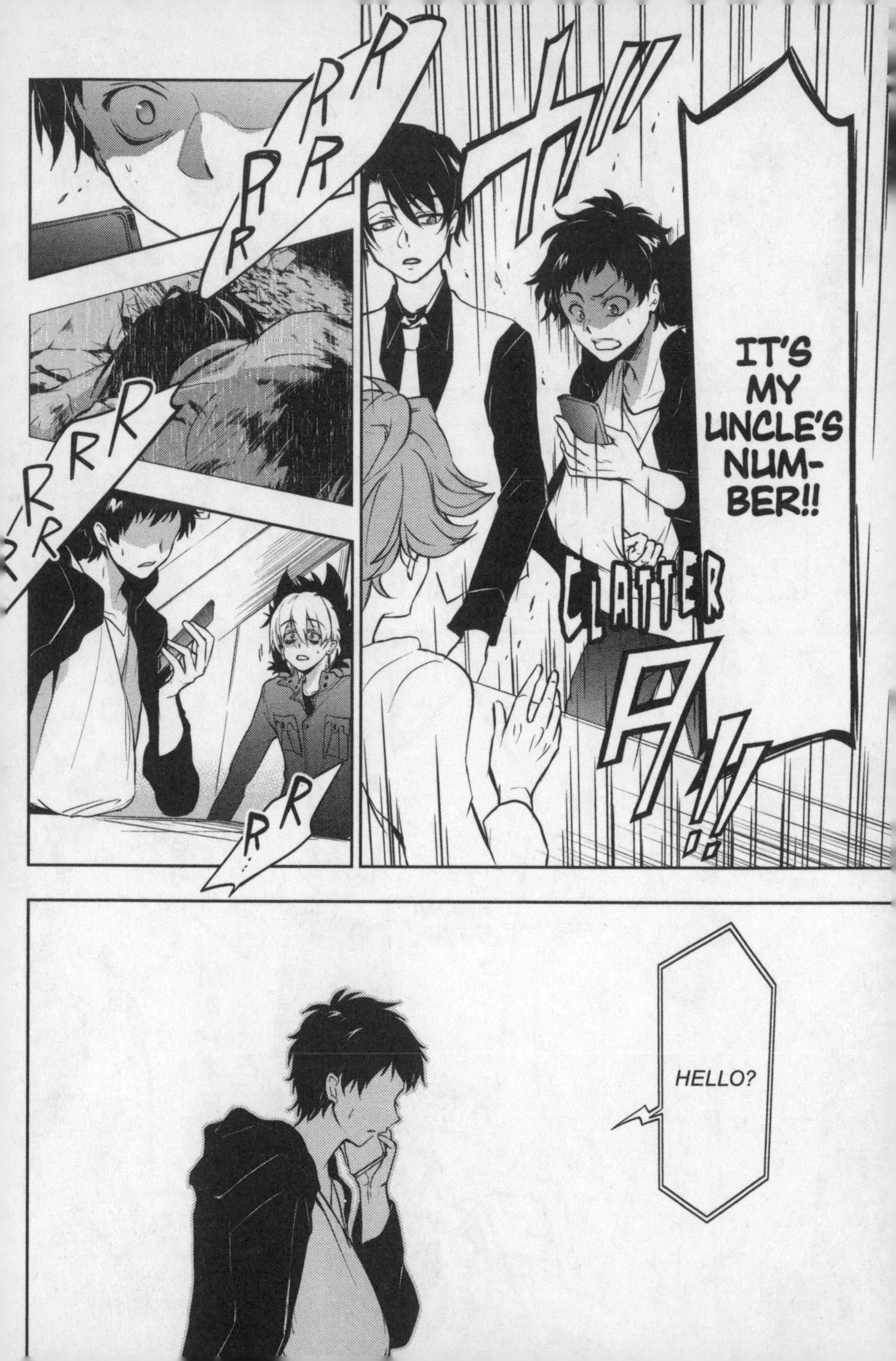
RRRRRRR
IT'S MY UNCLE'S NUM-BER!!
CLATTER
RRRRR
RR
HELLO?

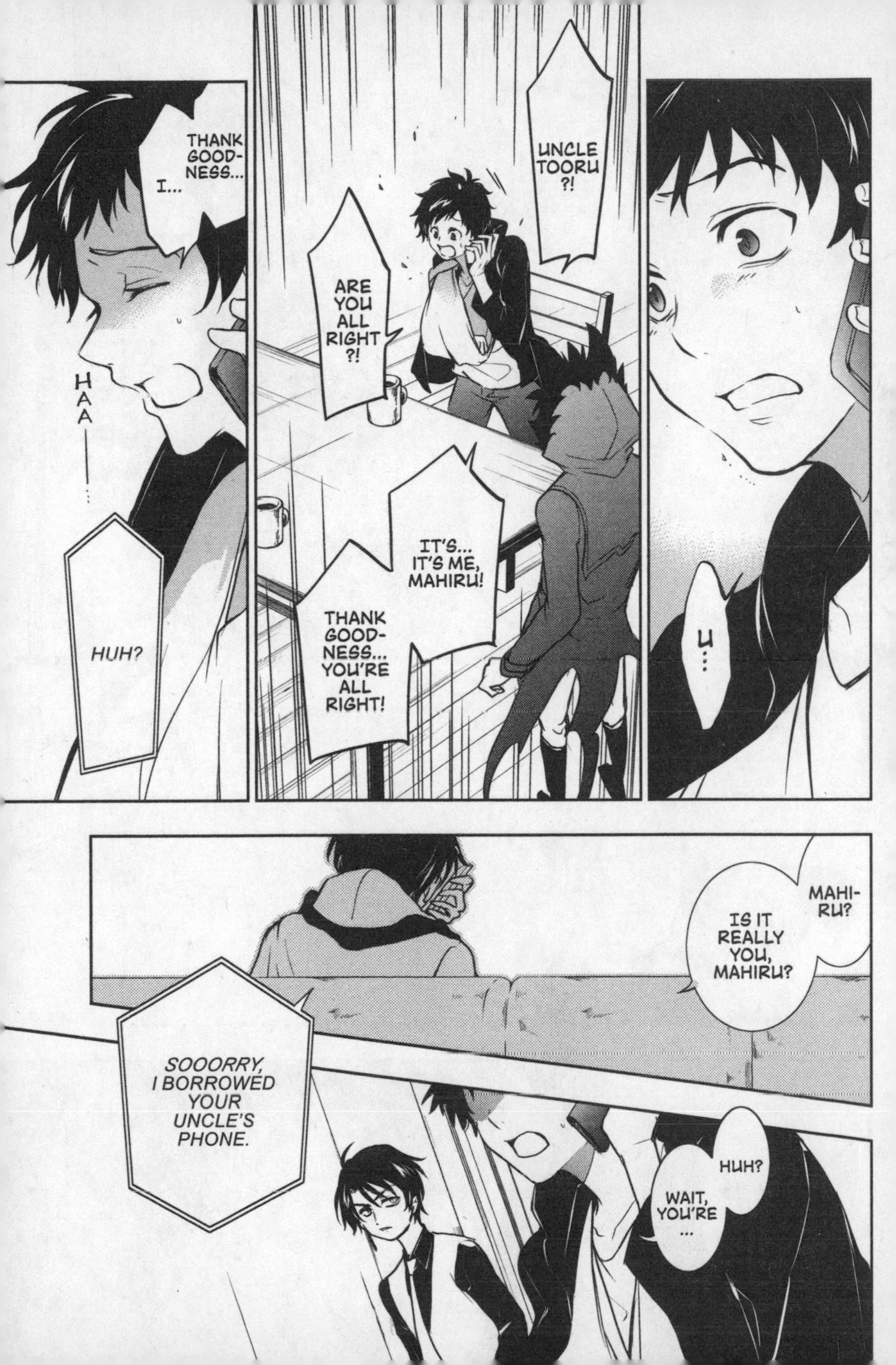
U...
UNCLE TOORU?!
ARE YOU ALL RIGHT?!
IT'S... IT'S ME, MAHIRU!
THANK GOODNESS... YOU'RE ALL RIGHT!
THANK GOODNESS... I...
HAA—...
HUH?
MAHIRU? IS IT REALLY YOU, MAHIRU?
SOOORRY, I BORROWED YOUR UNCLE'S PHONE.
HUH? WAIT, YOU'RE ...

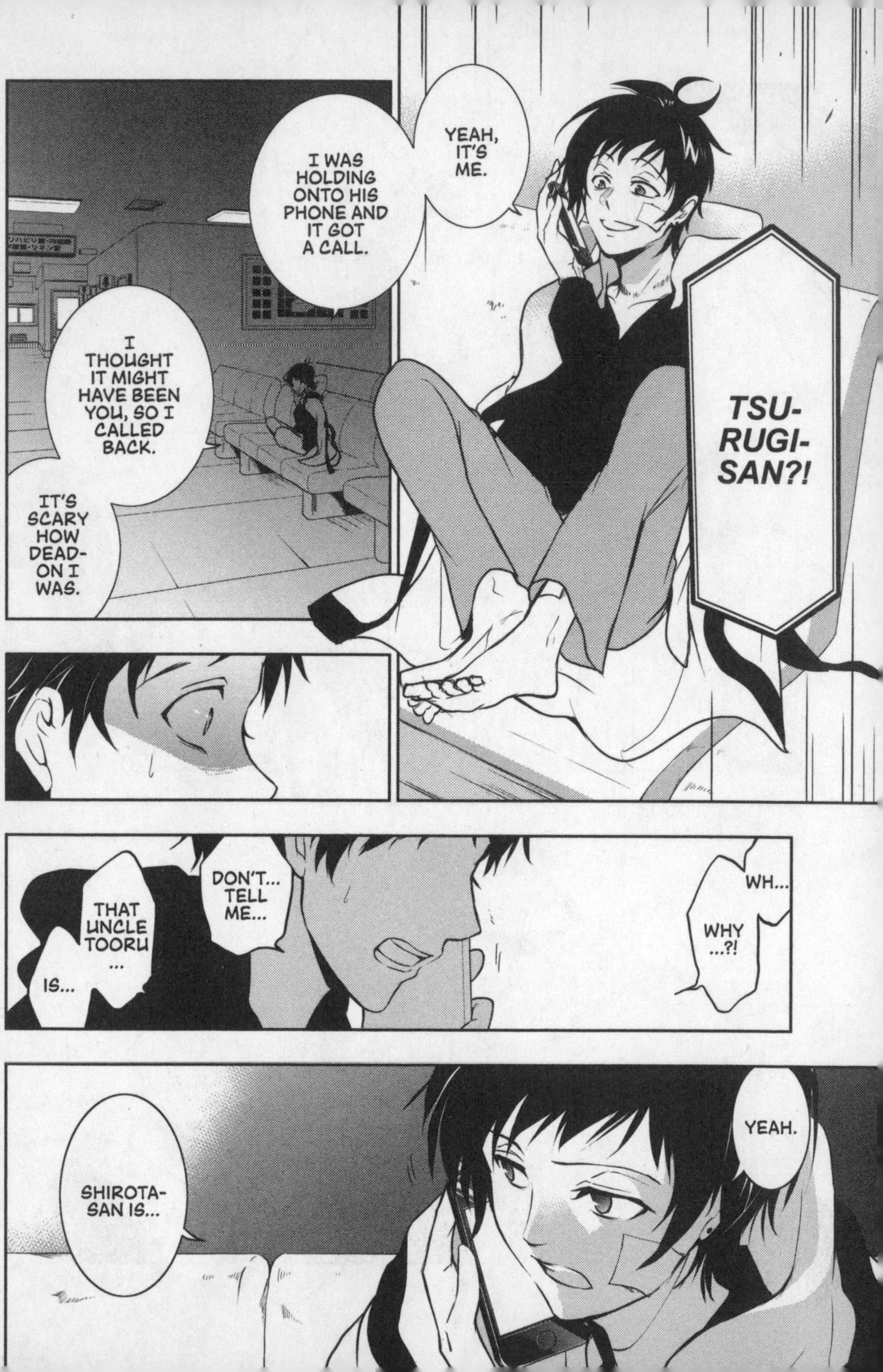
TSU-RUGI-SAN?!
YEAH, IT'S ME.
I WAS HOLDING ONTO HIS PHONE AND IT GOT A CALL.
I THOUGHT IT MIGHT HAVE BEEN YOU, SO I CALLED BACK.
IT'S SCARY HOW DEAD-ON I WAS.
WH...
WHY ...?!
DON'T... TELL ME...
THAT UNCLE TOORU ...
IS...
YEAH.
SHIROTA-SAN IS...

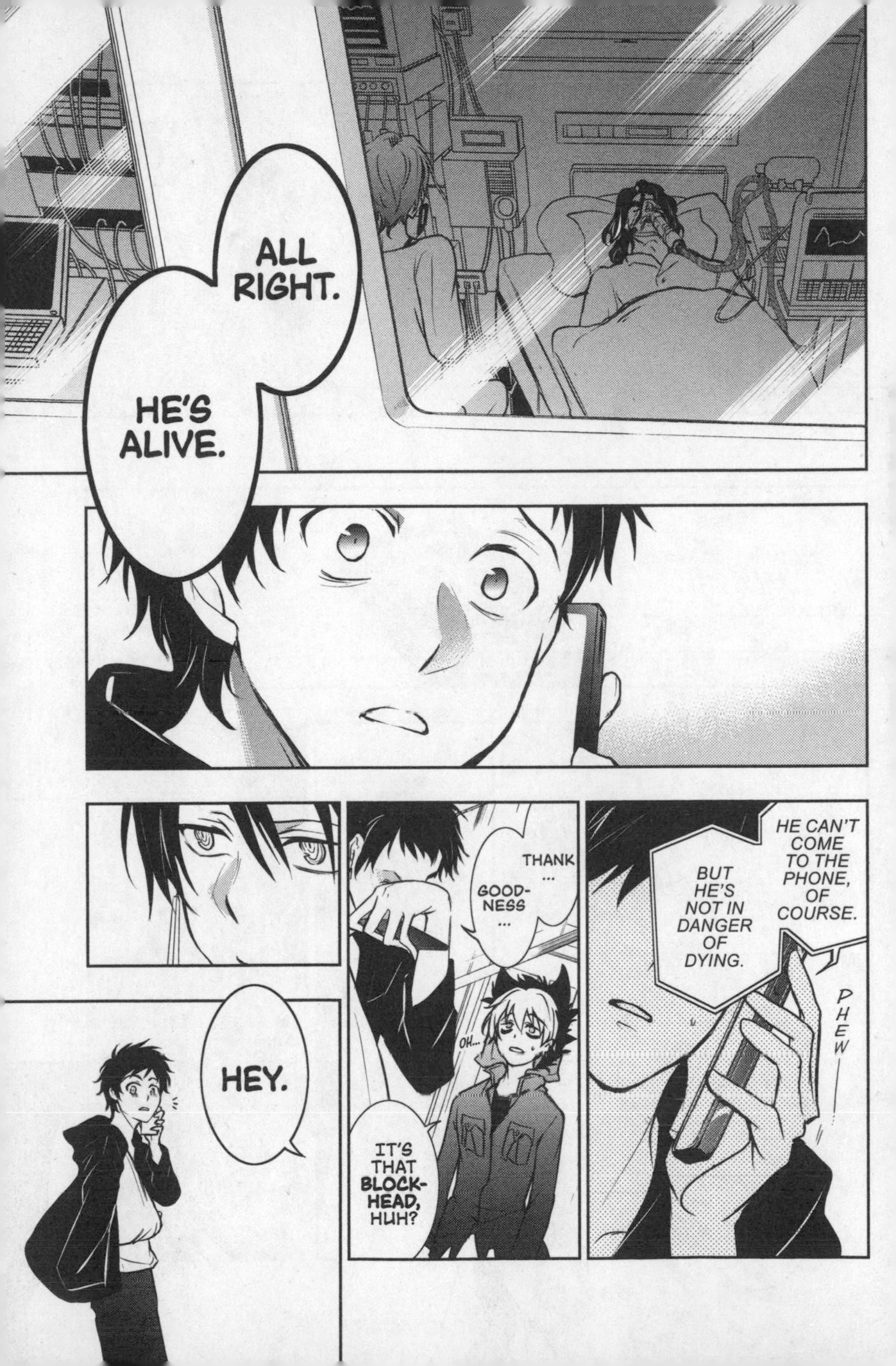
ALL RIGHT.
HE'S ALIVE.
HE CAN'T COME TO THE PHONE, OF COURSE.
BUT HE'S NOT IN DANGER OF DYING.
PHEW—
THANK... GOODNESS...
OH...
IT'S THAT BLOCKHEAD, HUH?
HEY.

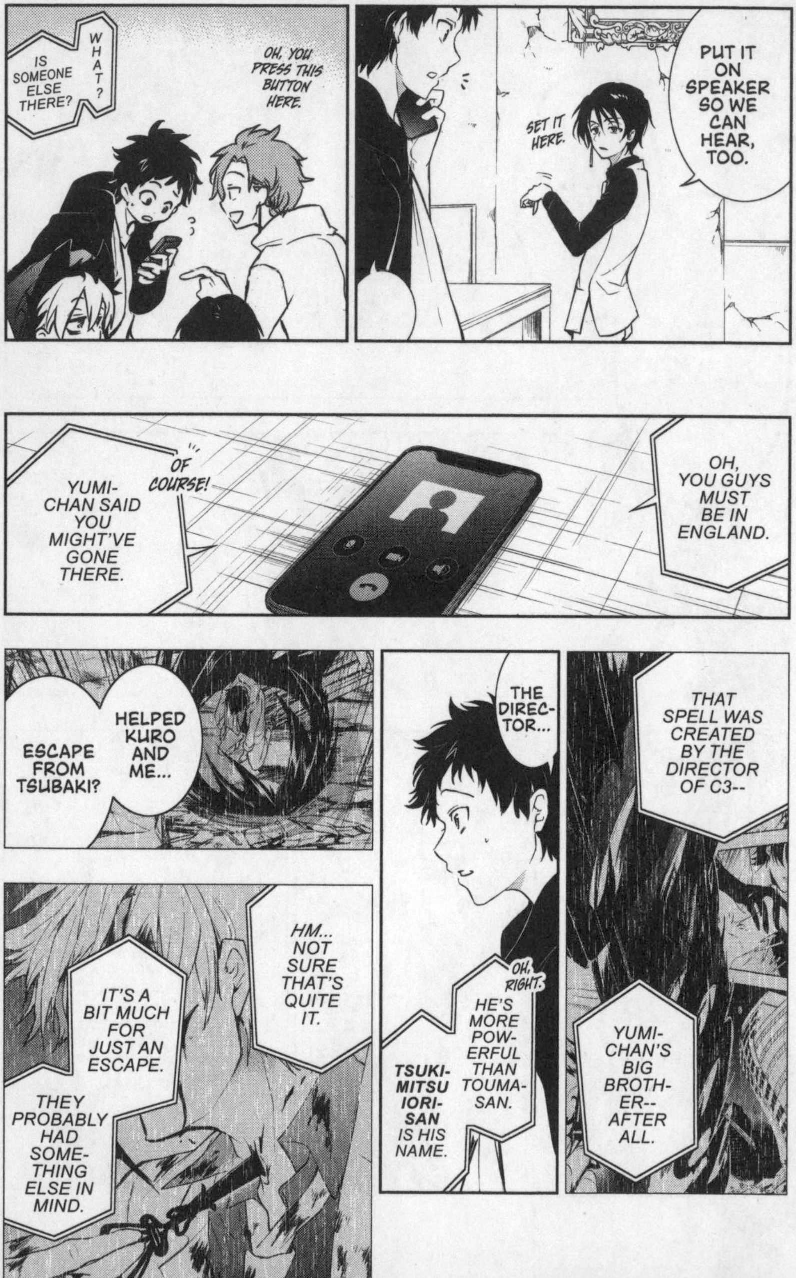
PUT IT ON SPEAKER SO WE CAN HEAR, TOO.
SET IT HERE.
OH, YOU PRESS THIS BUTTON HERE.
WHAT?
IS SOMEONE ELSE THERE?
OH, YOU GUYS MUST BE IN ENGLAND.
OF COURSE!
YUMI-CHAN SAID YOU MIGHT'VE GONE THERE.
THAT SPELL WAS CREATED BY THE DIRECTOR OF C3--
THE DIRECTOR...
HELPED KURO AND ME...
ESCAPE FROM TSUBAKI?
YUMI-CHAN'S BIG BROTHER-- AFTER ALL.
OH, RIGHT.
HE'S MORE POWERFUL THAN TOUMA-SAN.
TSUKIMITSU IORI-SAN IS HIS NAME.
HM... NOT SURE THAT'S QUITE IT.
IT'S A BIT MUCH FOR JUST AN ESCAPE.
THEY PROBABLY HAD SOMETHING ELSE IN MIND.

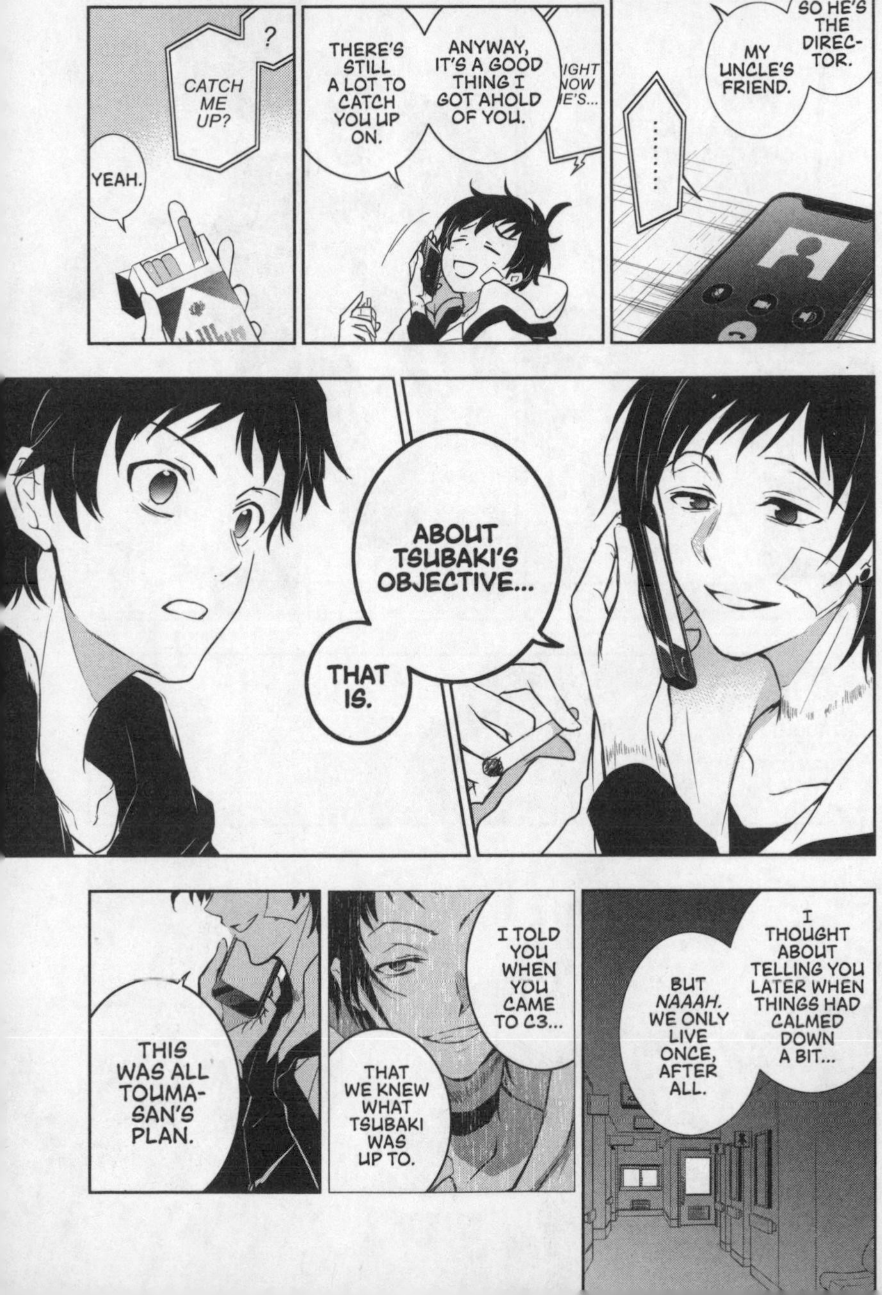
SO HE'S THE DIRECTOR.
MY UNCLE'S FRIEND.
......
ANYWAY, IT'S A GOOD THING I GOT AHOLD OF YOU.
THERE'S STILL A LOT TO CATCH YOU UP ON.
?
CATCH ME UP?
YEAH.
ABOUT TSUBAKI'S OBJECTIVE...
THAT IS.
I THOUGHT ABOUT TELLING YOU LATER WHEN THINGS HAD CALMED DOWN A BIT...
BUT *NAAAH.* WE ONLY LIVE ONCE, AFTER ALL.
I TOLD YOU WHEN YOU CAME TO C3...
THAT WE KNEW WHAT TSUBAKI WAS UP TO.
THIS WAS ALL TOUMA-SAN'S PLAN.

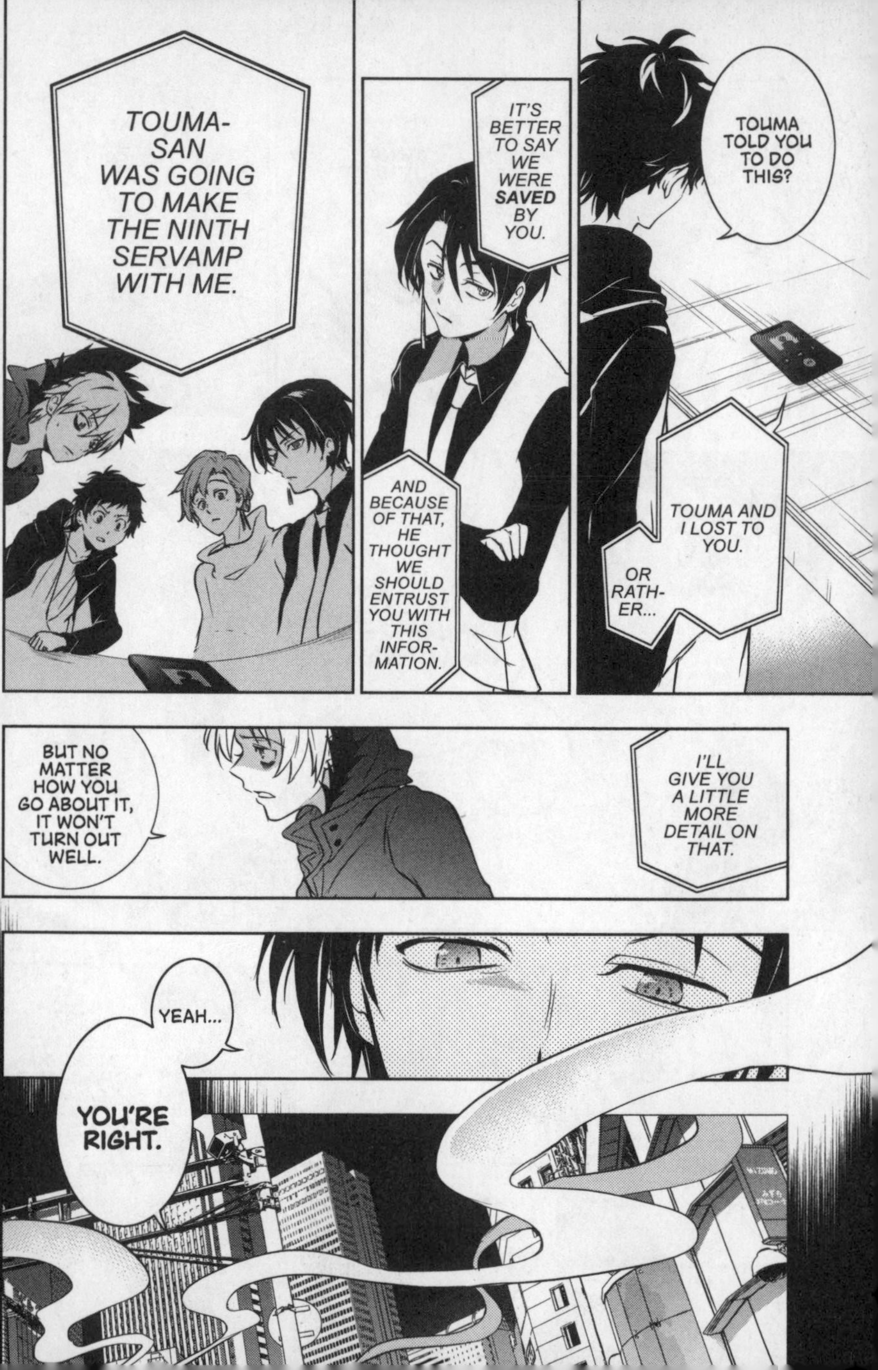
TOUMA TOLD YOU TO DO THIS?
TOUMA AND I LOST TO YOU.
OR RATH- ER...
IT'S BETTER TO SAY WE WERE **SAVED** BY YOU.
AND BECAUSE OF THAT, HE THOUGHT WE SHOULD ENTRUST YOU WITH THIS INFOR- MATION.
TOUMA- SAN WAS GOING TO MAKE THE NINTH SERVAMP WITH ME.
I'LL GIVE YOU A LITTLE MORE DETAIL ON THAT.
BUT NO MATTER HOW YOU GO ABOUT IT, IT WON'T TURN OUT WELL.
YEAH...
YOU'RE RIGHT.

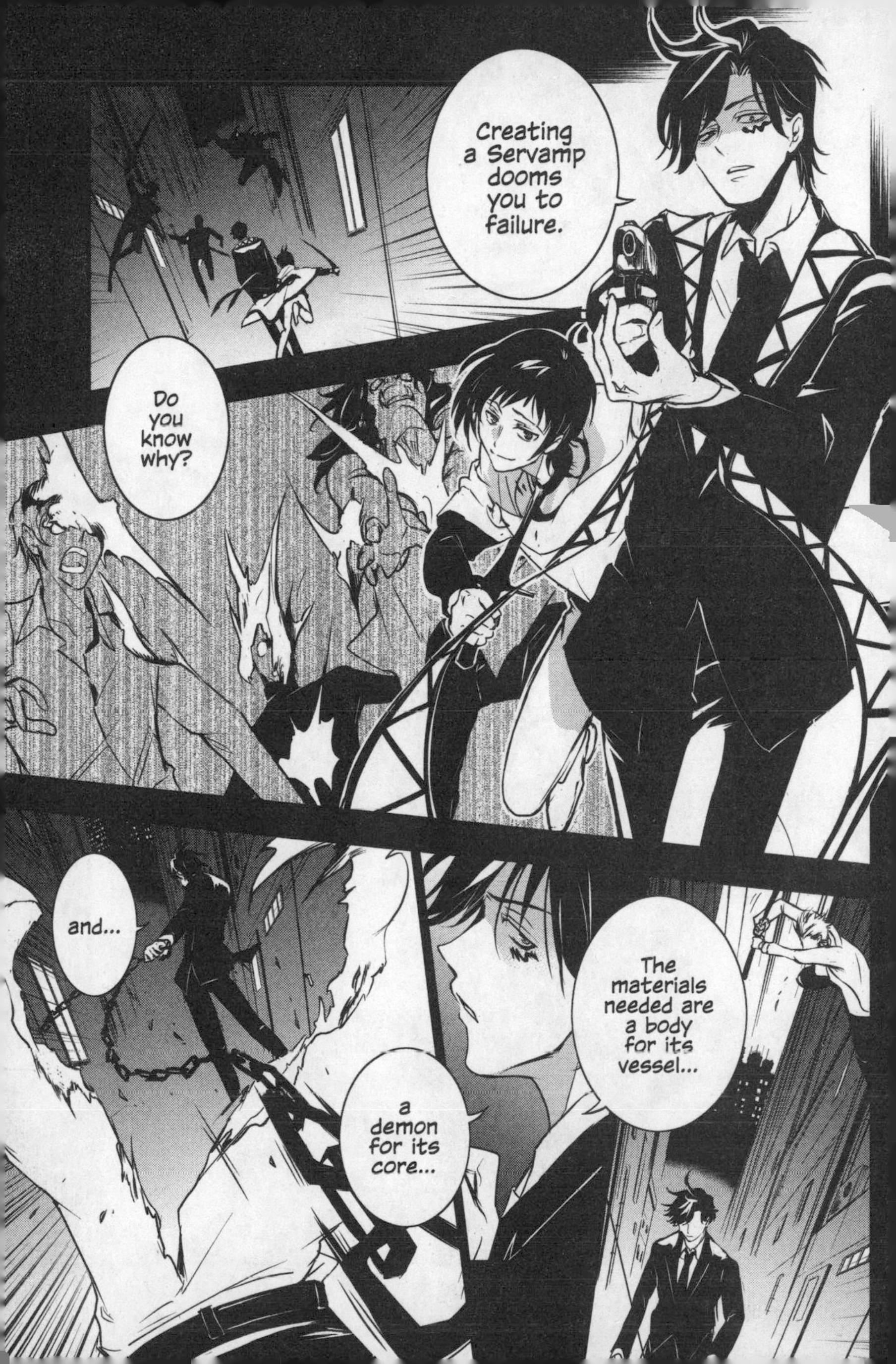
Creating a Servamp dooms you to failure.
Do you know why?
The materials needed are a body for its vessel...
a demon for its core...
and...

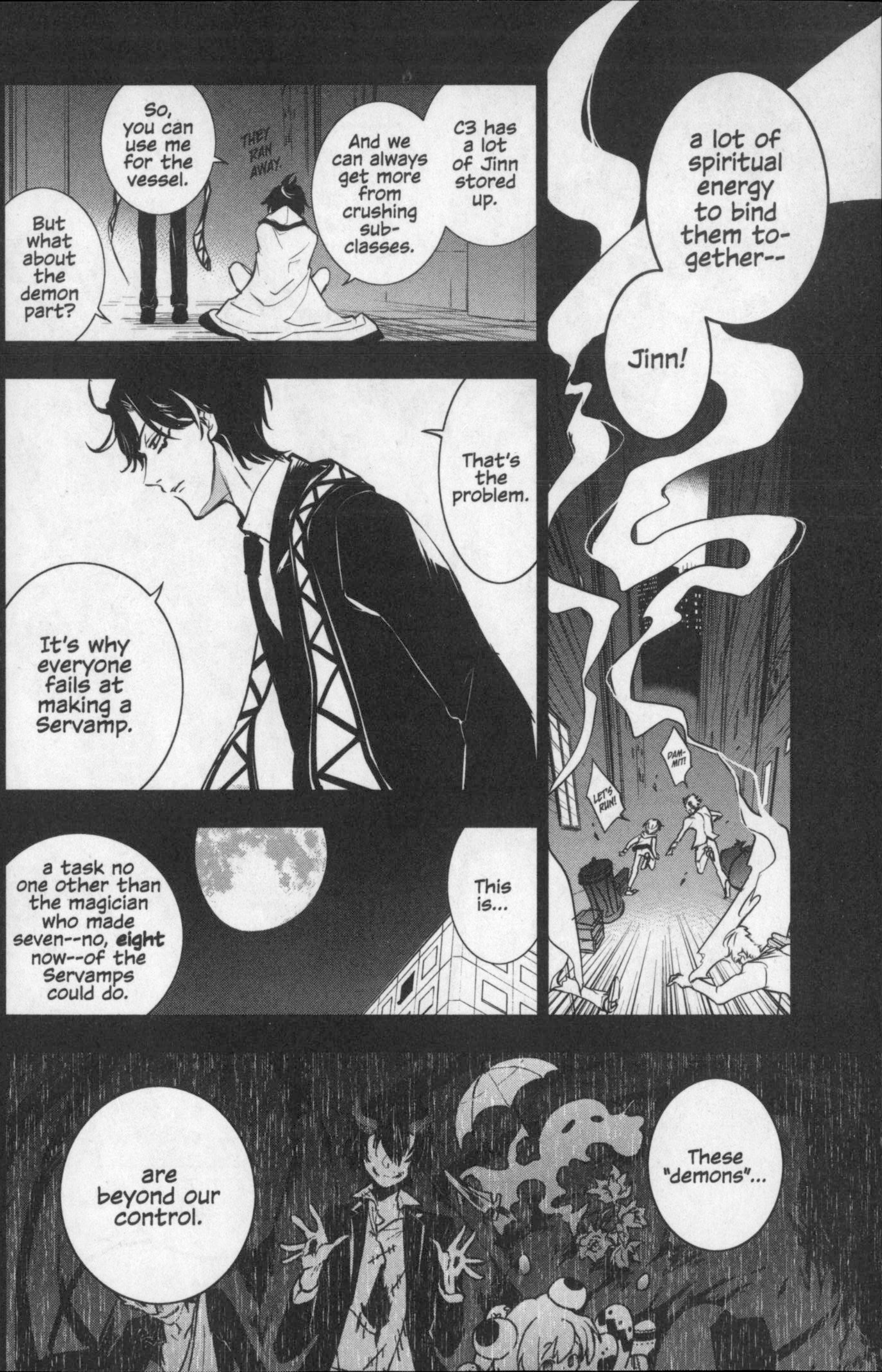

a lot of spiritual energy to bind them to-gether--
Jinn!
DAM-MIT!
LET'S RUN!
C3 has a lot of Jinn stored up.
And we can always get more from crushing sub-classes.
THEY RAN AWAY.
So, you can use me for the vessel.
But what about the demon part?
That's the problem.
It's why everyone fails at making a Servamp.
This is...
a task no one other than the magician who made seven--no, **eight** now--of the Servamps could do.
These "demons"...
are beyond our control.

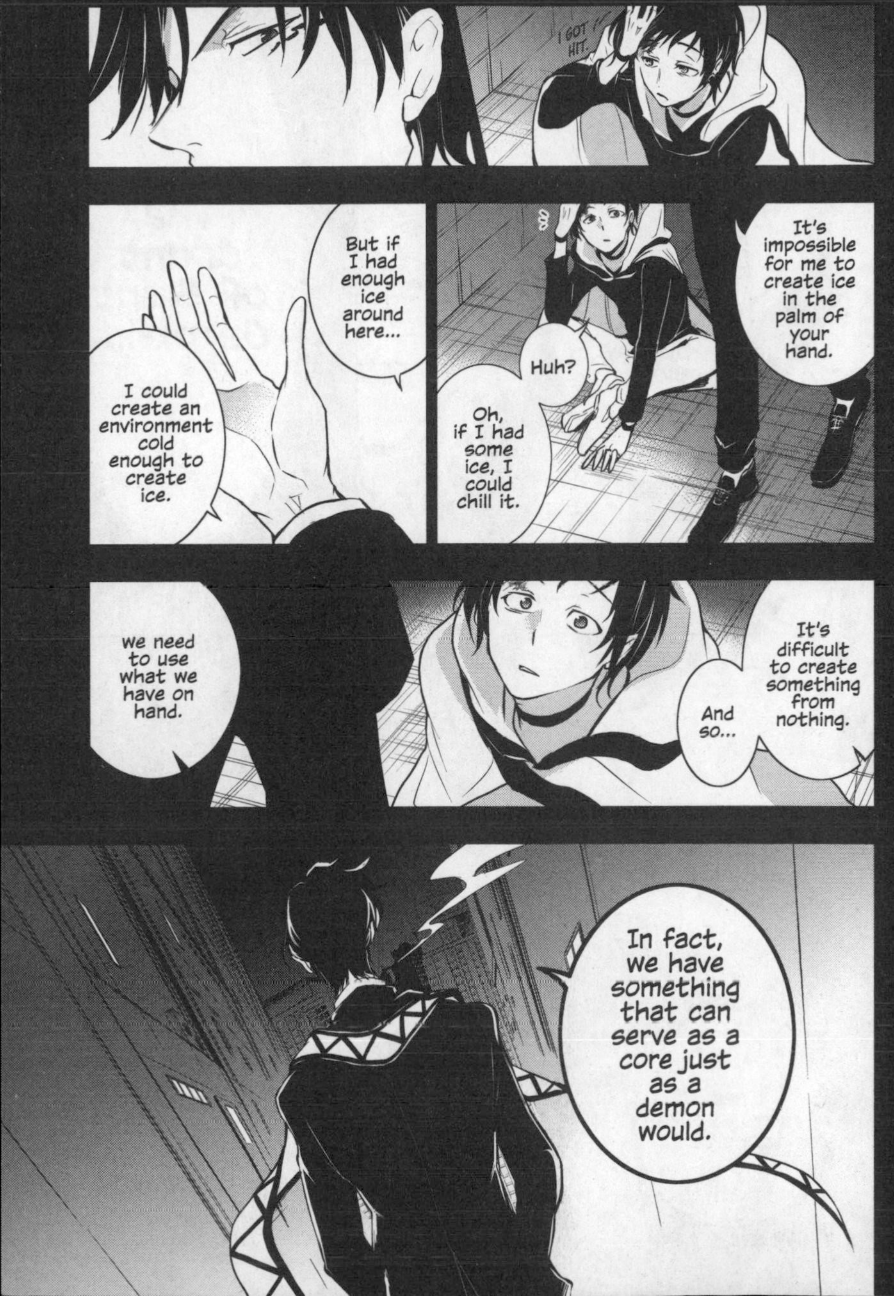
I GOT HIT.
It's impossible for me to create ice in the palm of your hand.
Huh?
Oh, if I had some ice, I could chill it.
But if I had enough ice around here...
I could create an environment cold enough to create ice.
It's difficult to create something from nothing.
And so...
we need to use what we have on hand.
In fact, we have something that can serve as a core just as a demon would.

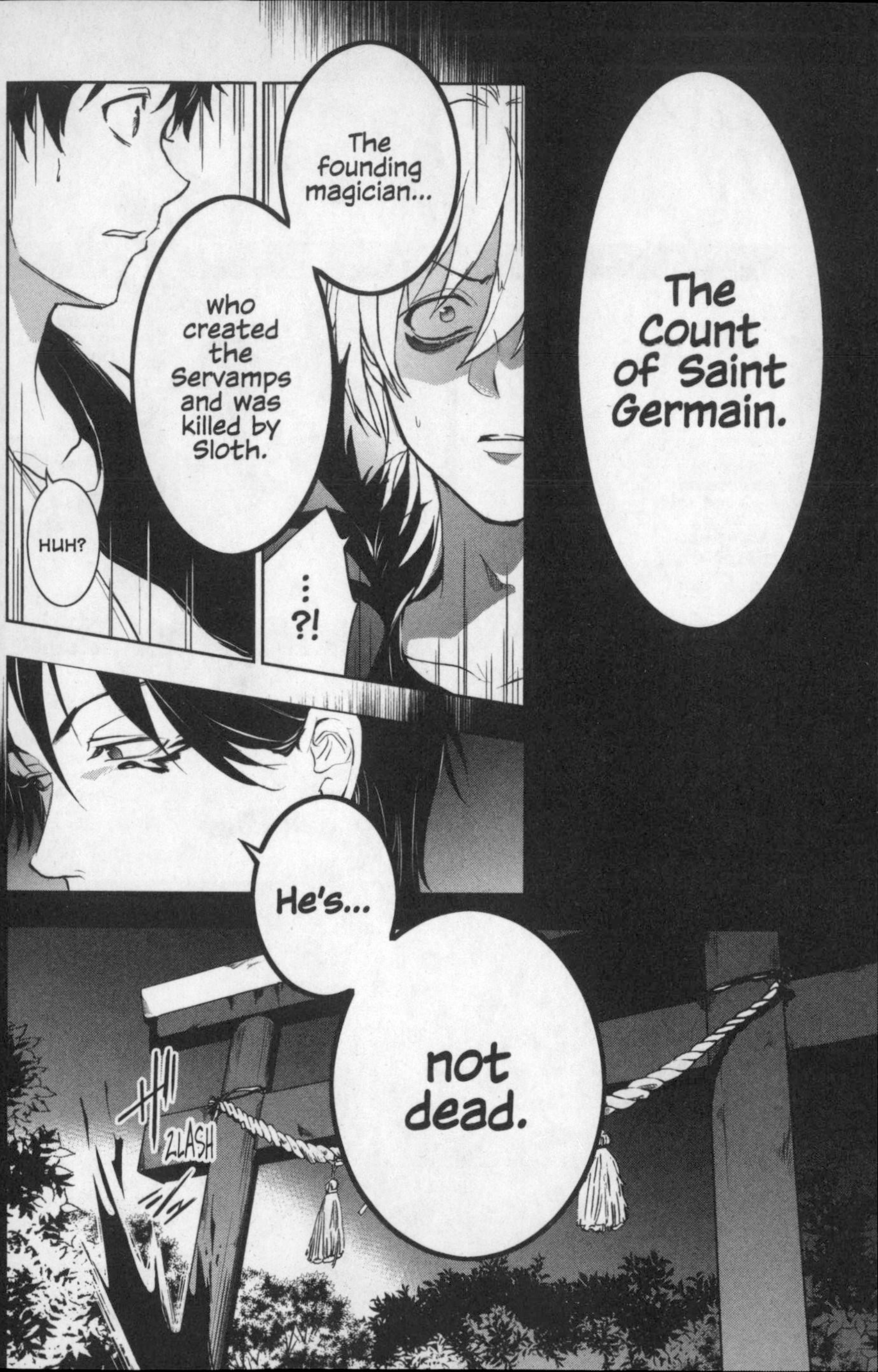
The Count of Saint Germain.
The founding magician...
who created the Servamps and was killed by Sloth.
...?!
HUH?
He's...
not dead.
ZLASH

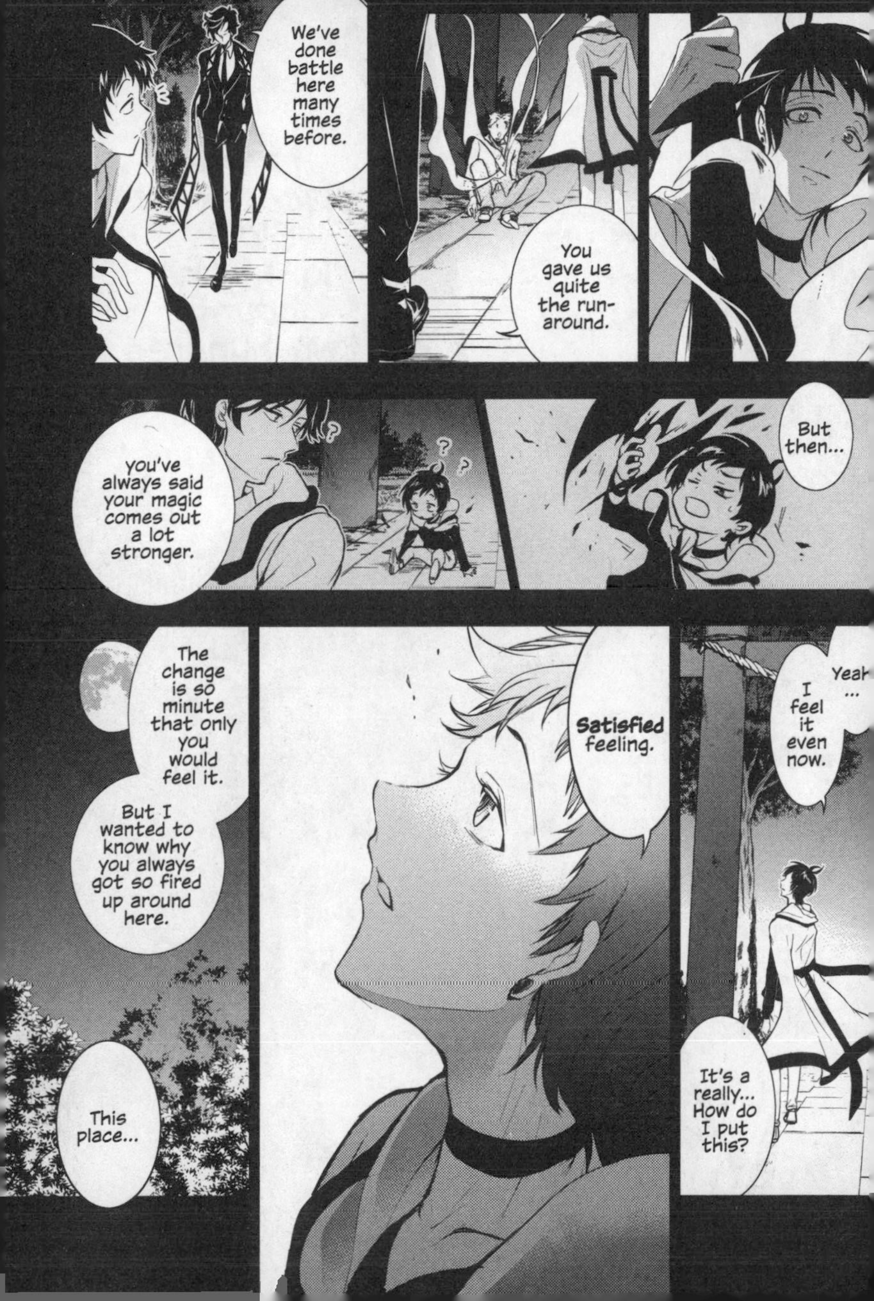
You gave us quite the run-around.
We've done battle here many times before.
But then...
you've always said your magic comes out a lot stronger.
Yeah... I feel it even now.
It's a really... How do I put this?
Satisfied feeling.
The change is so minute that only you would feel it.
But I wanted to know why you always got so fired up around here.
This place...

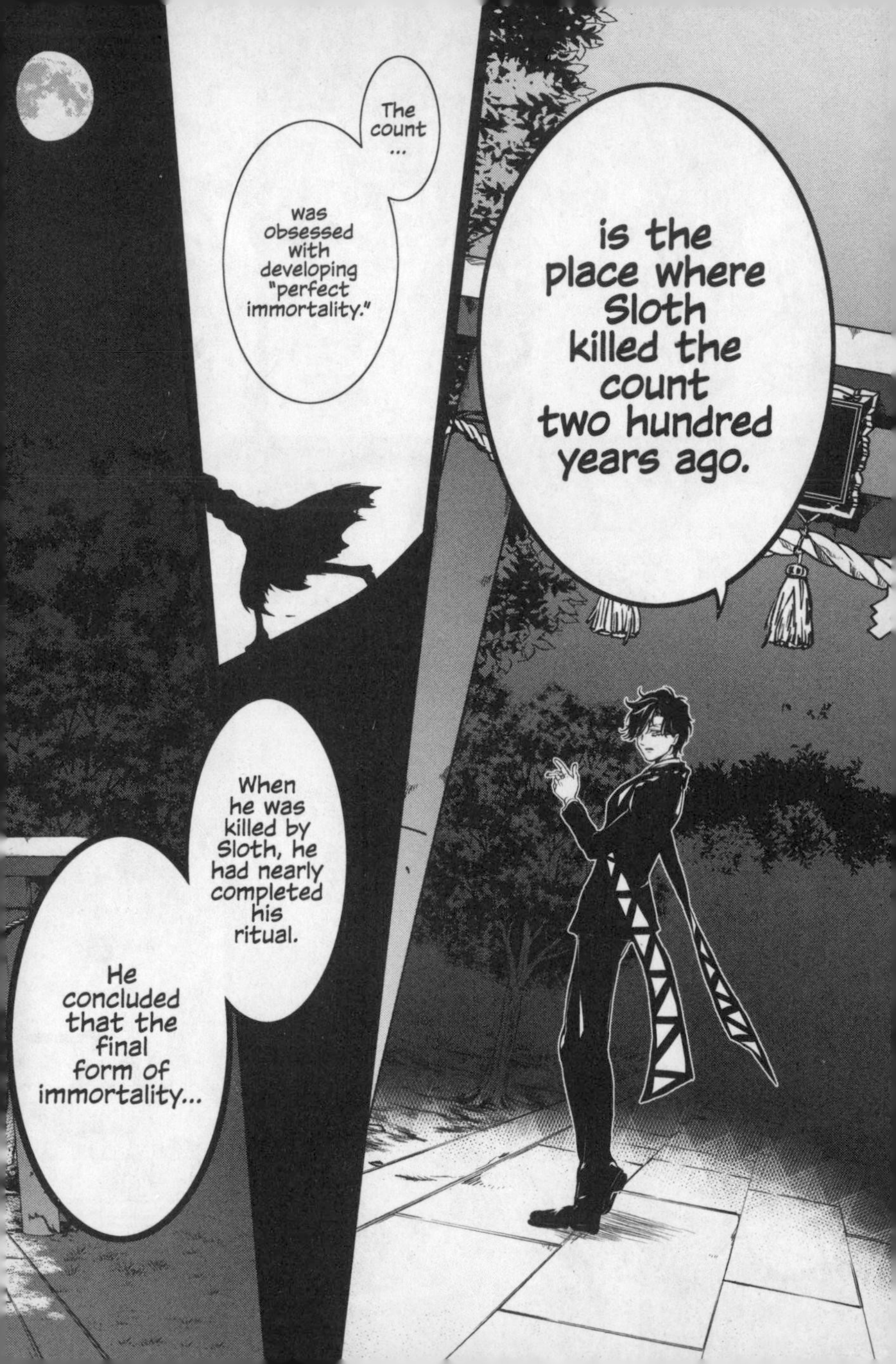
is the place where Sloth killed the count two hundred years ago.
The count...
was obsessed with developing "perfect immortality."
When he was killed by Sloth, he had nearly completed his ritual.
He concluded that the final form of immortality...

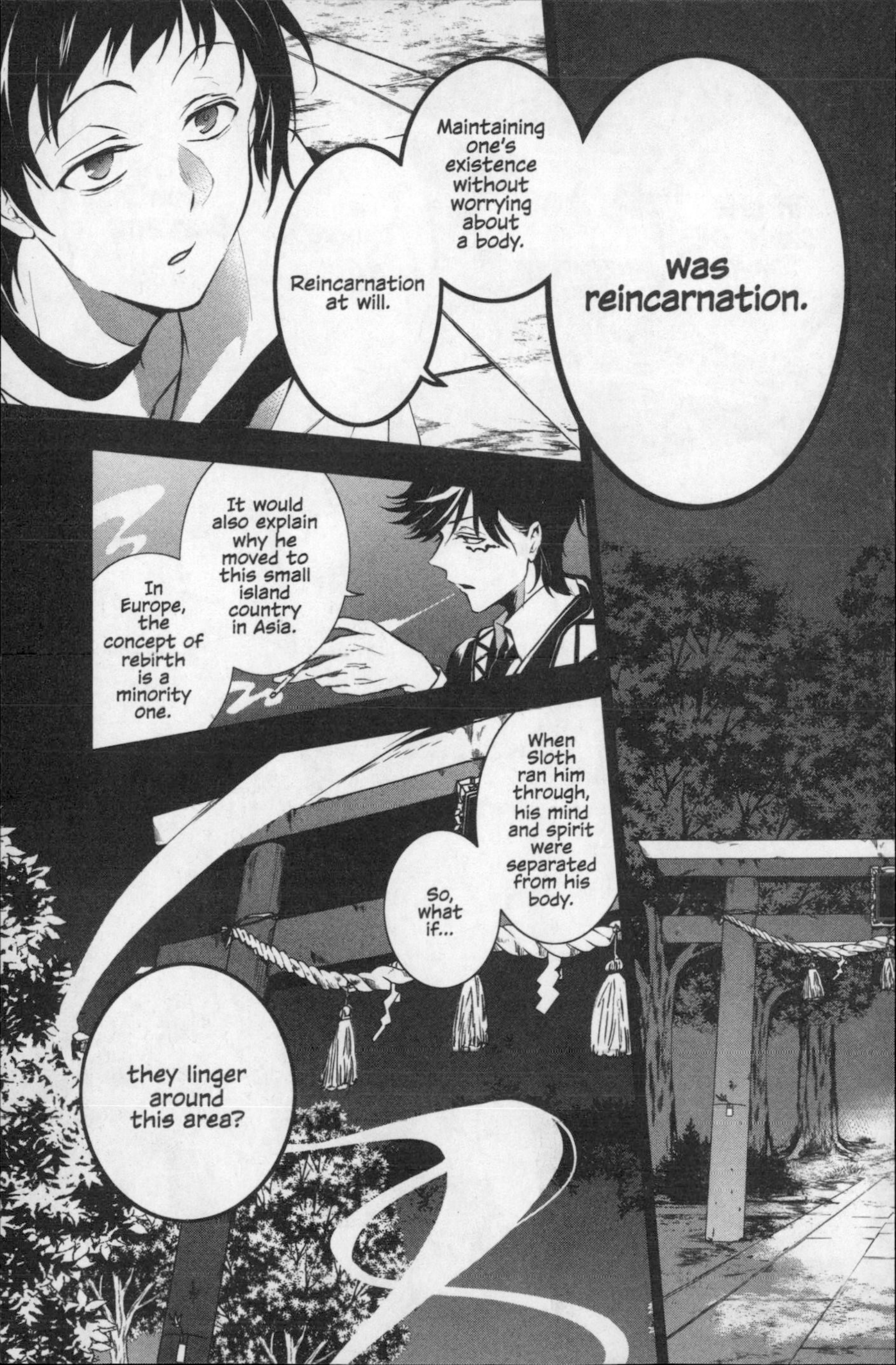
was reincarnation.
Maintaining one's existence without worrying about a body.
Reincarnation at will.
It would also explain why he moved to this small island country in Asia.
In Europe, the concept of rebirth is a minority one.
When Sloth ran him through, his mind and spirit were separated from his body.
So, what if...
they linger around this area?

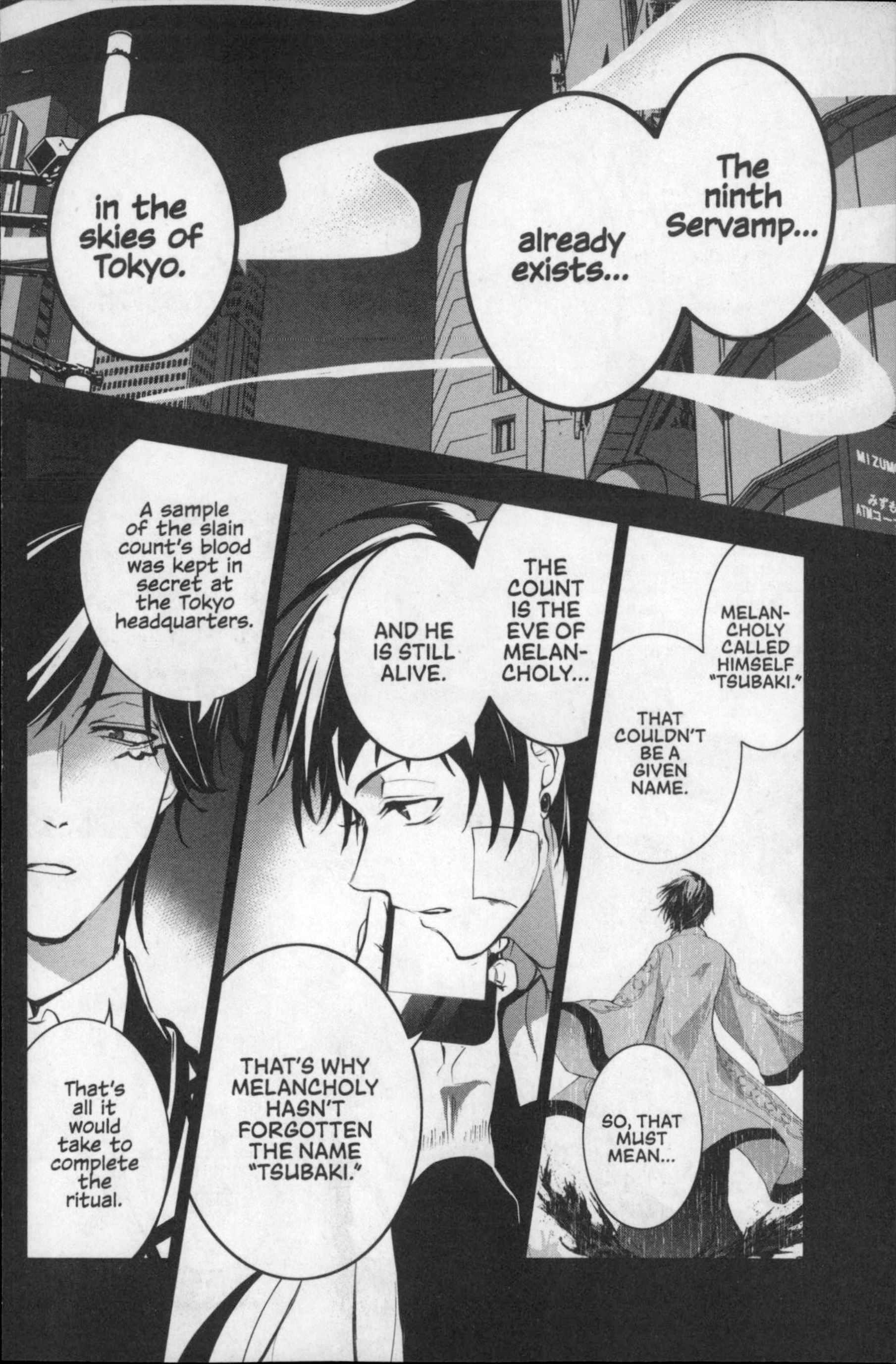
The ninth Servamp...
already exists...
in the skies of Tokyo.
MELANCHOLY CALLED HIMSELF "TSUBAKI."
THAT COULDN'T BE A GIVEN NAME.
SO, THAT MUST MEAN...
THE COUNT IS THE EVE OF MELANCHOLY...
AND HE IS STILL ALIVE.
THAT'S WHY MELANCHOLY HASN'T FORGOTTEN THE NAME "TSUBAKI."
A sample of the slain count's blood was kept in secret at the Tokyo headquarters.
That's all it would take to complete the ritual.

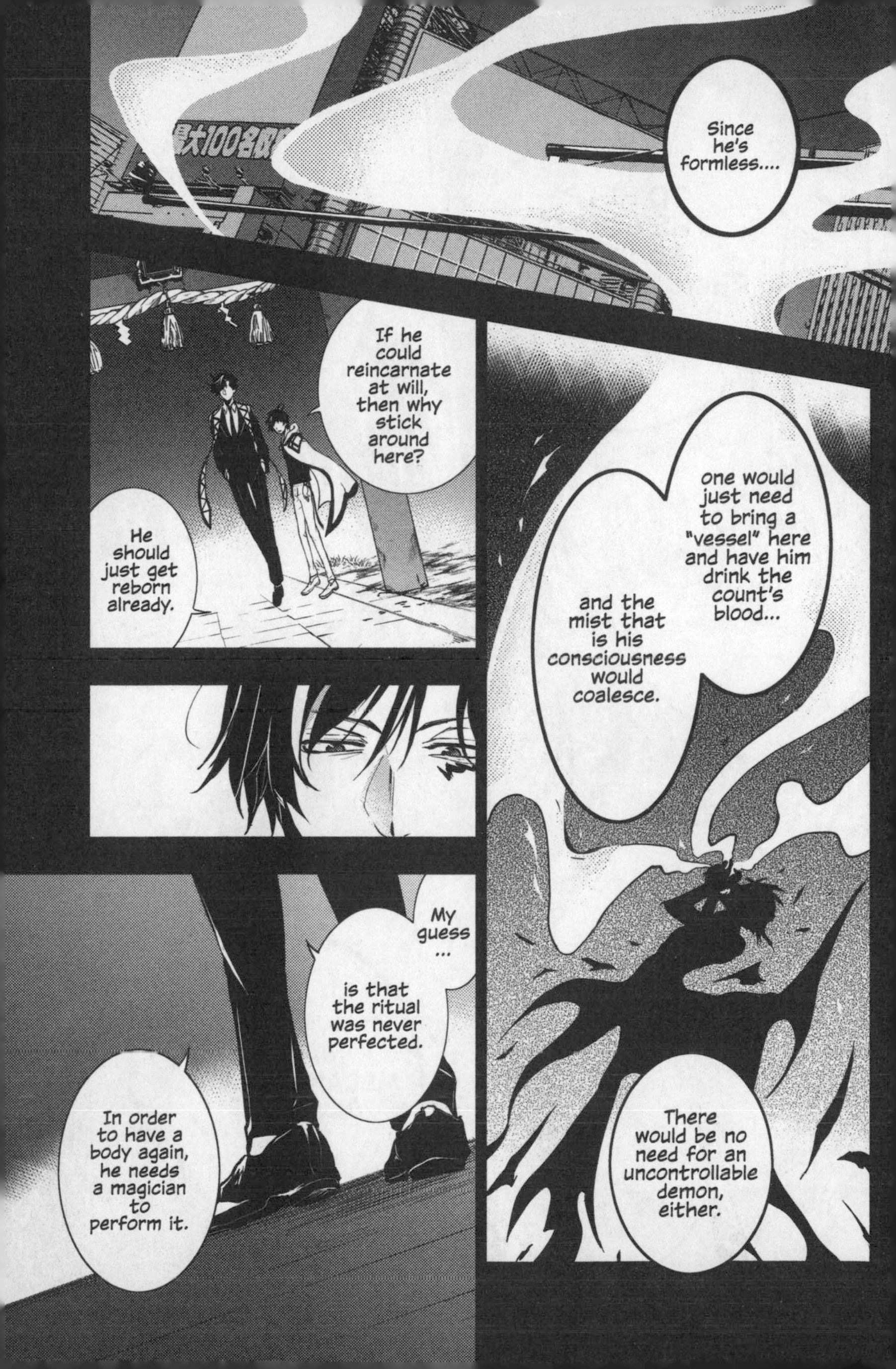

Since he's formless....
one would just need to bring a "vessel" here and have him drink the count's blood...
and the mist that is his consciousness would coalesce.
There would be no need for an uncontrollable demon, either.
If he could reincarnate at will, then why stick around here?
He should just get reborn already.
My guess ...
is that the ritual was never perfected.
In order to have a body again, he needs a magician to perform it.

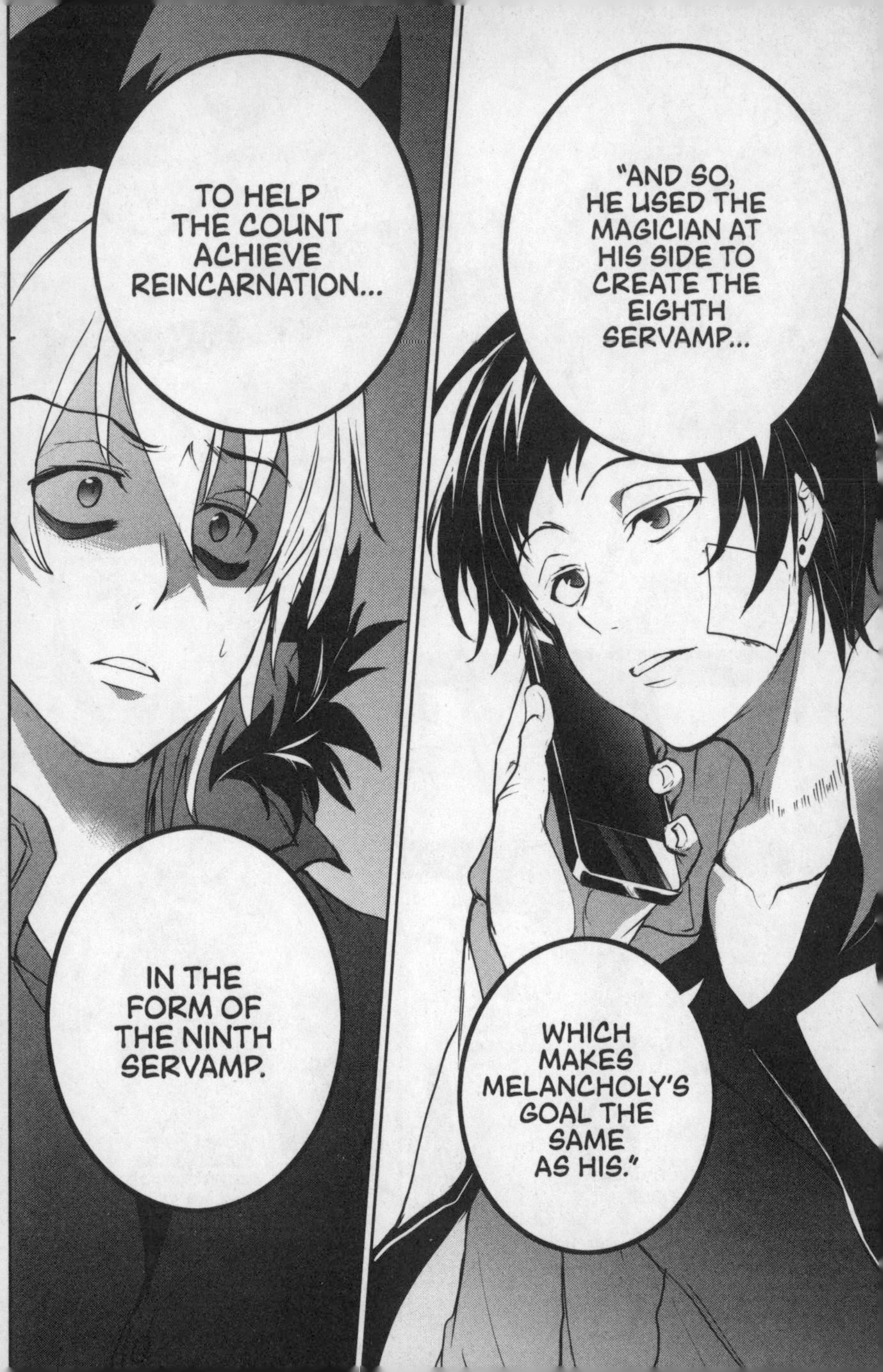
"AND SO, HE USED THE MAGICIAN AT HIS SIDE TO CREATE THE EIGHTH SERVAMP...
TO HELP THE COUNT ACHIEVE REINCARNATION...
IN THE FORM OF THE NINTH SERVAMP.
WHICH MAKES MELANCHOLY'S GOAL THE SAME AS HIS."

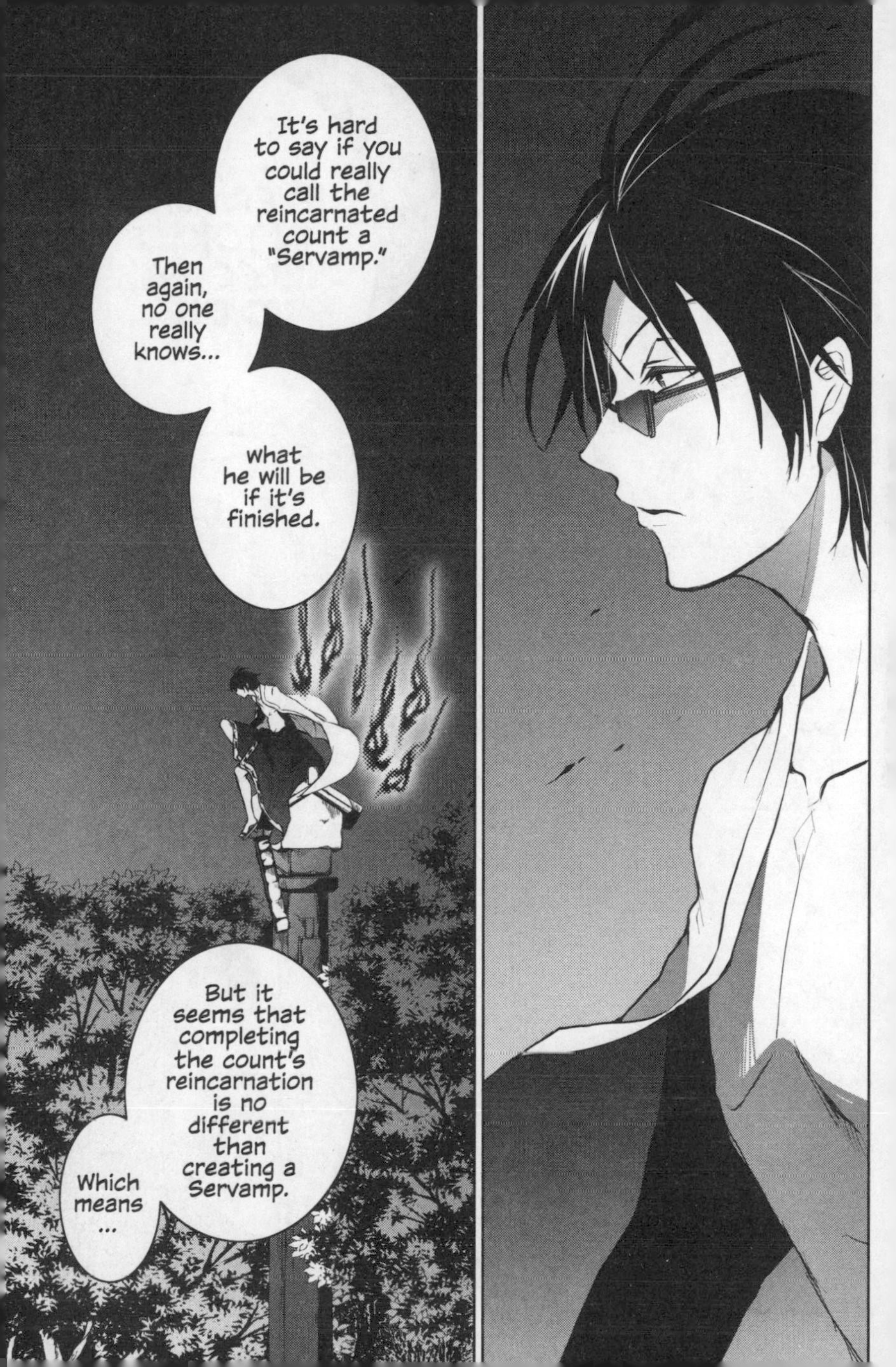
It's hard to say if you could really call the reincarnated count a "Servamp."
Then again, no one really knows...
what he will be if it's finished.
But it seems that completing the count's reincarnation is no different than creating a Servamp.
Which means ...

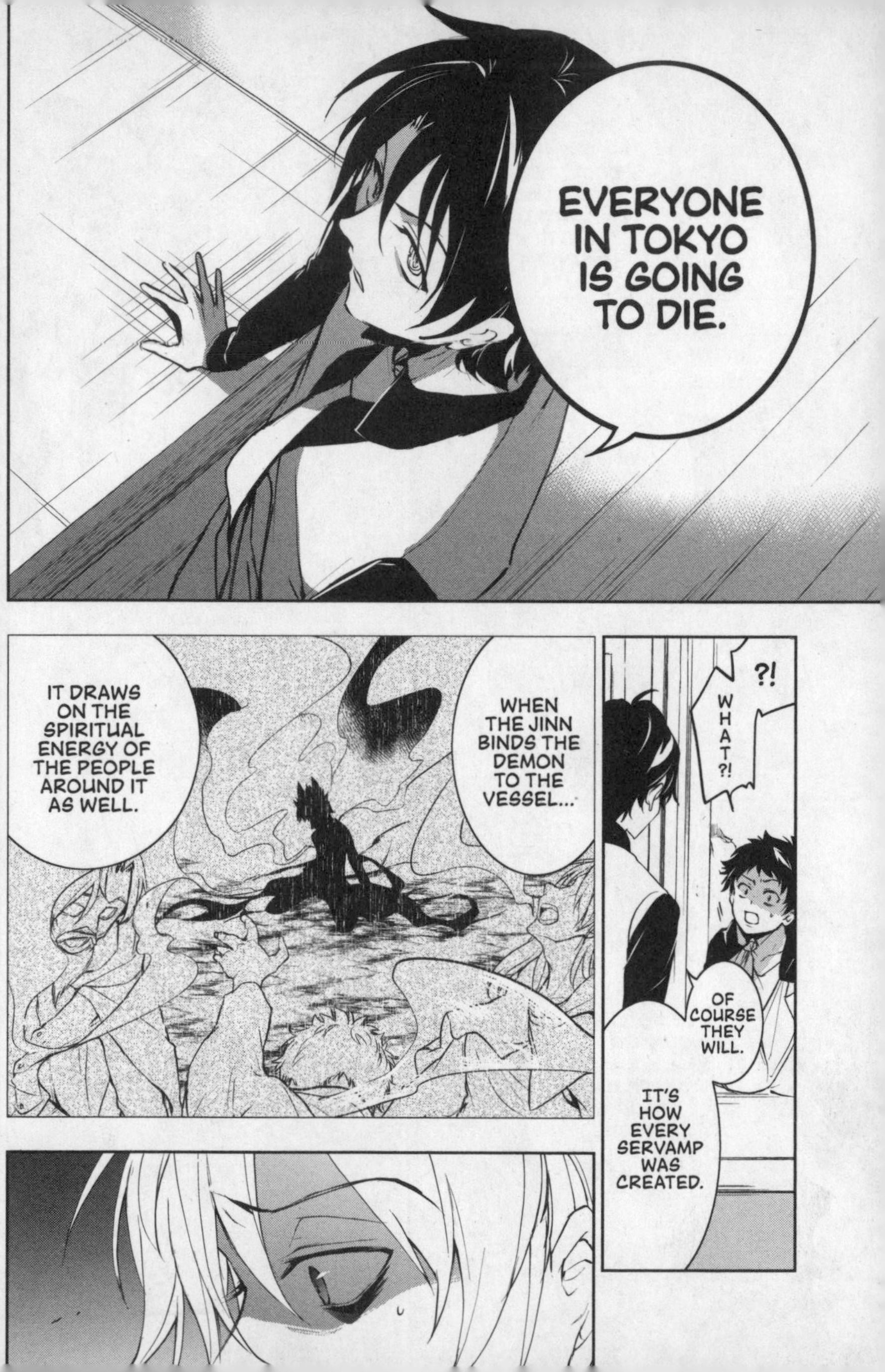
EVERYONE IN TOKYO IS GOING TO DIE.
?!
WHAT?!
OF COURSE THEY WILL.
IT'S HOW EVERY SERVAMP WAS CREATED.
WHEN THE JINN BINDS THE DEMON TO THE VESSEL...
IT DRAWS ON THE SPIRITUAL ENERGY OF THE PEOPLE AROUND IT AS WELL.

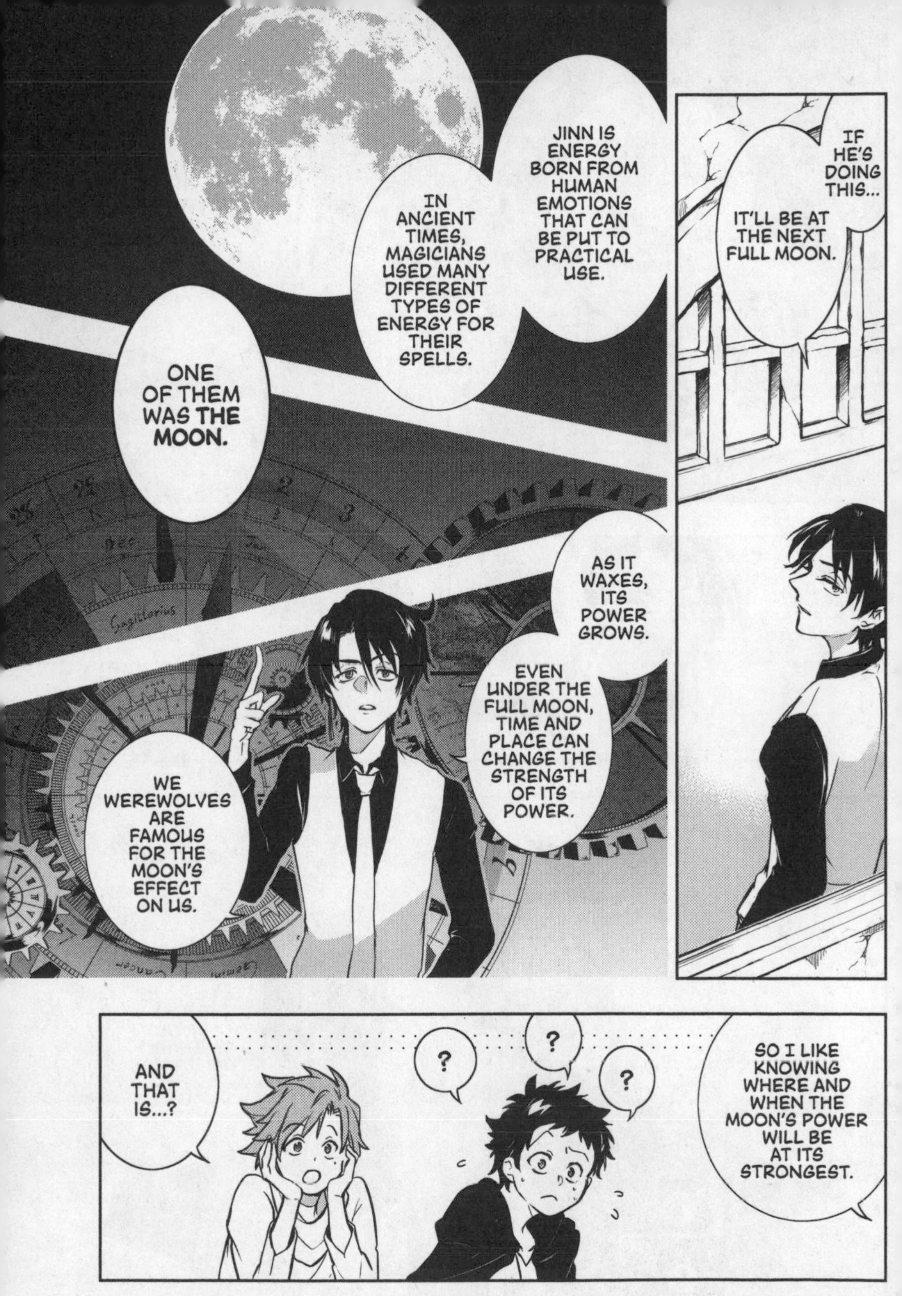
IF HE'S DOING THIS...
IT'LL BE AT THE NEXT FULL MOON.
JINN IS ENERGY BORN FROM HUMAN EMOTIONS THAT CAN BE PUT TO PRACTICAL USE.
IN ANCIENT TIMES, MAGICIANS USED MANY DIFFERENT TYPES OF ENERGY FOR THEIR SPELLS.
ONE OF THEM WAS THE MOON.
AS IT WAXES, ITS POWER GROWS.
EVEN UNDER THE FULL MOON, TIME AND PLACE CAN CHANGE THE STRENGTH OF ITS POWER.
WE WEREWOLVES ARE FAMOUS FOR THE MOON'S EFFECT ON US.
SO I LIKE KNOWING WHERE AND WHEN THE MOON'S POWER WILL BE AT ITS STRONGEST.
?
?
?
AND THAT IS...?

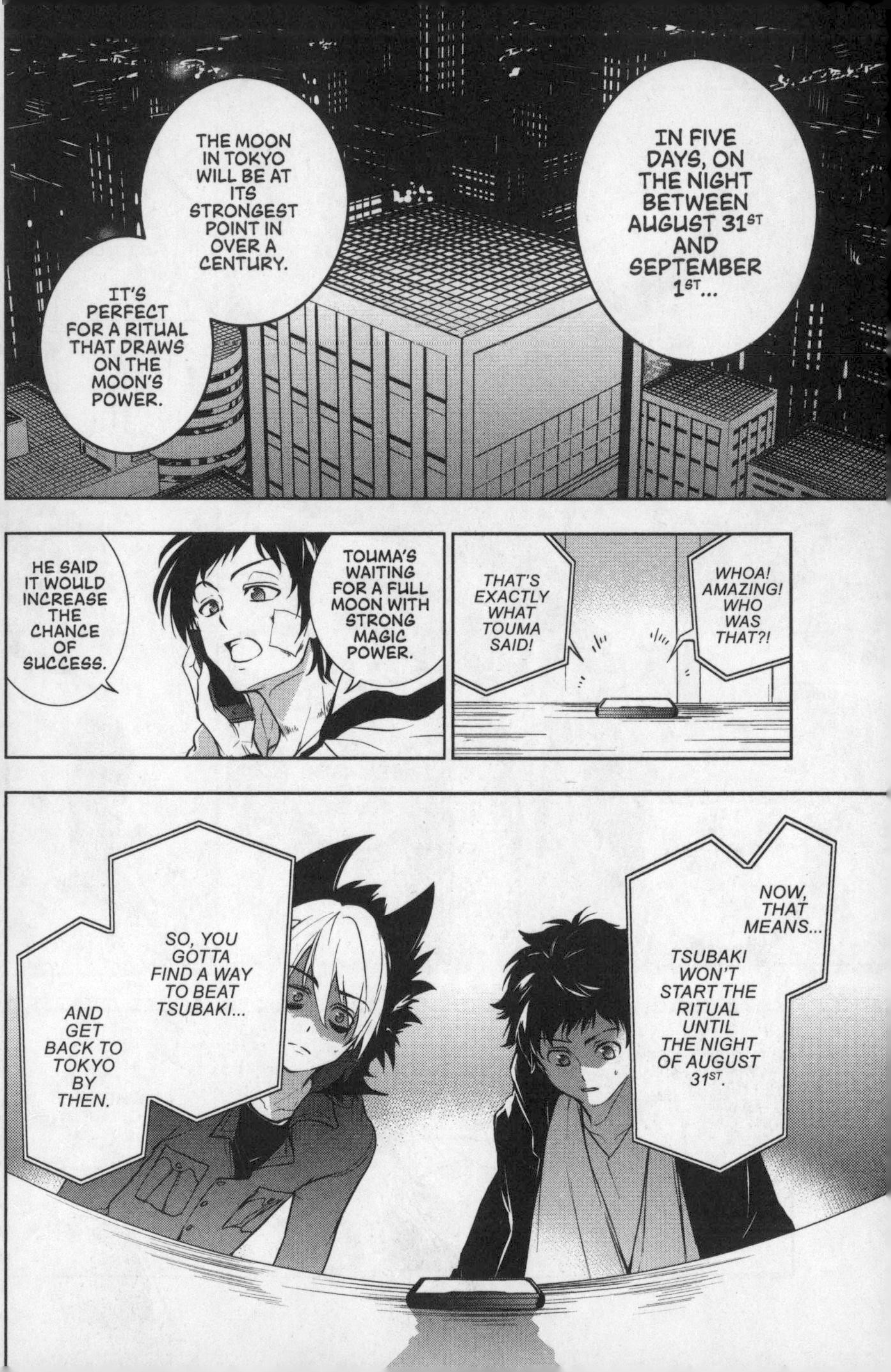
IN FIVE DAYS, ON THE NIGHT BETWEEN AUGUST 31ST AND SEPTEMBER 1ST...
THE MOON IN TOKYO WILL BE AT ITS STRONGEST POINT IN OVER A CENTURY.
IT'S PERFECT FOR A RITUAL THAT DRAWS ON THE MOON'S POWER.
WHOA! AMAZING! WHO WAS THAT?!
THAT'S EXACTLY WHAT TOUMA SAID!
TOUMA'S WAITING FOR A FULL MOON WITH STRONG MAGIC POWER.
HE SAID IT WOULD INCREASE THE CHANCE OF SUCCESS.
NOW, THAT MEANS...
TSUBAKI WON'T START THE RITUAL UNTIL THE NIGHT OF AUGUST 31ST.
SO, YOU GOTTA FIND A WAY TO BEAT TSUBAKI...
AND GET BACK TO TOKYO BY THEN.

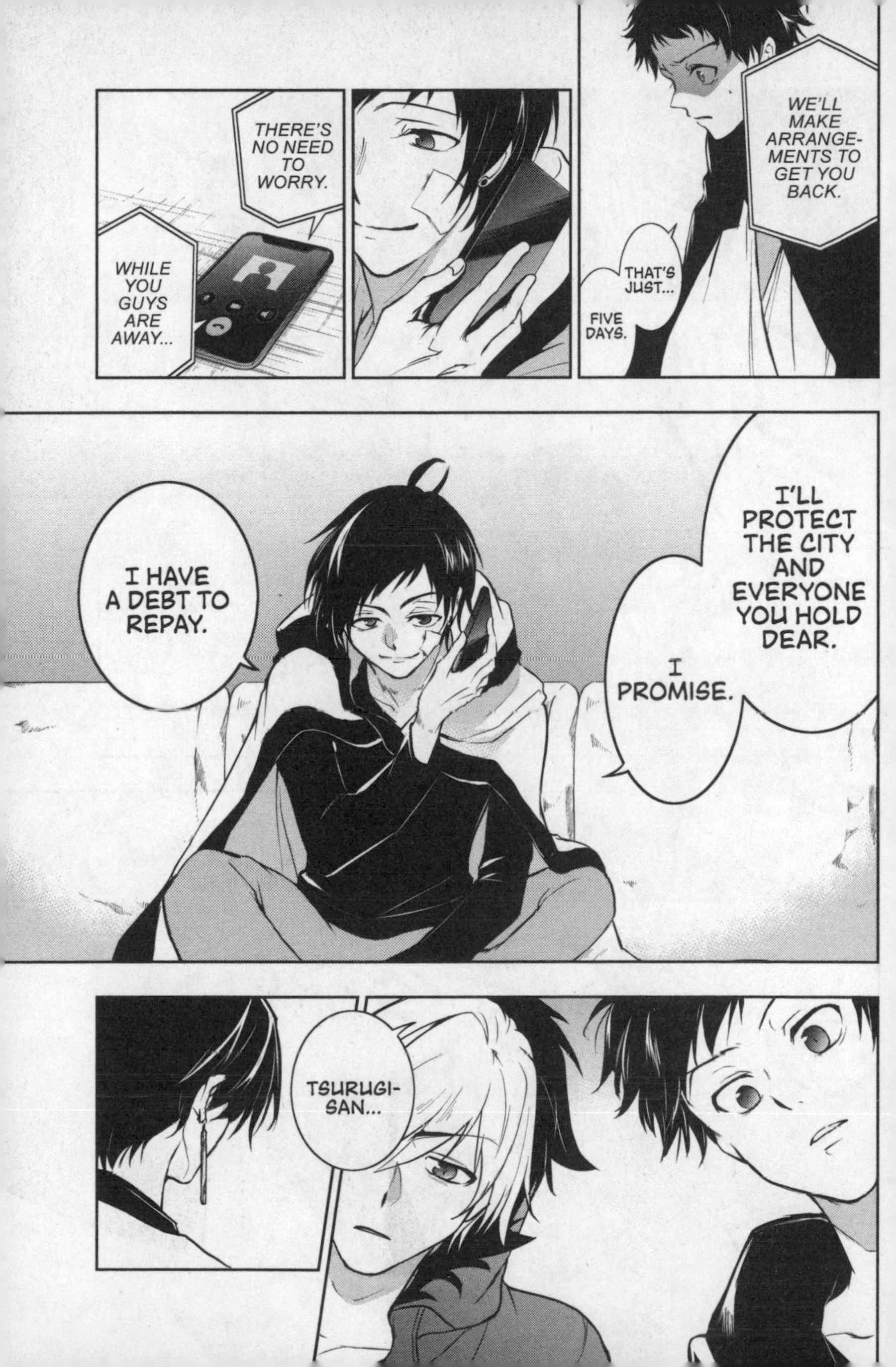
WE'LL MAKE ARRANGE-MENTS TO GET YOU BACK.
THAT'S JUST...
FIVE DAYS.
THERE'S NO NEED TO WORRY.
WHILE YOU GUYS ARE AWAY...
I'LL PROTECT THE CITY AND EVERYONE YOU HOLD DEAR.
I PROMISE.
I HAVE A DEBT TO REPAY.
TSURUGI-SAN...

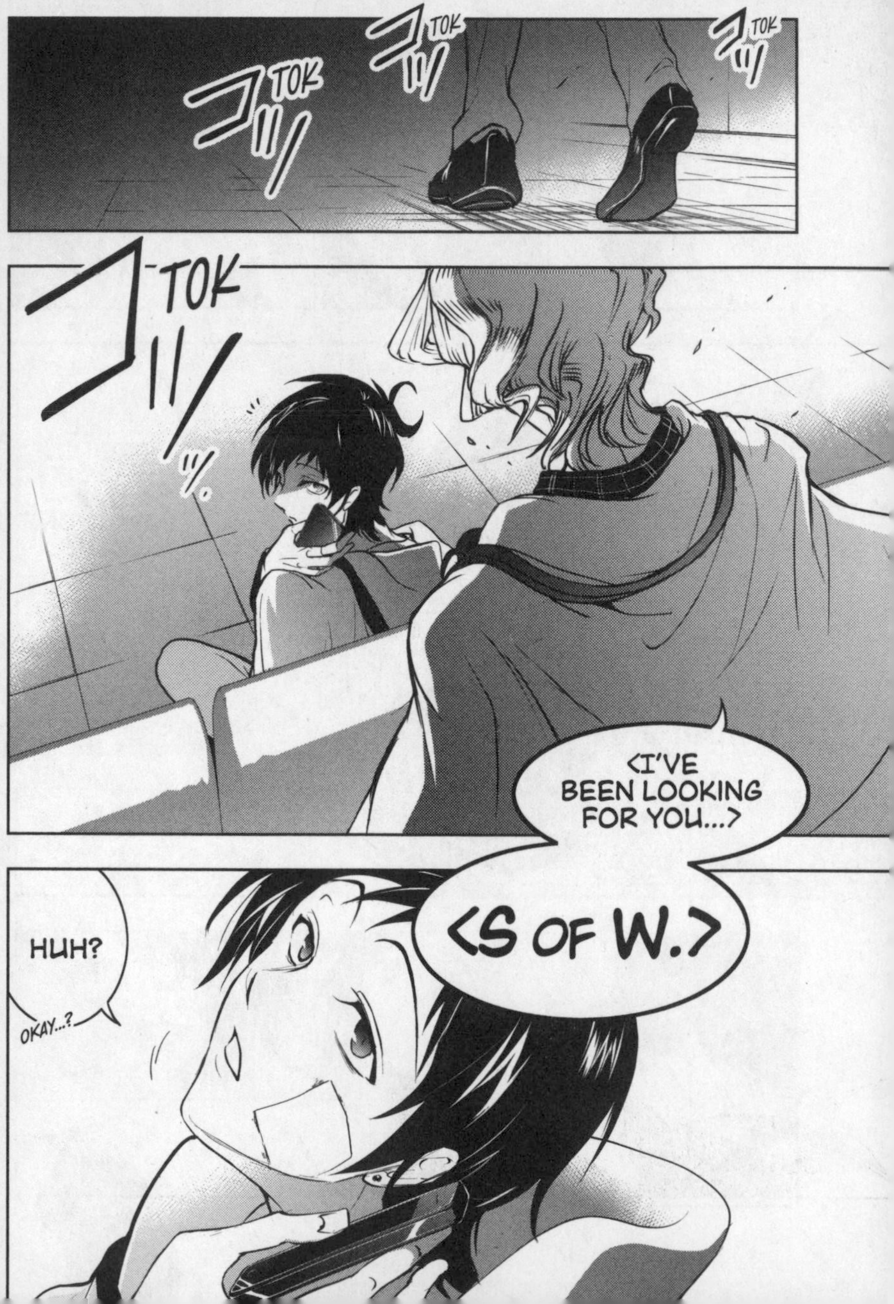
TOK
TOK
TOK
TOK
<I'VE BEEN LOOKING FOR YOU...>
<S OF W.>
HUH?
OKAY...?

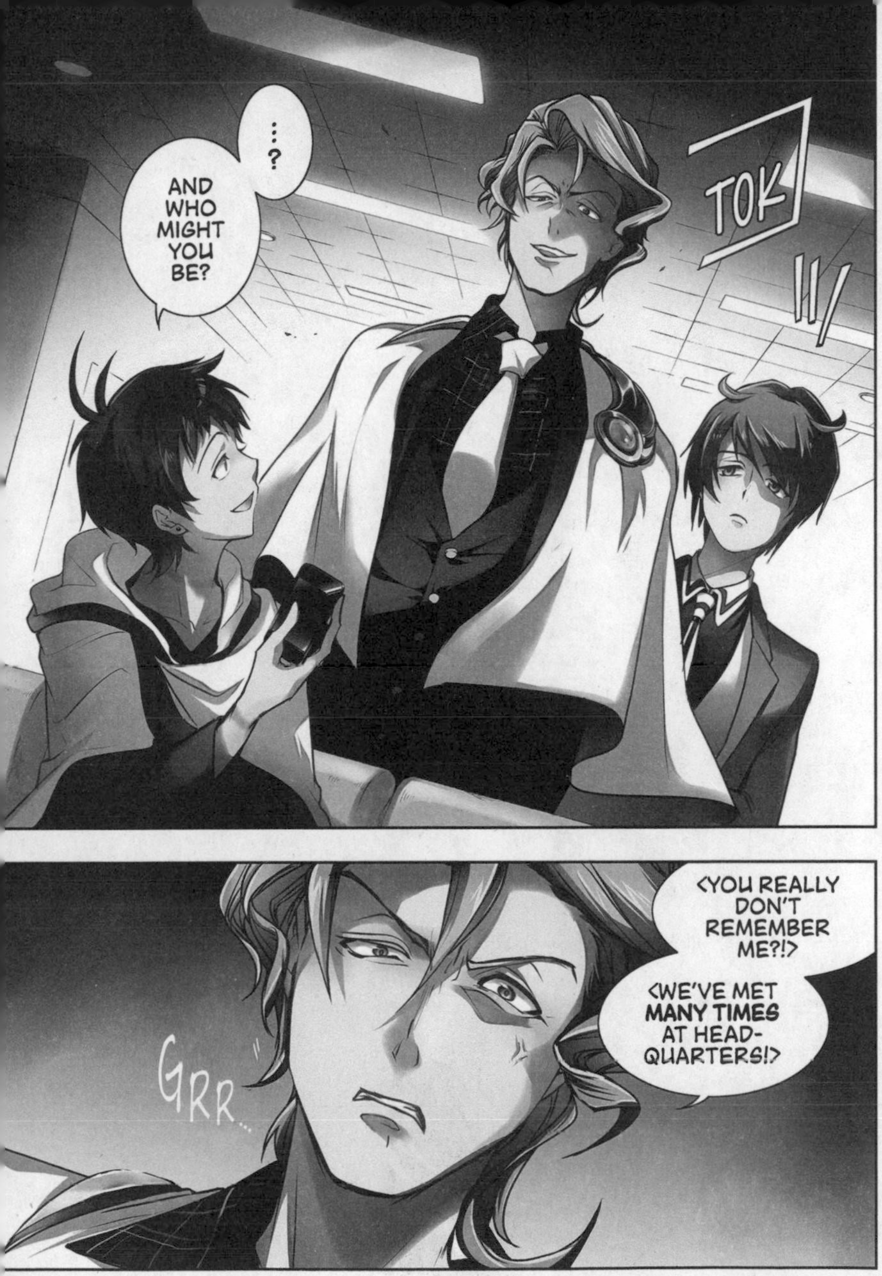
...?
AND WHO MIGHT YOU BE?
TOK
<YOU REALLY DON'T REMEMBER ME?!>
<WE'VE MET **MANY TIMES** AT HEAD-QUARTERS!>
GRR...

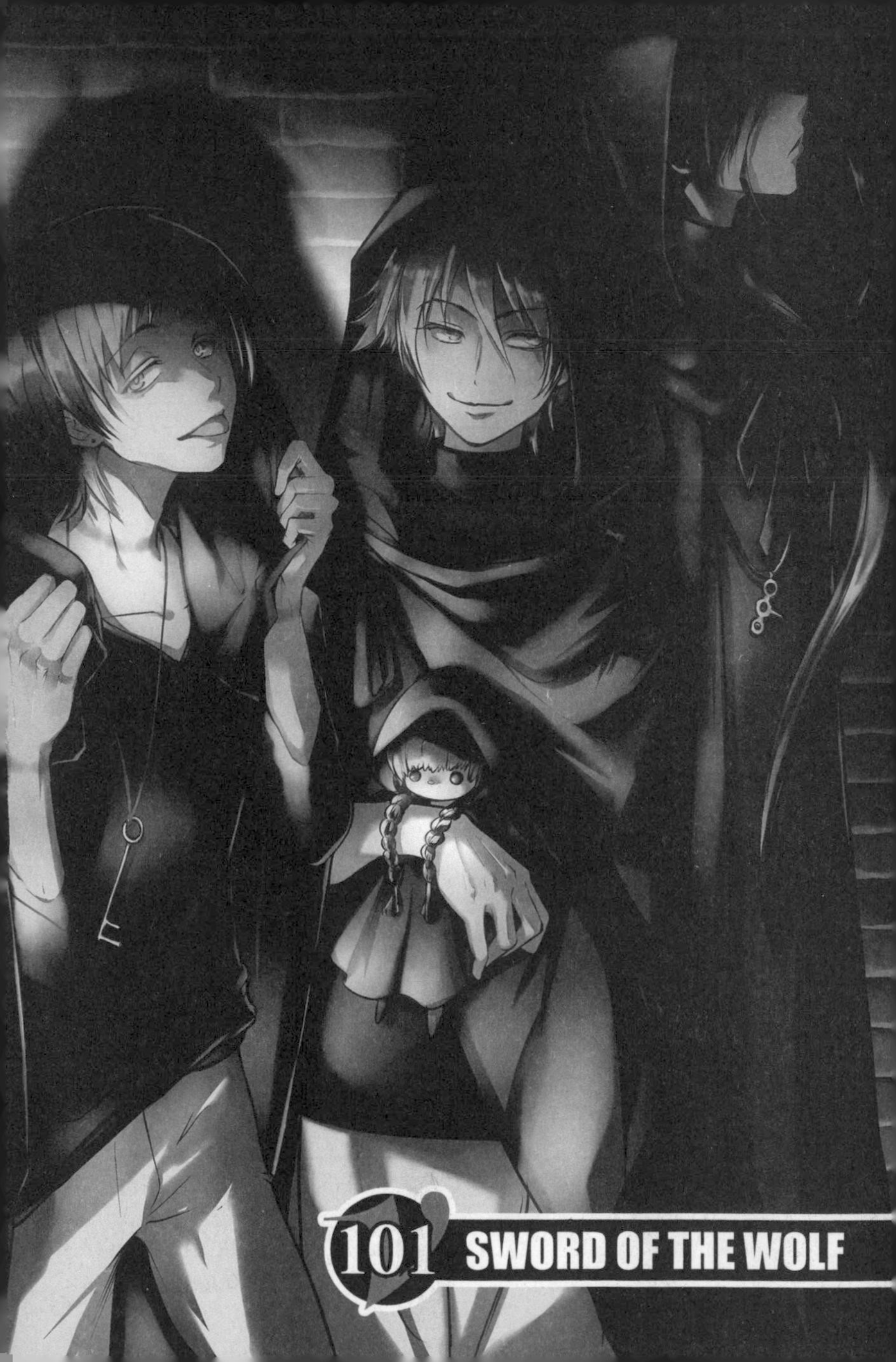
101
SWORD OF THE WOLF

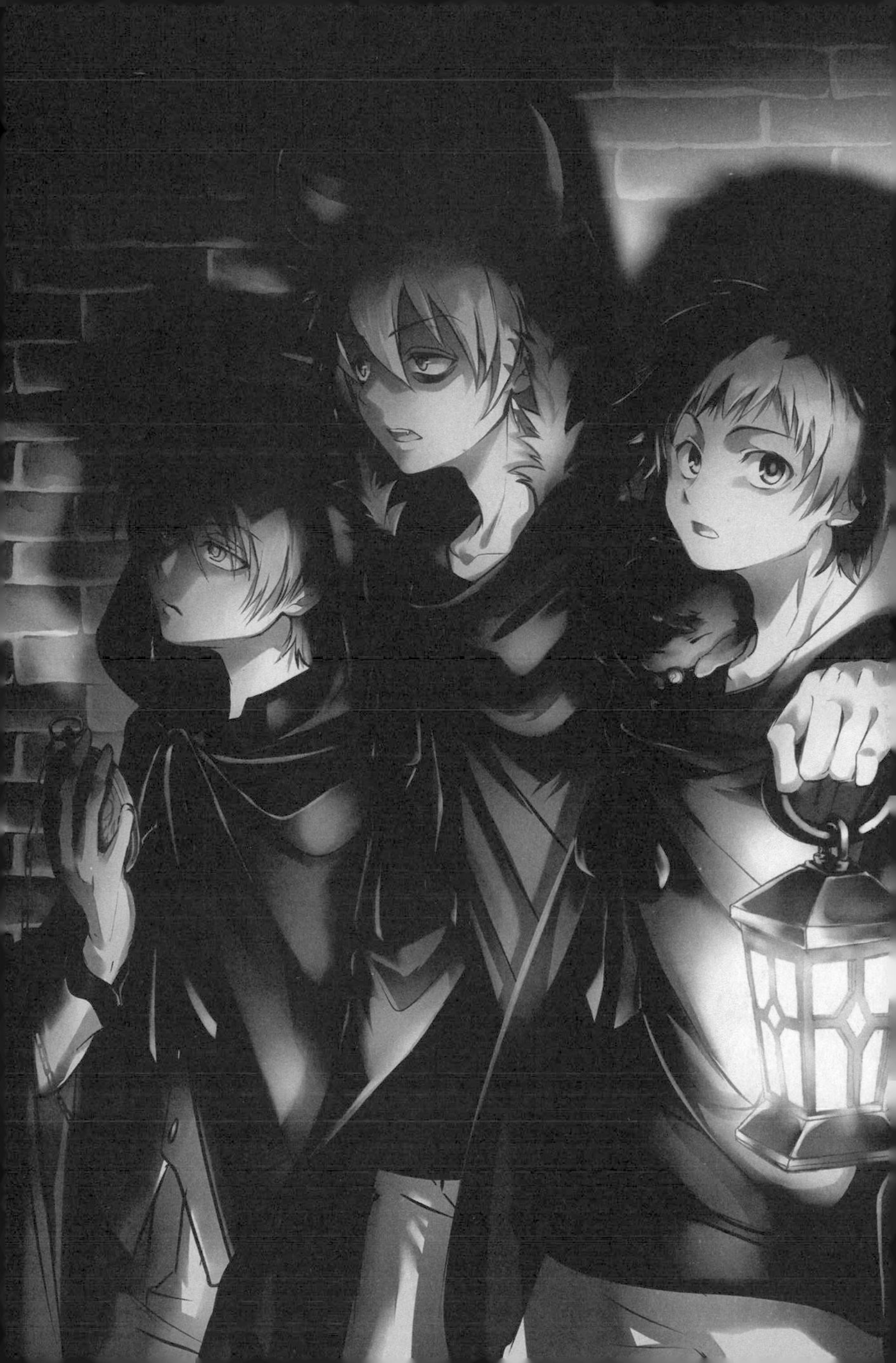

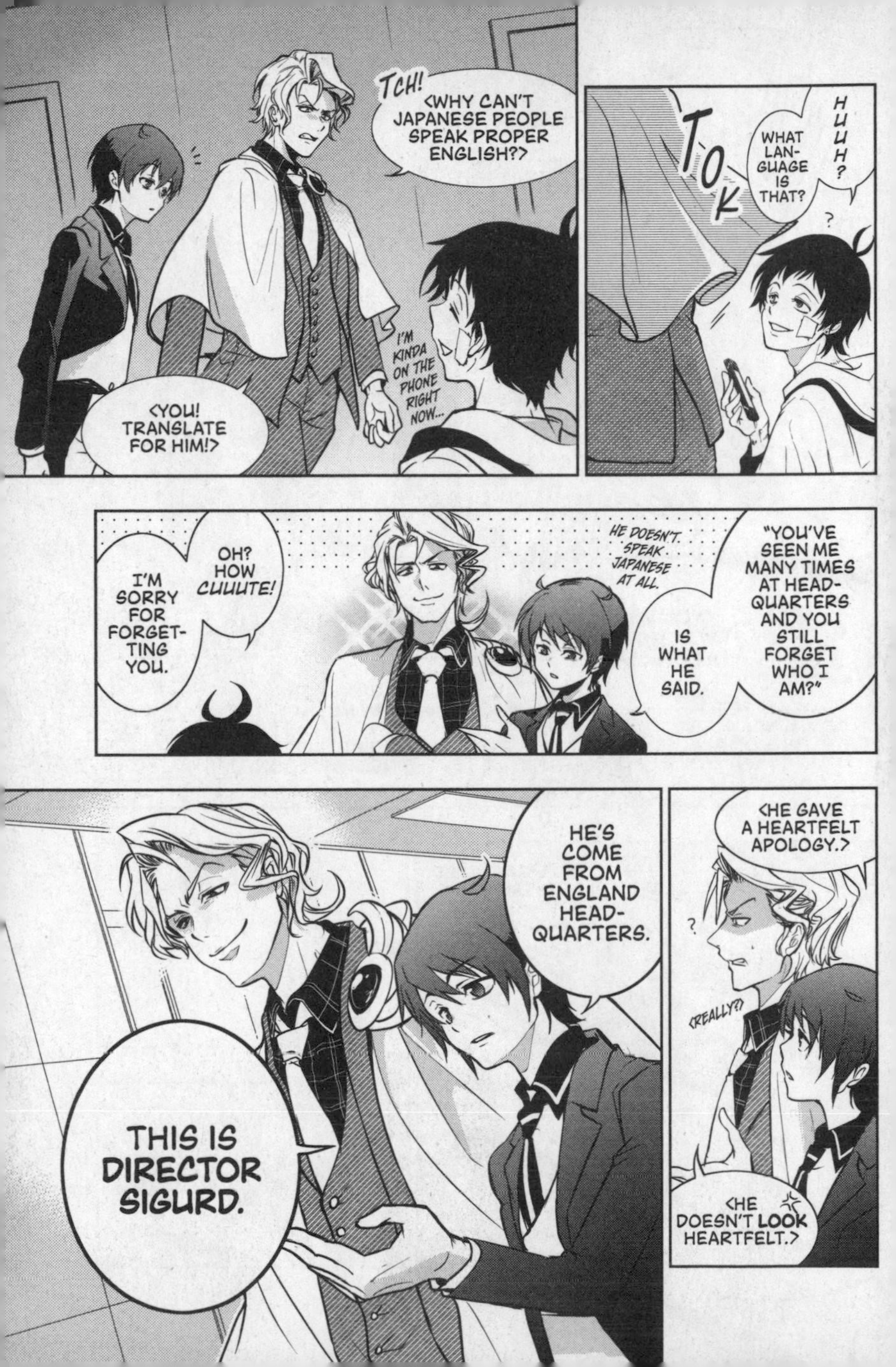
HUUUH?
WHAT LAN-GUAGE IS THAT?
TOK
?
I'M KINDA ON THE PHONE RIGHT NOW...
TCH!
<WHY CAN'T JAPANESE PEOPLE SPEAK PROPER ENGLISH?>
<YOU! TRANSLATE FOR HIM!>
"YOU'VE SEEN ME MANY TIMES AT HEAD-QUARTERS AND YOU STILL FORGET WHO I AM?"
IS WHAT HE SAID.
HE DOESN'T SPEAK JAPANESE AT ALL.
OH? HOW CUUUTE!
I'M SORRY FOR FORGET-TING YOU.
<HE GAVE A HEARTFELT APOLOGY.>
?
<REALLY?>
<HE DOESN'T **LOOK** HEARTFELT.>
HE'S COME FROM ENGLAND HEAD-QUARTERS.
THIS IS DIRECTOR SIGURD.

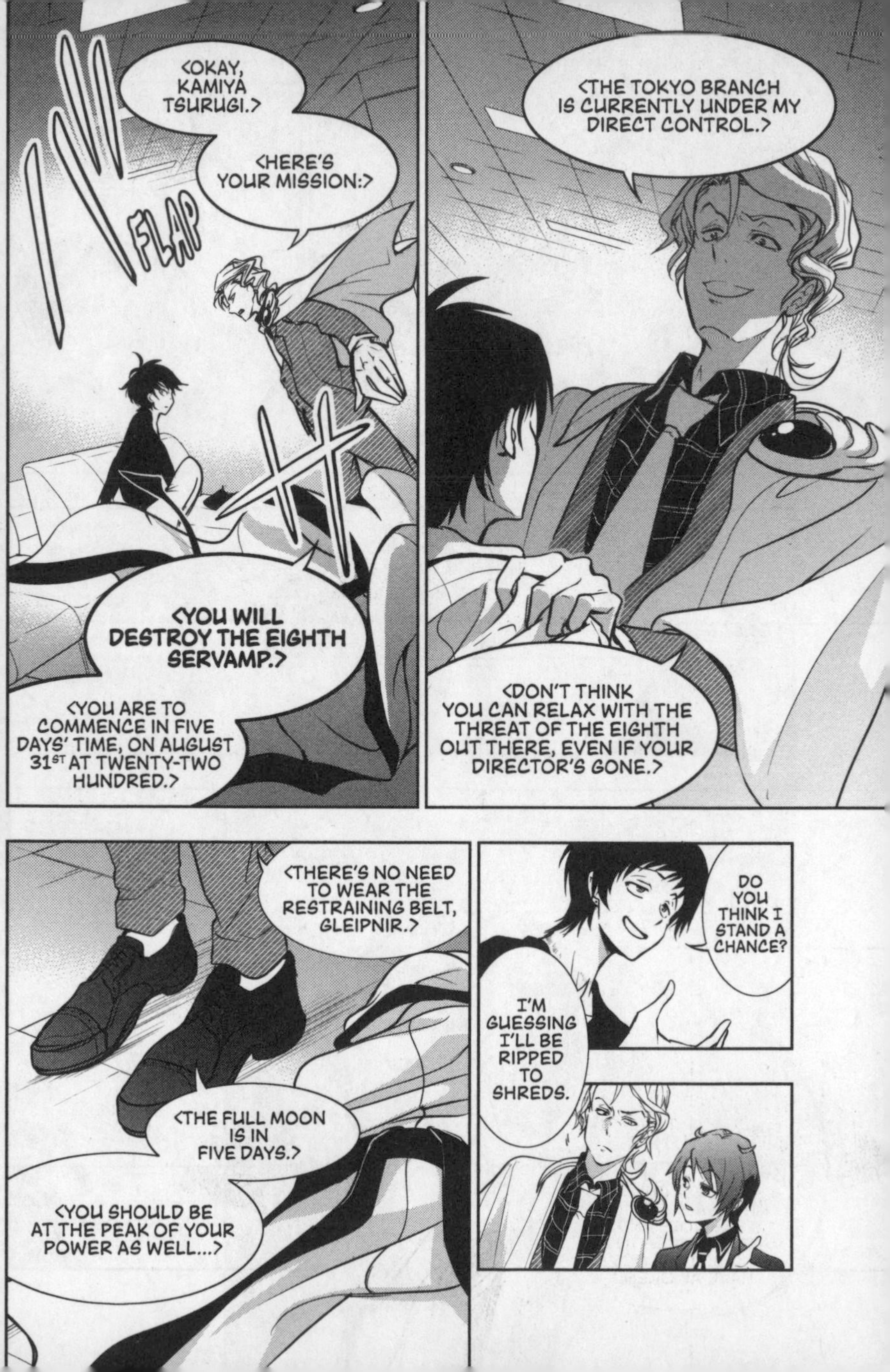
<THE TOKYO BRANCH IS CURRENTLY UNDER MY DIRECT CONTROL.>
<DON'T THINK YOU CAN RELAX WITH THE THREAT OF THE EIGHTH OUT THERE, EVEN IF YOUR DIRECTOR'S GONE.>
<OKAY, KAMIYA TSURUGI.>
<HERE'S YOUR MISSION:>
FLAP
<YOU WILL DESTROY THE EIGHTH SERVAMP.>
<YOU ARE TO COMMENCE IN FIVE DAYS' TIME, ON AUGUST 31ST AT TWENTY-TWO HUNDRED.>
DO YOU THINK I STAND A CHANCE?
I'M GUESSING I'LL BE RIPPED TO SHREDS.
<THERE'S NO NEED TO WEAR THE RESTRAINING BELT, GLEIPNIR.>
<THE FULL MOON IS IN FIVE DAYS.>
<YOU SHOULD BE AT THE PEAK OF YOUR POWER AS WELL...>

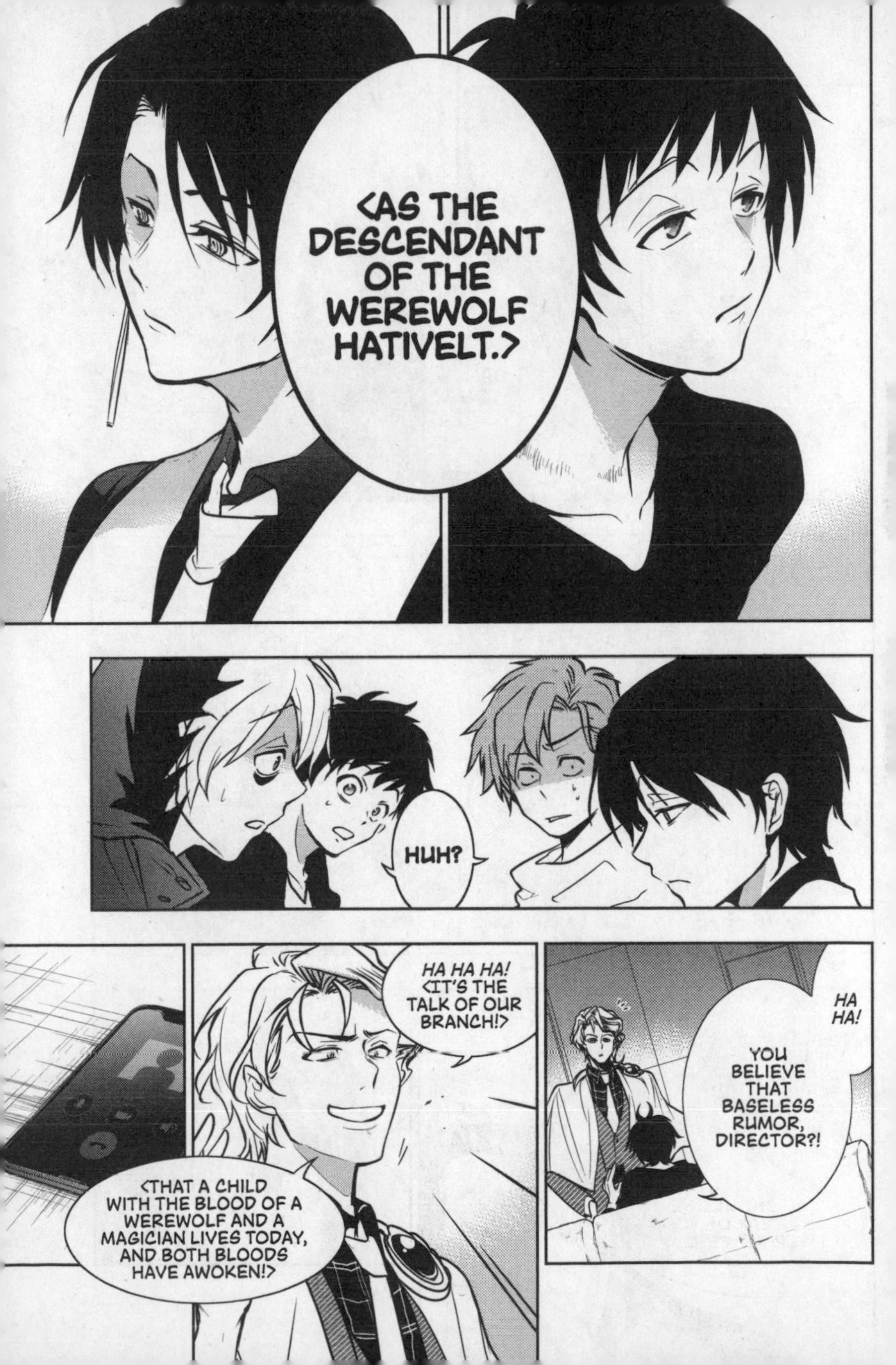
<AS THE DESCENDANT OF THE WEREWOLF HATIVELT.>
HUH?
HA HA!
YOU BELIEVE THAT BASELESS RUMOR, DIRECTOR?!
HA HA HA! <IT'S THE TALK OF OUR BRANCH!>
<THAT A CHILD WITH THE BLOOD OF A WEREWOLF AND A MAGICIAN LIVES TODAY, AND BOTH BLOODS HAVE AWOKEN!>

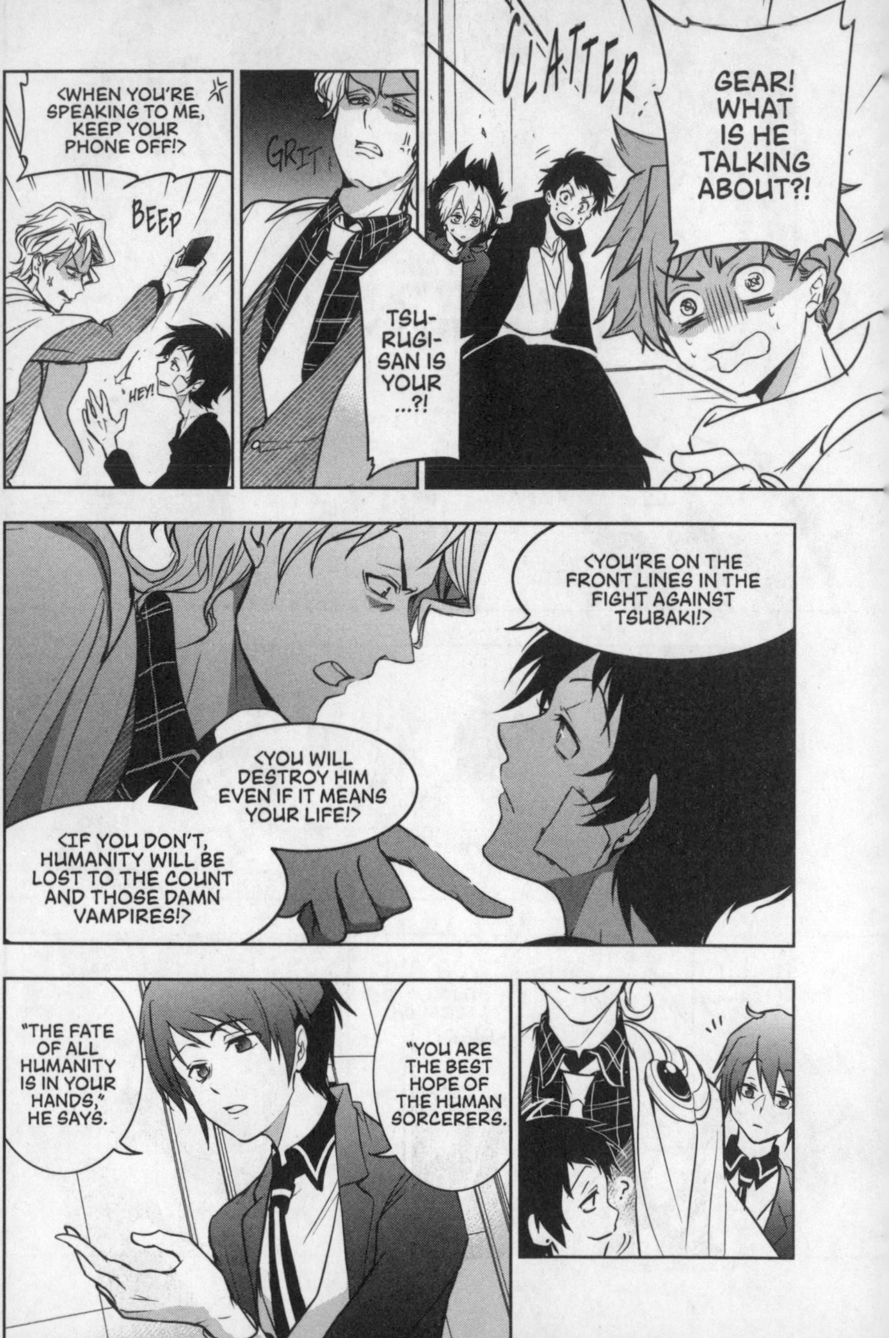
<WHEN YOU'RE SPEAKING TO ME, KEEP YOUR PHONE OFF!>
BEEP
HEY!
GRIT
TSU-RUGI-SAN IS YOUR ...?!
CLATTER
GEAR! WHAT IS HE TALKING ABOUT?!
<YOU'RE ON THE FRONT LINES IN THE FIGHT AGAINST TSUBAKI!>
<YOU WILL DESTROY HIM EVEN IF IT MEANS YOUR LIFE!>
<IF YOU DON'T, HUMANITY WILL BE LOST TO THE COUNT AND THOSE DAMN VAMPIRES!>
"YOU ARE THE BEST HOPE OF THE HUMAN SORCERERS.
"THE FATE OF ALL HUMANITY IS IN YOUR HANDS," HE SAYS.
?

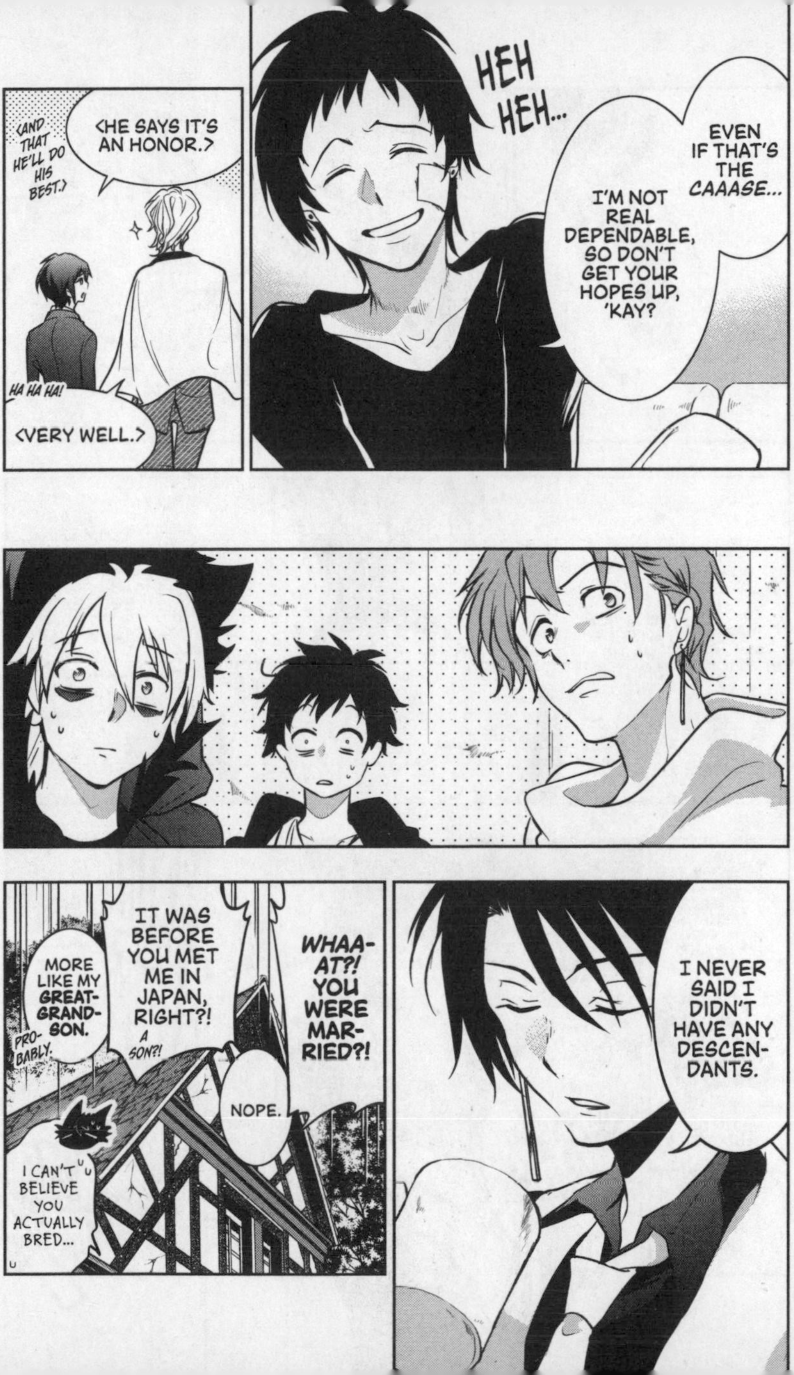
HEH HEH...
EVEN IF THAT'S THE CAAASE...
I'M NOT REAL DEPENDABLE, SO DON'T GET YOUR HOPES UP, 'KAY?
<HE SAYS IT'S AN HONOR.>
<AND THAT HE'LL DO HIS BEST.>
HA HA HA!
<VERY WELL.>
I NEVER SAID I DIDN'T HAVE ANY DESCENDANTS.
WHAAAT?! YOU WERE MARRIED?!
NOPE.
IT WAS BEFORE YOU MET ME IN JAPAN, RIGHT?!
A SON?!
MORE LIKE MY GREAT-GRANDSON.
PROBABLY.
I CAN'T BELIEVE YOU ACTUALLY BRED...

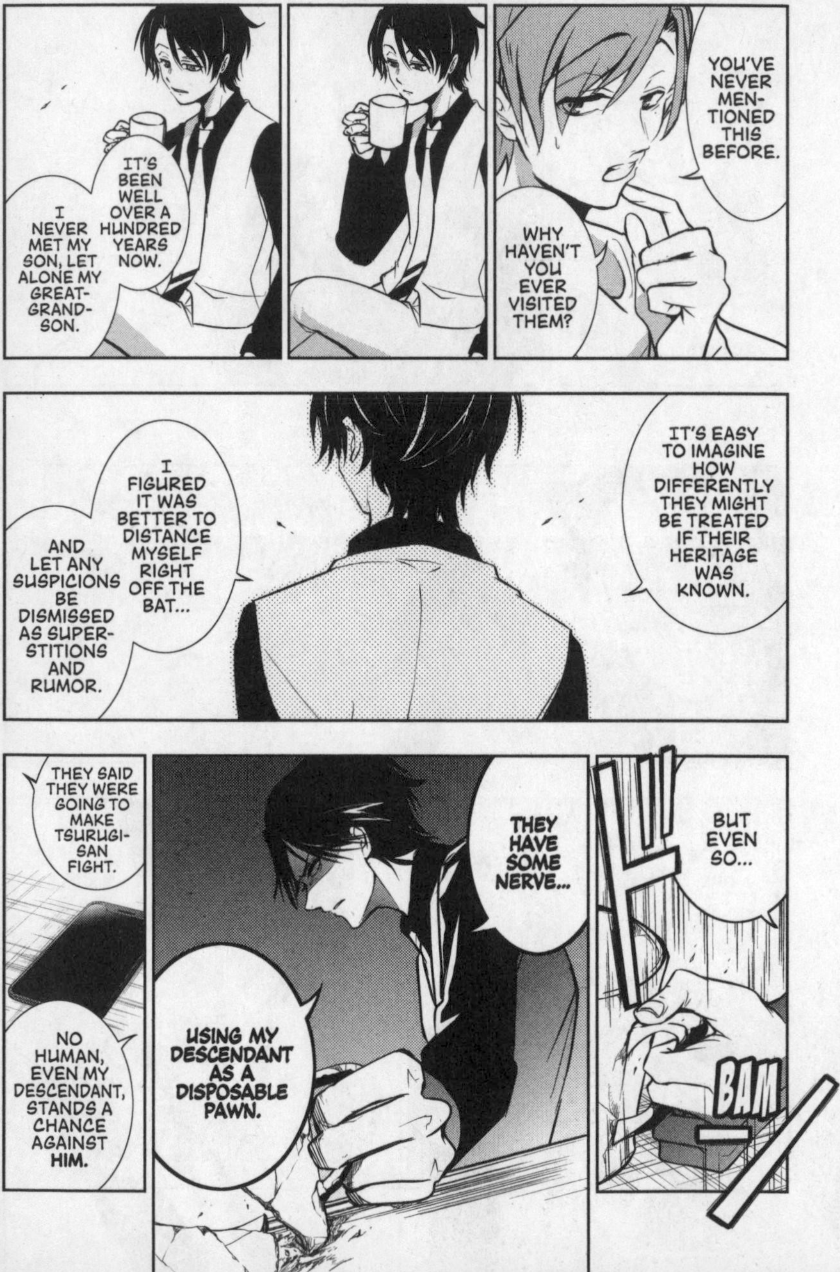

YOU'VE NEVER MENTIONED THIS BEFORE.
WHY HAVEN'T YOU EVER VISITED THEM?
IT'S BEEN WELL OVER A HUNDRED YEARS NOW.
I NEVER MET MY SON, LET ALONE MY GREAT-GRANDSON.
IT'S EASY TO IMAGINE HOW DIFFERENTLY THEY MIGHT BE TREATED IF THEIR HERITAGE WAS KNOWN.
I FIGURED IT WAS BETTER TO DISTANCE MYSELF RIGHT OFF THE BAT...
AND LET ANY SUSPICIONS BE DISMISSED AS SUPERSTITIONS AND RUMOR.
BUT EVEN SO...
BAM
THEY HAVE SOME NERVE...
USING MY DESCENDANT AS A DISPOSABLE PAWN.
THEY SAID THEY WERE GOING TO MAKE TSURUGI-SAN FIGHT.
NO HUMAN, EVEN MY DESCENDANT, STANDS A CHANCE AGAINST HIM.

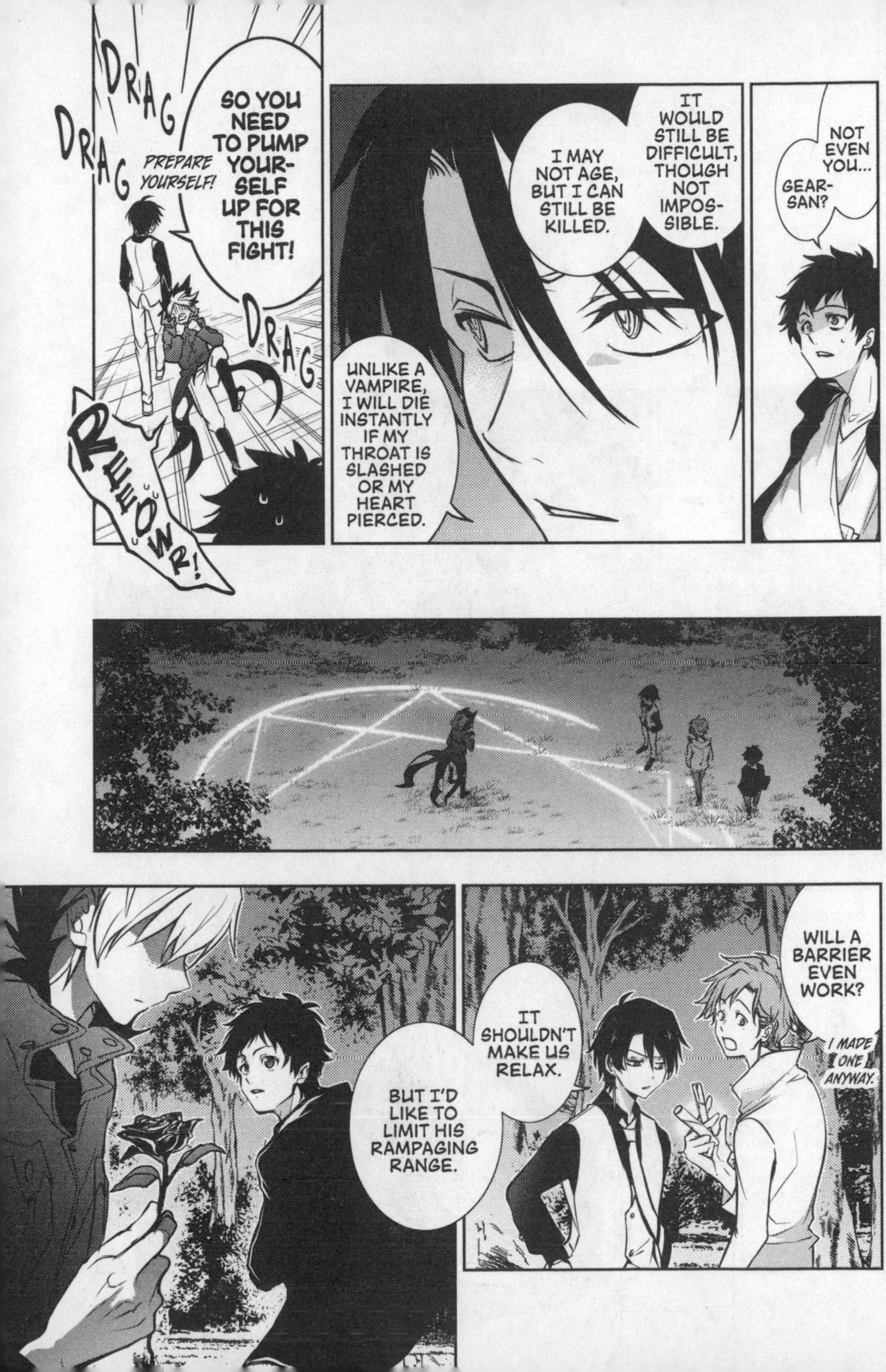
NOT EVEN YOU... GEAR-SAN?
IT WOULD STILL BE DIFFICULT, THOUGH NOT IMPOSSIBLE.
I MAY NOT AGE, BUT I CAN STILL BE KILLED.
UNLIKE A VAMPIRE, I WILL DIE INSTANTLY IF MY THROAT IS SLASHED OR MY HEART PIERCED.
SO YOU NEED TO PUMP YOURSELF UP FOR THIS FIGHT!
PREPARE YOURSELF!
DRAG DRAG DRAG
REEOWR!
WILL A BARRIER EVEN WORK?
I MADE ONE ANYWAY.
IT SHOULDN'T MAKE US RELAX.
BUT I'D LIKE TO LIMIT HIS RAMPAGING RANGE.

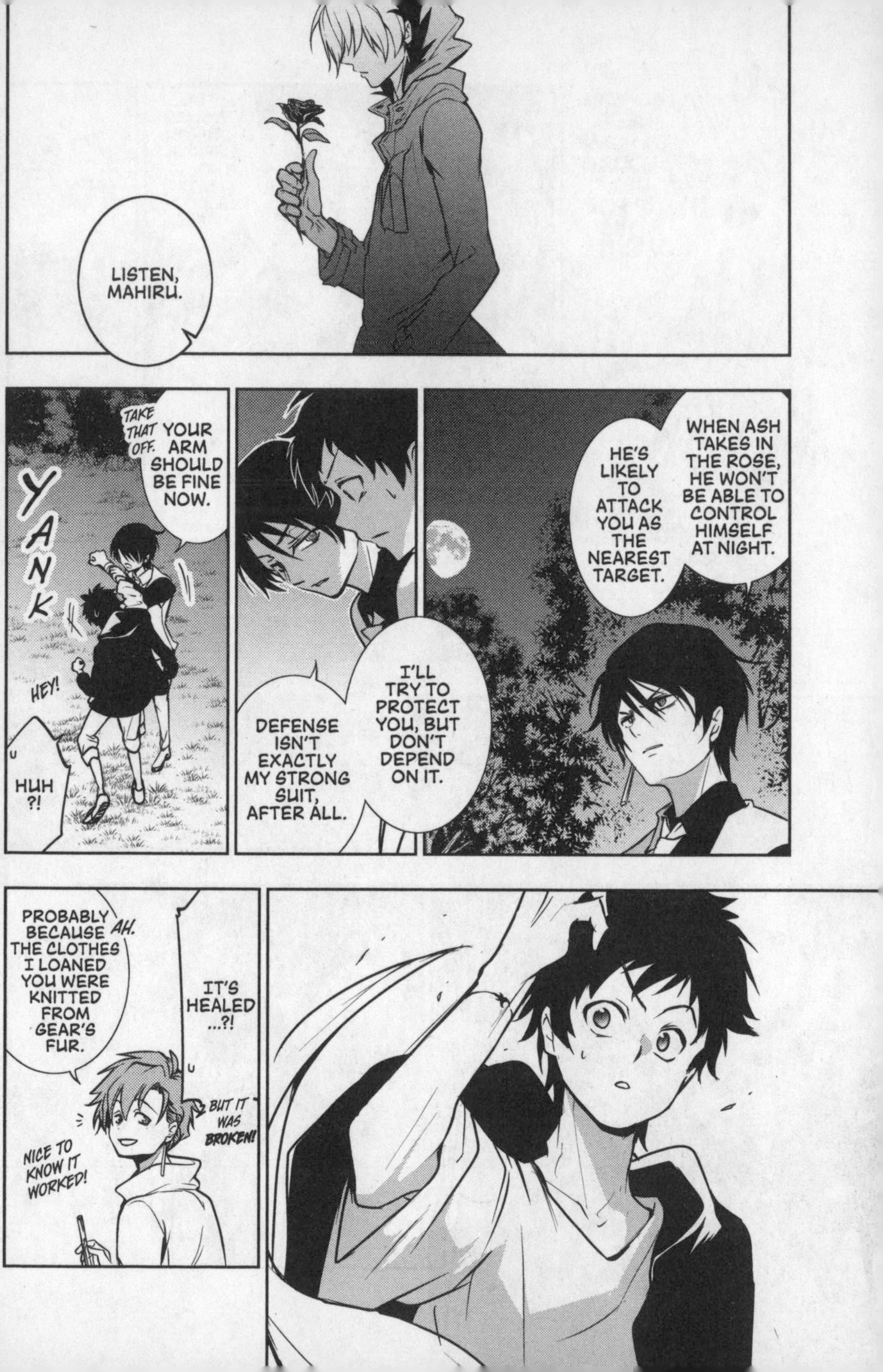
LISTEN, MAHIRU.
WHEN ASH TAKES IN THE ROSE, HE WON'T BE ABLE TO CONTROL HIMSELF AT NIGHT.
HE'S LIKELY TO ATTACK YOU AS THE NEAREST TARGET.
I'LL TRY TO PROTECT YOU, BUT DON'T DEPEND ON IT.
DEFENSE ISN'T EXACTLY MY STRONG SUIT, AFTER ALL.
YOUR ARM SHOULD BE FINE NOW.
TAKE THAT OFF.
YANK
HEY!
HUH?!
IT'S HEALED...?!
BUT IT WAS BROKEN!
AH.
PROBABLY BECAUSE THE CLOTHES I LOANED YOU WERE KNITTED FROM GEAR'S FUR.
NICE TO KNOW IT WORKED!

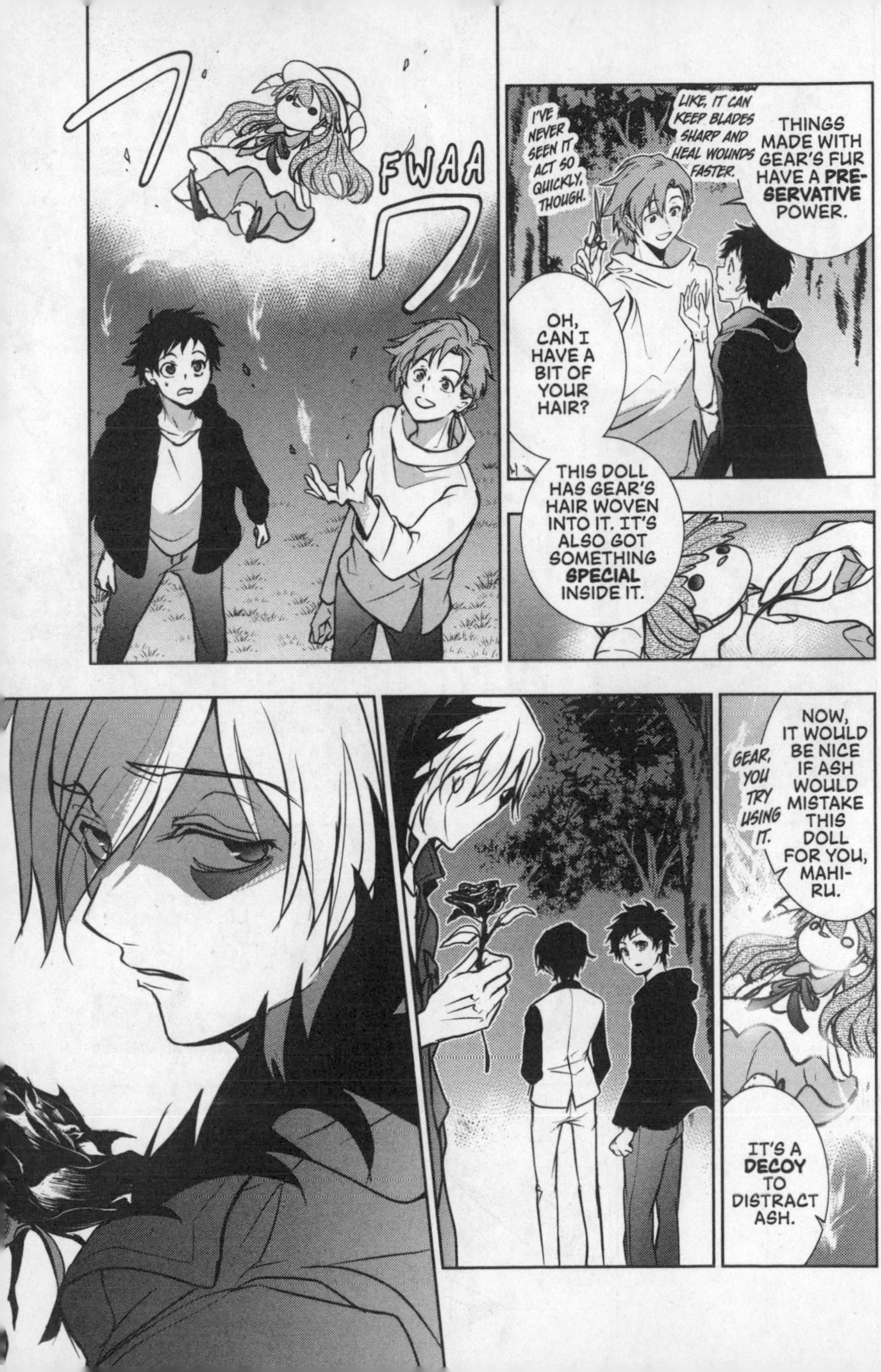
THINGS MADE WITH GEAR'S FUR HAVE A PRESERVATIVE POWER.
LIKE, IT CAN KEEP BLADES SHARP AND HEAL WOUNDS FASTER.
I'VE NEVER SEEN IT ACT SO QUICKLY, THOUGH.
OH, CAN I HAVE A BIT OF YOUR HAIR?
THIS DOLL HAS GEAR'S HAIR WOVEN INTO IT. IT'S ALSO GOT SOMETHING SPECIAL INSIDE IT.
FWAA
NOW, IT WOULD BE NICE IF ASH WOULD MISTAKE THIS DOLL FOR YOU, MAHIRU.
GEAR, YOU TRY USING IT.
IT'S A DECOY TO DISTRACT ASH.

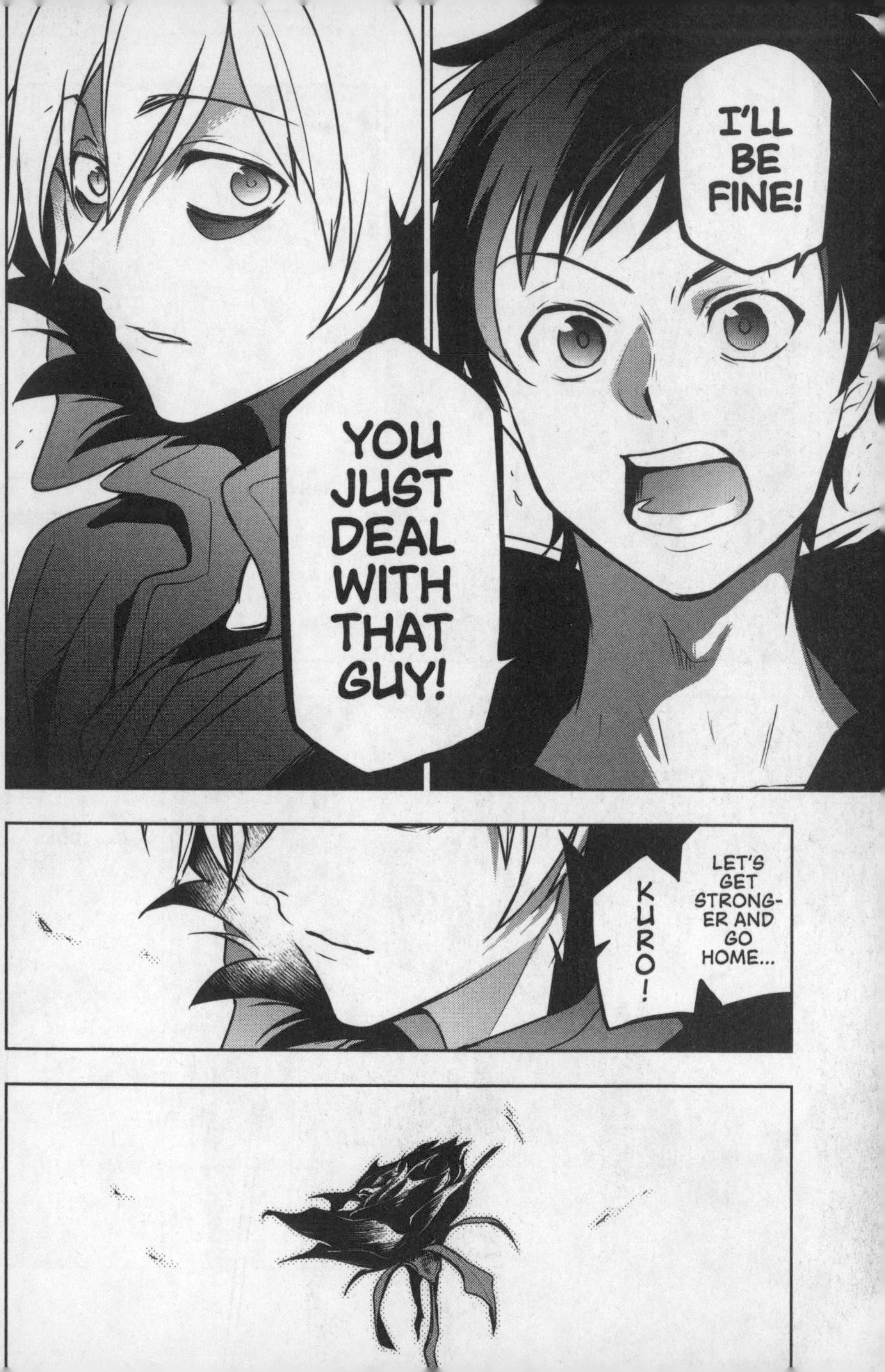
I'LL BE FINE!
YOU JUST DEAL WITH THAT GUY!
LET'S GET STRONGER AND GO HOME...
KURO!

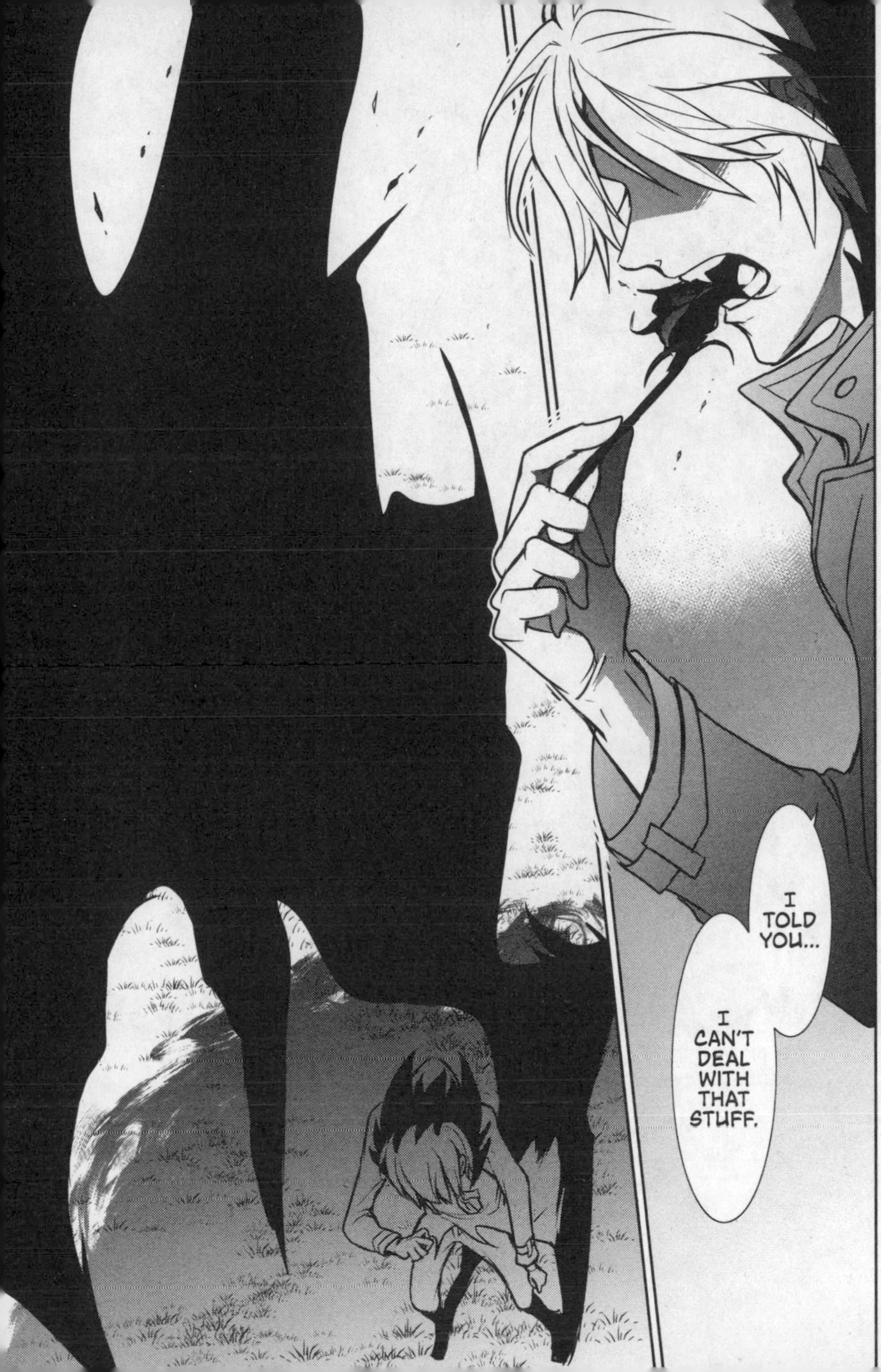
I TOLD YOU...
I CAN'T DEAL WITH THAT STUFF.

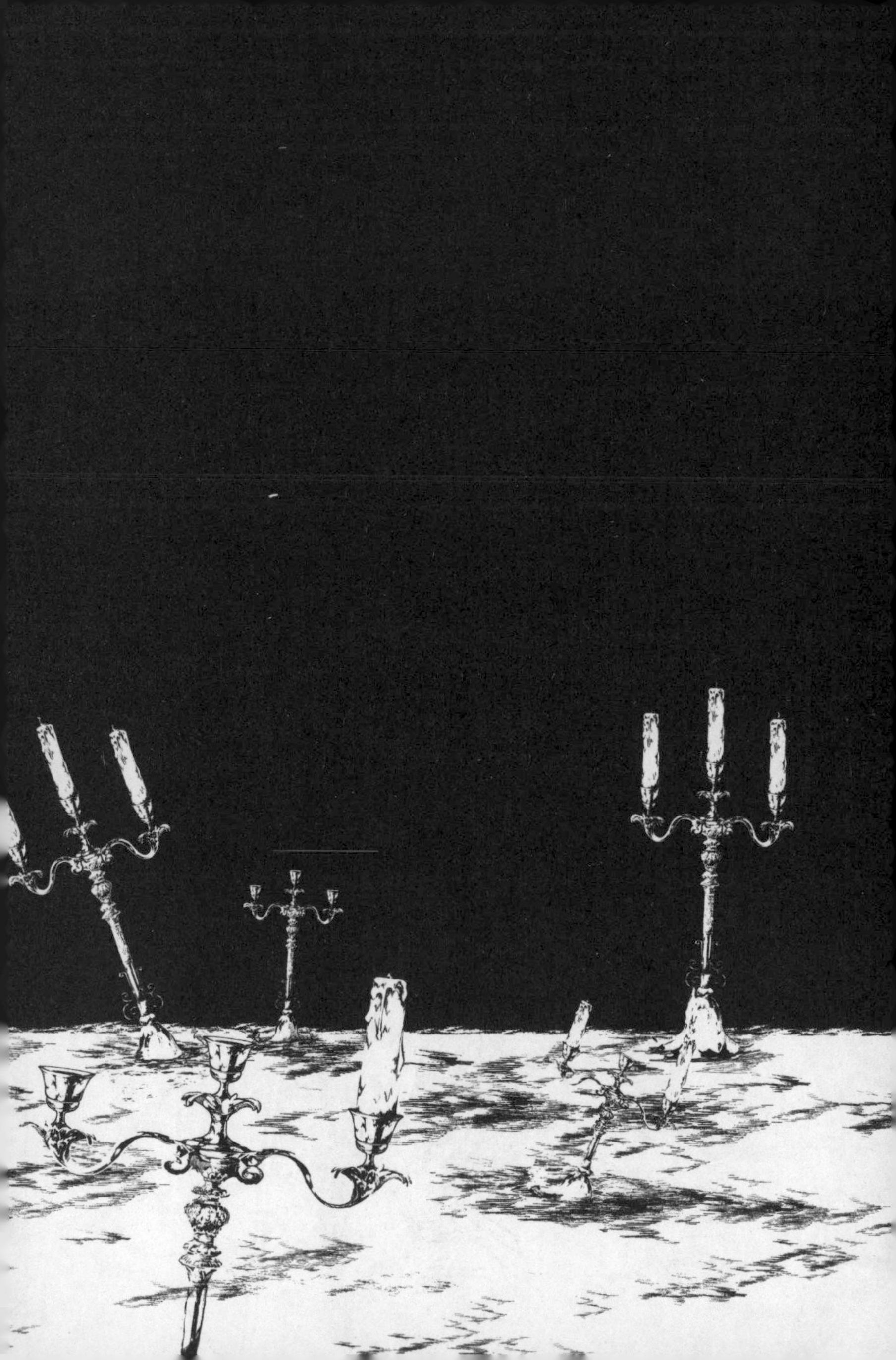

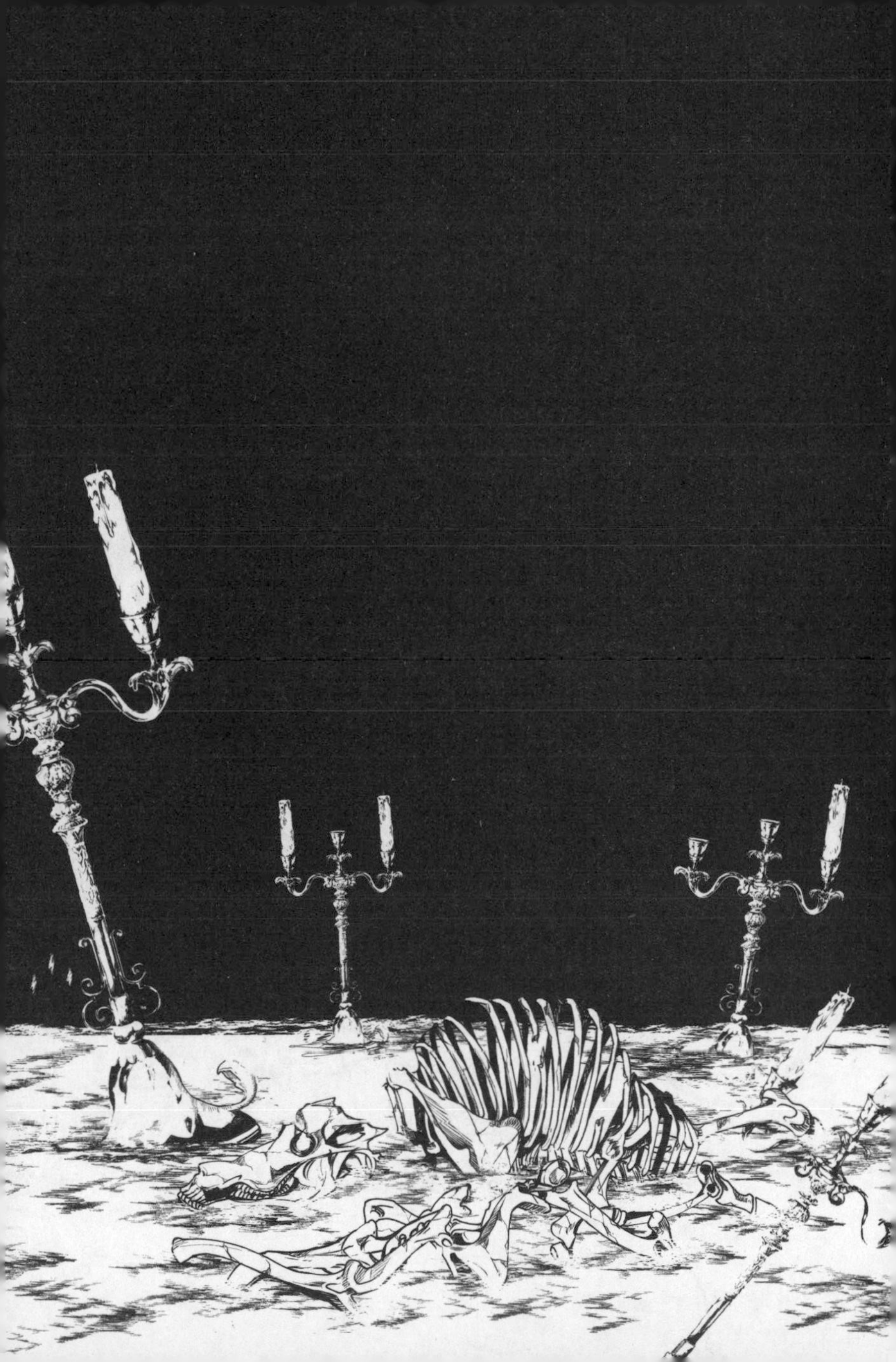

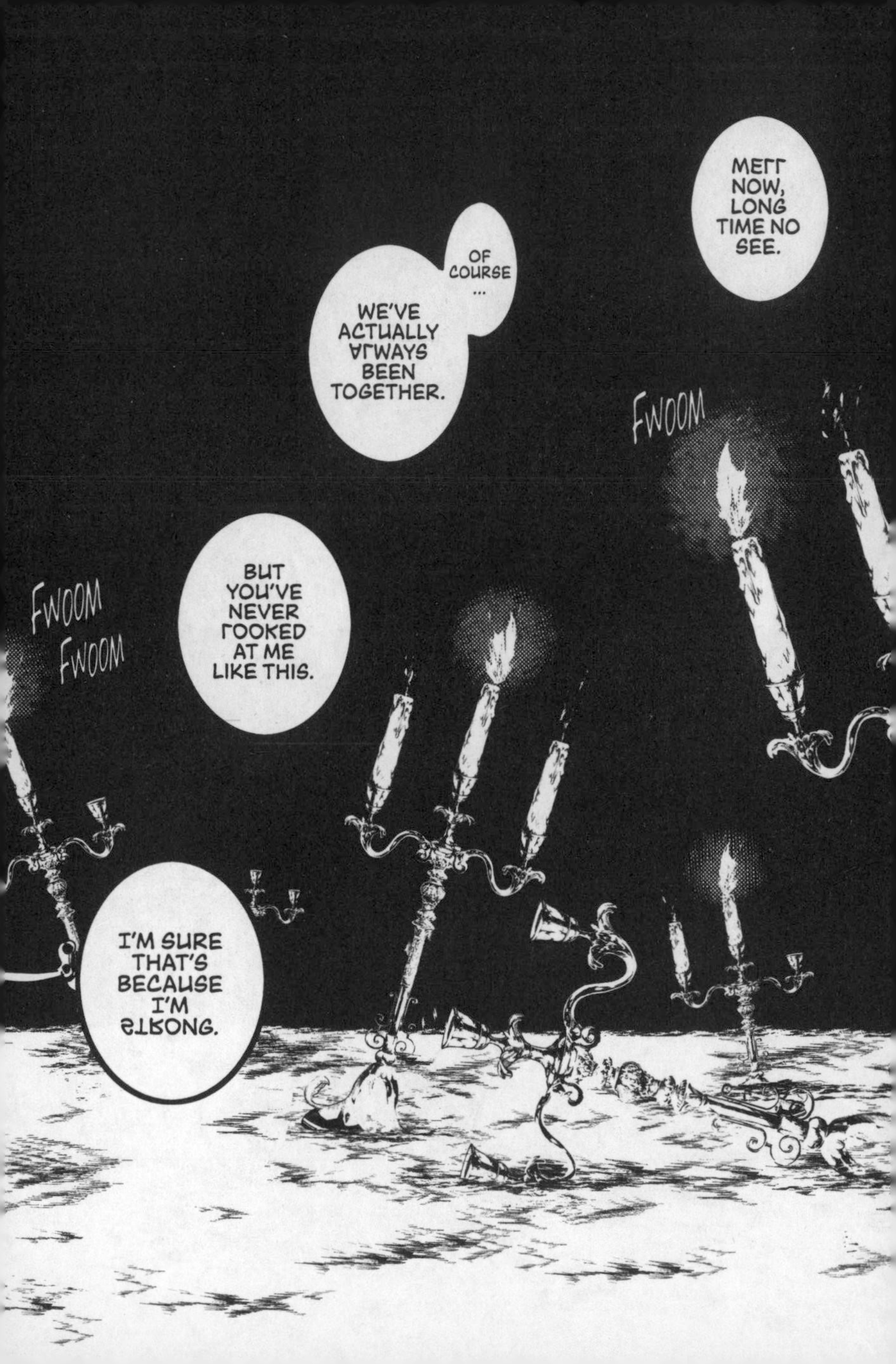
WELL NOW, LONG TIME NO SEE.
FWOOM
OF COURSE ...
WE'VE ACTUALLY ALWAYS BEEN TOGETHER.
BUT YOU'VE NEVER LOOKED AT ME LIKE THIS.
FWOOM
FWOOM
I'M SURE THAT'S BECAUSE I'M STRONG.

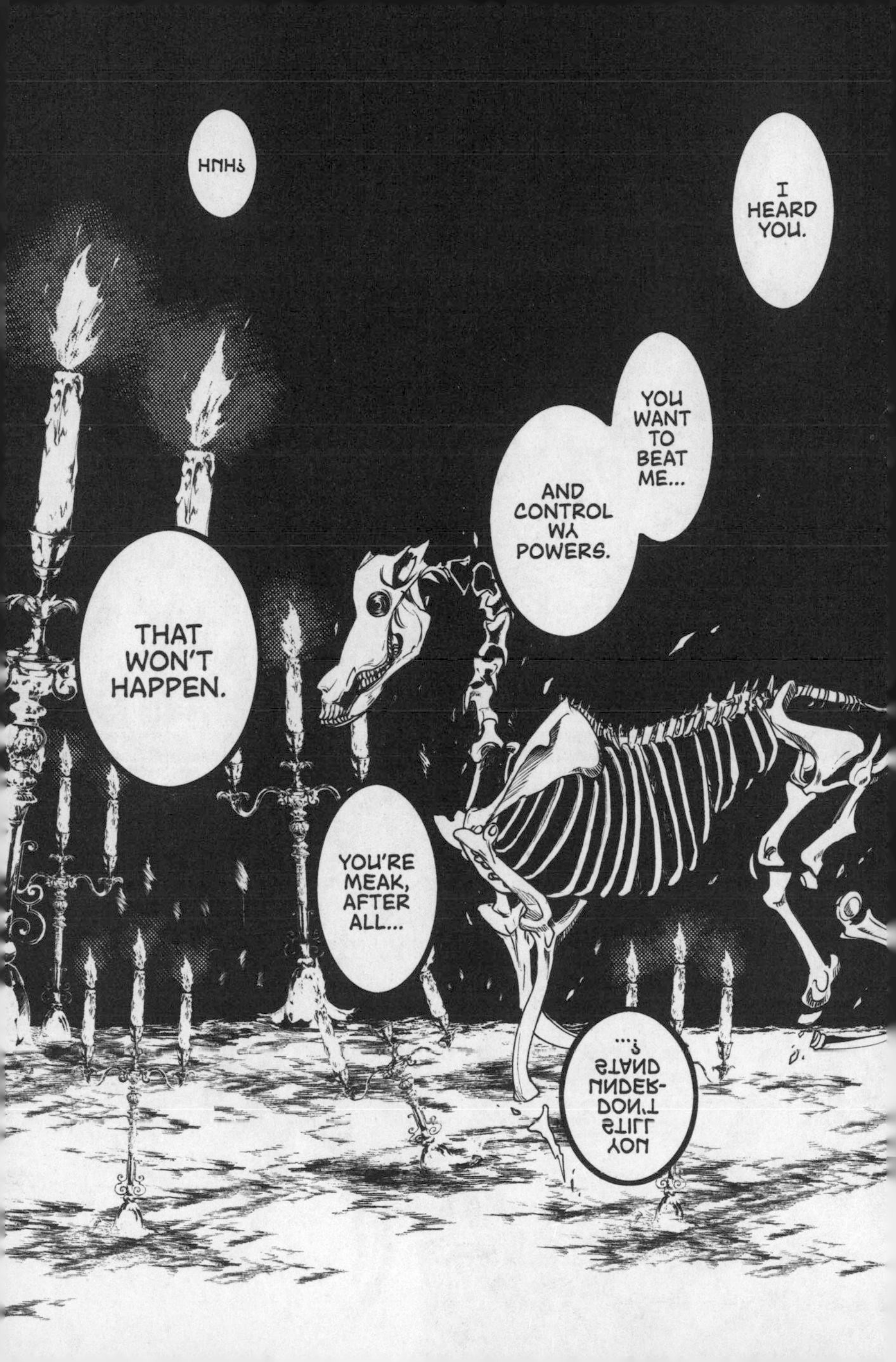
I HEARD YOU.
YOU WANT TO BEAT ME...
AND CONTROL MY POWERS.
HUH?
THAT WON'T HAPPEN.
YOU'RE WEAK, AFTER ALL...
YOU STILL DON'T UNDER-STAND...?

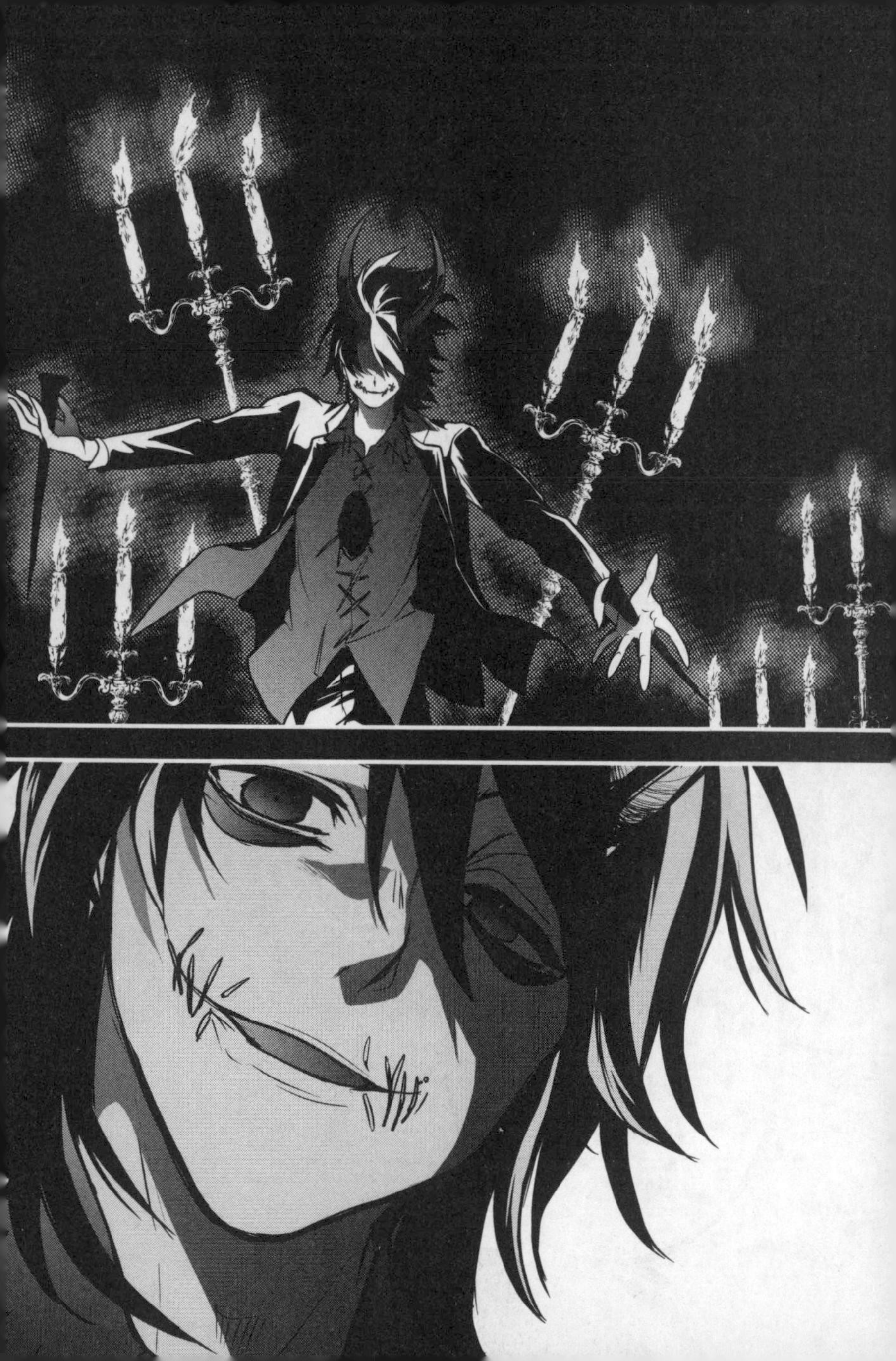

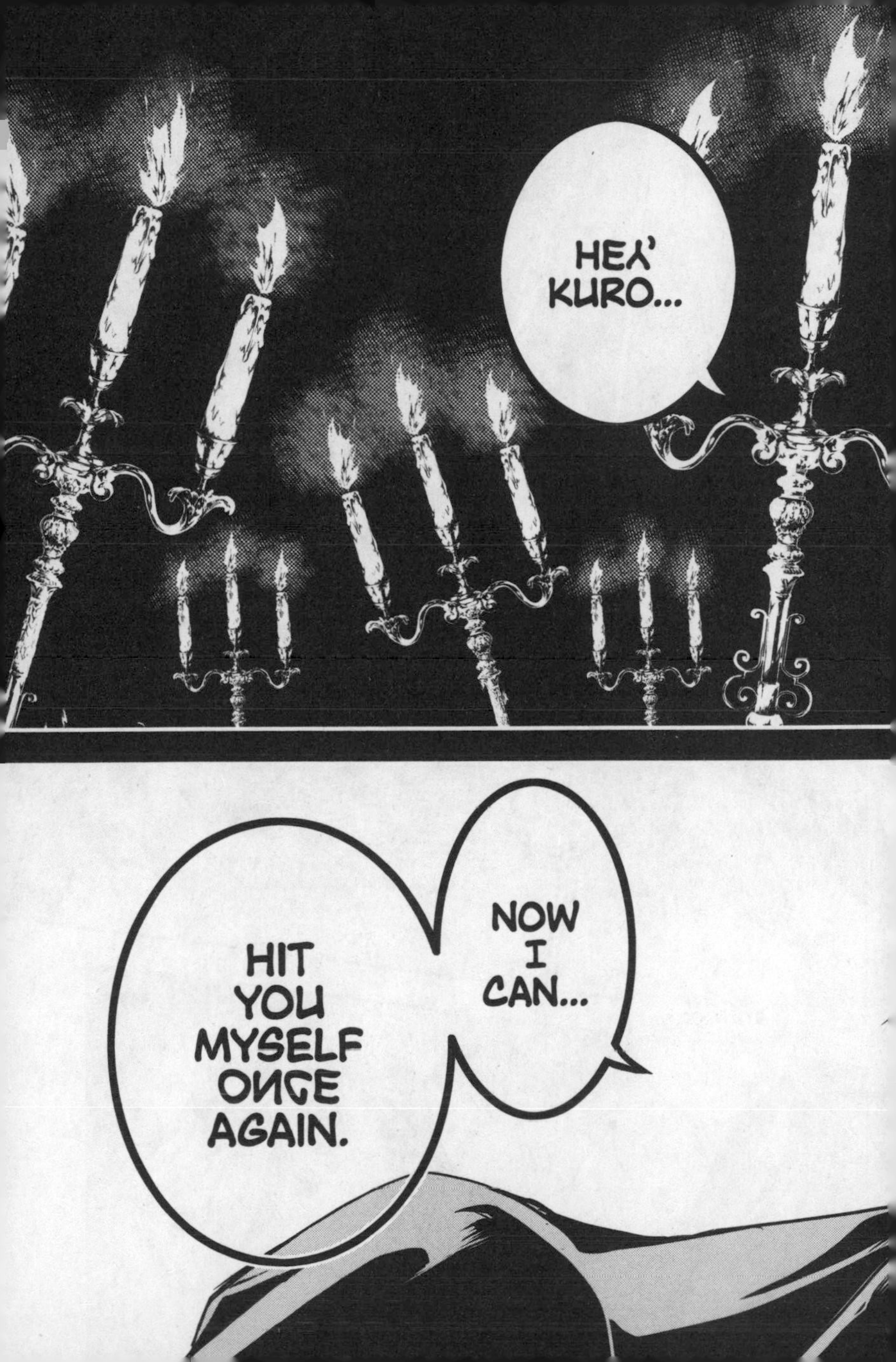
HEY, KURO...
NOW I CAN...
HIT YOU MYSELF ONCE AGAIN.

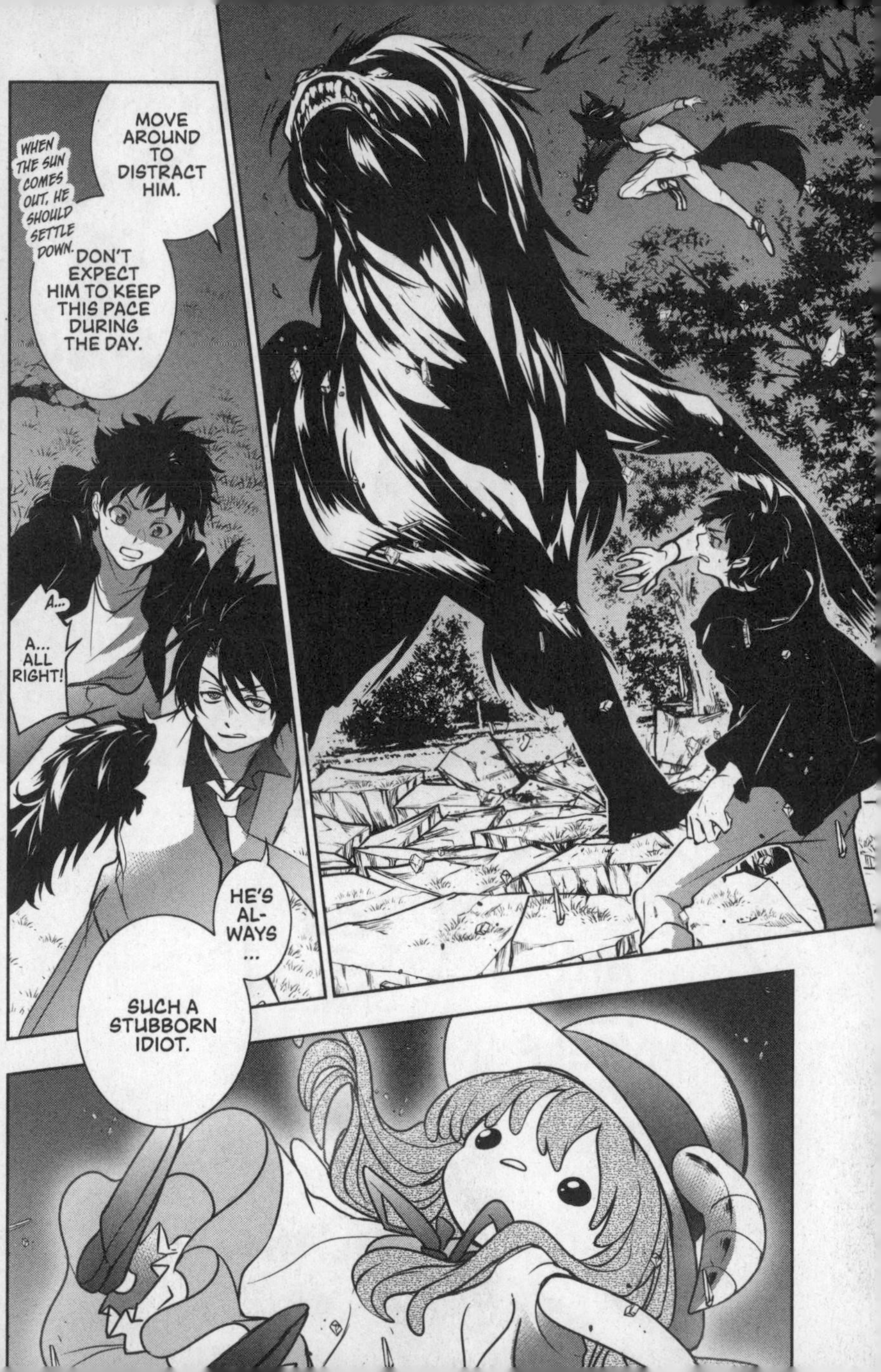
MOVE AROUND TO DISTRACT HIM.
WHEN THE SUN COMES OUT, HE SHOULD SETTLE DOWN.
DON'T EXPECT HIM TO KEEP THIS PACE DURING THE DAY.
A...
A... ALL RIGHT!
HE'S AL-WAYS ...
SUCH A STUBBORN IDIOT.

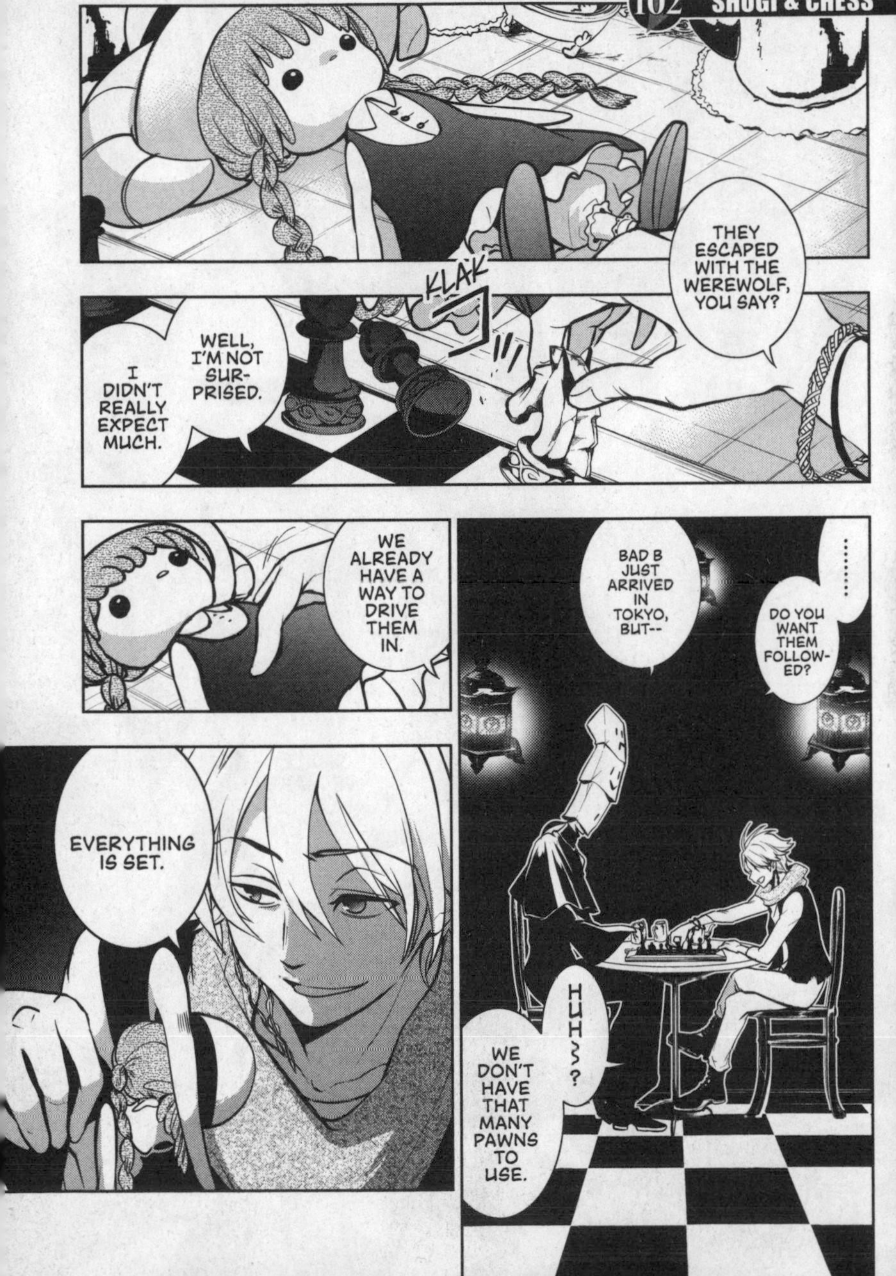
THEY ESCAPED WITH THE WEREWOLF, YOU SAY?
KLAK
WELL, I'M NOT SUR-PRISED.
I DIDN'T REALLY EXPECT MUCH.
......
DO YOU WANT THEM FOLLOW-ED?
BAD B JUST ARRIVED IN TOKYO, BUT--
WE ALREADY HAVE A WAY TO DRIVE THEM IN.
HUH??
WE DON'T HAVE THAT MANY PAWNS TO USE.
EVERYTHING IS SET.

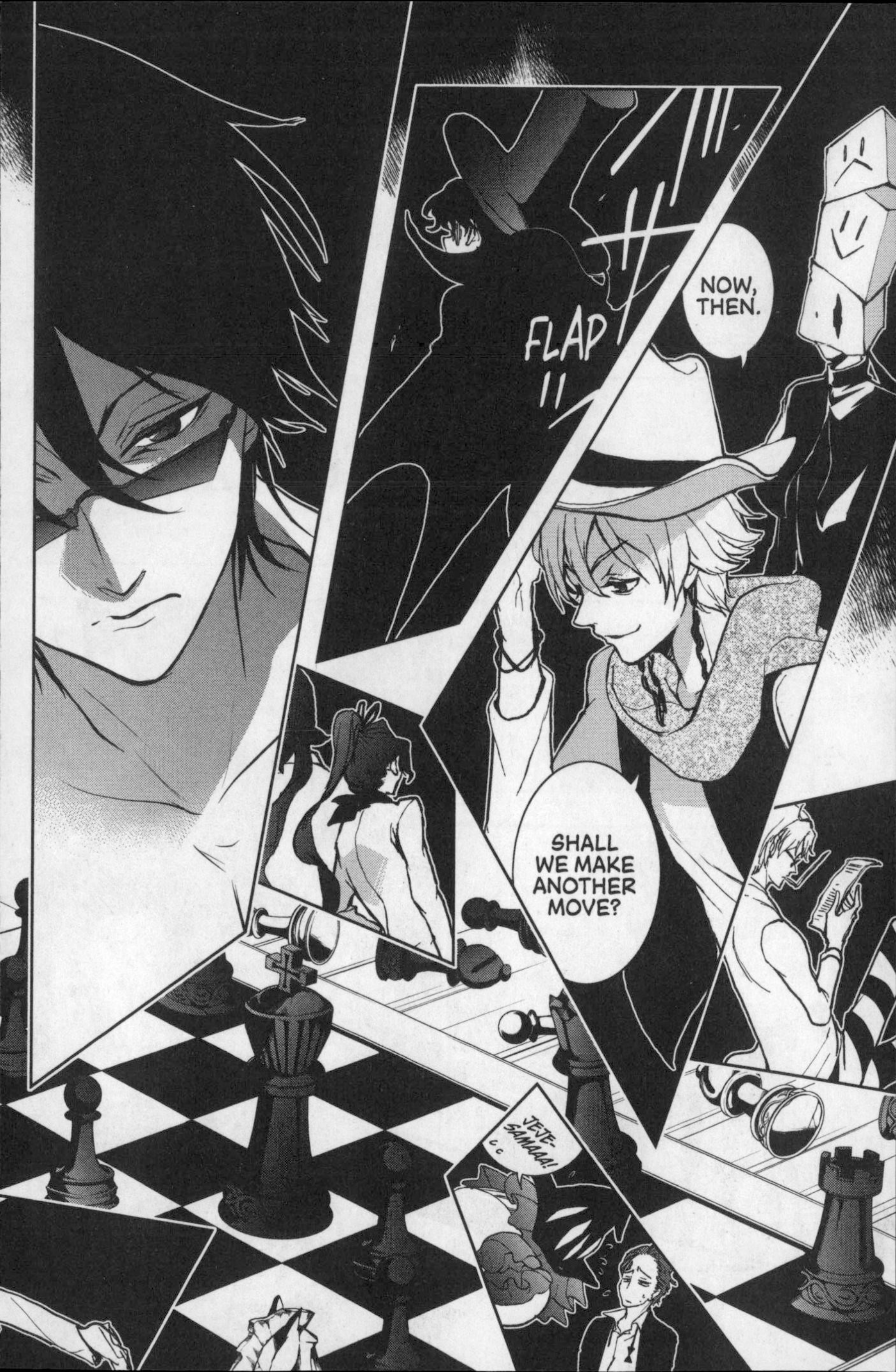
NOW, THEN.
FLAP
SHALL WE MAKE ANOTHER MOVE?
JEJE-SAMAAA!

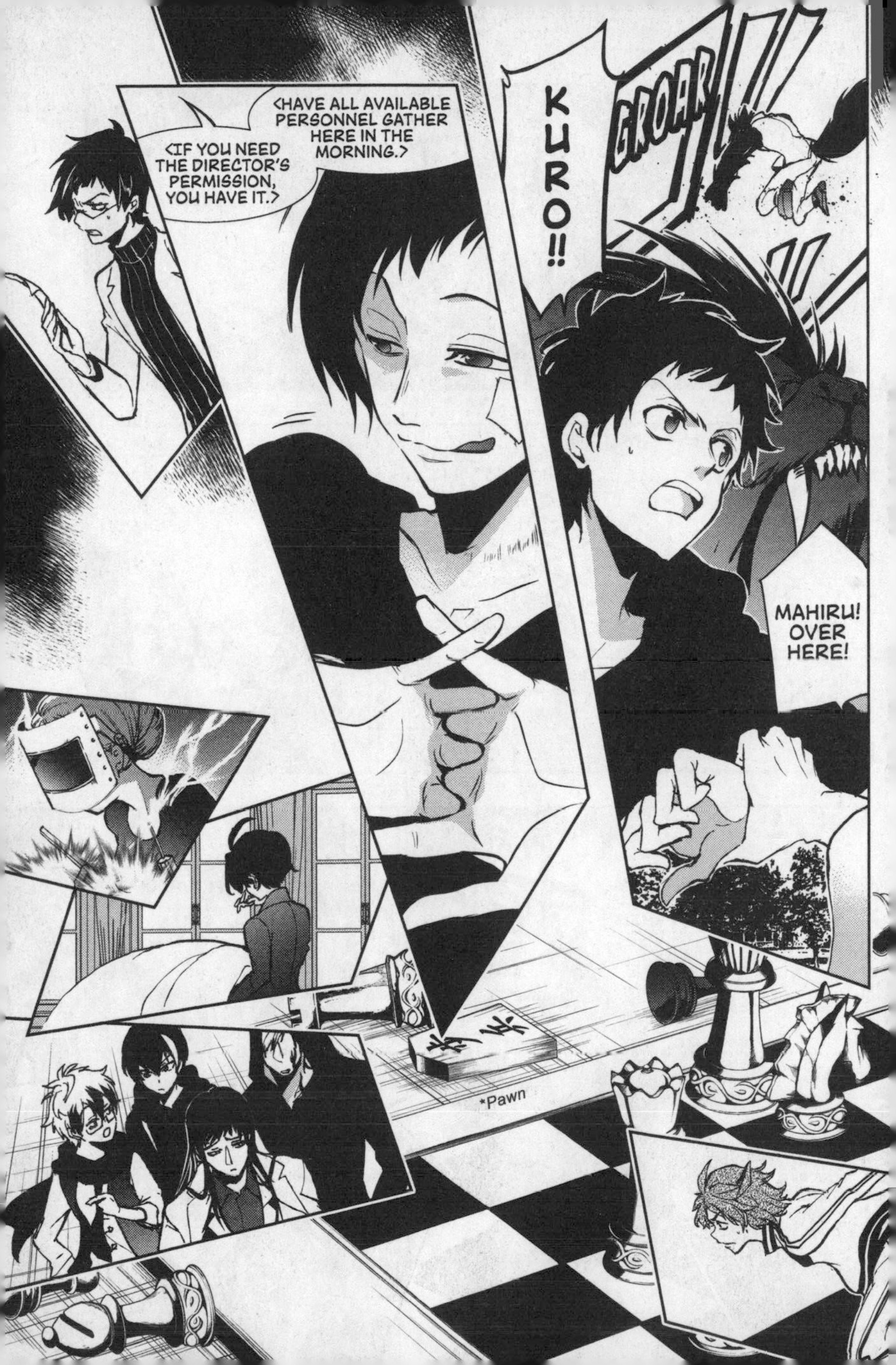

GROAR
KURO!!
MAHIRU! OVER HERE!
<HAVE ALL AVAILABLE PERSONNEL GATHER HERE IN THE MORNING.>
<IF YOU NEED THE DIRECTOR'S PERMISSION, YOU HAVE IT.>
*Pawn

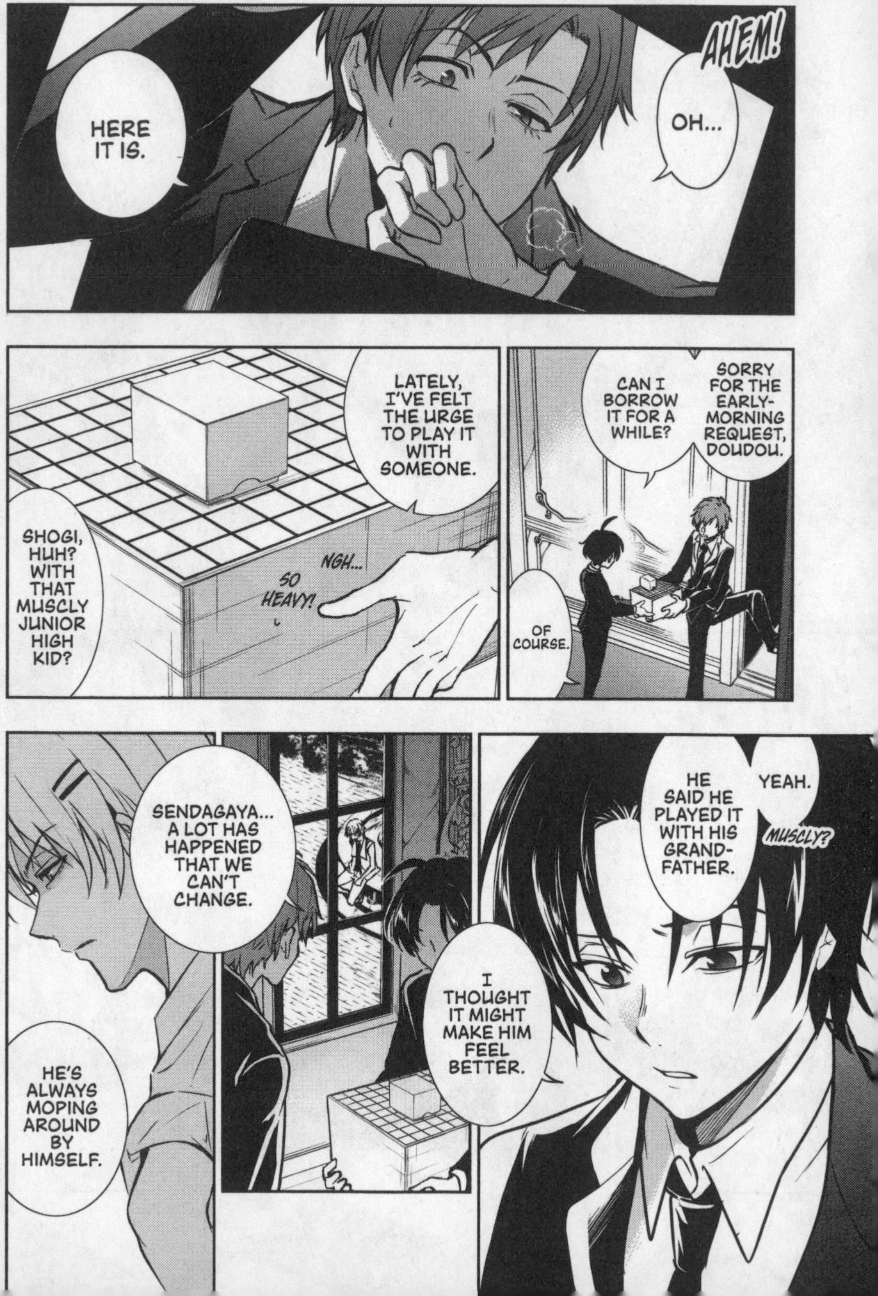
AHEM!
OH...
HERE IT IS.
SORRY FOR THE EARLY-MORNING REQUEST, DOUDOU.
CAN I BORROW IT FOR A WHILE?
OF COURSE.
LATELY, I'VE FELT THE URGE TO PLAY IT WITH SOMEONE.
NGH...
SO HEAVY!
SHOGI, HUH? WITH THAT MUSCLY JUNIOR HIGH KID?
YEAH.
MUSCLY?
HE SAID HE PLAYED IT WITH HIS GRAND-FATHER.
I THOUGHT IT MIGHT MAKE HIM FEEL BETTER.
SENDAGAYA... A LOT HAS HAPPENED THAT WE CAN'T CHANGE.
HE'S ALWAYS MOPING AROUND BY HIMSELF.

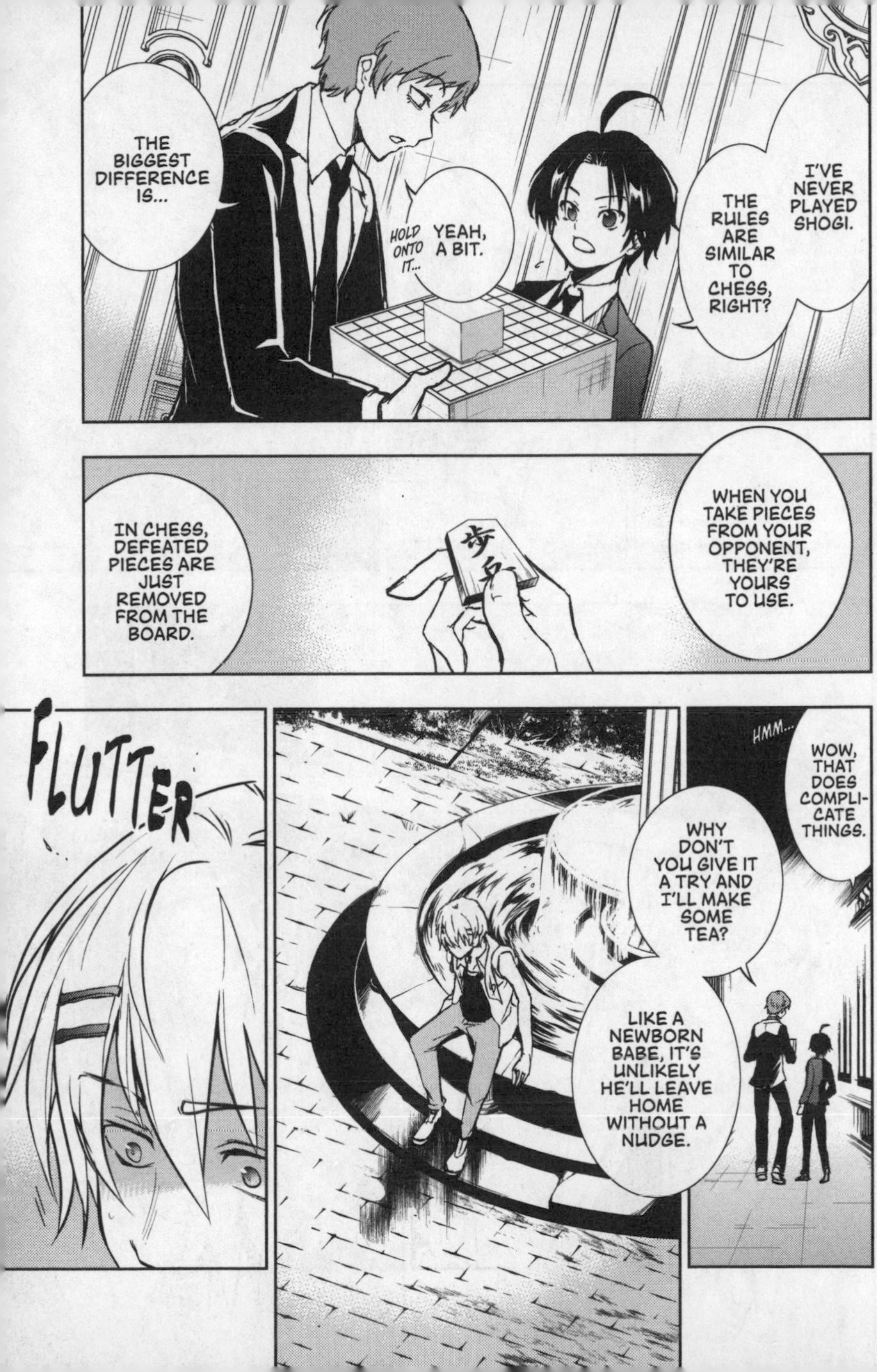
I'VE NEVER PLAYED SHOGI.
THE RULES ARE SIMILAR TO CHESS, RIGHT?
YEAH, A BIT.
HOLD ONTO IT...
THE BIGGEST DIFFERENCE IS...
WHEN YOU TAKE PIECES FROM YOUR OPPONENT, THEY'RE YOURS TO USE.
IN CHESS, DEFEATED PIECES ARE JUST REMOVED FROM THE BOARD.
HMM...
WOW, THAT DOES COMPLICATE THINGS.
WHY DON'T YOU GIVE IT A TRY AND I'LL MAKE SOME TEA?
LIKE A NEWBORN BABE, IT'S UNLIKELY HE'LL LEAVE HOME WITHOUT A NUDGE.
FLUTTER

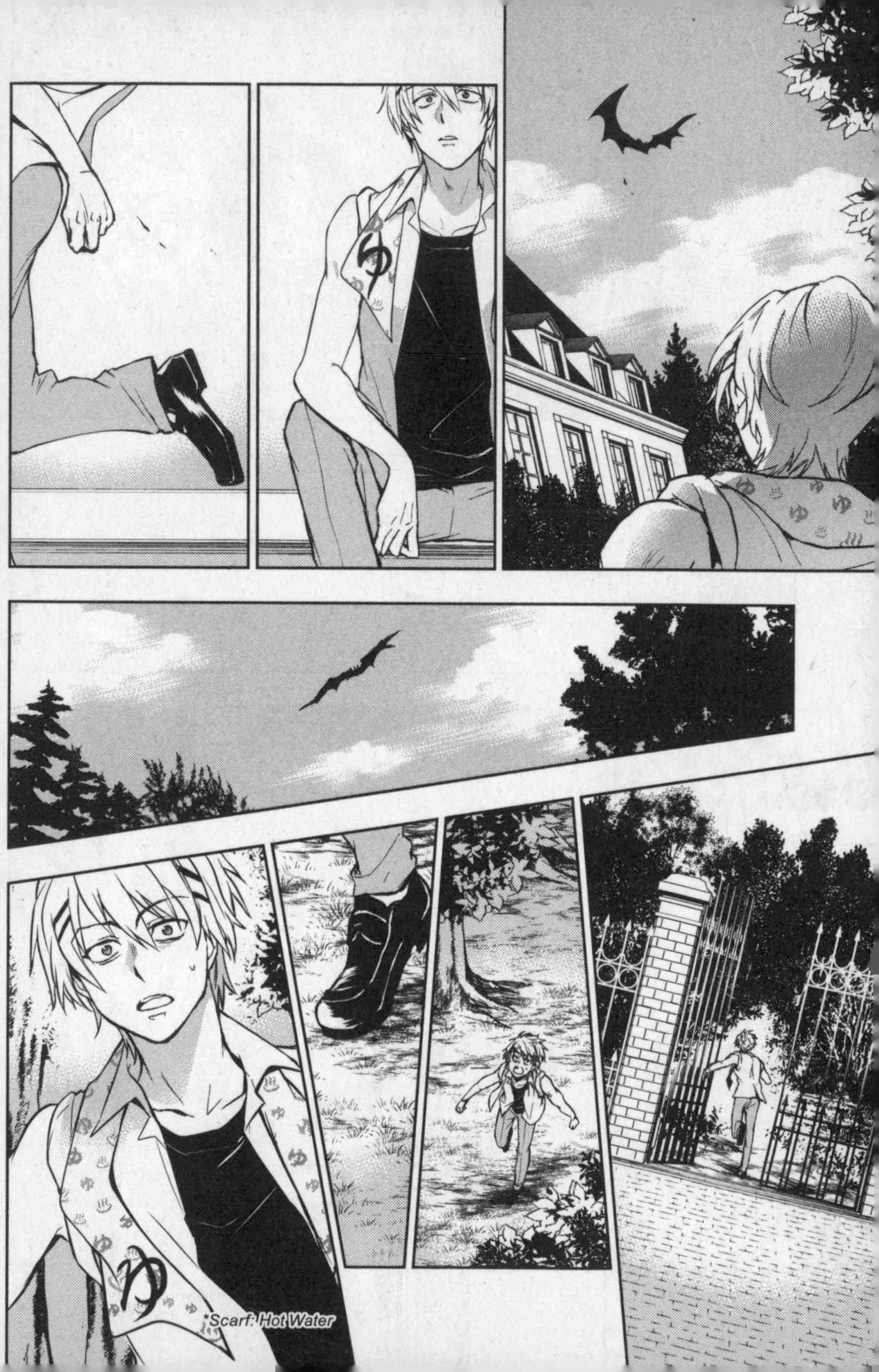
*Scarf: Hot Water

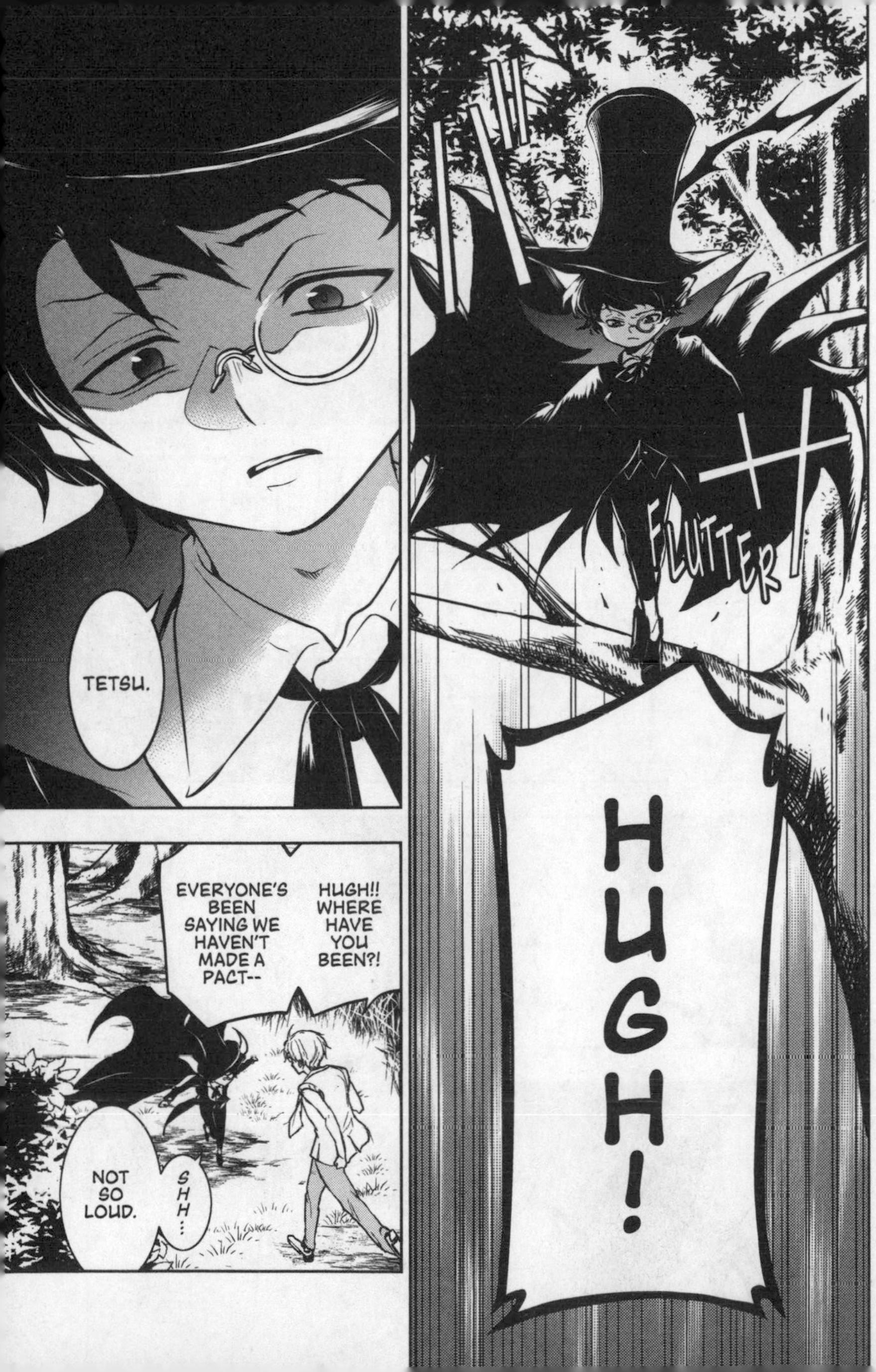
FLUTTER
HUGH!
TETSU.
HUGH!! WHERE HAVE YOU BEEN?!
EVERYONE'S BEEN SAYING WE HAVEN'T MADE A PACT--
SHH...
NOT SO LOUD.

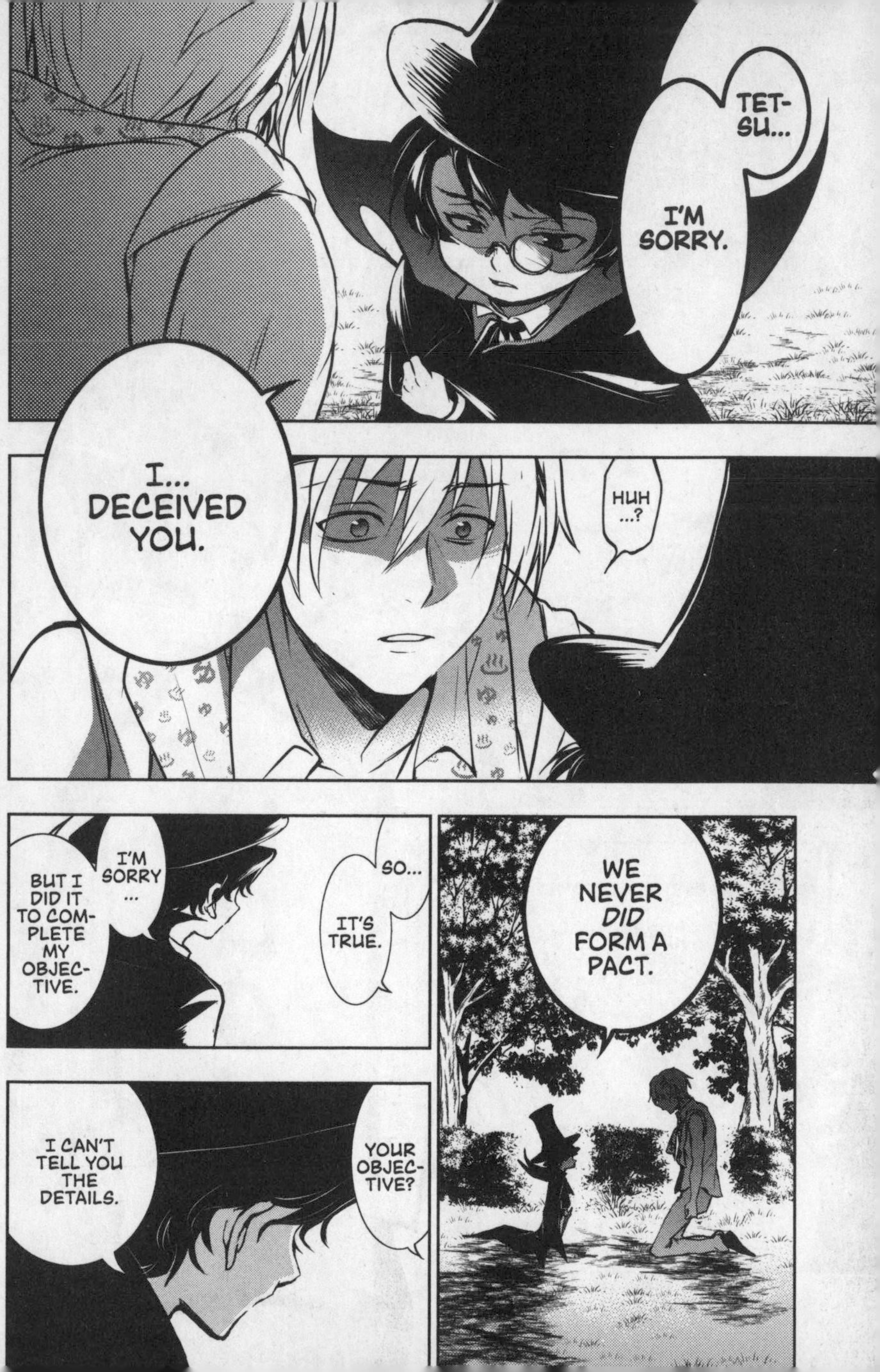
TET-SU...
I'M SORRY.
I... DECEIVED YOU.
HUH ...?
WE NEVER *DID* FORM A PACT.
SO... IT'S TRUE.
I'M SORRY ...
BUT I DID IT TO COMPLETE MY OBJECTIVE.
YOUR OBJECTIVE?
I CAN'T TELL YOU THE DETAILS.

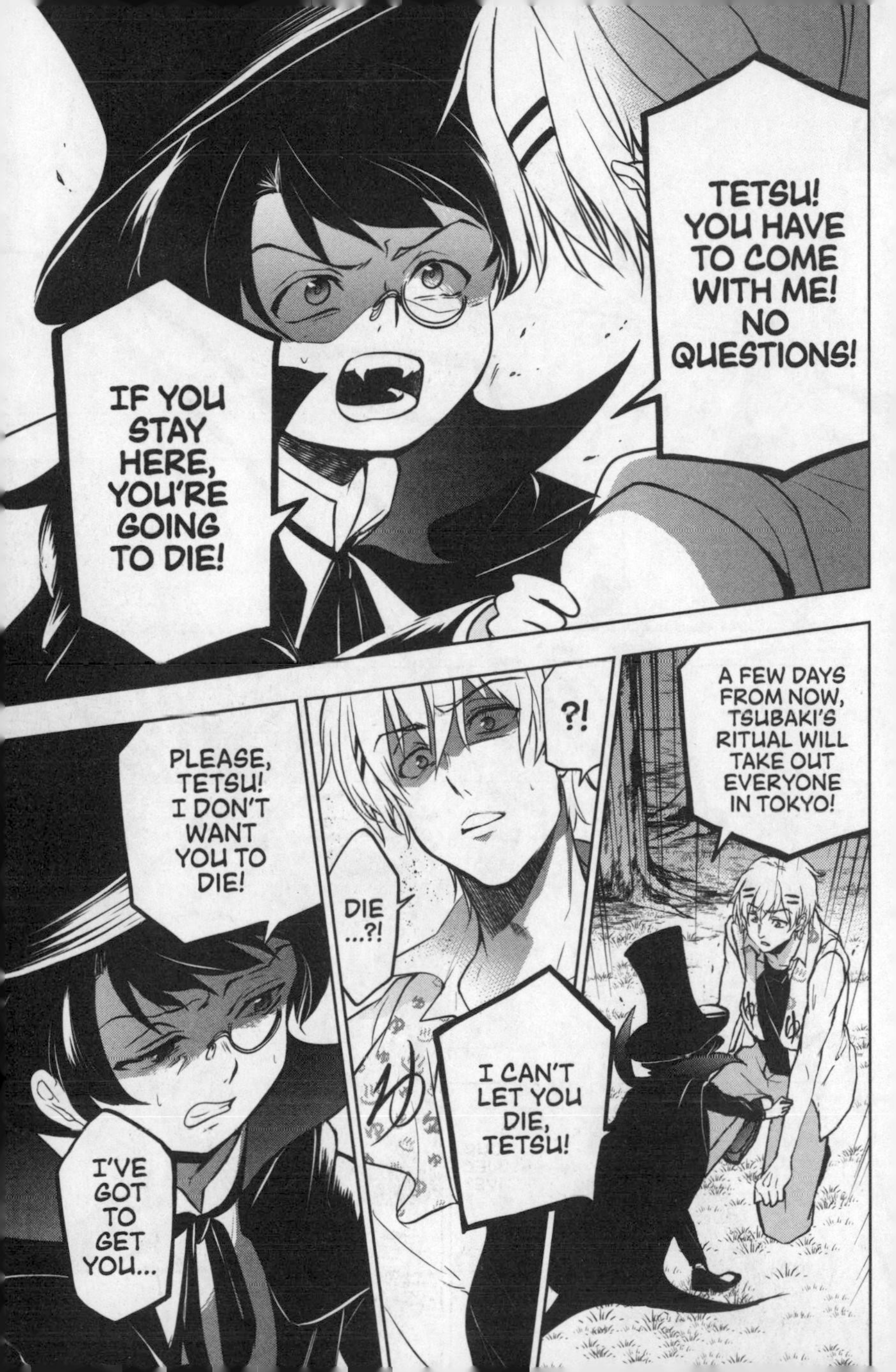
TETSU! YOU HAVE TO COME WITH ME! NO QUESTIONS!
IF YOU STAY HERE, YOU'RE GOING TO DIE!
A FEW DAYS FROM NOW, TSUBAKI'S RITUAL WILL TAKE OUT EVERYONE IN TOKYO!
I CAN'T LET YOU DIE, TETSU!
?!
DIE ...?!
PLEASE, TETSU! I DON'T WANT YOU TO DIE!
I'VE GOT TO GET YOU...

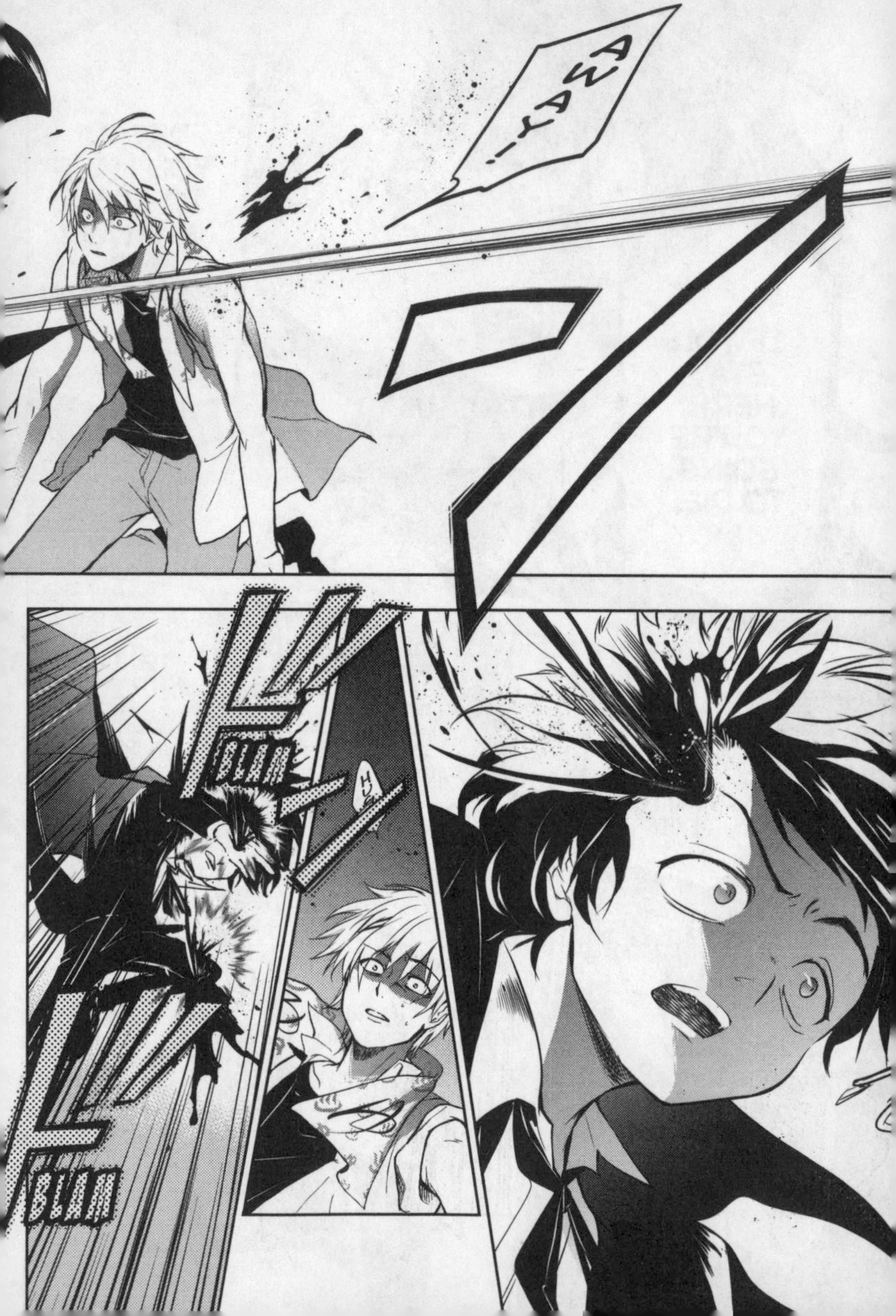
AWAY--!
BLAM
HU
BLAM

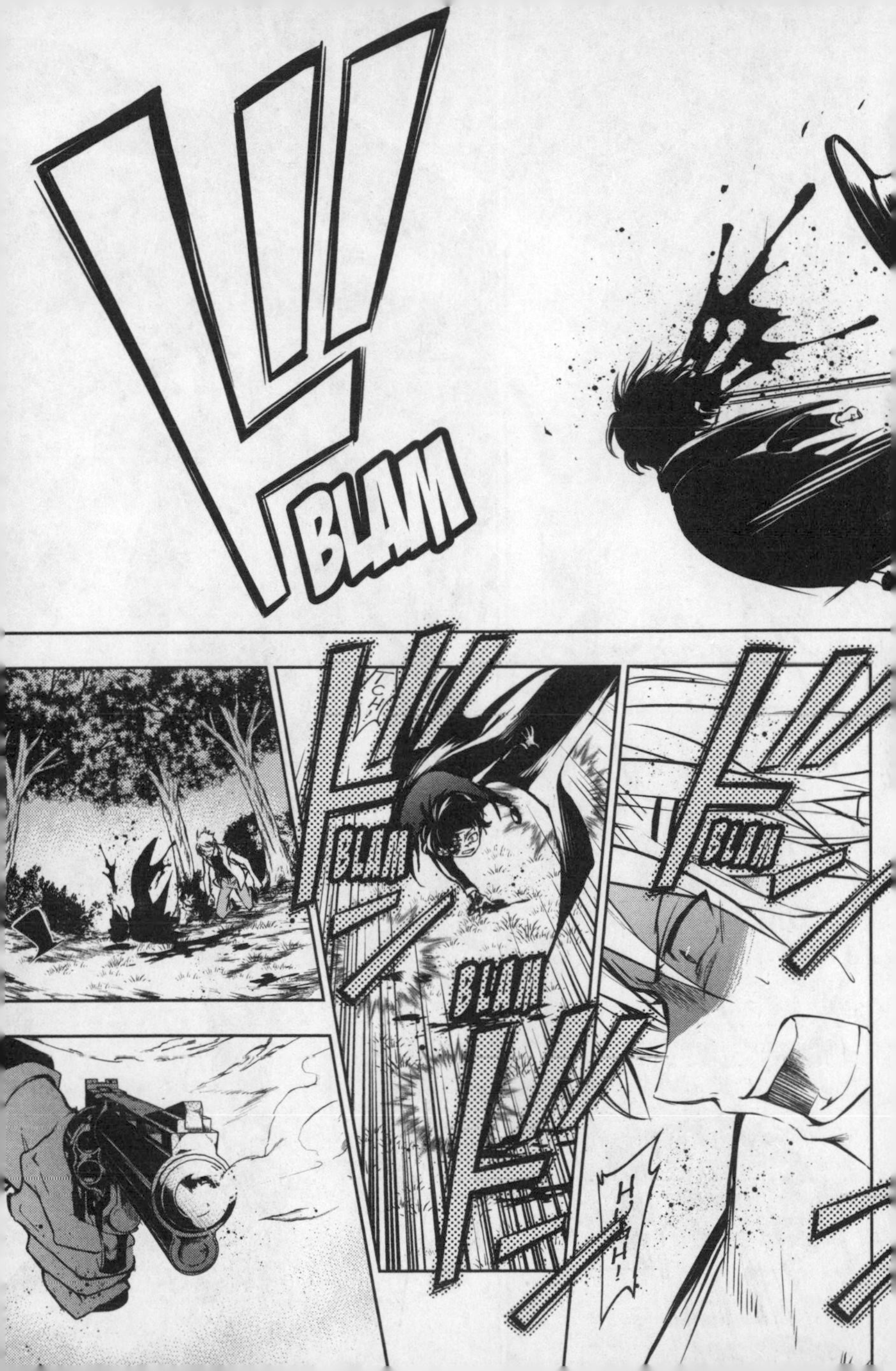
BLAM
BLAM
TCH!
BLAM
BLAM
H! H! H!

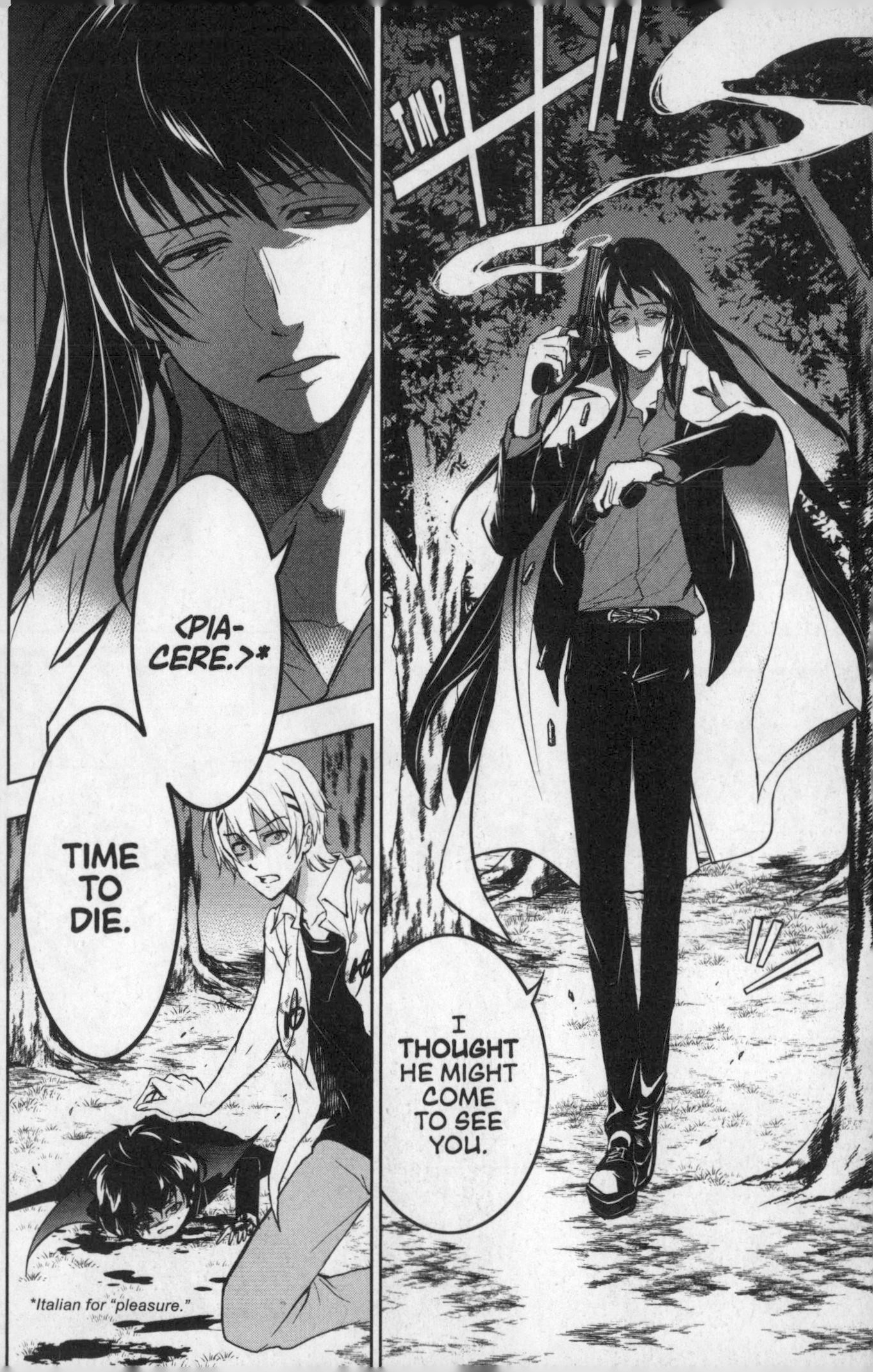
TMP
I THOUGHT HE MIGHT COME TO SEE YOU.
<PIA-CERE.>*
TIME TO DIE.
*Italian for "pleasure."

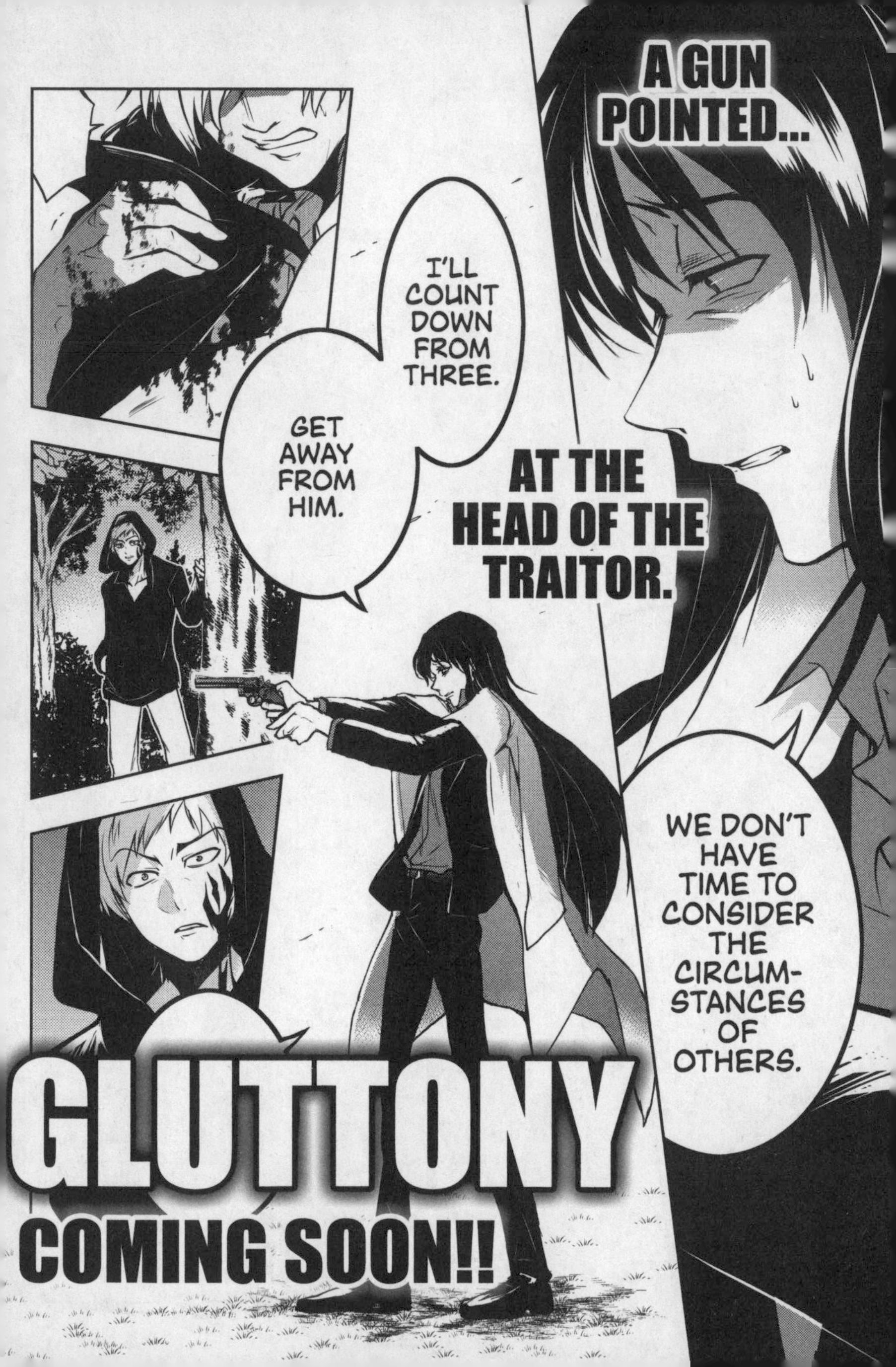
A GUN POINTED...
I'LL COUNT DOWN FROM THREE.
GET AWAY FROM HIM.
AT THE HEAD OF THE TRAITOR.
WE DON'T HAVE TIME TO CONSIDER THE CIRCUM-STANCES OF OTHERS.
GLUTTONY
COMING SOON!!

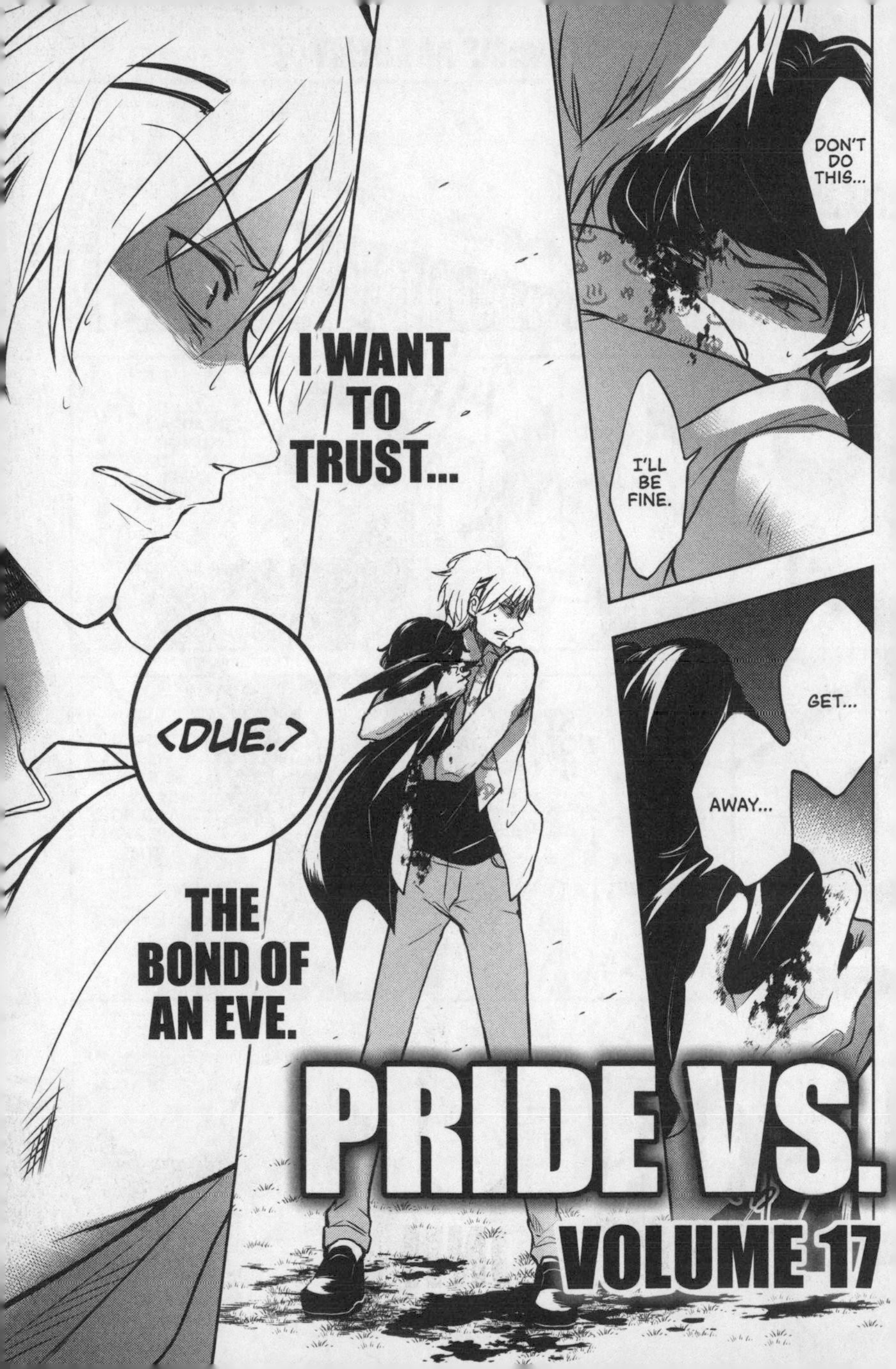
DON'T DO THIS...
I'LL BE FINE.
GET...
AWAY...
I WANT TO TRUST...
<DUE.>
THE BOND OF AN EVE.
PRIDE VS.
VOLUME 17

SERVAMP ACADEMY ⑧

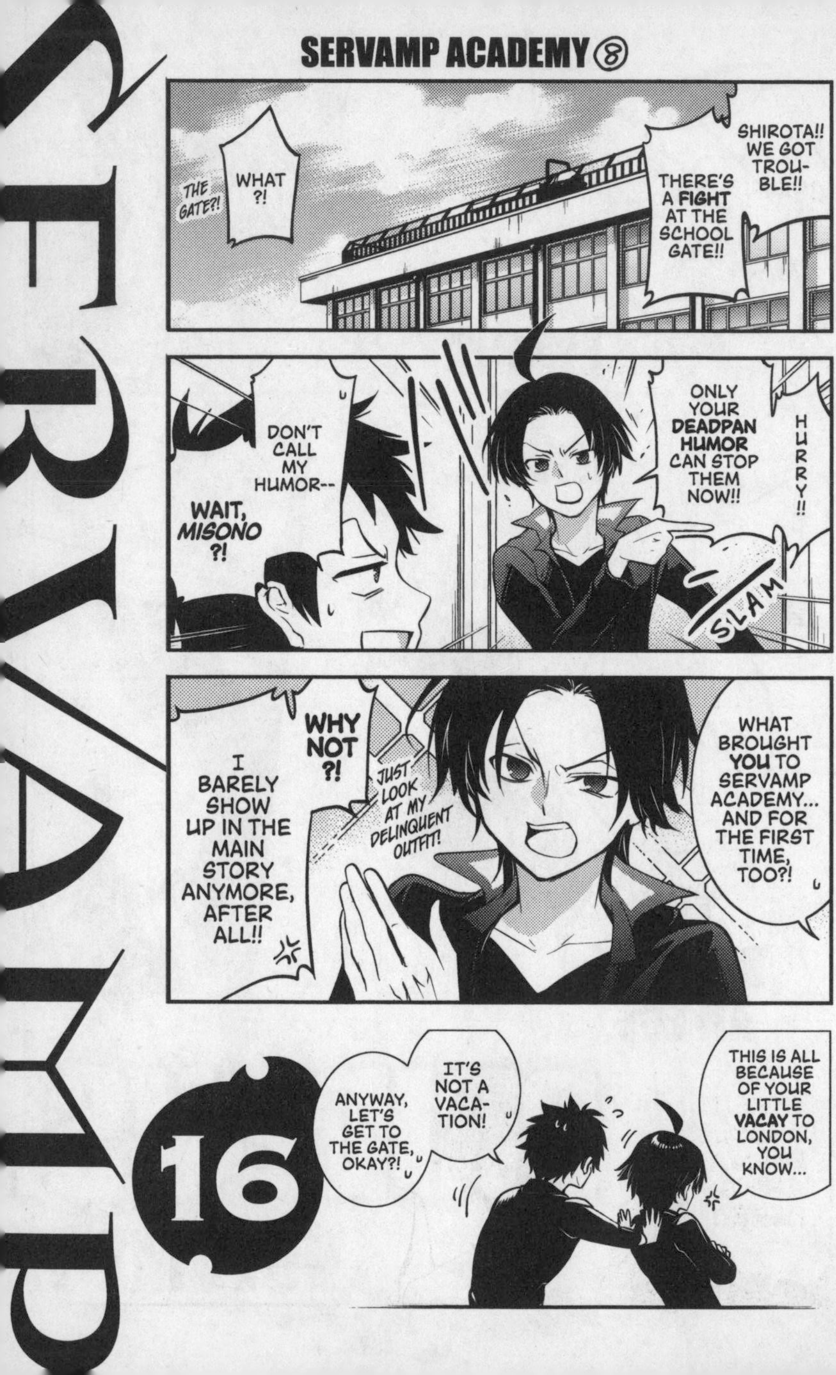
SHIROTA!! WE GOT TROUBLE!!
THERE'S A FIGHT AT THE SCHOOL GATE!!
WHAT?!
THE GATE?!
ONLY YOUR DEADPAN HUMOR CAN STOP THEM NOW!!
HURRY!!
SLAM
DON'T CALL MY HUMOR--
WAIT, MISONO?!
WHAT BROUGHT YOU TO SERVAMP ACADEMY... AND FOR THE FIRST TIME, TOO?!
WHY NOT?!
JUST LOOK AT MY DELINQUENT OUTFIT!
I BARELY SHOW UP IN THE MAIN STORY ANYMORE, AFTER ALL!!
THIS IS ALL BECAUSE OF YOUR LITTLE VACAY TO LONDON, YOU KNOW...
IT'S NOT A VACA-TION!
ANYWAY, LET'S GET TO THE GATE, OKAY?!

SERVAMP ACADEMY ⑨

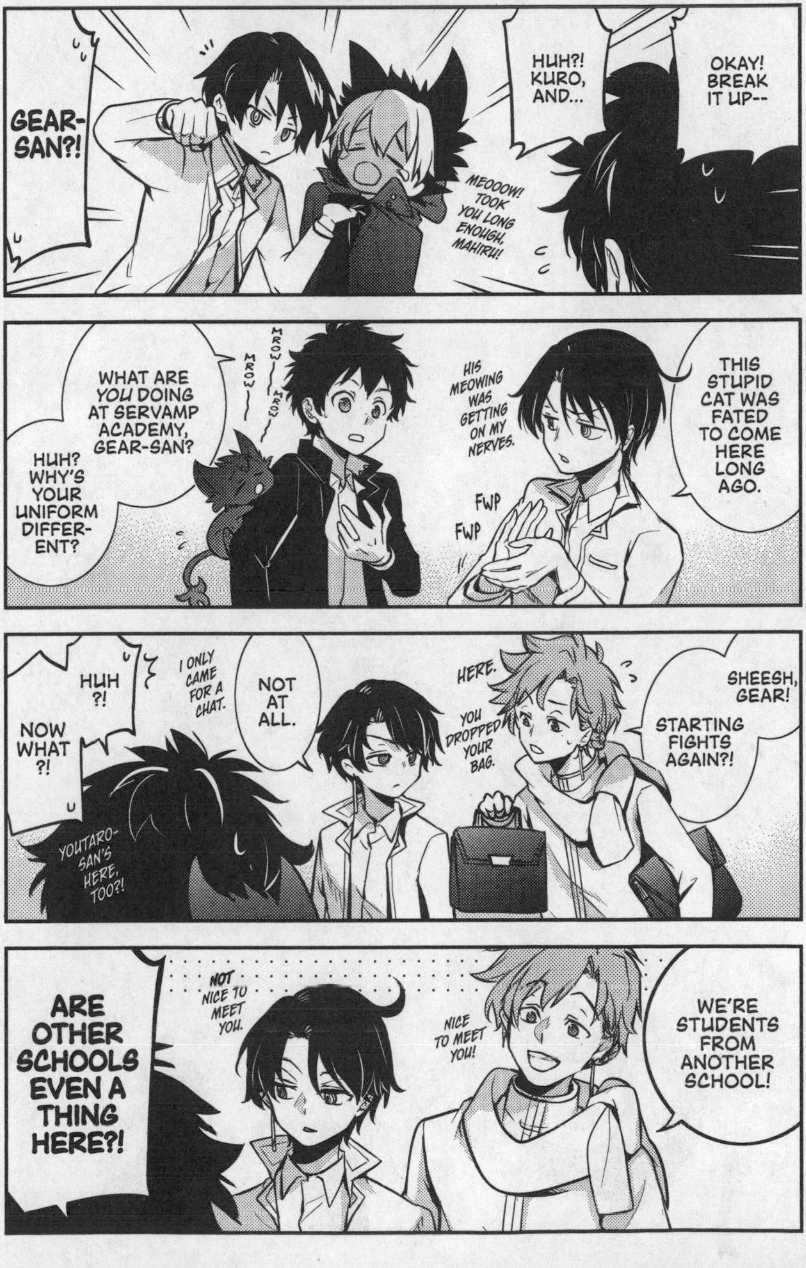
OKAY! BREAK IT UP--
HUH?! KURO, AND...
MEOOOW! TOOK YOU LONG ENOUGH, MAHIRU!
GEAR-SAN?!
THIS STUPID CAT WAS FATED TO COME HERE LONG AGO.
FWP
FWP
HIS MEOWING WAS GETTING ON MY NERVES.
MROW MROW MROW
WHAT ARE *YOU* DOING AT SERVAMP ACADEMY, GEAR-SAN?
HUH? WHY'S YOUR UNIFORM DIFFERENT?
SHEESH, GEAR!
STARTING FIGHTS AGAIN?!
HERE.
YOU DROPPED YOUR BAG.
NOT AT ALL.
I ONLY CAME FOR A CHAT.
HUH?!
NOW WHAT?!
YOUTARO-SAN'S HERE, TOO?!
WE'RE STUDENTS FROM ANOTHER SCHOOL!
NICE TO MEET YOU!
NOT NICE TO MEET YOU.
ARE OTHER SCHOOLS EVEN A THING HERE?!